DUCH
GEORG

CW00740352

Georgian Britain's Most Popular Woman
A New Study

Lindsey Porter

Lindsey Porter

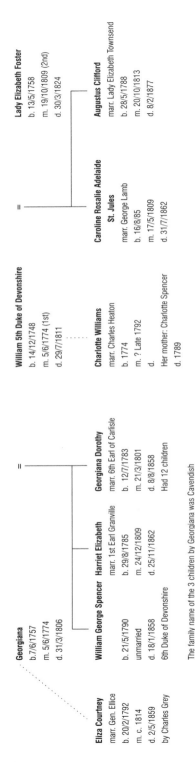

Lady Elizabeth Foster
b. 13/5/1758
m. 19/10/1809 (2nd)
d. 30/3/1824

Augustus Clifford
marr. Lady Elizabeth Townsend
b. 28/5/1788
m. 20/10/1813
d. 8/2/1877

Caroline Rosalie Adelaide St. Jules
marr. George Lamb
b. 16/8/85
m. 17/5/1809
d. 31/7/1862

William 5th Duke of Devonshire
b. 14/12/1748
m. 5/6/1774 (1st)
d. 29/7/1811

Charlotte Williams
marr. Charles Heaton
b. 1774
m. ? Late 1792
d.
Her mother: Charlotte Spencer
d. 1789

Georgiana
b. 7/6/1757
m. 5/6/1774
d. 31/3/1806

Georgiana Dorothy
marr. 6th Earl of Carlisle
b. 12/7/1783
m. 21/3/1801
d. 8/8/1858
Had 12 children

William George Spencer
b. 21/5/1790
unmarried
d. 18/1/1858
6th Duke of Devonshire

Harriet Elizabeth
marr. 1st Earl Granville
b. 29/8/1785
m. 24/12/1809
d. 25/11/1862

Eliza Courtney
marr. Gen. Ellice
b. 20/2/1792
m. c. 1814
d. 2/5/1859
by Charles Grey

The family name of the 3 children by Georgiana was Cavendish

Guidelines Books & Sales
11 Belmont Road, Ipstones, Stoke on Trent ST10 2JN
England Tel: 07971 990 649 Email: author.porter@gmail.com

1st Edition ISBN: 978-1-84306-559-3
© Lindsey Porter, 2015

Design: Mark Titterton
Printing: Berforts Information Press Ltd, Eynsham, Oxford

Picture Credits

CONTENTS

Acknowledgements

I wish to thank all those who have assisted me in the production of this work, particularly Helen Maurice Jones, who has listened patiently for over three years to the detail of the progress of this book and acted as a sounding board where interpretation of material needed discussion.

I am indebted to His Grace the Duke of Devonshire and the Chatsworth House Trust for access to the Devonshire Collection Archives, plus the following Collections Department staff for their ongoing assistance: Mathew Hirst, James Towe, Aidan Haley, Charles Noble, Diane Naylor, Louise Clarke, Stuart Band (retired) and Andrew Peppitt (retired); Martin Price, working on the Lady Spencer-C Howe correspondence; Pam Bater (Friends Of Chiswick House); Fellow Devonshire Collection Archives researchers Ralph Lord, Philip Riden & Cliff Williams for sharing findings; Esme Whittaker (English Heritage); Peter Gaines; Nicola Dixon; David Neave re Londesbrough; staff at the British Library & Parliamentary Archives; Dr JH Rieuwerts; and for post-research assistance: John Mills, Marjory Ide, Liz Hardy, Stella & Phillip Porter.

Chronology

Destinations are for the family unless stated
Abbreviation: Dss: the Duchess

1774

5.6.74	Marriage, Georgiana Spencer – William Cavendish
16.6.74	Dss's Presentation at Court
c. Sept 74	To Chatsworth
c. 9.1.74	To Hardwick
7.11.74	At Londesbrough
	Mid Dec To Althorp

1775

?Jan 75	To London
Early Apl	To Bath
Late May/ June	To Spa and Paris
27.7.75	To England
EarlyAug	To Chatsworth, smallpox at Edensor
1.10.75	Dss has miscarriage
Late Oct	To London

1776

25.7.76	To Chatsworth via Whittlesea Mere
30.7.76	Total eclipse
Oct 76	David Garrick at Althorp
2.10.76	To Welbeck for 2 days and then to Londesbrough
c. 16.10.76	To London via Althorp
1.11.76	Dss at House of Commons: American Debate

1777

8.5.77	Dowager Dss Katherine Devonshire died
30.7.77	To Chatsworth; 'the bed chambers are almost compleat'
4.8.77	To Hardwick and Nottingham Races
7.8.77	Back at Chatsworth
14.9.77	Local earthquake in Peak District
27.9.77	To London
6.10.77	To Brighthelmstone (Brighton)

1778

23.2.78	Dss leaves Wimbledon Park for Chiswick
24.2.78	Dss contracts scarlet fever
18.4.78	Family at Devonshire House
May 78	Duke with Derbyshire Militia, Coxheath Camp, Kent
	Dss to Chatsworth
7.7.78	Dss's 21st birthday
11.7.78	Dss to Coxheath but takes house in Tunbridge Wells by 17/7/78
	Duke has affair at the camp with Lady Jersey
4.11.78	Duke still at the camp

1779

	To Europe, ?Spa, and return in September
1.10.79	Duke and Duchess at Warley Camp, Essex
22.11.79	Duke still at camp, but not permanently there

1780

28.3.80	Duke and Duchess go to Milton

	House (Fitzwilliam's), Duke goes on to Derby, ?at Chatsworth
20.4.80	Refurbishment at Devonshire House complete
7.5.80	Charlotte Williams goes to live at Devonshire House
June 80	Gordon Riots, London
30.7.80	Duke and Dss at Portsmouth (Militia Camp)
c. 5.9.80	Duke ill and leaves Portsmouth for Chatsworth
27.11.80	Dss's sister Harriet marries Lord Duncannon

1781

11.2.81	Arrive at Hardwick, leaving for marriage, below
6.3.81	Lord Althorp, Dss's brother, marries Lady Lavinia Bingham
26.7.81	Leave Devonshire House for Plymouth (Militia Camp)
1.8.81	At Plympton House (being rented)
27.8.81	Dining on HMS Royal George at Torbay
4.9.81	Dss launches HMS Anson at Plymouth
7.9.81	Lord Richard Cavendish dies in Naples
16.10.81	Still at Plymouth
Xmas	Probably at Devonshire House
28.12.81	To Althorp

1782

1782	Duke and Dss of Portland leave Burlington House
22.5.82	At Bath, ? left London 20th
23.5.82	Met Lady Elizabeth Foster
May/June	National epidemic of influenza
End July	At Plympton again
15.11.82	Leave Plympton for Hot Wells, Bristol
3.12.82	Dss pregnant, her sister too
25.12.82	Bess Foster & Charlotte Williams leave Dover

1783

22.2.83	Dss liaising with John Carr re refurbishment at Chatsworth (in London)
6.7.83	Birth of Harriet's son Frederick
12.7.83	Birth of Georgiana Dorothy (Little G)
1.9.83	Family arrive at Chatsworth
22.10.83	From Chatsworth to Hardwick
29.10.83	1st Earl Spencer dies
Xmas	At Bath

1784

?Feb	Arrived in London from Bath
17.3.84	Dss with Little G. Opera House playing 'The Reine de Golconda', with a march composed by the Dss
21.6.84	Duke meets Samuel Lapidge at Chiswick re garden alterations
13.7.84	To Compton Place, Eastbourne to return 17/7
22.7.84	Bess Foster in England with Charlotte
29.7.84	Dss at Roehampton (sister's)
12.8.84	Dss to Chatsworth from Newmarket with Bess and Charlotte
18.8.84	Dss at Ball in Derby, wearing a muslin chemise 'with fine lace that the Queen of France gave me'
1.9.84	Duke invites Dr Erasmus Darwin to stay at Chatsworth
6.9.84	Dr Johnson and Dr Taylor of Ashbourne at Chatsworth Public Day
2.12.84	Bess leaves England for France

1785

Mar 85	Wimbledon Park destroyed by fire
June 85	Dss writes to Bess 'how much I do love you – I cannot live without you'
11.8.85	Duke writes to Bess, expressing his love, very passionately
16.8.85	Caroline St Jules born at Vietri near Salerno

Mid Aug	Duke to Chatsworth leaving Dss at Devonshire House
29.8.85	Henrietta (called Harriet) born at 10 pm. Known as Haryo
1.10.85	Christening of Haryo
13.11.85	Birth of Caroline Ponsonby
Dec 85	Play 'The Duchess' at Drury Lane Theatre

1786

14.8.86	The Great Hotel, Buxton, opens for business
Sept	Bess returns to England
23.9.86	Family at Chatsworth (1)
Pre 5.10	Separation demand following Martindale's claim
23.10.86	To Buxton
4.11.86	To Hardwick with Bess. 4th – 13th, Duke shooting at Welbeck but staying at Hardwick (2)
Mid Dec	To Buxton again, two separate visits were recommended

1787

? 22.1.87	Left Buxton for London
6.2.87	At Devonshire House, William Ponsonby born
Late June	?at Chiswick
July	At Bath
Early Aug	To Chatsworth
Mid Aug	To Bolton Abbey
End Aug	To Chatsworth
21.11 87	Returning to London
c. 26.11	Dss has a miscarriage

1788

Mid Feb 88	At Devonshire House
21.2.88	Bess left Dover for France
End Mar	At Chiswick back to London
End April	Ditto, ? packing
19.5.88	To Buxton
22.5.88	To Chatsworth
26.5.88	Augustus Clifford born in Rouen
End May	Back to Buxton

June	To Holywell House, St Albans
11.7.88	Theft of diamonds and coins at Devonshire House
25.8.88	Duke leaves Holywell for Chatsworth
14.9.88	Dss ditto
5.10.88	Bess expected at Chatsworth
5.11.88	Centenary celebrations, Glorious Revolution, Chesterfield
5.11.88	Duke's steam winding engine started, Ecton Mine. First outside Cornwall & Lake District
Early Nov	To London via Welbeck for the shooting (3)

1789

19.6.89	To Paris, arrived 23/6, left c.10/7. Bastille fell 14/7
14.7.89	Arrive in Brussels and proceed to Spa
Early Oct	Leave Spa for Brussels

1790

Early 90	Duke returns to England
11.3.90	Duke goes back to Brussels with daughters
4.5.90	Lady Spencer travels to Brussels
9.5.90	Family leave for Paris
21.5.90	Marquis of Hartington born
30.5.90	Dss takes her baby to visit Queen of France
10.8.90	Party return to England

1791

2.5.91	Marquis christened in London
Spring	Dss in affair with Charles Grey
Mid May	Dss conceives Grey's child
June	Dss travels to Bath with her sister
Sept/Oct	Duke receives letter suggesting he calls on his wife
Pre 11/10	Duke demands his wife's exile
12.12.91	The Dss's party in Lyon, France
28.12.91	They reach Marseilles

1792

20.2.92	Dss gives birth to Eliza Courtney in Aix-en-Provence
3.3.92	Dss and Bess Foster in Toulon
July	Charlotte Williams returns to England
End May	Dss arrives in Geneva. Party travels on to Lausanne
End Aug	Sir Charles Blagdon arrives stimulating Dss's interest in science
6.9.92	Dss still in Lausanne
Early Nov	All of the party south of the Alps
11.3.92	Lord Duncannon becomes 3rd Earl of Bessborough

1793

21.1.93	France declares war on Britain
May 93	Duke asks Dss to return home
3.7.93	Duke receives the DCL from Oxford University
Early Aug	Dss and Bess Foster reach Bolognas`
16.9.93	Dss reaches Ostend
18.9.93	Dss lands at Dover
End Nov	To Bath

1794

Jan	Return to London; Bess still in Bath on 13.1.94
? Feb	To Oakley, Bedfordshire; Dss in London, 12.2.94; Bess 30.1.94 [4] Exceedingly cold winter
2.5.94	Lord George Augustus Cavendish dies
12.5.94	Centenary of the Dukedom
3.6.94	Dss of Portland dies
June	To Chatsworth
Early Aug	Return to London from Chatsworth
Mid Aug	Lady Spencer and Harriet land at Harwich
Dec	Dss's brother, 2nd Earl Spencer, appointed First Sea Lord
? Dec	Dss joins sister in West Teignmouth, Devon

1795

Late April	Duke joins Dss at Stonehouse near Plymouth
12.5.95	Family leave Devon for London
Early Sept	To Bognor, (Susssex) and Goodwood
9.10.95	Return to London (Bess to Goodwood) from Bognor
Xmas	Chiswick

1796

13.1.96	Fire at Chiswick
Early Jan	Bess returns to London
Mid July	Dss plans to join mother in Worthing and then to go to Chatsworth
Late July	Dss suffering from eye infection, ? Cavernous Sinus Thrombosis
Nov	Augustus Clifford enters Harrow School
Late Dec	At Chiswick
18.12.96	Lord John Cavendish dies

1797

Late Jan	Dss miscarries
June or Jul	Family at Bognor
Early Aug	Duke at Chatsworth
11.8.97	Duke moves to Bolton Abbey
16.9.97	Dss to Chiswick
11.11.97	To Hardwick for Christmas

1798

July	Hartington enters Harrow School
Sept-Dec	At Chatsworth
Xmas	? at Chiswick

1799

Jan 99	At Chiswick
Sept	Hartington ill & goes to Margate with Bess Foster

1800

21-22 May	Little G's Presentation at Court
11.6.00	Dss rejoins social society: party for 800 at Devonshire House

12.7.00	Public Breakfast at Chiswick for 900 (Little G's 17th birthday)
15.12.00	Lord Morpeth proposes to Little G at Chatsworth

1801

7.2.01	Dss & Little G to London from Chatsworth
21.3.01	Little G marries Lord Morpeth
20.6.01	First balloon flight over London, sponsored by Dss and others
27.8.01	To Londesbrough, leaving 2/9 for Hardwick and then on to London
3.9.01	Arrive Hardwick
7.10.01	Leave London for St Albans
9.10.01	To Hardwick, Haryo unwell, delaying departure for Castle Howard
21.10.01	Leave for Castle Howard, stopping at Londesbrough on the way (5)
Xmas	Chatsworth

1802

March 02	Return to London, delayed by Duke's gout
18.4.02	First grandchild born, George Morpeth
29.4.02	Peace signed with France (Peace of Amiens)
May	Mdme Recamier in London
24.8.02	To Ramsgate (& Goodwin Sands)

1803

5.1.03	Morpeths sail for France and Paris
24.4.03	Bess Foster arrives in Dover from Paris
28.4.03	Haryo presented at Court along with Caroline Ponsonby
17.5.03	Britain declares war on France
25.8.03	Haryo's 18th birthday
21.10.03	Lord Frederick Cavendish died
12.11.03	Arrival at Bath

1804

27.2.04	Return from Bath
End Mar	To Chiswick for Easter
Sept 04	Hartington recouperating at Hastings with Bess Foster and Caroline St Jules
Dec 04	Young Roscius appears on the London stage

1805

May 05	Hartington leaves Harrow
3.6.05	Caroline Ponsonby marries William Lamb (future Lord Melbourne)
20.7.05	Emily Lamb marries Lord Cowper
23.7.05	Dss with eye infection, goes to Chiswick
10.11.05	Lord Duncannon marries Lady Maria Fane
4.10.05	Dss leaves Chiswick for Brocket Hall via St Albans
21.10.05	Trafalgar
Xmas	At Devonshire House

1806

9.1.06	Nelson's funeral
22/23.1.06	William Pitt dies
28.2.06	Dss hosts her last party
22.2.06	Pitt's funeral
5.3.06	Dss goes to Court
6.3.06	Dss's last appearance at a friend's party
9.3.06	Dss has jaundice
31.3.06	Dss dies, 3.30 am
10.4.06	Interment, Derby
29.7.11	Duke dies
30.3.24	Duchess (Bess Foster) dies

1

Introduction

This book covers, in far greater detail than previously, the family life of a legendary Georgian lady: Georgiana, Duchess of Devonshire, wife of the 5th Duke. It presents for the first time a different story about her and the story about her husband. The evidence has been there all along: this is the true story.

The material available for researchers is chiefly letters written by or to the Duchess, but even here, her son culled and burnt many of them twenty years after her death. The amount of material on the Duke is frankly very little in comparison. Nonetheless, enough survives to give a good account of his contribution to our heritage, although the 20th century saw the needless destruction of the achievements of both the Duke and the Duchess at Chiswick House.

The material garnered together for this book stretches beyond the surviving correspondence (of which over 2,000 items survive). It includes much more material which has lain untouched in the archives. A decade and a half of research at Chatsworth has enabled much more to be learnt, putting detail of both the Duchess and her husband into a much broader context.

A significant bonus has been the discovery of material providing details of the provenance of books, paintings and other items now in the Devonshire Collection Archives at Chatsworth. Although there are not a lot, it has given us a better understanding of the couple's contribution. This needs to be viewed alongside the Duke's creative endeavours, some of which were initiated at the suggestion of the Duchess.

But why legendary? Well, in just over 30 years of married life (not always blissful, one must admit), the Duchess did pack in a lot and some of it unwillingly (her exile in 1791-93 for instance).

She married one of a small clutch of elite aristocrats who could claim to be amongst the richest in England. It was, however, more than that, William Cavendish, 5th Duke of Devonshire, had a dynastic background few could equal. Bess of Hardwick and the King Maker, the first Duke, were amongst his ancestors. His father had been Prime Minister; his home was a palace – Chatsworth. Good marriages had brought much landed property to the Dukedom. In addition to Chatsworth, there were six other seats in England, and a minor one, supported by 40,000 acres nonetheless, in Ireland. The six included three of the finest houses in London, one arguably amongst the very best – Devonshire House in Piccadilly. The couple lived in a semi-regal status, the Cavendish crest upon the coaches instantly recognizable.

Unfortunately, the Duchess was a compulsive spender, of which gambling losses generally featured to a small degree, although more so in the early part of her marriage, when she was way off the rails. To suggest these debts were a major contributor all her life is wrong. From the mid- to late- 1780s to 1800, she avoided the London night life for a lot of the time. From 1800, she re-engaged, quickly establishing herself as the leading socialite in London.

Everything she did was reported in the 'fashionable' columns of London's largest selling newspaper, the Morning Post. Not only that, it was immediately after the Royal Circular. The clamour for detail about her, to see her, to have her on your guest list reached an abrupt halt with her untimely death in 1806. For the first time, her life in those final glittering years is given in these pages. Fortunately for her, her husband put up with her profligacy, even paying much of it. Her partying was seemingly also underwritten by him, especially when she was hosting her own events at either Devonshire House or out amongst the countryside at Chiswick.

She was a legendary figure then, but contrary to current popular belief, she was not a legendary beauty. What contributed more to her persona was her charm, grace, dignity and consideration for others. She also enjoyed a laugh but was equally happy talking with luminaries such as Dr. Samuel Johnson, C.J. Fox (who became a close friend) and Edward Gibbon, let alone the best scientific minds in the country. In the last years of her life, she was probably the most popular woman in the land. With no shortage of admirers, she learnt the cost of a physical relationship (with Charles, later Earl Grey) in a man's world. At a time when her young family needed her the most, she spent nearly two years parted from them.

From 1782 to the end of her days, she lived much of the time in a *ménage à trois* with Lady Elizabeth Foster. It was a complicated arrangement, with both women sharing an affection for each other greater than the love either perhaps had for Duke at times.

In terms of talent, she was fluent in French and probably Italian. Artistically, she was a poet, praised by Coleridge, could draw and paint, played music, rode horses and appreciated the value of sea air, to the cost of visits to the national heart of the family – Chatsworth, situated about as far from the sea as one can get here. She also had a flair for interior design, an interest in early 18th century Anglo-French furniture, picture hanging and garden design – all very much part of a man's prerogative, except with her husband who used such activities to keep her actively engaged away from London society.

Perhaps an important legacy was her encouragement for young artists, whom she helped by giving them commissions and introductions to other aristocratic patrons, including the Prince of Wales. Other interests included sketching, poetry, reading (along with the Duke), mineralogy (she was an avid collector) and even fishing occasionally. Yet above all she was an eminent hostess. There were at least 900 people at her daughter Little G's (Georgiana's) 18th birthday party at Chiswick, the Duchess playing a leading part in the decorations, even in their production. This event was shortly after the ball to celebrate Little G's presentation to the King and Queen, when 800 people arrived at Devonshire House.

Regrettably she was plagued by ill health, notably headaches (?migraine) and found conception difficult, at least with her husband if not Charles Grey, although her lifestyle may have been a contributing factor. It took 16 years to produce the much vaunted family heir at the age of nearly 43 years. She nearly lost the sight of an eye having caught what is now considered to be CST (Cavernous Sinus Thrombosis). Luckily for her she contracted the non-fatal variety and was very fortunate not to have died ten years earlier, in 1796. However, what finally brought on a fatal illness was liver disease.

She created changes in fashion, couldn't resist an extra diamond or two, mixing socially and occasionally harmlessly flirting with the men. More seriously, her home became the notional heart of the Whig Party, with Charles J. Fox regarded as a close friend. She kept abreast of politics and events affecting the national interest, especially naval success, sending Nelson gifts after his victories via the First Sea Lord, Earl Spencer (her brother). She was equally at home accompanying the Prince of Wales for a stroll at different assemblies, balls etc, with her arm on his.

She was instrumental in using her popularity to gain victory for C.J. Fox in the 1784 Westminster election. Dispensing kisses for votes to itinerant tradesmen created a sensation but perhaps not so frequently as we believe, for in the middle of the election she left London for St. Albans and her sick mother. The poll was swinging away from Fox when she was urgently requested to come back. She did so and Fox was returned. Richard Sheridan was helped through his first election as M.P. for Stafford although there the bribe was more compromising (cash instead of kisses). Her value as an instrument of party politics was well understood and valued (at least by the Whigs).

The final years of her life had an increasing amount of partying as head of the 'fashionables' of London society. The Duchess lengthened the season, continually changed the theme of events, changed the style of her dresses etc. Even the style and furnishing of carriages became a status symbol to the ever increasing cost of hosting several assemblies every season. She was determined to retain her elevated position. She kept the number of other events she went to (usually with a Devonshire House entourage) strictly under control, she was no longer a young woman and these events were largely nocturnal affairs, lasting to 7.30am.

Occasionally, the Duke ventured out too, especially where he was interested in being with the hostess, including the Duchesses of St Albans and Gordon, the Marchioness of Abercorn and Mrs. Maria Duff. Catherine, Duchess of St Albans was the Duke's cousin. Her brother Frederick married Georgiana Devonshire's sister Harriet and succeeded to the title of Earl of Bessborough. The Duchess of St Albans' other sister Charlotte married the 4th Earl Fitzwilliam, another relative, all of whom feature in these pages. It was in this way that the Devonshires maintained their influence and patronage. Much of the detail on this period (1801-06) is highlighted for the first time.

Despite much being written on the Duke relating to his shy nature and even describing him as an aristocratic brute, he was nothing of the kind. His reputation has been tarnished by several authors with no firm or convincing evidence to justify it. In fact he put up with his wife's debts with moderation and with patience. There appears to be no evidence that he ever lost his temper. This issue is discussed in detail because it is necessary to have a clear understanding about the basis of his character, how he was perceived as a result of that and how it affected his marriage. What is clear is that they enjoyed a good relationship (other than at the time of the pregnancy by Grey). Upon their reconciliation, the Duke went out of his way to keep his wife contented and busily accepting work to fulfil, which challenged her fertile mind.

The only area where he could have done more was to have helped her to clear her debts sooner, but she kept him in the dark and for much of the time he was oblivious of the mire she was in. Even his mother-in-law observed that the couple enjoyed a loving relationship in 1788 and again in 1797 (see Appendix 1).

The exact situation of her debts is given in full for the first time. It not only shows how enmeshed she was, but the effect it had on unwitting lenders or suppliers. A measure of the affluence within which she lived is also given with details of consumables in a 14-week stay at Chatsworth in 1798. But the purchases she liked to make were her pieces of jewellery. From 1799-1806 she spent at least £7,000 on this alone and figures for some years in this period are not included at all (i.e. are not known).

Following her marriage, the Duchess found that she was the centre of attention and played on this to the full. Free from the bonds of probity and discipline under her mother, she found and embraced the excesses of social pleasure. Moreover, her husband patiently put up with it. This continued until 1782, when she met Lady Elizabeth Foster. She was probably more intelligent than most of her aristocratic contemporaries. Quickly getting her feet under the Devonshire's table, both of her hosts seem to have started spending more evenings at home. Further domesticity followed the birth by the Duchess of two girls in 1783 and 1785. Having found themselves in the French Revolution in 1789, they moved to what is now Belgium and the Duchess conceived again, with a baby boy giving the Duke the heir he craved for, in 1790. Banished abroad for conceiving Charles Grey's child in 1791, she did not return to England until September 1793.

Thereafter the Duchess returned to domesticity, spurning the night life, or much of it, and instead devoted her time to her growing children, still sharing her husband with Bess Foster. However the Duke's ardour and passion for the latter was evaporating and he and the Duchess grew much closer. From 1796 and the completion of two significant extensions to Chiswick House, much more time was spent there. The Court Presentation of daughter Georgiana (Little G) in 1800 saw the Duchess re-engaging with her social life, partying away and rapidly becoming the leader of the fashionables, a position she relished and maintained until to her death.

Her Husband: The Duke of Devonshire

This story also shows that far from finding his real enjoyment only within the walls of Brooks's Club, the Duke was a consummate countryman. He loved shooting whenever he could (there is however some evidence to suggest that he may not have been a very accurate shot). He used to go to Welbeck Abbey, just for a change, his sister's home, on his own or with his own company, taking his beaters with him and using Hardwick as a base. He rode frequently when he was in the country, fished the waters of his own and friend's estates and regularly when at Chatsworth, would take his wife out for a ride after dinner. He also rode to hounds and kept his own pack, even hiring them when necessary when militia camp life permitted it.

He was to be found at the annual race meetings of Derby, Chesterfield (where he owned the course) and Nottingham. As well as cards, he also loved billiards, with of course a bet upon the outcome. His mother-in-law was a worthy opponent.

As a young man, he may have enjoyed the tables and conversation at Brook's and other clubs. But following his marriage, he spent a lot of time away from London. From the mid-1790s, whilst in town, he frequently lived twelve miles away at Chiswick, not Devonshire House, in Piccadilly, where they could host parties on a magnificent scale. Chiswick was a place preferred by the whole family, especially after the building of the two wings there from the mid-1790s. By this time, playing cards at home was a preferred choice, often as a result of gout and stomach ailments restricting his activities.

As for Hattersley's comment (see Chapter 3) about the Duke's gambling and *'the sexual adventures which interrupted [it]'*, he gives us neither detail or even a backing-up reference to support it. Foreman's view of the Duke's early relationship with his wife is similar.

A careful study of the evidence over a prolonged period offers us an alternative view of the relationship of the Duke and Duchess. It points to a loving one and a marriage that worked, yes even one initially damaged by the Duke's affair with Lady Jersey in 1778 after four years of marriage and his love for Lady Elizabeth Foster in 1784. And not forgetting the Duchess's relationship with Charles Grey. Yet we need to remember that the sanctimony of marriage in those far off days did not have the rigidity of it as perceived today, let alone the fact that women were always subservient to their husband.

So long as it did not break the calm surface of 18th century respectability, in a lot of households morality embraced a more flexible posture. This book projects the available evidence of the Duke's character and relationship with his wife as objectively as is possible. It will be for you, the reader, to judge whether it passes muster in terms of historical accuracy. What is certain is that there is no presumption included except where it is indicated and the facts are presented in as wide a context as has been possible. This is to all intents and purposes the true story.

So Why Then A New Book?

This is a story about a Duchess who lived in the limelight which her husband preferred to avoid. It creates a fascinating portrait of a family life played out with one of its partners being one of the most celebrated women in the country, the other partner virtually unknown then let alone now, in comparison.

This was not a marriage that raced on through chance and change, but this story does present a remarkable insight into what aristocratic family life was like in Georgian England. It was cocooned in many respects from the rigours of a more recognisable way of life. Yet it was still subject to worries over illness, children and other domestic concerns, let alone invasion by the French, rioting, being caught up in three revolutions no less and shot at.

It was not a marriage made in Heaven either. With a *ménage à trois*, infidelity and the Duchess's extravagance beyond one's wildest of dreams, it did have its moments. But then it is a lucky marriage that doesn't.

It is a story told from a different perspective, supported by material not previously used, which sheds new and interesting light on a paragon of her age. It shows how her husband, castigated by other writers, did much to enable his wife to achieve what she did, with patience, understanding and generosity of his wallet. Not many other men would have done this which such composure. From the naivety and exposure of a carefree spirit in her early married life, suffering from her infidelity with Edward Grey, to her final years when she maintained her pole position of the London social scene through sheer (if not ruthless) determination and to hell with the expense, this is the true story of Georgiana, Duchess of Devonshire, together with her family.

The Achievements of the Duchess

Although some of her activities have been well documented, she is less known for other areas in which she developed more than a passing interest. If nothing else, it portrays an enquiring mind and a desire to promote or otherwise assist people whose paths crossed hers and where she could see she was able to help their progress.

Aspiring young artists were given commissions and introductions, as high as the Prince of Wales. These included Anne Darmer, Richard and Maria Cosway, James Barry plus Thomas Hardy, who not only did portraiture but also worked on the Chapel and the Painted Hall ceiling at Chatsworth in 1783-84. Because of the interest in her, the Duchess became one of the most painted women of her time. A portrait of her by Maria Cosway was exhibited at the Royal Academy in 1782 and brought her (Cosway) much acclaim.

By 1792, she was developing an interest in science (see the detail of her meetings with Sir Charles Blagden at Lausanne below). It is quite probable (but currently a presumption), that Blagden told her of Dr. Thomas Beddoe's work on the use of gasses for the treatment of diseases. Whilst she was still abroad in 1793, Beddoes started work in Bristol on this, with a desire to establish a research facility there. Within twelve weeks of arriving home from exile, she was in Bath, ostensibly because her daughter Little G was ill, and went to see Beddoes. How she knew of his activities is not clear, but Blagden, with his research background, could have told her, especially as he may have known that Sir Joseph Banks, the President of the Royal Society was against giving assistance (Blagden was the Society Secretary).

Beddoes wrote to Dr. Erasmus Darwin following her visit to tell him '*she had showed a knowledge of modern chemistry superior to what he should have supposed that any duchess or any Lady in England was possessed of '*. [1] Bergman goes on to state that the Duchess established her own small laboratory to study geology and experiment in chemistry. The Duchess wrote a couple of times to try and persuade Banks to support Beddoes but he remained blinkered in his rejection of support. Even James Watt, the inventor, received a similar negative response. It would be interesting to discover how else the Duchess progressed her interest in science.

Whilst at Lausanne in 1792, she met with several leading exponents of chemistry and mineralogy and impressed them with her knowledge of such subjects. In 1799, White Watson arranged mineral specimens in three specially made cabinets at Chiswick House, which are now at Chatsworth, the minerals and other specimens she collected now arranged and catalogued by the Russell Society.

Additionally, she read a lot, often writing to her mother to tell her which books she was leafing through. She often read with the Duke and Bess Foster and sometimes the Duke read to the other two. She wrote poems regularly, including a long one on her experience crossing the St. Gothard Pass in 1793, which was acclaimed by Coleridge, and was translated into three languages. Her book The Sylph was published and was also well received.

From an interest in early Anglo-French furniture, which survives at Chatsworth, the Duke left her to furnish Chiswick in 1794-95, which she also did in Anglo-French style. From this led requests by the Duke for her to be responsible for rehanging paintings at Chiswick and Hardwick, together with garden design, especially outside the newly completed east wing at Chiswick.

Her interests in politics, especially with the Whig Party saw her getting involved in the 1784 election (but none after that). She did however, continue helping/advising where she could and became the Whig's principle hostess. However, much of the detail on this has been covered elsewhere and is not repeated here, except where a different conclusion is offered. As her children, and several more who attended school lessons at Devonshire House, grew older, the Duchess taught them several subjects herself including: poetry, reading, dancing, an appreciation of music, the opera and ballet, plus drawing and painting. Her musical talents included the piano and the harp, sending a man to France to purchase the harp belonging to her close friend, the executed French Queen.

The Duchess was a co-sponsor of the first balloon flight across the capital, by M. Garnerin, a Frenchman, and she held annual musical subscription concerts etc. Then there were her assemblies and her position as the leader of the ton, which are considered under the chapters covering 1801-06. Finally, but not necessarily the least or the last highlight of what she achieved, was her interest in philanthropy. She founded the school in the village of Edensor, near Chatsworth; was a subscriber to a girls' charity school at Chesterfield and supported various women and at least one schoolboy at Cheltenham.

Nomenclature

In this text, 'the Duke' refers to William, 5th Duke of Devonshire. His wife is referred to as 'the Duchess'. Their oldest daughter, also called Georgiana, is referred to as 'Little G' (her nickname) and her younger sister Harriet by her nickname, Haryo (Hary as in Harry). Lady Elizabeth Foster is referred to here as Bess Foster, although the girls called her Lady Liz while the Marquis of Hartington, at least as a boy, called her Lizzy. The whole family always referred to the Marquis as Hartington or Hart in correspondence. Countess Spencer (later Dowager) was known as Lady Spencer and is so called here.

Maintaining Accuracy

Regretably, it will be clear that this work identifies, if not completely, the discovery that other descriptions of the activities and feelings of the Duchess and the Duke are at variance to what can reasonably be attributed as the true position. It is sadly disappointing, especially when it appears to have been written without any supporting evidence or with a reference quoted but one which is at variance to the text alleged to have come from it.

In this book, the projection of the truth has been paramount. Presumptions have been flagged up. It is hoped that this work acts as a platform from which further study may be made with confidence of its validity. At all times I have striven to relay primary and other sources without embellishment other than to offer the reader the opportunity to consider the effect of what happened, although not necessarily give the answer or result. For example, at Nelson's funeral, where and how do you park 681 coaches and c. 2,000 horses around St Paul's Cathedral?

This book represents the true story of the Duchess and her family and a reasonable representation of the way of life and the times which affected the life she lived.

Lindsey Porter 2015

2

The Spencers, the Dukedom and the Duke

Lady Georgiana Spencer was born on the 7th June 1857, the daughter of the Hon. John Spencer and his wife Georgiana, (some sources state that her name was Margaret Georgiana, but on her birth and death records, her coffin plate and on her memorial, she is called Georgiana only. [1]. She was the daughter of Stephen Poyntz of Midgham House, Berkshire and his wife Anna Maria née Mordaunt. Their principal country house was Althorp in Northamptonshire. His father, also called John, and with a wife also called Georgiana (née Carteret) had received as a wedding present Wimbledon Park, just outside London and inherited Holywell House at St. Albans from his grandmother, Sarah, Duchess of Marlborough. She had died in 1744 leaving John's father £250,000, plus 27 landed estates in 12 counties with a capital value of £400,000 and rental value of £17,000 net p.a. Additionally, were paintings, the Marlborough silver and Sarah's jewellery with the diamonds worth £12,000 alone. In addition was the paternal inheritance of Althorp and Wormleighton together with Sunderland House, Piccadilly. A condition of the bequest was that John (senior) should not take up any post or office under the Crown. However, his death in 1746 saw the properties and much of the bequest passing to his son. [2]

The latter married Georgiana Poyntz on 20th December 1755 the day after his 21st birthday and shortly after that commenced building Spencer House (in 1756) at 27 St. James's Place. Today it is one of London's earliest and finest surviving Palladian houses. Their oldest daughter, Georgiana, was born at Wimbledon the following year on 7th June 1757. Their son George was born on 1st September 1758 and was followed by Harriet on 16th June 1761. There were two other daughters who did not survive, Charlotte, born 1765 and died the following year and Louisa, born in 1769 and died shortly afterwards.

It was early in 1774 that the 5th Duke of Devonshire, one of the most eligible bachelors in the country proposed marriage to Lady Georgiana Spencer, who was then 16 years old. Within weeks, she was to be married to a man ten years older than she was, whose gross income when he was 16 years old was £65,000 p.a. and who lived in a palace (or rather two: Devonshire House and Chatsworth in Derbyshire). She had £4,000 p.a. to spend and had the responsibility of a ducal household to run.

She was soon married to a Duke, living in a semi-regal state, propelled to the pinnacle of society. Moreover, she was married to a man who literally had no concept of the value of money. His wife's extravagant spending has to be seen in this light. It had no meaning to him, strange though it may seem. No wonder if her mind was in a complete whirl.

It was not just that the Duke had no concept of the value of money. The main houses were full of valuable treasures even if the furnishings were tired. Everything she would have, everything she did would be of the best. She would have been used to a privileged life at Althorp but now she would be one of the most elegantly dressed women in the country, adorned with the finest jewellery, known and feted wherever she went. Georgiana Spencer was now marrying into the Cavendish dynasty. She was now becoming Duchess of Devonshire. It didn't get much better than that even if you married into royalty.

The Dukedom

Over the last couple of centuries, the Duke has attracted a lot of comment relating to his character, with a lot of emphasis on a little detail because that seemed to be all there was to go on. This chapter looks primarily at the man and his Dukedom, so that the basis of the marriage is seen in what is perceived to be the reality.

The 5th Duke had inherited estates in London including Burlington House, Piccadilly, leased property north of Oxford Street, London and Burlington House, Chiswick plus Devonshire House, a rather plain looking Palladian fronted house, also in Piccadilly with a three acre rear garden. It fronted Green Park, now the site of Green Park Underground Station, virtually opposite The Ritz Hotel. It was however, sumptuous internally and with rooms capable of taking nearly a thousand people – and from time to time did so. In Yorkshire, he had Londesbrough Hall, near Pocklington, south-west of York, one of the finest houses in Yorkshire. To the west, the Bolton Abbey estate, with the Abbey remains and many acres in the area of the Yorkshire Dales, including the Grassington area lead mines, plus much of Wetherby, brought in further income. There was a huge estate in Ireland centred on Lismore Castle. It had 32,550 acres in Co. Cork, 27,400 acres in Co. Waterford and just 3 acres in Co. Tipperary at its height in Victorian times, possibly less in the Duke's days.

Nearer home, so to speak, were the several estates in Staffordshire and Derbyshire including Hardwick Hall and, of course, Chatsworth, the notional heart of it all. He also had the valuable copper mine at Ecton on the Wetton estate south-west of Hartington, worked in hand (i.e. with the profits, rather than a royalty of c.10%, going to the Duke) since September 1760. In that year the profit was c. £5,000 per annum. Two decades later it would be nearly five times as much.

So much for the dukedom, what about the man?

Background Of The Duke

His Character

Much of the printed sources give a warped view of the Duke and his character and therefore provides a slant on the Duchess's relationship with him which is now judged to be incorrect.

Not very much material survives to allow one to build a reasonable understanding of what the Duke's character was really like. Pearson, [3] suggests that he was 'congenitally bored with life' and for one reason or another, this perception of him seems to have pervaded a sense that this was the bedrock of everything he did or chose not to do. However an obituary of him survives from a cutting from the Dublin Correspondent, an Irish newspaper, of 1811. It is unattributed, but it is clearly by someone who knew him well. It includes details of the second of his two speeches in the House of Lords, which apparently was not recorded verbatim at the time. Yet the writer was able to quote Latin comments from the speech 13 years later.

The obituary highlights his good points, however 'his common habits, founded on the best of virtues which came so easy to him, acquired an air of indolence and indifference which was far from his real disposition'. He was clearly well read with a good memory. 'His knowledge of the classics, both ancient and modern, was extensive and very accurate'. A proverb of his era was the phrase 'to know Shakespeare as well as the Duke of Devonshire'. No person's opinion was more highly valued and his judgement was often relied upon, whether on literary matters, poetry, fine arts or even discretion of conduct. Apparently he was quite witty. His manners were reserved and perhaps, with the best of intentions, could appear cold, masking kindness and a demeanour which displayed grace and dignity. The Prince of Wales found him to be a valued friend and confidant and it is clear that many others did too.

The obituary writer seems to have known his man when he wrote *that 'his modesty produced a habitual shyness as to make him renounce every degree of action that required an effort'.* Herein lies the link to descriptions the Duke's character has been saddled with – boredom, apathy, etc. This work makes little contribution to our knowledge of his dalliances – from lowly Charlotte Spencer (no relation to his first wife) to the First Mistress of France and his *ménage à trois* with the two women he married, but it would seem that there was a feature of his life where sex displaced shyness let alone modesty.

This shyness appears to have rippled through Georgiana's perception of the Duke's early interest in his children. It was no doubt influenced by the worry of the arrival of two daughters and a continuing absence of a son and heir. In 1788 the Duke wrote to his wife: *'You cannot doubt my whole life being dedicated to them* (the children) *if it was recognised'.* [4] The absence of a son was preying on the Duchess. A month earlier, she had written to her mother a sad note on how she felt about Chatsworth itself, which reflects her mood, no doubt induced by the Duke's worry over the matter: *'I do think that nothing in beauty that equals Chatsworth, I like a number of places better – I believe if I had a son I shd (sic) like it best of all; but there is something in its not being my children's that makes me fancy it is not mine'.* [5] The son he craved for was eventually born 15 days short of their 16th wedding anniversary. The birth day was the 21st May 1790. Thirteen years later, in 1803, the Duke seems to have realised, if not before, that there was a limit to all this dedication to children.

The Duke's oldest daughter, Georgiana, (known as Little G), had gone to Paris, leaving her son George Howard in the hands of his grandparents at Devonshire House. Haryo (the Duke's younger daughter Harriet) wrote to her sister on 15th January 1803 to tell her that her pride and joy came down to the dining room each day to have a dessert. Haryo continued that he *'has unfortunately taken a most violent fancy to Papa* (the Duke), *who though very civil to him, will neither play at peep-bo or creep creep'.* [6]

Moreover, the Duke's shyness never left him. The family decamped to Ramsgate in October 1802. They attended two balls one week, described as being *'very crowded, hot and disagreeable'* by Haryo. Attendance had been encouraged by the Duke. She described him as *'in love with all the Mannerses'* (i.e. the Manners ladies, the Rutland family). *'Their chief attraction is that they save him the trouble of speaking and I defy the most determined chatterer to edge in a word, especially if Mrs. Duff takes him in hand and therefore Papa, who does not quite come under that denomination may be silent not only conveniently but necessarily'.* [7] But then the Duke had a soft spot for Mrs. Duff, who died 20th December 1805 at the tender age of 30 years old. She was married to James Duff, who succeeded as 4th Duke of Fife, and was sister to the other Manners girls present.

He also retained an eye for the ladies: while at Ramsgate the Duchess of St. Albans (his cousin) dined with the Devonshires. Harriet wrote: *'it really was too ridiculous to see Papa and her flirting the whole evening and as she is terribly deaf, he was obliged to repeat all the little gallantries and small talk two or three times and to the amazement and amusement of us all'*. She described the Duchess of St. Albans as being *'in very great beauty and what I confess surprises me seeming perfectly happy. The Duke* (i.e. her husband) *is the most hideous, disagreeable animal I ever met with'*. [8]

In 1844, the 6th Duke (the 5th Duke's only son) wrote his Handbook about Chatsworth, describing the main rooms etc. His bedroom had been his father's bedroom and it gave him (the 6th Duke) the opportunity to reflect on his father: *'Here slept he, and when informed that the house was on fire, turned round to sleep on his other side, observing that they had better try to put it out – Am I wrong to record such anecdotes as these? No – for it gives me an opportunity to add, that such apparent apathy was only on the surface of the most generous and noble feelings that could exist – feelings that made him reply to Mr. Heaton, the old and crabbed auditor when he said "My Lord Duke, I am very sorry to inform Your Grace that Lord Hartington appears disposed to spend a great deal of money" – "so much the better Mr. Heaton; he will have a great deal to spend". Sir Robert Adair in a sketch of my Father's character, says that his goodness was a deliberate resolution of the mind, grounded on a love of justice. Fox said he preferred his judgement to that of anyone; and another person wrote "he had apprehension, judgement and perspicuity in their very highest degrees: his ideas were rapid and took unforeseen directions".* [9] From two who knew him well, there is nothing derogatory here.

It is strange that the 6th Duke remembers this quote about Heaton. One wonders if the 6th Duke also remembered that Heaton's reason for saying this was because the Duke's response shows that he did not realise the opposite was true: the 5th Duke was running short of net disposable income because of debt. The comment about the fire in the night is understandable if it was in the kitchen wing on the north side of the house. If it burnt down, it would not affect the structure of the main house.

No-one at the time seems to have suggested that he had a sense of limited confidence borne from the loss of maternal affection when aged six and paternal guidance when aged 16. What his father had provided him with was wealth beyond the jaws of avarice, although he did not live long enough to appreciate the extent of his legacy. Between 1760 and 1790, profits from the Ecton copper mine yielded £297,000 largely tax free revenue. Investments in landed property saw a big rise in annual gross income flowing from this. The effect, if any, this had on his character is difficult to judge.

The copper mine did produce evidence of the Duke's inner strength and determination: he visited the mine in 1783 and went underground. Perhaps it was because his father had done so in 1763, but nonetheless it certainly showed some backbone to his character. Having walked in about 1,000 feet on the flat in the main access level, they reached a large excavation with the top of a shaft visible and with two large and noisy water driven engines.

He descended at least to the 34 fathoms level (204 feet down) where he inspected the mine horses drawing up 80 gallon wooden barrels loaded with stone, water or copper ore. The stone was emptied at that depth into boats on a canal. Their only light would be a candle each, although perhaps more light was available in the area of the horses and boat.

Nonetheless the descent this far (and he may have gone deeper, but perhaps unlikely) needed strength of character and no small measure of determination. He could hardly allow himself to turn about and go back or show any measure of discomfort or panic. [10] It is interesting to compare this with his speaking (or rather the lack of it) in the House of Lords. He only made two speeches in the House. Yet his father had held public office and would have made many public speeches, but the necessary measure of resolve was absent in the son. At least the resolve to do it rather than to not do it. No resolution here to follow in father's footsteps.

By contrast he must have been pleased with Vice-Admiral Lord Nelson's warm description of his illegitimate son Augustus Clifford by his later wife, Lady Bess Foster: *'a fine young man who will be an honour to his country … it is not his brother officers alone, but all the sailors, all love him who come near him'*. [11] A far cry, one suspects from the father. Augustus joined the Navy when he was 12 years old, in 1800. He was knighted in 1830 and created a baronet in 1838. His half-brother, the 6th Duke, obtained for him, after some opposition by King William IV, the appointment of Black Rod in the new Parliament of 1832. He held the position until 1877, the year of his death. [12]

A further contrast however, where the shyness showed its apparent limitation, occurred in August 1778. Edmund Burke wrote that *'I found the Duke of Devonshire in Camp* (the military camp at Coxheath, Kent, the Duke being the Colonel of the Derbyshire Militia), *whose composure, the effect of a natural good temper, the best circumstances and perhaps a just estimate of the value of all human affairs was a perfect contrast to the sickly impatience of the Duke of Grafton'* (Colonel of the Suffolk Militia). [13] While there, the Duke appears to have had an affair with Lady Jersey, while his wife was in the camp until Lady Spencer put a stop to it. The Duke (of Devonshire) was the Lord Lieutenant of Derbyshire and was Colonel of the county militia as a result of that.

At least the Duke's friends knew how to handle him. In December 1775, Lady Clermont, a close friend of Lady Spencer, wrote to Georgiana to say she was sending a letter by Mr. *Rigby 'who intends making the Duke and you a visit tomorrow I send it by him and beg you will remind the Duke (if he should not think of it) of asking him to dinner'.* The Duke, in fairness on this occasion, probably did not need advice from Lady Clermont. On one of the Public Days the following August, the Duke met some people in the garden (a Dr. King, his wife and friend) and asked them to dinner that evening. They had been to Spa, which was known to the Duke, and had struck up a conversation around this.

It is interesting to note that the Duchess told her mother *'the Duke is very proud of what you say of him indeed he deserves it …'*. [14]

So What Was The Problem?

The 5th Duke's symptoms of his shyness, or perhaps more quietness within his family, created an excessive reserve, plus an apathy of creative expression or action; producing the belief that he had bouts of downright boredom. The Duke probably did not appreciate just how people generally thought of him. Very few would presume to tell him. He was possibly blissfully unaware of his reputation and if he did know it, one gets the impression that his way of life extended to failing to consider its implications; in other words its effect on him, practically or emotionally, meant nothing.

His shyness was congenital not compulsive. Unfortunately, it made him appear to some to be cold when he actually was not. It is often quoted that even his younger daughter (known as Haryo) at one stage apparently found it difficult to engage him at dinner unless it was talking about his or her dogs.

In fact this dining room difficulty portrays his problem rather well given that he had made it clear to the Duchess that he was *'dedicated'* to his children, when the girls were aged 5 and 3 respectively in 1788. Yet this one incident can easily be taken out of context and indeed has by some writers. As their children grew up, he had them reading to him over breakfast. Little G recorded how she had stayed up late as a young teenager with her father. We cannot assume that he had little contact with them. At the same time (1794), he was also playing with his daughters and admiring Little G's drawings. A little later, there is evidence of the whole family together and of his time spent with his three children.

Yet at other times he clearly opened up. Georgiana of course knew of this other side of his character. She wrote cheerfully about going to the wedding of Mr. Eyre of Hassop Hall (north-west of Chatsworth) to Lady Mary Bellasise, Lord Falconberg's sister. *'She is very old and ugly but seems a very good kind of woman. I thought the Duke would have burst out a laughing when she came in, it seem'd such a joke her being a bride'.* At least the Duke knew his place; but then he was known for his exemplary manners. [15] The month before, there was a full eclipse of the sun and the Duke animatedly explained its motions using a salt cellar for the sun, a guinea for the earth and half guinea for the moon. Clearly the Duke's demeanour was not all reserve as these two examples show and their marriage worked because of this. [16] It is just a pity that there are not enough records like this to persuade the sceptics!

Moreover, the precise nature of the various house accounts record work done and payments made for it. There is no indication as to the direct involvement of the Duke or the lack of it. However in 1776 – 77, the Duchess records in her correspondence that the Duke had overseen improvements to 'bedchambers', dressing rooms etc. These were at Chatsworth, Londesbrough and Devonshire House and a surprise to her on finding that the changes had been made in her absence. Moreover, she was happy with the changes and also noted that a further change was underway at Chatsworth. Here the Duke was arranging for changes to the furnishings in the drawing room for their next visit *'which will be a great improvement'*. [17] More importantly, he authorised much work to the interior of the family rooms at Chatsworth in 1783. He was certainly involved with the work here, if only because of the interference in the project by his wife.

This is important as it shows the Duke closely involved in making alterations to three of his houses. Moreover, as result of encouragement by the Duchess, he was personally organising the building of two wings and alterations to the gardens at Chiswick in the late 1780s and he insisted on being involved in matters concerning his Irish estate in the 1790s. Interestingly, Joseph Farrington recorded a conversation with John Spencer, the second son of Lord Charles Spencer (a son of the 3rd Duke of Marlborough and a relative of the Duchess) on 6th September 1800. He (Farrington) described John Spencer (then aged 32) as being *'a good scholar and a man of genius with a considerable practical talent'*. He then added: *'Mr. Spencer is much acquainted with the Duke of Devonshire, who he says is a very good scholar and has read extensively and possesses an excellent memory. He is slow in conversation. He has a perfect knowledge of his own affairs and is of a kind and liberal disposition.'* [18]

This note that he was running his own affairs marks an important change, probably encouraged by his wife after he had admitted to her that the opposite was the case in 1783. In support of this, the following year (1784), the Duke personally took charge of garden alterations at Chiswick. On 19th June, he insisted on the Duchess going with him there from Devonshire House, despite her being unwell with severe toothache. This was quite probably to boost his confidence and is an indicator of the confidence he had in her. Two days later she accompanied him back there again to meet Mr. Samuel Lapidge, the garden designer employed for the work. After the Irish estate was brought under direct

English management in 1791, the Duke insisted on being told exactly what was going on over there and when he felt it necessary, on a weekly basis. [19]

The Duke's capabilities were clearly significant as was the loss of potential achievement. A few days before the birth of his first child, Georgiana Dorothy, the Duke had a discussion at Devonshire House with the Prince of Wales, which was followed by a subsequent discussion by the Prince with C. J. Fox in the next room to Georgiana. As he left, the Prince observed *'there is the man* (i.e. the Duke) *whose generous and feeling heart and right head and understanding may be repos'd in without fear – and that's the man whom if his indolence did not get the better of him ought to govern this country'*. [20]

Are We Misrepresenting Him?

It would therefore appear that we may be in danger of doing the Duke a mis-service in our assessment of his sociability. So little was written about his character by those who really knew him that what was written is seized upon as though it is the truth and often not in the proper context. Unfortunately this includes the comment by Haryo about the Duke and his dogs and people like Mrs. Delaney with whom he did not socialise and who therefore did not know him when the veil of shyness was dropped. The number of people who regularly joined him at his social gatherings would not keep going if he was not good company. What we do not have is a description of him by one of those people, but this point must not be overlooked.

However, Haryo stated in 1809 that having crossed the barrier and got him started in conversation, everything was fine and that should not be forgotten. Even the Duchess's letters to her mother say little about him – probably out of deference, although that seems strange today. But then she often did not give any detail on her children either, let alone Bess Foster. However the Duchess did give a pointer to what he was like when relaxed.

Mention has been made about the Duke meeting Mrs. Eyre of Hassop Hall. The Duchess expected the Duke to laugh. The Duke knew his manners, but it points to what she was used to seeing. Similarly, while out on Calton Pasture, just downstream from Chatsworth, with friends in 1784, the Duke made them laugh with his antics trying to get one of the guests, Col. Crawford, to run uphill, knowing that he generally avoided running at all.

It looks as though it did not take much to make him happy. Also in 1784, a Mr. Munday accompanied the Duke to Chesterfield Races. The former's family had previously owned the Races prior to their purchase by the Duke from Mr. Munday (sic, ?Mundy) who was a local Tory leader. The Duchess wrote that he could not have paid the Duke a better compliment than simply accompanying him that day. A similar thing happened when the Duke found Dr. Samuel

Johnson in the Chatsworth garden on a Public Day. The two sat under lime trees enjoying a prolonged and impromptu discussion together. The amount of detail to support any view of his character is not much but this is because the amount of detail on the man in its entirety is equally little. There are definitely some pointers to suggest that amongst friends the Duke was good company. Hattersley goes so far as to state that he was *undoubtedly an insensitive and autocratic brute*. [21] This author has seen no evidence to support Hattersley's view which in any event is not substantiated. In fact, just the opposite was the case. See Appendix 1 for extracts from the Duchess's letters referring to the Duke.

At the end of the 1760s, the Duke was 22 years of age. The next decade saw him settling down into married life. It also saw his income rising with the copper revenues and the beginning of his investment plan. It was to be a defining chapter in his life.

On another issue, there is a tantalising glimpse of another aspect of the Duke. His commercial understanding may have been more limited than we might have expected. There is a story that Sir Joshua Reynolds told Julius Angerstein (the father of the National Gallery) that on one occasion when he (Reynolds) met the Duke, the latter asked why he did not retire, being so successful. Reynolds had to explain the difference between himself and the Duke! Reynolds had the privilege of being able to go to Devonshire House any time he pleased to look at the pictures. There were numerous old masters all over the house.

Finally, it needs to be remembered that the 6th Duke recorded that he had destroyed an 'immense' amount of his parent's letters. Our opinion of both the Duke and the Duchess has to be judged in this context. Our knowledge of the couple and Georgian aristocratic family life may well have been enhanced significantly had he not done so.

3

The 1770s: Marriage and Married Life

Enter Georgiana

It is not clear what brought the Duke and Georgiana Spencer together, but Bessborough states that it was at Spa in the Austrian Netherlands. The latter was a popular holiday destination for the British aristocracy. No doubt whatever created the encounter, Lady Spencer would have made the most of it. They were in a sense neighbours, as Spencer House was just opposite Devonshire House, the former backing onto the edge of Green Park. The Duke's in-laws did not however use it regularly.

The Spencers had been in Spa in the Autumn of 1772, when Georgiana was 15½ years old. Was the Duke there too? It is possible, for talk of a possible union between the Duke and Georgiana were circulating in 1772. The family moved from here to Paris, reaching there on 28th October and staying for two weeks. Her diary shows that essential elements of her character were already beginning to define themselves. On the day of arrival, at the Hotel de Radziwill, she was measured for a new robe, a pair of stays and a pair of shoes. She was soon noting that she had run out of money. She was also soon having dancing lessons, although presumably her parents picked up that cost. Both at Spa and in Paris, her parents were associating with the upper layer of aristocracy and members of the royal family. On the 4th November, her parents are noted as having returned from Fontainebleau, where presumably they had an audience with the King and Queen of France. Perhaps this is why in 1789, when back in Paris, she very quickly was associating with royalty and upper members of the French aristocracy.

Back in 1772, Georgiana had soon developed a friendship with the Comptess Amelia, particularly admiring her skill with the harp: *'I never heard anything so delightful, so much taste and so much expression ... I was extremely sorry to bid adieu to (her). I believe her being here adds greatly to the other motives that make me doat (sic) on Paris, a little self love may be another ingredient and in short, friendship, self love, love at dissipation and amusement...'.* [1] Georgiana became proficient as a harpist and later acquired the harp of the executed Queen, Marie Antoinette. As for dissipation and amusement, she was to lift this to a much higher plain after her marriage.

The Wedding

Shortly before the wedding, Lady Spencer described her daughter in a letter to a Mrs. Henry: *'she is amiable, innocent and benevolent but she is giddy, idle and fond of dissipation'.* Lady Spencer went on to add about Georgiana – *'she is a lovely young woman, very pleasing in her figure but infinitely more so from her character and disposition. My dread is that she will be snatched from me before her age and experience make her by any means fit for the serious duties of a Wife and Mother as the Mistress of a family'.* This letter of January 1774 was inadvertently never sent and when re-found three weeks before the wedding of Georgiana to the Duke, Lady Spencer continued it: *'My words are verified about Georgiana who is indeed to be taken from me much sooner than I think either for her advantage or my comfort as I had flattered myself I should have had more time to have improved her understanding and with God's assistance to have strengthened her principles and enabled her to avoid the many (? shares) that vice and folly will throw in her way.'* [2] In other words, although she agreed to it, she did not think that her daughter was ready for marriage.

One wonders what it was that determined the Duke to turn his future to such a potential partner. He must have been dazzled by her, despite her adolescence; her personality dominated perhaps by a captivating fragrance. Yet even her looks were called into doubt. Her mother referred to her figure in a positive tone, as one might expect. However, Wraxhall considered *'her beauty consisted in the amenity and graces of her deportment, in her irresistible manners, and the seduction of her society ... her face, though pleasing, yet had it not been illuminated by her mind, might have been considered ordinary.'* [3] He also held a forthright view of the Gainsborough portrait of her (with hat and feather) *'which probably does not represent any Dss of D at all ...'*

The Duchess admitted to her laziness later that year whilst at Londesbrough which the 4th Duke's wife had brought to the Devonshires through the death of her father and mother, Lord and Lady Burlington. *'I am ashamed to own how lazy I was this morning'.* Visitors (Sir Charles and Lady Thompson and Miss Hotham) had arrived and been let into the house *'before I knew anything about it … to complete my Distress another Coachful arrived of People I had never seen before'*. Her distress was to continue when she eventually went downstairs to receive them. *'As I could not have much to say for myself and that some of the Company were talking about things I new (sic) nothing of I made the silliest figure you can conceive and J* (? Lord John) *says I broke all the Rules of Hospitality in forgetting to offer them some breakfast'*. At least she offered dinner to yet more guests who turned up later the same day and stayed the whole evening. Prior to their marriage, they did have the opportunity of going away to Longleat, possibly the only time it happened: *'I recollect both of you saw it before you were married'*. [4]

Under the marriage settlement, the Duchess was to receive £4,000 per annum plus £1,000 per annum paid from specific estates. [5] Prior to the wedding, the Duke decided to buy a new coach and four coach horses to take him to Wimbledon Park for the ceremony. The coach maker charged £564 *'for new carriages etc'* and the horses cost £252. Even more was spent on liveries for the coachmen and other servants amounting to £766. This amounted to £1,582 in all and any other celebration costs at Devonshire House lie hidden in other expense headings and cannot be separately identified. The Duke's sister, the Duchess of Portland, found that she was to have more to do in the preparations for the marriage than she imagined or wished. She was to be consulted about the jewels and furniture but felt *'I shall be cautious how I give my advice as it can only be from civility that it is asked.'* It is worth noting that a married labouring couple working at the Duke's Ecton Copper Mine would be earning c. £23 pa between them. [6]

On 5th June 1774, the Duke and Lady Georgiana Spencer were married. Between February and May, the Duke had asked for her hand in marriage. It could not have been any later (indeed it was probably early in the year) in order that the bride's preparations could be completed and the marriage terms agreed. Financial arrangements concerning the new wife and future children would have to be settled on specific estates so that the income required would be protected. [7] In other words, the income from specified estates (or part of it) would be pledged as a guarantee as the source of income for the Duchess etc.

In the event, the wedding ceremony, which was to have been on the bride's 17th birthday, took place two days earlier, at Wimbledon Park. It was agreed to do this to avoid an assembly of a crowd beyond the gates. The Duke's gift to his bride was diamond jewellery. A month after the wedding, the Duchess received a letter from a relative, the Hon. Diana Sackville of Stoneland Lodge (now Buckhurst) in Sussex. She wrote that she had received *'a long description of the magnificence of your jewels'*. The Devonshire Collection Archives include a box of very small notebooks, presumably small enough to go into a muff.

One item in a notebook endorsed 'Various Memorandums' has a list of her wedding clothes, although it was written some years later (? c.1782). It states: *'The whole of what I paid for my wedding clothes is £3,649. 5s. 6d'. It then lists: 'My Loop print suit; My Valenciensse [Do]; My presenting Do; My trimming & suit complete; My wedding night cap & shift; My Bruxelles lace Apron'.* [8] This gives us a tantalising glimpse of her wedding trousseau and is the only known reference to it to survive. It cost her father an awful lot of money.

Her *Valenciensse* may refer to her wedding dress. Valenciennes lace came from that town in northern France and was very fashionable. Its main feature are patterns etc on a continuous piece of diamond shaped mesh or ground. She used Brussels lace however on the initial clothes and bedding of her two girls. The decision to bring forward the wedding to avoid the gathering of crowds etc. was probably at the suggestion of Georgiana's parents. They had married on 20th December 1755. That ceremony *'was performed privately in his mother's dressing room at Althorp and nobody in the house, though near 500 people, knew anything of the matter until the Saturday following'.* [9]

Following the wedding, which may have also been brought forward to allow more time to complete arrangements for the presentation of the Duchess at the Palace levée, her dress for that event had still be to be completed. Ribbon needed could not be obtained by Lady Clermont (her mother's friend) who sent a substitute, hoping it would do instead. The Countess wanted to be present when the Court gown was tried on in order to fit it to the wedding diamonds, which suggests that it was a different dress to her wedding dress. [10]

The extent of the wedding jewellery is not well understood. The main item was a stomacher. [11] Thus it was a relatively long and large assembly which Lady Spencer referred to as 'your diamonds' the day before the levée (see below). They would have sat on the front of her dress, necessitating a good corset underneath to flatten her breasts and create a flat platform upon which the jewels would lie. The stomacher would have been too long to dangle in front of her, swinging about below her bust. Hence Lady Clermont's comment of fitting the Court gown to the stomacher. It may have passed to Lady Georgiana, (Little G) the Duchess's oldest daughter; Haryo, is known not to have possessed many jewels. Whatever happened to it is unknown.

At the time of her death in 1806, some of the Duchess's wedding jewellery was held by Parker, a pawnbroker of Crane Street, off Fleet Street. He had been holding for nearly a year a watch and chain covered with diamonds and three rows of very fine quality pearls which were confirmed as being part of the wedding jewellery, purchased at a cost of £1,000.

Following the marriage of the 8th Duke to the Duchess of Manchester (the Double Duchess), she had much of the Chatsworth jewellery broken up to make a new tiara. Consequently there is little if anything remaining known to be earlier than the late 19th Century. Likewise there is little of a descriptive nature and it is necessary to rely on paintings and the accuracy/clarity of what is depicted. As a result, virtually nothing is known of the Duchess's jewellery other than a few surviving invoices, chiefly dating from the last years of her life.

First Days Together

A few days after the marriage, the Duke was seen out with his friends and this has been seized upon as though this is something significant in judging him. However the forthcoming levée at the Palace gave self-opinionated critics an opportunity to fire across the Duke's bows and whether justified or not, the mud stuck. The day before the levée, the Duchess received a letter from her mother, the wedding couple having gone back to London. It was full of advice from a concerned parent: '*I beg you will take care to be at Lord Jersey's by half an hour after four at the latest ... if you go in your chair, let it be in the morning one and do not let your servants put on their best liveries* (to avoid attracting attention one supposes). *I will send your diamonds to you as soon as I come to Town. I think you might wear the pearl earrings and necklace today as it will be better not to put on the diamonds till tomorrow but that may be just as you like best. I send this to Chiswick for fear the Duke of Devonshire should not be yet up that you may put him in mind of the levée for which I have some fear he will be too late and that will make your presentation to morrow very awkward*'. [12] This may suggest that she knew the Duke was going somewhere else first.

The Duchess presumably went with her parents or alone. Lady Spencer's ill feelings proved correct for the Duke was four hours late, almost missing the event. The Spencer's embarrassment must have been hard to conceal, just with the delay, the reason hopefully taking longer to leak out. If nothing else, this surely must indicate a complete lack of sensitivity by the Duke for leaving his young wife alone under such circumstances a week after her wedding. She was bound to be nervous, rightly expecting the support of her husband on such an occasion. With all eyes on her waiting to be introduced to the King (or Queen), he should have been with her.

However that does not infer that he was ill-mannered. That is one aspect of his character which is clear. The interfering Mrs. Delaney wrote that the only grace the Duke possessed was that of his dukedom but she was going too far. We do not know why he was late and in his favour, Lady Spencer wrote to the Duchess at the end of October 1774 to say that Lord Richard Cavendish (the Duke's younger brother) had dined with them the day before '*and added that the Duke did not express it so much as you* (the Duchess) *he believed he was no less happy than yourself*'.

The Duchess's parents completely believed him. Moreover, she continued, saying *'he likewise spoke in the highest manner of what both your Papa and I have been more and more convinced of the more we have seen the Duke. I mean his most excellent judgement and understanding'*. Clearly they were at ease with him ... *'you are married to a man whose temper, disposition and good sense put it in your power to be happy ...'*. Yet Lady Spencer does not seem to have rested until she had a confirmation from the Duke that he was happy with her. He wrote to her to that effect: *'I'm writing this letter to you, partly to convince you that you was mistaken in thinking that I was too lazy ever to write letters ... I shall allways (sic) be very happy if I can think I deserve your friendship of esteem'*. [13]

Following the wedding it was usual for the bride to spend time visiting many aristocratic ladies who would have been expecting the visit. There must have been quite a few for the cost of carrying her sedan chair about was £215. It is interesting to make a comparison of the average household costs per annum of Devonshire House for the three years prior to 1774 (i.e. 1771-73) and the three years afterwards 1775-77: £6,657 against £10,586. [14]

The Relationship of the Duchess and her Duke

Hattersley writes that in 1774, after three months of marriage that *'there is nothing in her* (i.e. the Duchess's) *letters to suggest that she was even remotely enthused in her new state. There was very little for her to be excited about. Her husband ... was one of the dullest men in society'* [1]. Foreman states *'three months into her marriage, Georgiana could not help but suspect the true nature of the Duke's feelings for her. He was kind in a distant sort of way, but he was naturally reticent and she soon realized that they had little in common. Her innocence bored him and Georgiana was too acute not to notice his lack of interest in her'*. [2]

The first two writers project, perhaps more strongly, a view which has been around for a long time. It ignores the fact that lots of letters, which may have told us more of him, were destroyed. Mrs Delaney was one of many who were happy to project a view which is not justified. She was not part of his set. It is easy for contemporary observers to write negatively about a shy young man taking the backseat at social gatherings. Especially when, through no fault of his own, he finds himself to be one of the richest men in the country when aged 16 years, foisted into the upper reaches of society without the guidance and support of his parents.

Hattersley goes on: *'But in later life, he seemed hardly able to show real enthusiasm even for the sexual adventures which interrupted his only true joy – gambling at Brooks's Club. Every activity was a bore.'* It creates for us an understanding that the Duke was incapable of feeling for others and had little interest in life or perhaps other than his sex life. As will be seen, the Duke had many interests. Where Hattersley gets his information to confirm that the Duke found every activity was a bore is not clear. His two chapters on the 5th Duke are moulded around this portrait of a dismal almost lifeless individual. All three writers share a common feature: the evidence suggests otherwise. Chapman on the other hand paints a different picture, quoting a letter from James Hare to Bess Foster, stating that the Duchess's best interests would be served if left entirely to the Duke's kindness and generosity. Hare was one of the Duke's closest friends and he would have been in a position to know better than most. [3]

His shyness may well have projected an image of *'dullness in society* 'as Hattersley puts it. But when did dullness in gatherings of society grandees have anything to do with one's love for another? Furthermore, the Duke's marriage had been arranged without much courtship. It is hardly surprising if in fact the newlyweds were still finding their feet together after twelve weeks. Yet Foreman tells us that ': *three months into her marriage, Georgiana could not help but suspect the true nature of the Duke's feelings for her. He was kind in a distant sort of way, but he was naturally reticent and she soon realized that they had little in common. Her innocence bored him and Georgiana was too acute not to notice his lack of interest in her'.*

She fails, like Hattersley, to quote any reference to support these comments. She also overlooks the comments by Lady Spencer, the bride's mother, that she was being *'snatched from her'* before she was ready for marriage. If she was so unready, was she competent to judge the Duke's feelings as a partner, let alone for his wife? Especially as she was only 17 years old two days after she married. What would she be expecting from her innocence being merged with the duties as mistress of such a large household overnight alongside the expectations of her married status in the bed of man she barely knew?

Hattersley rightly states that the Duchess rarely referred to the Duke in her correspondence. She does so in general terms but both she and her mother were always aware that the mail was liable to be read by servants or even mislaid while being delivered. Sometimes she did so, but in French. It would be unsafe to read much into this. She likewise did not mention her children that often or in detail. Moreover we only have the rump of her correspondence: her son burnt the bulk of it in 1826.

It is important that the relationship between the Duke and Duchess is correctly understood when the volume of evidence is slight. However, there is a repetitive theme, which keeps reoccurring through the Duchess's correspondence across the years of her marriage. It is the words written about the Duke in that letter of December 1774. Hattersley does himself no favours in incorrectly describing the

Duke as *'undoubtedly an insensitive and autocratic brute'*. From your author's perspective, the evidence points to the opposite being the case. He gives no reference to any source material for this either. See Appendix 1 for quotations in the Duchess's correspondence about the Duke. There are not that many, but there is a theme to them.

Moreover, the nature of the relationship expressed after six months of marriage was sustained, despite hiccups on both sides. It is worth reflecting that the Duchess may be seen to have potentially done more to poison their marriage through her debts than the Duke ever did through his shyness. It is a sign of the strength of their feelings for each other, especially after the birth of their son, that it survived at all.

To Chatsworth

Several weeks after the wedding, they set off for Chatsworth in Derbyshire. It took four days or so to make the journey and with the addition of the Duchess's staff, there would have been around a couple of dozen people involved, plus the Duke's horses (the Duchess was to develop her own team in due course) and the dogs.

The House was full of guests, including Lord and Lady Spencer. Unfortunately the latter suffered a miscarriage while she was there. Unable to face the others present, they left early in the morning of 22nd September for Althorp. Lady Spencer left a letter for the Duchess writing: *'pray take some opportunity of telling the Duke how much your Papa and I have been touch'd with the kindness and attention he has shown us'*. On the way back, they stopped off at Matlock to eat. The inn was so thick with smoke (probably from the fire) that Lady Spencer was relieved by it. It gave everybody sore and red eyes, disguising in her case the fact that she had been in tears at her own misfortune, losing a child literally in more ways than one. [15]

An early event after arrival was a Public Day when the House was open to visitors to be introduced to the Duke and Duchess and to receive (free) hospitality. Across the country these were in decline owing to the cost, but this was not a consideration for the Duke. The Public Day at Chatsworth was held twice each year, three weeks apart and in the autumn. Such events help to develop new friendships but perhaps more importantly maintained a link with the populace, especially local squires etc who could be relied upon to use their voting influence on his behalf.

On 19th July 1788, Lady Spencer went to the Public Day at Hatfield House: *'both Ld & Lady Salisbury seemed to take pains to be civil to everybody and I thought it less formal and disagreeable than these sort of things generally are'*. [16]

Of people of note to the Duke and Duchess, only Dr. Denman, the Duke's doctor from nearby Middleton who was kept on an annual retainer of c. £30 per annum, had turned up on the Public Day (25th September). Shortly afterwards, guests started to arrive. Three days later, the Duchess wrote to her mother to say *'our Party is growing up and up – it consists of Mr. FitzHerbert, Mr. Lite and Mr. Giardini has composed a new trio for me extremely pretty but requires practising'*.

It is interesting that an early guest was William FitzHerbert of Tissington Hall. He had accompanied the Duke on his Grand Tour to Italy in 1768 (with Mr Lyte) and they were of the same age and clearly good friends. Also like the Duke, he had lost his mother at an early age; he (FitzHerbert) was four when she died. William FitzHerbert was a Gentleman Usher to the King, a barrister at law and recorder of Derby. He was created a Baronet on 22nd January 1784 and his descendants still live at Tissington Hall where Sir Richard is the current Baronet. William married on 14th October 1777 Sarah Perrin of Jamaica (she died in 1795), the only daughter of William Perrin. They had four sons and two daughters. [17]

Moving On To Hardwick

The Duke and Duchess moved to Hardwick in October 1774 and were joined there by the Duke's uncles and William FitzHerbert. They (excluding the Duke, who constitutionally was barred) went to an Election Ball in Derby soon after their arrival and there they met William's only sister. The Duchess was impressed by her. Writing to her mother she said: *'she is not handsome but has (a) very engaging manner and the Meynells give her a very high character. I shall be very glad to take all the notice I can of her for she has now no father nor mother and being so blest as I am in two such Parents, I cannot help feeling for those who are depriv'd of their nearest friends'*. [18] In September 1776 William FitzHerbert joined the Chatsworth house party for a few days and the Duchess wrote of him *'he is so good humoured, sensible and unaffected (sic) that it is impossible not to like him'*. [19]

On the 12th July 1774, Dr. Samuel Johnson accompanied by Mr. and Mrs. Thrale and their ten year old daughter (later Lady Keith) visited Chatsworth. The Thrales *'were not struck with the house ... it fell below my ideas of the furniture'*. There is also an inference that the Devonshire Arms at Edensor did not come up to the mark either: *'a bad inn'*, but the name is not given. However Johnson was taken up by one of the Duke's horses: Atlas. He was *'very handsome and very gentle'*. Johnson said *'of all the Duke's possessions, I like Atlas the best'*! [20] There is no mention of the Duke and Duchess being in residence or having just married. It would appear that his next visit was on 6th September 1784, when they met him. Boswell does not mention the Duke and Johnson meeting in London, or the Duke being a member of The Literary Club, where Johnson was its President and Lord Althorp, the Duchess's brother, was a member.

Hardwick Hall was built by the Duke's famous ancestor, Bess of Hardwick. It stands on a high ridge south of Bolsover, an ancient and perhaps then a draughty house, but nonetheless loved by generations of the Cavendish family. No sooner had they arrived and the Duchess went off to Derby to the Election Ball (mentioned above) on the 8th, changing at Mr. Gisburn's house into a demi-saison silk dress, trimmed with *'Gause and Green Ribbon'*. Her evening did not start off too well, as she was greeted on arrival by *'F on the stairs'* (Uncle Lord Frederick Cavendish who was staying at Hardwick) *'extremely drunk'*. If he was after a dance, he did not get one, as she stood up to dance with Tom Coke, the son of the retiring MP (who decided to stand for Norfolk rather than Derby).

The Sunday night Ball was held in the Assembly Rooms, built in 1764. It had been funded by a group of local people chaired by the 4th Duke. The assemblies were held regularly with more at the time of the Derby Races and subscriptions were taken in advance for a certain number of evenings. They were usually well attended by Derby socialites. [21] However on the night of the Ball nobody was refused at the door and the Duchess recalled in a letter to her mother: *'the Ball Room was quite full of the Daughters and Wives … in check'd aprons etc'*. It would have presented quite a contrast to the fine silk or muslin draped elegant Duchess whom they had come to see.

Being a peer, the Duke was not allowed to be seen doing anything which may be construed as influencing the election, which is why he had remained behind. Although supposedly not permitted, bribery of the electorate was rife. Even miners from the Duke's mine at Ecton went off to Derby in 1784 to spend the Duke's money on ale etc for votes. There were also the Whig supporters amongst many who were better off, who sat above the salt although never meeting the Duke except perhaps on one of the Public Days. One such person was the school friend of Dr Johnson who lived at Ashbourne: the Rev. Dr. Taylor. He lived in Church Street at The Mansion and he was a Prebendary of Westminster and Rector of Bosworth. At Ashbourne he was a Justice of the Peace.

During the winter of 1775, he had distributed £200 to the poor out of his own pocket. He had *'considerable political interests in Derbyshire, which he employed to support the Devonshire family, for although the school fellow and friend of Johnson, he was a Whig.'* Boswell wrote: *'His size and figure and countenance and manner were that of a hearty English squire, with the parson superinduced: and I took particular notice of his upper-servant, Mr Peters, a decent grave man, in purple clothes and a large white wig, like the butler or major-domo of a bishop.'* Maintaining his influence with people like Dr. Taylor who would have, in turn, influence over a number of voters, was important in returning the Duke's nominee to Parliament. [22]

The Duke therefore had to rely on his wife and his brothers to help the Devonshire nominated candidate. What better way of seducing votes than to have her turn up that night on the eve of the general election. Even her first dance partner (see above), Tom Coke of Melbourne Hall south of Derby, was the son of the expected local candidate. It is possible that that had been pre-arranged, may be by Uncle Frederick who was in Derby ahead of her. Countess Cowper (the Duchess's grandmother) wrote to her after the Ball stating that her dancing had been much admired *'as it is beyond ye common run'*. [23]

In her eagerness to dance she rose onto the dance floor with young Mr. Coke and was kept waiting for *'almost ten minutes in the middle of the Room before they could make the Musick to play a minuet and when they did they all of them play'd different parts – I danced Country Dances with Mr. Coke .....'*. It must have been hilarious. She probably skipped the hunting the following day, but her practice was to ride daily after breakfast. The day after (Tuesday) she joined the Duke and possibly all three of his uncles (who had another election meeting on the Thursday), in fishing in one of the Hall ponds. Successfully, too, obtaining *'carp larger than any I ever saw'*. On the Thursday, the Duke and Duchess rode together to call on a Mrs. Hallows and Lady Hunloke, of Wingerworth Hall, who was pregnant and not well. Although going unannounced, they were both at home. That week Lord Edward Bentinck lost his seat for Nottinghamshire, held under the patronage of the Duke of Portland. The Duchess told her mother *'I am sorry for it for my Dear Duke of Portland's sake for whom you know I have so serious a passion'*. [24]

The quote about 'F' being extremely drunk is the entirety in the Duchess's letter. Foreman writes: *'The Duke's brothers were already drunk by the time she arrived and Lord Frederick Cavendish almost fell on her as she climbed the stairs to the assembly room'*. The source quoted, letter 28 of 9/10/74, makes no reference to these additional comments. This is important in two ways: like the Duchess, the uncles were there to elicit support, literally buying votes if necessary. One uncle being drunk was bad enough, all three would likely do more harm than good, negating the good work the Duchess was undoubtedly doing for the cause (i.e. assisting the election campaign of the Duke's candidate). For her part, she would be doing what her mother had been up to the same week, at that point unknown to her. However if all three uncles were drunk, surely her letter to her mother would have indicated as such, let alone if Frederick had almost fallen on her. The source quoted appears to be incorrect.

It would be easy enough to dwell too much on this if it was a singular example. However, Chapter 2 of Foreman's book covers the days after the wedding. She states, for instance, that: *'the road had dwindled to little more than a bumpy track by the time the cavalcade of wagons and baggage carts reached Derbyshire'*. There had been plenty of reasonably good turnpike roads in the county for a generation and Lady Spencer recounted to her daughter about the good surface on the turnpike to Buxton from Ashbourne for instance.

Public Days, we are told, were held weekly, an error also made by Chapman. They were held twice a year when the Duke and Duchess were in residence, on Mondays three weeks apart in the autumn. In one year, an exceptional third one appears to have been held. They were an opportunity for the populace, whoever they were, to meet the Duke and Duchess during the time that they were in residence. There would be little point in holding them when they were not there, which was most of the year. Against this background, there follows the comment referred to above, relating to the couple's early relationship: *'three months into her marriage … they had little in common.*

Some idea of the Duchess's routine is possible: riding after breakfast; music lessons; taking further lessons on drawing *'from the delightful Mr. Thomas'*. Into this was the necessity of sitting in conversation with callers although that did not stop trips out as necessary. For example, on one occasion from Hardwick after tea, the Duchess rode over to Chesterfield to buy books, followed later by dinner for which the Duke and Duchess changed into more formal clothing. They tended to play cards in the evening. The Duke's activities remain a mystery but would include outdoor activity with staying guests (usually the men), dealing with estate matters as required with John Heaton plus other issues which cropped up. These included sorting out scrapes within the family on financial matters, rearranging family trusts, marriage settlements etc. Heaton was kept very busy, but was never employed by the Duke, being self-employed. Their meetings must have been fairly frequent, although letters survive showing that the Duke was also kept up to date by post.

Clearly the Duke and Duchess were going out together visiting etc. The Duke would also have had other calls on his time. Visitors seeking his support within the community, for example was one. For instance, he seems to have been involved in the building of Derby Hospital as he paid the account of its architect, Thomas Pickford. He was also Lord Lieutenant of Derbyshire following his father. It isn't clear to what extent that placed a demand on his time beyond the summer military camps.

He was summoned to the House of Lords in c. 1769 taking his seat following his return from France in early 1770. There is virtually nothing in the estate accounts to indicate that he made many formal visits to his estates, although he did use his various family homes, except the relatively small house at Lismore Castle in Ireland, Londesbrough in Yorkshire (south west of York near

Pocklington) and Burlington House close to Devonshire House in Piccadilly, which in 1771 was rented to his sister and her husband, the Duke of Portland.

Londesbrough

By the autumn of 1774, the Duchess had established a routine of letter writing to her mother who was keen to know everything she could of what was happening in her daughter's life. While at Londesbrough, the post took two days to get there and the service was seven days a week. Her mother continually gave her encouragement as she settled into her new role as a Duchess and in charge of the household. Writing to Londesbrough a month before Christmas, she wrote: '*I am delighted with you and the Duke for going to the village church. If you were both to do it constantly wherever you are you cannot imagine how much good your example would do …*'. [25]

It is clear that The Duchess liked the old house at Londesbrough, initially preferring it to Chatsworth. She described the gardens: '(they) *appear to be laid out something in the style of Chiswick as that was the favourite taste of Ld. Burlington*'. In the house '*I found here a very good piano forte & Mr. Evans* (who was the Prebend of York and there when they arrived) *says there is a good harpsichord and an excellent master who comes to a family near us – I shall certainly take lessons of him as it will be a sure method of keeping up my music.*' [26]

Bad weather however prevented them from going out as much as she would have wished. It is also clear that the couple were getting on well. Together they played music, the Duke on the violin and The Duchess's music master being '*a very tolerable second*'. They made return visits to people who had called to see them as was usual practice and at least once were '*rejoiced*' to find that a rather formal lady – Mrs. Bethel – was not at home.

To recap on their movements: a few weeks after the wedding, they went to Chatsworth where they stayed until moving on to Hardwick on about 9th October 1774. On 7th November they were at Londesbrough (going from Hardwick) and then in mid-December they moved on to Althorp. Their movements from there are less clear. They could have stayed there for Christmas. In those days it was no great social occasion as it is now and only the one day was observed. Often the daytime was occupied being hospitable to visitors calling, sometimes clearly without any warning, the call expected to be reciprocated. Friends or relatives would often come for days on end, presumably by arrangement, hunting, shooting and fishing being popular pastimes for the Duke. The latter and the Duchess made music together with the Duchess also having music lessons from her music master. They both did a lot of reading and the Duchess would have been encouraged in that at Althorp by her mother, who seemed to read as often as she could. Church on Sundays was a regular part of the week for the Duchess and she mentions going with the Duke and when opportunity allowed, with her mother.

It is likely that she soon found herself playing cards in the evening with the Duke (and her mother too), except the latter knew when to stop, confining her play to one or two rubbers of whist etc. and never games of chance. Finally, the Duke was getting on with his father-in-law, staying with him (and hunting) early in 1775 when both their wives were absent but not together.

This image appeared in an appreciation of the late Duke in 1811, written by Sir Robert Adair. It is an engraving of Anton von Maron's painting of 1768 -69 when the Duke was in Rome on his Grand Tour. It has been altered to include the Duke's Garter Star, which dates from 1782 when he became a Member of the Order of the Garter

4

Early Days

A Change of Scene and Pace: London, early 1775

Having moved from Londesbrough to Althorp in mid-December 1774, it is not clear where they spent Christmas. However it is clear that they had gone on to London early in 1775. An undated note probably was written at this time by the Duke to his wife: '*I am going to sup in St. James's Place and I have sent you the carriage that you may come in it if you like it. Devonshire*'. Georgian formality saw close relatives using their title when writing. The Duchess's father when writing to her signed off with 'Spencer'. Whether she went isn't clear but another note, this time from the Duchess to her mother in February shows her distraught at his nightly absences.

Her mother was probably at Wimbledon Park when she received this note: '*As the Duke dines at Almacks, if you will give me leave if you have not people with you to come with you I shall be very glad, may I come in a nightgown or will you have me in my polonaise*'. [6]

What was it that drove her to write so frantically to her mother? Presumably it was late and she was in her nightgown. She could clothe herself up to her polonaise (an underskirt with a bodice attached). Her dresses must have required assistance from her maid, probably because they were fastened or laced up on the back and her maid was not available. Devonshire House was an extremely large house for an eighteen year old girl to want to spend too many evenings there on her own (servants excluded). As a result of this, it may be that she started going to Almacks with the Duke, as may be judged below, or having card parties at home. However there was nothing discreet in her socialising, although her miscarriage in 1775 may have made her more circumspect about her behaviour.

After her night at the Derby Assembly Room Ball, the Duchess must have been looking for an opportunity of repeating it and Devonshire House was the ideal venue. She was clearly wanting to get on with organising it and just prior to Easter the Duke wrote to her from Althorp. He had clearly been expecting to hear from her and it appears she had been keeping him waiting. *'what a naughty little wretch you are to have wrote to me once since I came here for I don't reckon your first for anything as it was not above four lines. Lord Spencer intends to stay out of town till after Easter Hollydays (sic) and expects Lady Spencer to come to him and I hope you will come with her as I have told Ld. Spencer that I will stay with him so that I think you cannot have the Ball till after Easter week ... as it will as well that we should be in town four or five days before, in case of having to ask people etcetera ... (having been hunting) I cannot write anymore or read this over again to look for mistakes. Devonshire.'*

A letter survives from the Duchess of Portland, probably to her husband, which possibly puts this letter a little more into its proper context. Unfortunately it is undated but it states that there was to be a *'superb ball at Devonshire House the week after Easter ... The Duke of Devonshire has had a fever and looks very thin and ill'*. [7]

The Duke could not have been too pleased with the quality of the beer at Devonshire House for he called for the Chatsworth brewer, Richard Holden, to go down there. Huge quantities of wine and beer were kept at the houses although the turnover at Devonshire House would have been greater than at the others owing to the level of entertaining there. (see Chapter 24, Life at Chatsworth)

The Duchess in Debt, 1775

She had not been writing because she had been gambling and losing badly. This presumably in the short time they had been in London and at least some of it at Almack's Club. One gets the impression that her projection into London society had not been handled properly by the Duke. There is a widespread understanding that the Duchess had gambling debts. However that is only part of the picture. She was a compulsive spender too, having little or no regard for her allowance. To the Duke she was just a girl and she received a significant amount of patient acceptance, her excesses put down to that by a man living behind his barrier of shyness. Yet her reputation for excess was well founded.

Nonetheless the Duchess faced a significant dilemma; she did not have the money to pay the debts. She wrote to her mother on 13th April 1775 (only about three months after arriving in London): *'I begin to grow uneasy about money for I don't think I can well tell the Duke and if any of his family was to know it they would be more certainly very angry about it. If it was possible to borrow the money just to get out of the scrape now, I think I would better tell him next year or any time than at present'.* [8]

This raises certain questions: Did she think she was pregnant and not wishing to follow her mother who had lost two babies did she really mean to tell him in 1776? Was the Duke content to allow his wife's excesses to come under the scrutiny and comment of his uncles, allowing them to be his mouthpiece? The Duchess received back a letter of admonishment from her mother from Wimbledon Park, the letter sent the next day, clearly shocked by what had happened and understandably not as patient as the Duke. She worried about its effect on him: *'the Duke of D. from any mistaken tenderness persists in not dictating to you the things he wishes you to do and not contradicting you in any thing however disagreeable to him'.* The letter focuses on the Duchess's duty to others and in particular, the Duke, her parents and her younger sister etc., but also hints that she will help out with the money needed. [9]

The Spencers sent the money and the Duchess, no doubt then in repentant mood, told the Duke, who repaid her parents. Trying to appease the latter, she wrote *'you can not conceive how seldom Almacks ... are thought of ...'.* She also told them *'it is like every thing else he does, but consider my dearest Mama how all these marks of his goodness must attach me to him ...'.* Experience was to prove otherwise. There is an indication that the amount of the debt was £3,000. The Duke's personal account book does not mention Lord Spencer, but there is a payment noted as 'P'd the bearer' £3,000 on 29th June 1775. There are no other payments like this which could be an alternative.

The Duchess's father, 1st Earl Spencer inherited immense wealth, which he spent unwisely. His descendant, Charles Spencer states that he *'was a man of generous and amiable disposition, spoiled by having been placed at too early a period of his life, in possession of what then appeared to him in exhaustible wealth...'.* [10] This could easily have been written about his daughter and her attitude to money and spending it. Although she was directly not a very wealthy woman, this did not stop her spending, ever hopeful from an early age that her husband would eventually pay for her largesse.

Her father spent an estimated £120,000 on the 1768 election and even more on Spencer House in London. All this resulted after his death in 1783 in his widow, Lady Spencer, confined to a £4,000 annuity and the house at Wimbledon Park to live in. The Duchess's sister Harriet experienced much of her life in similar circumstances. The Bessboroughs lived in a large house with empty pockets and much debt, like many of their contemporaries.

On the15th April 1785, the Duchess of Portland reported to her husband that the Duke (and presumably the Duchess) had gone to Bath to drink the waters. It must have been decided upon rather suddenly as a dinner at Devonshire House on the 16th had been cancelled *'as the Ponsonbys are engaged'*. [11]

The Duchess may not have known that in addition to the loss of money paid out to cover her debts, the Duke had another financial problem that year. A Mr. Collins had been declared bankrupt owing the Duke £6,718. Although some of this was recovered, the Duke lost £4,296 plus his legal fees (to John Heaton). [12] It is difficult to understand what this was for other than knowing that £964 was on the Devonshire House estate and £5,754 on the Burlington Estate. Was he the Collector of Rents?

Other Events in 1775-76

Having paid his father-in-law the £3,000, the Duke appears to have decided, probably in late May/early June, that it might be best to go away for a while to Spa, then in the Austrian Netherlands, now Belgium, a favourite destination for the Spencers particularly. With the latter there too, maybe the Duchess would quieten down for a while. The Duke and Duchess returned on 27th July leaving the Spencers behind, who appear to have stayed until early October when they moved to Paris. After a ten hour passage across the Channel to Dover, they hastily drove towards Sittingbourne. They probably stayed at an inn there and changed their horses, hired in Dover. From there they went on to Welbeck Abbey, a home of the Duke of Portland and the Duke's sister, Dorothy, before reaching Chatsworth early in August.

The Duchess found that there had been some changes within the house, but not in the Park. Her *'little dressing room has been entirely new furnished and is extremely very pretty'*. [13]. They went off to Chesterfield Races (where the Duke annually provided a £50 plate, as at Derby) just prior to a large house party at Chatsworth. There was an outbreak of smallpox in the village (presumably Edensor) and children there had been inoculated. Lady Spencer enquired if the Duchess had been to enquire how they were getting on *'but not to go into the houses as sick rooms and sick houses are things I beg you will always avoid'*.

The Duchess had been nowhere near, partly because they were well (from enquiries she had made) and *'I could not have gone for the 1st time about the Village without being guided by Mr. Barker and the poor old man never had the smallpox so that he has been confin'd here but as I fancy all infection is now over I will go there very soon'*. Nonetheless, her mother knew the necessity of being seen in the village as soon as it was safe to do so.

Relations with the Duke were good: *'the Duke is in very good spirits – I sincerely hope he is contended (sic) with me, tho if he is not he said as if he is to me how much he seems to make it his business to see me happy and pleased – with so much reason as he had had to be discontented at such a number of things*

I have very little right to expect it … I flatter myself that you must know that it (my heart) is capable of being sincerely touched especially by the unmerited goodness of people I love'. [14]

No doubt the Duke was enjoying his Chatsworth house party. Lord and Lady Jersey were there, together with Lord Egremont; Mr. Fitzpatrick; James Hare; Felix Gardini (their musician) was expected; Lady Diana Sackville; Mrs. Shipley and the Duchess's friend and socialite Miss Lloyd whom she collected from the stage coach in Derby (possibly the London – Manchester coach, which stopped there). Also expected was Lady Melbourne, with her 5 year old boy, but without Lord Melbourne. She was apparently going to her father's house in Yorkshire. Amanda Foreman relates that after the birth of his heir, the latter allowed his wife to follow her sexual pursuits as she wanted. It brought titles and positions to him. She gained a reputation as a serious predator, especially where another woman was to lose by it.

She possibly displaced Lady Jersey as the Prince of Wales' mistress, bearing his child, George Milbanke in 1784. She had four children of which only the first and last appear to have been with her husband, the other two by Lord Egremont.

If she was a serious sexual predator of men, she presumably had the Duke in her sights, even if she was unsuccessful. Yet we know he had had a woman like her before – Madame du Barry – and was content to marry just as his mistress appears to have had his child. He was soon to have a very open affair with Lady Jersey at Coxheath Military Camp whilst his wife was living with him on the base. [15] Lord and Lady Jersey did not stay long however, leaving Chatsworth on the 2nd September.

It is easy to make an assumption here but the probability was that the presence of Lord Egremont and Lady Melbourne was because of a relationship between the two. Nonetheless, the Duke must have been the centre of attention for many a female eye. His power, position and pockets deeper than most must have ensured that. On 1st October 1775, the Duchess had a miscarriage. The Duke wrote that day to advise her parents, adding that Dr. Denman had told him that she was *'surprisingly well and that he has not often seen a woman in her situation whose health seemed to have suffer'd so little'.* [16]

The sad news was told to a visitor two days later by a gardener who also commented that it was alarming because of Lady Spencer also having had several miscarriages. The visitor was Frances Cust writing to her mother, Lady Banks, from Belton Hall, Grantham; she was on her honeymoon and wife of Sir B. Cust. She described Chatsworth as being *'not well furnished'.* [17] Interestingly the gardener had been told the miscarriage had happened on the 2nd. Ironically, the Duke's sister had had a baby girl about that time. She was called Charlotte and the Duchess was one of her godmothers. [18]

It is interesting to see that the impression left on Mrs. Cust, following her trip to Chatsworth to look around the house and garden as a day visitor (as distinct from an invited guest), was the lack of good furnishings. She would not have seen the private apartments where improvements had commenced to the Duchess's taste (see above). With the death of the Duke's mother in 1754, 6½ years after her marriage, it looks as though little, if anything had been done to improve the house interior. This was to change in 1783. Later still, the Duchess was still continuing to buy small items. Her purchases ranged from cheese graters to barometers from John Whitehurst of Derby (the latter being still in the house). The refurbishment of 1782-83 and the purchase by the Duke of Reynolds' now famous painting of the Duchess and Little G as a baby were among the most significant items. The painting was brought on the baggage cart from Devonshire House in 1800 when the family came in September to stay until after Christmas. Two French tables arrived from her mother in 1775, possibly for the Duchess's *'little dressing room'*.

Further afield, storm clouds were gathering across the Atlantic in the American colonies. William Penn had arrived in August and presented a petition seeking a resolution of conflict. Generals Burgoyne and Gage had been recalled and Parliament was to meet to discuss the crisis on 31st October. The Duchess thought it was wonderful news *'for the chance there is of its bringing us all together soon'*. The Duke and Lord John Cavendish made plans to return to London. They must have been away for c. five months.

Over in Paris the recall hadn't gone down too well with Lord Spencer who felt the need to write to his daughter after the miscarriage: *'...I do not at all relish the beginning of winter again in London so easily for this abominable meeting of Parliament which I suppose you have no objection to* (the man certainly knew his daughter). *But I cannot help lamenting it upon your account too as I am afraid of your having so much more of all the racketing which did you a great deal of harm last year.*

However I hope you will be a little more cautious especially after the accident (the miscarriage) *you have had or you will entirely lose your good looks if not especially your constitution and indeed my Dear Georgiana you have already experienced that you have a kind and generous husband who deserves that you should preserve your health and beauty for him. I suppose the Duke of D will not be inclined to stay longer in Town than is necessary and I shall certainly, as soon as the American business is finished, get down to Althorp where I hope we shall have a good deal of your company this year if he does not go back to Derbyshire or Yorkshire...'*

His spirits were not raised on viewing the sea at Calais. Although Admiral Harland, the ships' captain, had decided to sail, the prospect of a sick-inducing

10 – 12 hour passage to Dover was too much. Recall or not he decided to wait for fairer weather [19]. The Duchess's admonishment wasn't over either. She received a rather stern letter from Lady Clermont, her mother's friend: '... *what possessed you child to miscarry, don't let me hear of such a thing again'.* [20] She would appear to have been of the belief that it was a symptom of her behaviour, not for any medical reason.

The return from Paris could have done little to improve Lady Spencer's spirits either. She had already complained to the Duchess that it was '*one of the dullest seasons I ever saw, no* (? Parties), *no Breakfasts ... no Races, in short nothing but Balls that tire every Lady and* Pharoh (gaming) *that ruins them'*. The jibes from Lady Clermont continued, albeit with assurances of continuing love etc.: '*...I sometimes forget that you are a* <u>sober</u> *Duchess and think I am talking to the wild Lady Geo.'* Whatever the latter had got up to that Spring was still haunting her at the end of the year. Meanwhile Lady Jersey, who ultimately had at least ten children in all, was probably having another when Lady Spencer visited her just prior to Christmas. Lady Spencer recorded that she looked very well '*but is monstrously big and rather fat'.* [21]

1776: Cementing Relationships

Although Lord Spencer hoped to get away from London after the recall of Parliament, it is not clear what the Duke's activities were until the middle of 1776. In the month that saw the 13 American colonies declaring independence (on 4th July), he and the Duchess returned to Chatsworth on the 25th. [22] They had been at Wilton House, the home (then as now) of the Earl and Countess of Pembroke, near Salisbury. It was then the home of the 10th Earl, married to the Duchess's aunt Lady Elizabeth Spencer, the daughter of the 3rd Earl of Marlborough. Elizabeth was the sister of Lady Diana Beauclerk (previously Sackville). Diana had a daughter Elizabeth who married her cousin, Aunt Elizabeth's son, George Augustus who became the 11th Earl. [23] From this it would appear they probably left London in June, having spent eight months there.

On the way back to Chatsworth on 25th July 1776 the Duke and Duchess went to a regatta on Whittlesea Mere, south-west of Peterborough. It was one of the largest inland lakes in the country in the then county of Huntingdon, where the Duke had an estate. It extended in size for 3½ miles from west to east and 2½ miles from north to south, but was shallow, being no more than 7ft/2.3m deep. It was the last of the large fenland lakes which had been drained chiefly in the previous century. It is now agricultural land, being finally drained by 1850. In the summer it was c. 1,870 acres /756 ha in extent but nearly doubling in size in winter. It appears to have been used for regattas by the aristocracy.

In 1774, George Walpole, 3rd Earl of Orford had nine boats on the water for a month for his friends, so the event the Duke attended may have been something similar. (24)

If the Duke had reason to go back to Chatsworth on account of the good weather, he was not to be disappointed. On 28th July, writing to her mother, the Duchess stated: *'Chatsworth is reckoned to be in its full beauty this summer, the plantations* (now Stand Wood) *are much grown, the verdure is remarkably green and the river full smooth and clear'*. That evening she, accompanied by the Duke, passed the time driving behind her four little ponies up to the tower above Stand Wood, which had been built by Bess of Hardwick, and into the wood.

The new woodland extended into former moorland and away from the valley. It is probable that this also included the valley-side behind the house for she wrote *'when it grows will add very much to the boldness of the hill'*. It was one of the few external changes made to the land around the house, although the Duchess also wrote later that the valley-side had been smoothed. (25)

These were not the only alterations however for more work had been done on the private apartments. Again, writing to her mother in the same letter, she wrote: *'I looked over the appartments they are much improved. I have settled all your rooms – yours is to be the blue and my father's if he likes it the room he had before, as Ld Richard does not come I intend my sister should have his room as a bed … may be put up in his dressing room, so it is next door to me'*.

On their return back to the house after the visit to Stand Wood, they were met by Lord Carlisle, Mr. Storer and Mr. Boothby. Country seats were like inns for the aristocracy. That evening they played cards at commerce, which is about as close as the Duke came to commercial work. Taking advantage of the glorious day, they rode out in the morning before having to return, for Monday 29th was a Public Day. There were only five visitors, including Dr. Denman, their consulting doctor.

No sooner had they all gone *'we set out on an amazing walk up to the stand and down the plantation it quite a glorious day and we made Mr. Storer sing to us all the way. The evening was spent at commerce* (both Duke and Duchess had become infatuated with it) *before supper and some whist afterwards'*. They repeated this on the Tuesday. *'Chatsworth really looks so beautiful they are all in raptures with it'*. The good weather continued but there was a diversion that evening, 30th July 1776. After supper they opened the windows and watched the total eclipse, the last one until 15th May 1836. It began just after 10p.m and lasted until 1.30a.m. (26)

Within a couple of days some of the guests were expected to leave but with the anticipated arrival of the Duke's sister, the Duchess of Portland, the stream of visitors was endless. A couple of nights before the second Public Day found them enjoying themselves with a musical evening, a popular pastime, with the Duke and Duchess playing with Felix Giardini and Mr. Borghi and other friends forming an audience of yet more guests.

The following Monday, 5th August, was the second Public Day, causing the Duchess (and probably the Duke) to rise and dress earlier than usual. There were more visitors this time, despite a change in the weather to rain. Visitors included General Gisburn and his wife, a pretty Irish lady (whom the Duchess had stayed with at the time of the 1774 Ball at Derby) and Lord Scarsdale with Mr. Curzon (probably his son) from Kedleston Hall near Derby. Another visitor was regular guest Sir Harry Hunlocke (sic), actually Sir Henry Hunloke, 4th Baronet. He married Margaret Coke on 21st December 1769 and died 15th November 1804. He lived at nearby Wingerworth Hall, an elegant three storey nine by seven bays house set in 2,600 acres. [27] After his death, Margaret moved to London and lived at Saville Row until her death in 1821. She became part of the London social scene and on the Duchess's guest list.

Margaret came from Longford Hall, west of Derby. Her brother Thomas Coke was later the 1st Earl of Leicester of Holkham, MP for Norfolk and well known for his improvements to agriculture. [28] Apparently Sir Harry *almost cried with joy'* when the Duchess said to him that *'Mr. Garrick was to come into Derbyshire'.* Tom Coke was the Duchess's dancing partner at the Derby Ball in September 1774 and it was probably through him that she met his sister Margaret and Sir Harry, the latter developing a friendship with the Duke. Thomas went on to marry just four days after the Duchess's miscarriage, which no doubt prevented their attendance on 5th October 1775. Details of David Garrick's visit to Chatsworth have not survived. Nor have many of the letters written between the Duchess and her mother over the next couple of years. In October 1776, Garrick was at Althorp where Lady Spencer found that he *'keeps me constantly employed either in laughing or in puzzling at his sharads'* (charades). [29]

On 2nd October 1776 the Duke and Duchess left for a couple of days at Welbeck Abbey (his sister's house) before continuing on to Londesbrough. Also going there were the Duke's Uncle Frederick and Mr. & Mrs. Ponsonby. These three were enjoying a very good relationship with the Duchess particularly. She told her mother that she was *'quite in love'* (no physical sense) *with Lord Frederick's charming presence and good humour and Mrs. Ponsonby's good nature, liveliness, consideration for others etc'.* Horace Walpole described Lord Frederick as being *'by far the most agreeable and possessed the most useful sense of the whole family'.* [30]

The Duke rode and the Duchess went in the chaise to York where they were joined by the other three for the final few miles to the south-west to Londesbrough. They were there for only a couple of weeks, paying visits together in the morning and entertaining their neighbours in the evenings. Then they packed up again and headed off for Althorp on their way to London, probably in late October. They had been joined by Lords John and George and they all left with regrets. At least the Duke had kept his wayward wife from London for at least the previous six months. For the Duke it was back to the House of Lords and for his wife an incessant round of daily socialising, going to plays, the opera and late night suppers. This time she appears to have heeded her mother's advice. She started telling her of her losses – ten guineas here, twelve there; this was affordable.

The Duchess also went to the American debate in the House of Commons on 1st November 1776 with Lady Jersey. The Duke had a box at the opera. Amongst his usual inner circle of friends (which included the Melbournes) were Charles Fox, Sir Charles Bunbury, Lady Pembroke, Lord Carlisle, Lord Fitzwilliam plus Mr. Fitzpatrick. Lord Egremont wasn't mentioned but was likely to be there as the Duchess described him the following day as 'being very handsome'. Just what the Duke was up to isn't recorded, but if he wasn't keeping his eye on his wife, her father was; dining with her 'tete a tete' on several evenings. The Duke was certainly socialising with her on some nights out. What was recorded was: *'with regard to play I have done nothing that signifies*, (i.e. of consequence), *the Duke of Devonshire has been very good and shown great virtue for he has not up very often at Almacks and yet has never play'd but once and then only for … 20 minutes'.*

Lord Carlisle was the 5th Earl of Carlisle. His father's first wife was Lady Frances Spencer, daughter of the 3rd Earl of Sunderland and Lady Annabel Cavendish, who died young. His second wife was Lady Margaret Caroline Leveson-Gower, daughter of the 1st Marquis of Stafford who gave birth to the 6th Earl. She was the grand-daughter of the canal builder, the 1st Duke of Bridgwater. The 5th Earl, Frederick Howard, born 28th May 1748, was appointed a Privy Counsellor in 1777 and a year later, the Commissioner to negotiate with the colonists in America. [31] Their son, Lord Morpeth, later the 6th Earl, married the Devonshire's oldest daughter, Georgiana, (Little G) in 1801.

William, Marquis of Kildare (who met the Duke in Turin in 1768) also met Lord Carlisle in that Italian city. He wrote to his mother: *'I can't say I miss Lord Carlisle, as he is certainly a great coxcomb* (conceited person) *and what is worse is that (he) despises everybody, especially foreigners. He would not allow there was a sensible person here, which is a thing he could not judge of, as he never opened his lips to any of them.'* [32]

Lord Fitzwilliam was the 8th Earl Fitzwilliam, born 30th May 1748. He married

Lady Charlotte Ponsonby, the daughter of William Ponsonby and Lady Caroline Cavendish on 11th July 1770. The latter was the 5th Duke's aunt, so the 8th Earl was married to the Duke's cousin.

Who were Mr. and Mrs. Ponsonby? Probably William, son of the Rt. Hon. John Ponsonby (1st Earl of Bessborough) and Lady Elizabeth Cavendish, sister of the above-mentioned Lady Caroline. William married Hon. Louise Molesworth on 26th December 1769. He was MP for Bandon in Ireland and *'kept the best hunting lodge in Ireland at his seat Bishops Court, Co. Kildare, where he lived in the most hospitable and princely style'*. Unfortunately his mother left his father John in 1778 *'the poor man breaking his heart at parting with so sweet a woman and allows her £300 a year, which he cannot by any means afford'*. She returned to England. [33]

Most of the Duke's closest friends were clearly members of his extended family with a few others whose names crop up frequently in these pages. It was in this way that the Dukedom maintained its influence through regular contact and the power of patronage. Two other friends were 'Mr. Storer' and Mr. Hare'. Mr. Storer was Anthony Morris Storer (1746-99). He was educated at Eton (1754-64), where his contemporaries included Charles Fox, Lord Carlisle and Lord Fitzwilliam.

He was connected with the 'macaronis'. These were fashionable young man in the late 1760s-early 1770s which also included Fox, Carlisle and James Hare, all later guests with him at Devonshire social gatherings. He was a great collector of books, amassing some 2,800 books as well as early prints, some rather rare. Many of his prints were by Joshua Reynolds. He bequeathed his collection to the Eton College library where it remains as its 'crowning glory'. [34]

James Hare (1749-1804) went into politics at a time when one-tenth of all Etonians went on to the House of Commons. He was MP for Stockbridge (1772-74) and for Knaresborough, where he held it care of the Duke's patronage, let alone the voters, from 1781-1804. When he died the Duke paid for a memorial to him in Walcott Church (? in Kent). The Duke's son by Lady Bess Foster, Sir Augustus Clifford, described him as *'the tallest, thinnest man I ever saw, his face like a surprised cockatoo and as white'*. [35] During 1776, Reynolds painted the portrait of the 5th Duke which hangs at Althorp.

The end of 1776 saw the Duchess's aunt, Lady Pembroke, complaining that she had rheumatism in her knees. The continual round of partying and dancing which her niece enjoyed was not for her. She lamented that if the winter was as bad as 1775, there would be no running on the ice for her. *'I shall be shivering on the bank, pale with envy, while you are all hopping and dancing and eating in the gocarts'*. [36] The Duke would have advised her to do what he did for his rheumatism: go to Buxton and bathe in the waters there.

The Duchess and Debt, 1776

The carefree approach to these letters may indicate a solution to a problem which must have been causing the Duchess some significant stress all year long; more mounting problems of debt. This time they were her domestic debts, although the fact that her pin money clearly had gone could be because she had used it to pay undeclared debts to the Duke in 1775. She eventually told an unsympathetic mother who asked for all the bills so that she could see exactly what was going on. She made a list of them and sent it back. Debts to the end of 1775 amounted to £1,700. These included bills to milliners: £320; hairdresser: £40; merciers: £228; shoemaker: £23; and staymakers: £25, totalling £636. The other tradesmen's bills do not have their business type indicated by Lady Spencer.

The latter estimated additional bills to Lady Day which would increase the total to £2,000. On top of that were a few additional items including gambling debts for which in total she had added £500, making £2,500 in all. She recommended that the Duchess asked the Duke for assistance: '*if the Duke would let you have £3,000 it would possibly clear you to Lady Day last and then the remaining quarter you might by care during the summer pay off yourself – but less than £2,500 will not do even to clear you to Christmas last – for heavens sake think seriously of these things*'. [37]

The gambling debts had been clearly kept separately by Lady Spencer and it seems unlikely that her daughter would have misled her, the wrath of her father being a likely consequence, let alone a tirade from her mother.

5

A Social Life 1777-79

Pleasures At Chatsworth

Only three letters survive at Chatsworth for the period January – July 1777, all three from the Duchess to her mother. In January they went to a glittering birthday party which was 'extremely full'. The party was for John (Jack) Townshend, the second son of the 1st Marquis Townshend, Field Marshal George Townshend. He was born on 19th January 1757 so the event was to celebrate his 20th birthday. It was another ten years before he married Georgiana Poyntz, a relative of the Duchess. He died in 1833, a month or so after his 76th birthday. His wife was divorced from William Fawkner, who may be the man who simultaneously attended functions of the Devonshire's inner circle of friends in the late 1770s. This is presumably where he (Jack) met her. He became a Whig MP in 1780 but was a casualty in the 1784 Election. He became a Privy Counsellor in 1806.

The Duchess described him the following July *'a very amiable young man* (a few months older than her) *he has great parts tho' not such brilliant ones as Charles Fox and I dare say he will make a very good figure hereafter. He is but just twenty now, tho' he has the appearance of being older'*.

She described a few of the most magnificent dresses: *Lady Melbourne in white satin with great Draperys (sic) of Puce and gold gauze and sable; Miss Warren who had the same on Pink Satin, Ly Catherine Genley who had a white petty coat with silver gauze and a Box coloured gown. There were very few fine drest men – the Duke of Devonshire coat was light green with Roses in poulletes, the Duke of Hamilton, Sir Harry Featherstone in green and pink and George Hanger who was to be all complicity in a plain grey coat with Pink enamelled (sic) buttons set around with something like Diamonds – a plain silk hat etc'.* [1] It was not all good fun however. Someone was brash enough to steal Sir George Warren's ensignia of the Order of the Bath off his jacket. It was set around a large sapphire.

On 8th May 1777, the Duke's paternal grandmother died. She was born Katherine Hoskins and married the 3rd Duke on 27th March 1718. She had become Duchess on 4th June 1729 and raised seven children. The Duchess makes no reference to her in her surviving letters. Following her death, the Duke would have had a saving of £2,500 pa as her annuity of this amount under the 3rd Duke's will ended.

The nocturnal social life was highlighted a little later, together with the rigidity of life and custom within the Devonshire household. One day the Duke did not get up until 5pm (presumably following a late night) and the servants would not raise the Duchess until he was up. Once she was up, it took her until 10pm to be dressed, when she went out to Lord Maras', presumably with the Duke. She was supposed to be meeting her mother after that, but the hour was too late to do so. The following month saw Frances, Lady Clermont restyled as Countess of Clermont on 10th February. She was c. 44 years old at the time. She kept an ever watchful eye on the Duchess, thinking nothing of reproaching the latter even from Paris, but in a friendly way. [2]

By July, the Duke and Duchess were house visiting and out of London, going from Brocket Hall (the Melbourne's) to Milton House, the home of Lord & Lady Fitzwilliam, before heading to Chatsworth at the end of the month. They rested there over the weekend, had a Public Day on the Monday and after everybody had gone, drove to Hardwick on their way to Nottingham Races. The Duke drove part of the way himself. He had bought the Duchess six new ponies from the Duke of Portland to add to the four she already had. No doubt he wished to try them out himself. Perhaps it was the first time they had had a chance of using his 20th birthday present to her (her birthday was the 7th June).

They spent two days at the Races, spending three nights at lodgings taken by the Duke of Portland. The racecourse had a reputation for being *'the most beautiful one in England'* with quite an attractive stand. After the racing, they went to a Ball, leaving late (midnight on the first day) to go to the Duke of Portland's for supper. The Duchess was the only woman there on the first night with at least 16 men, some of whom went on to Chatsworth afterwards. Exhausted each night, she was relieved to be heading back to Chatsworth despite the five hour journey. Back at Chatsworth on 7th August, Lord George Henry (whose unfancied horse appears to have won at Nottingham) and Horace Walpole came the following day, but twenty four hours later Walpole had to leave in a hurry. In even a bigger hurry was his daughter, who had run away with an officer in the Guards. [3]

A non-stop round of entertaining guests and visitors to Chatsworth plus another Public Day was followed by the Derby Assembly Ball. The Duchess went by herself, staying at General & Mrs. Gisburn's again. After a little dancing, she left for supper and the pleasure of an early night. Derby Races were attended the next day, The Duchess going with Mrs. Gisburn, *'she seems a quiet sickly good natured woman above five and twenty'*. Then it was back to the Ball and socialising once more.

Charles Fox as well as the Duchess returned to Chatsworth on the following day, 14th August 1777. She had a soft spot for him and of course he enjoyed the Duke's support (and that of his sponsored MPs) in the House of Commons. Fortunately for us, she chose to disclose to her mother her thoughts about him: *'the great merit of C. Fox is his amazing quickness in seazing (sic) any subject he seems to have the particular talent for knowing more about than what he is saying and with less pains than anybody else – his conversation is like a brilliant player at billiards the strokes follow one another piff paff and what makes him more entertaining now is his being here with Mr. Townshend and the Duke of Devonshire for their living so much together in town makes them show off one another – their chief topic is Politicks (sic) and Shakespeare – as for the latter they all three seem to have the most astonishing memory for it'*. [4]

Foreman suggests this about Fox: *'Though he very quickly frittered everything away, Fox could always count on friends like the Duke to support him financially and politically'*. [5] The latter is certainly true, but there is only limited Chatsworth-based evidence to suggest the former and only in the last seven years of Fox's life.

Although the Duke later kept £1,000 in cash at the bank, he did not have access to much extra cash without recourse to John Heaton to provide it. However he does appear to have made an exception with C.J. Fox, who received £500 on 5th January 1779 and a further £1,000 just over six months later. In 1800, the Duke took out an annuity on Fox's life (today we call it a life assurance policy) which was paid until Fox died in 1806. The total was a staggering £6,118. A further £150 in 1807 may well have been a subscription to a memorial fund. [6]

For the latter part of August 1777, Derbyshire was blessed with both sunny and very hot days, with an ever continuing stream of guests. In the middle of the month an accident occurred at Chatsworth which now gives us information for the first time on part of the garden – probably outside the doors from the Orangery shop (although the Orangery building is much later). Now the ground slopes down from the 1st Duke's Greenhouse to the gravel path which runs the full length of the house on the east front.

In 1777, the upper ground was much more level with a stone retaining wall 12 – 14 ft (say c. 4.5m) high facing the east front. Sir Charles Bunbury and

Jack Townshend ran a race towards that corner of the garden from the foot of The Cascade. Not knowing of the wall's existence, they ran straight off it. Fortunately, no bones were broken, but they were indisposed for some time afterwards.

Thomas Smith's painting of 1743 of the house and its grounds shows the Salisbury Lawn apparently sloping down to the gravel path. The current steps rising up to the old greenhouse must mark where this wall existed and that the profile of the northern end of the lawn was possibly re-levelled after 1777 as a result. The inference is that they were running on grass right up to the wall.

Much of August 1777 was spent entertaining at Chatsworth. Visitors left for York Races or arrived from there. The latter included the Duke of Dorset on his way to Lord Derby's house at Knowsley near Liverpool. He stayed three full days before moving on. The Duchess described him: *'I have always looked upon him as the most dangerous of men for with that beauty of his he is so unaffected and as a simplicity and persuasion in his manner that makes one account very easily for the number of women he has had in love with him'*. Charles Fox, Jack Townshend and Lord Robert Spencer went to shoot at Woodlands (the area of Birchinlee Pasture, now above Ladybower Reservoir, upriver from Chatsworth) with more shooting at Hardwick. There were also days spent at Chesterfield, Derby and Nottingham Races. [7]

If this was not enough, there were horse races above Calton, across the valley from the House, between horses of the Duke and Jack Townsend and running races between various men including Charles Fox. Felix Giardini serenaded them all in the evenings with 'charming solos' of music. Sir William Boothby [8] hung about waiting for a response from Lady M. Churchill, whom he had written to asking for her hand in marriage. He was declined and later married Rafaela de Gardo in May 1781. An ex-Major in the 51st Foot, he probably met her while in the Army. She was from Mahon, Minorca, and they had four children.

He is less well known compared to his little descendant (? his granddaughter/ or daughter of his nephew), Penelope Boothby, daughter of Sir Brooke Boothby of Ashbourne Hall. She died on 19th March 1791, three weeks before her 6th birthday. Her reknown and lifelike tomb carving may be seen in Ashbourne Church, Derbyshire. Carved by Thomas Banks, it is a fine piece of work. Penelope had been painted by Reynolds in 1788, the painting being known as the *Mob Cap*. It is one of the most well-known child portraits of the Georgian period.

Meanwhile, early in September, the Duke was wondering about going to Brighthelmstone, now Brighton. He was thinking that bathing in the sea would be beneficial to him; the Duchess also liked the idea. All it was wanting was for the Duke to make his mind up. On 11th, Lord & Lady Clermont had arrived from Trentham Hall in Staffordshire, Lady Clermont going with the Duchess to meet Lord & Lady Jersey at Matlock. Despite finding that his wife had been having further extra-marital affairs, he was in good humour.

On 14ᵗʰ September 1777, there was an earthquake, felt at both Leek and Ashbourne, south west of Chatsworth. In all probability, this would also have been felt just north of the road between the two towns at the Ecton Copper Mine. Given that the mine was c. 1,000 feet deep at that time, it would have been a worrying experience for the Duke's miners. [9] If they knew about it, it did not deter the Duchess and guests a few days later.

In the middle of September the Duchess led a trip to Castleton Cave (now known as Peak Cavern). The entrance was then shaded by wood and a number of old women were employed in making pack thread (used to make the large saddle bags used on pack horses, one each side and of one hundredweight capacity each). In the entrance cave they went through a small door into a much lower passage where they dropped down a steep slope, unable to stand up, to reach water. Leading the others, the Duchess crossed over the stream *'in a kind of trough'*. She said she had to lie *'down in the boat and it seemed as if I was leaving one part of the world to go to a new one'*.

They passed *'another stream over which we were oblig'd to be carried … we crossed the water seven times more by the help of stepping stones and at last go to where the rock and the water closes – they have some hopes by the help of gunpowder of pursuing the opening further, nobody has ever been able to venture under this rock, nine years ago a Mr. Day attempted it but was twice nearly drowned … this place is 700 yards from the entrance'*. Note: Today, the route has been extended, exposing a cave system of 10.3 miles / 16 kms and the deepest natural vertical descent in the country of Titan at over 656 ft /200m. The rope walk where the *'old women'* worked may still be seen. Nearly 240 years later, the cave is still open to the public. [10]

Back To London

They had left Chatsworth on 27ᵗʰ September 1777 for the Melbourne's at Brocket Hall. There were no other guests; the Duke went fishing on the estate – presumably with Lord Melbourne – and no doubt the Duchess spent her time with Lady Melbourne who was seven months pregnant. No child is recorded from this pregnancy. Either there was a family tragedy or it was illegitimate and not brought up in the Melbourne household. [11] They arrived at Devonshire House on the 30ᵗʰ and stayed in London before setting off for Sussex on 6ᵗʰ October. The Duchess makes no mention of going out to gamble and she also deliberately kept away from it at the seaside. They regularly went out (in London) to see a play. She took little John Ponsonby (her nephew) to see the Harlequin Skeleton where they laughed so much *'that the whole house observ'd it*'. It must have been good because she went again the next day – presumably with the Duke and other adults this time.

While at Devonshire House, Lady Clermont had arrived during the day only to find the Duchess still in bed. She received a good telling off for it: '*I was scolded*'. At last, the Duke decided to go to Brighthelmstone in Sussex. Now the socialising took a different turn as they reached there on 6th October 1777. Unshackled from the responsibility of feeding and entertaining at the inn Chatsworth had become, they had time to enjoy themselves with a small circle of friends also there. They took a house in West Street. By their standards it was rather small, but the largest available. There is a distinct theme running through the detail of the visit that, as in London, the Duchess was behaving more responsibly. Her miscarriage may have been the catalyst for this, as mentioned above. Even so, she had to wait eight years after that before her first child was born. Does that infer that the highlife which preceded her miscarriage did not prejudice her pregnancy, which had more to do with a condition similar to her mother?

Socialising at the Seaside

At the beginning of October 1777, the Duke wrote to Lady Spencer in Paris. He was considering going on from Brighthelmstone to France. The Duchess was more than happy at the prospect. No doubt her mother would have been personally glad of it but she clearly suggested otherwise. She was anxious to return to England as soon as possible – presumably for safety's sake. She also told the Duchess that the latter's gambling and other debts there made it prudent that she stayed away. They therefore made do with the Sussex coast. The Duke was going there with the hope that the sea water would be beneficial to the both of them, although the weather and sea temperature would not be at its best. A visit in the hot weather of the previous August would clearly have been more beneficial.

By her own standards, the Duchess was turning over a new leaf: '*I get up very early*'. Before breakfast, she drank the local mineral water (on the advice of two doctors) and went into the sea. After breakfast she went out visiting. She usually seems to have done this in the Duke's company when they were away and where they were reciprocating a visit to them. As the bulk of her comments in her letters relate to gatherings of women, the men were no doubt occupied on other things and probably also together.

Following the visits, she rode, drank another glass of mineral water, went walking on the Steene and ate buns at the Cook's Shop. After dinner, the circle of friends descended on the Assembly Rooms. The Duchess lamented that the weather was rather cold, she never played at cards, and there was nobody to flirt with. [12]

On 24ᵗʰ February 1778, a day after moving from Wimbledon Park to Chiswick, the Duchess contracted scarlet fever. Lord Spencer wrote to advise her brother on the following Friday from his home in St. James' Place, London *'I am going back directly to your mother who is there and you know is easily terrified upon such occasions. Doctor Warren however assures me that he sees no dangerous symptoms, but she must of course have a long and disagreeable illness ... do not regard anything that you may see in the Newspapers...'* At the beginning of April her brother (Lord Althorp) received a letter from his grandmother, Lady Cowper, to tell him that his sister had recovered *'and Harriet* (his sister) *did not catch ye disorder tho she slept w(i)th her ye night she was taken ill'.* In fact she was on the mend by mid-March but confessed to her brother that the illness has frightened her for a few days. [13]

The Derbyshire Militia Camp, 1778

Letters thereafter are almost totally missing until the Duke took the Derbyshire Militia to its summer camp in May 1778 at Coxheath, Kent. Also missing is an account of the Duchess's 21ˢᵗ birthday on 7ᵗʰ June 1778. The impression given by his wife's letters portray the Duke as enjoying his role. However his life was somewhat different to the life of his men in camp. His wife went to be with him in July and their tent was the largest she had ever seen.

It had a dining room, an even larger area for a bedchamber which had two recesses at each end which provided servants' accommodation consisting of a further bed chamber, dining room and kitchen. Somewhere, perhaps in the opposite recess, was the accommodation for the Duchess's servant, Betty. The tent must have been of some size, not only did it accommodate dinner parties, the Duke even had a fire in it on cold nights! The Duchess may not have had a room of her own for on one occasion she was almost in public view when she got undressed, although her bed may have been moved because of the rain. Initially, she was confined to the tent with a swollen face.

The Duke had his own tent made for the Coxheath camp, costing £282. The brazier to keep the tents warm, trunk and carriage of it all to Coxheath cost another £152. However the Duke's expenses at the camp amounted to £541. On the 4ᵗʰ May, the Duchess reported that the *'men look amazingly well, they have just got spatterdashes and shirts and I believe are to begin firing soon. There is a vacant company which the soldiers call mine – I intend to make it a very good one, it is kept vacant to see if some of the gentlemen here about wish to come in'.* [14]

The inner circle of the Duke's social life at the camp included two of the younger Colonels. These were Lord Cranbourne, son of the 6ᵗʰ Earl of Salisbury, and Colonel of the Herefordshire Militia [15] Another was Lord Cholmondeley, later 1ˢᵗ Marquess of Cholmondeley, and Colonel of the Cheshire Militia. His father had been a Lt. Colonel in the 65th Regiment and his great-grandfather was Robert Walpole, Prime Minister 1721 – 42.

The General at the camp was General Robert Sloper who was deployed to Ireland that year (1778), possibly from Coxheath. The following year he was sent to India, rising to the rank of Commander-in-Chief, India, in 1785. The Duchess wrote to her mother to say that he wasn't very popular, but several times the Duke and the Derbyshires won his approval, saying that *'he wished the rest of the line was like them'*. [16]

The Colonels were required to do night-time picket duty, checking the perimeter camp guards, although the Duke appears to have handed the job on to a subordinate en route. On 3ʳᵈ and 4ᵗʰ November 1778, King George III and the Queen visited the camp. The Duchess reported that the Derbyshires looked better than one could have hoped considering the age of their clothing. The Duke and other commanders dined with the King, The Duchess on the other hand spent two hours in the Queen's tent, chiefly standing up (as she had been all day) and bored to death.

It was during this Camp that the Duchess took to parading the women up and down in quasi-military style uniforms. It was while all this was going on that the Duke is alleged to have had a relationship in his tent with Lady Jersey. consequently, it is not clear whether the Duke was able to travel to London where, on 25ᵗʰ August 1778, Lord Richard Cavendish (his brother) moved a Bill to repeal an Act which disabled Catholics from any interest in lands previously forfeited because of their religion. [17] This may have been on behalf of the Duke and he certainly would have approved of it.

The Duchess's Perceived Personality

The above text gives examples of aspects of her life in general, but little was written about her London social life, other than general comments from her parents about her dissipation (from her mother) and her racketing (from her father). There is however, more on her personality plus some criticism of her.

In 1778, an anonymous author produced an astonishing document called a 'Letter', but over 100 pages long. It was published as a book. It is likely to have been written by someone sympathetic to her, but despairing of her lifestyle. Frankly, today most of it appears as dry as dust, but a section in conclusion at the end sums up her lifestyle and the effect of it:

'Inspired with an uncommon vivacity of temper and having experienced no medium between the parental control and the boundless indulgence of a Husband, her Grace yielded to the delusions which played around her, and suffered herself to be tempted into a rage after pleasure, which, at once, blasted

all the fond expectations concerning her. Fashion submitted its capricious fancies to her control and she was delighted to direct them.

Flattery was continually at her ear and she encouraged its adulations. Vanity prepared her Temple and she became the Priestess of it. Pleasure solicited a place in her heart and she gave up the whole of it to that deluding Syren – while Discretion and good sense, finding themselves deserted and unnoticed resigned their care...' This critisism extended into other areas too: *'Those marvellous hats, which Gainsborough had immortalised were specially censured. Nor was the lady's public appearance 'in the dress of the nursery' approved. Her levity, her lack of dignity, her vanity, all came under what was rather the paternal slipper rather than the lash of the satirist.* [18]

Three years later, C.J.Fox wrote somewhat more concisely of her:

'And thou young, fair fantastic Devon
Wild as the Comet in mid-heaven [19],
which seems to be something of an endorsement.

Walpole was kinder; he had met her at a ball at the Lady's Club on her return to London early in 1775. *'It was all goddesses instead of being a resurrection of dancing matrons as usual. The Duchess of Devonshire effaces all with out being a beauty; but her youth, figure, flowing good nature, sense and lively modesty and modest familiarity, make her a phenomenon'.* Wraxall and Fanny Burney were all of the same opinion as Walpole so far as her beauty was concerned and of course, this is supported by the many portraits of her. *'Her features were not cast in a classic mould. Her hair was touched with red, which in those days was not the colour hair should be. She had the affectations of her age, would pose, coquette, intersperse her conversations with unnecessary snatches of French. But there was something beneath the powder and patches. Certainly she was irresistible. It was not long before she was the most admired and most discussed woman in the realm. Discussion did not necessarily imply admiration...her costumes were daring, her conduct, it seems not always discreet'.* Nonetheless, this author, Bickley, allows that she had *'wonderful vivacity, gaiety, radiant charm, which had given her ... her undisputed position'.* [20]

The Duchess's health problems continued through to the end of the decade, as did her apparent obliviousness of the effect on others of her money problems. Returning from their European trip in 1779, the Duke and Duchess were detained for three weeks at Helvoetsluis, now in Holland, *'over indispositions picked up'.* It was sufficiently bad enough to stop them sailing for England and the 21st birthday celebrations of her brother in September 1779.

Soon after their return to London, she stopped her coach in the street, having seen Dr. Graham to *'tell him to attend and to do his best to cure either one or two of her Grace's servants... Her black or Malatto Hairdressing servant, in a dangerous and very obstinate fever at his lodging in Jermyn Street for several weeks and furnished him with expensive medicines (at a charge of ten guineas) and to a Scotsman her footman for a considerable time... for some old and obstinate pains, weakness etc in the knee or knees (charged five guineas)'*. The Duchess never paid the bill and in 1788, Dr. Graham, then living in reduced circumstances in Edinburgh, was forced to ask Earl Spencer if he would pay his sister's bill. [21] At her death it was found that there were 129 creditors owed less than £50 each.

Militia Duty 1779

Upon his return to England around the end of September 1779, the Duke immediately resumed his duties as Colonel of the Derbyshire Militia, this year at Warley Camp in Essex. As usual, the Colonels of the regiments had orders to take the picket duty – the last round of security checks before the night watch took over. On the 4th October (their 4th night there), two men were found injured, one with stab wounds. A subaltern of the Middlesex Regiment was responsible for it. If that was not bad enough, the following night there was a fire in a stable. John Heaton had taken a house near to the camp in order to discuss business with the Duke, which had arisen while he was abroad. Heaton's servant had put their two horses in the stable and they were lost in the fire.

Foreman states [22]: *'The strain of anticipation* (of invasion) *was reflected in the drinking and debauchery that went on after dark: during one all night party the stables burned down and six horses were killed'*. No reference is given for this statement and none has been seen by this author. The Duchess's correspondence does not appear to mention all night parties at the barracks.

The night before the fire there was a Ball but the number of people present was so small that there was no dancing and the Duke and Duchess played cards (commerce). Sleep was disturbed that night by a report by *'the out piquets of the 59th'* (of the Middlesex Militia) of a stabbing. The Duke must have been involved because it was his duty to formerly notify the Camp Commander, General St. Johns of the incident. Whether the Ball was at the barracks is not clear, but it probably was as the Duke was on piquet duty that night, although he had delegated authority for part of the duty to the two field officers. That night the Duke was not at any party; let alone an all night one, he was in bed and was *'wokd very early'* with details of the incident. This indicates that the Duchess was not out partying either.

The following night, the October 1779 was the night of the fire, when Foreman states there was an all night party. Yet the Duchess spent the early part of the evening sketching for two hours. After dinner, she played cards. Lord

George (? Cavendish) won 150 guineas, the Duke lost 30 and the Duchess lost just $3^1/_2$ guineas, Writing to her mother, she *'came home to supper, hardly sat down and heard a cry of turn out the piquets upon which the men all ran out of the tent. Fire at the rear of the Cheshires'.* The Duke must have been with her when she had returned to the tent; she would not have left ahead of him and good manners would have ruled that he escorted her back. If there was another ball that night, they would not have gone back for supper, it would have been available at the event. Nor would they have been playing serious card games in the middle of a drunken, debauched mob.

Foreman's 'drinking and debauchery' suggests a breakdown of discipline, which is not suggested in any of the Duchess's correspondence. Nor is there evidence to suggest that the Duke's inner circle at the camp was involved in it. As this circle centred on the younger Colonels, the excessive drinking would therefore have to have been amongst the lower ranks and toleration of this seems unlikely without direct evidence to prove it. [23] So on what does Foreman base her comments?

Upon returning to London, during November 1779, the Duchess found herself spending more time with Lady Jersey than she would have preferred. However the latter was in the final throws of pregnancy and gave birth to Sarah Villiers on the 15th November. A month before, the Duchess had written to her mother: *'tho' I love her tenderley* (sic) *I have learnt to feel a kind of uneasiness in being with her and cant tell her so'.* After the ending of the relationship with the Duke at Coxheath camp a little over a year previously, she had not wasted much time getting pregnant again. [24]

So as the decade moved towards its conclusion, the Duchess appears to have been more careful in her socialising, or at least more discreet and probably more careful with her expenditure. Given that so much has been written about the Duchess's excesses, it is worth noting when she was in London and able to do so. It is much less than one might be led to believe:

1775	? January – late May/early June
	October – December
1776	January – ? June
	Late October – December
1777	? January – July
	30th September – 6th October
	? November – December
1778	? January – mid February
	? March – May
	November – December

From this list, it would appear that the Duchess must have been partying to excess during late October to mid-summer in 1775-76 and 1776-77. Thereafter, she would appear to have been in London for a similar period in 1777-78, but it is known that she was leading a quieter life at this time. Care needs to be taken about her partying afterwards. This is supported by Mrs Delaney, writing to her niece, Mary Port of Ilam Hall, north of Calwich Abbey the home of the former's brother on the Staffordshire border south west of Ashbourne, Derbyshire. The letter stated that *the Duchess of Devonshire is much quieter than she was and is always home before the Duke*. [25] Reports may be true or alternatively malicious gossip. Certainly she spent more time being more careful. However it does not mean that she was being more prudent with expenditure overall.

6

Changing Times 1780-81

Riots and Marriages

The 1770s had ended with the Duchess leading a much quieter life accompanying her husband and this continued into the 1780s. There was to be a watershed when she opened her arms embracing what her mother called '*dissipation*'. The year 1780 was when strides were made in the Duke's new investment programme. The construction of The Crescent hotels and mineral baths complex began at Buxton; the fires were lit in the new battery of copper smelting furnaces at Whiston, eight or so miles south of the Duke's rich copper mine at Ecton in North Staffordshire; and the Duke spent £21,500 purchasing a couple of coal mines to supply the smelter and associated other activities.

It was a decade which saw improvements at Chatsworth and developments in the gardens at Chiswick. This was to be followed by major development work at the latter with the construction of two major wings. Once complete, Chiswick House hosted lavish garden parties with nearly 1,000 guests arriving for a mid-day 'breakfast' at one of them. The opening of the Spa hotels and the redeveloped mineral water baths saw the Duke and Duchess using Buxton to find relief from gout (the Duke) and headaches and other ailments (the Duchess), with some success.

This decade saw the Duchess giving birth to two daughters with her sister providing more little ones. It also saw the the loss of dear family and friends: notably the Duchess's father, Earl Spencer and the Duke's brother, Richard, and his uncle, John. The Duchess's sister, Harriet, married Frederick Ponsonby. Frederick's father and uncle had married two sisters, aunts of the Duke. The latter had children by both his wife and mistress. The Duchess steered clear of any complications herself but embraced politics (the Whig party), socialising and debt. Her life became scandalous but she appears to have avoided the personal scandal of liaisons. The Duke lived in her shadow. John Heaton, the Duke's agent, lived in the shadow of the Duke doing his best to increase his gross wealth while the Duchess did her best to reduce it.

It was also the decade when the friendship between the Devonshire's and Lady Elizabeth Foster developed. It was to have a profound effect on all three of them. Chapman and Dormer have produced a scholarly work on Bess Foster, much of it from surviving letters etc. Regarding Bess, Chapman says: *'of her love for the Duke and Duchess and of her fidelity to them in thought, word and deed, I am entirely convinced'.* [1]

April 1780 saw the Duchess sitting for James Barry's portrait of her, due to be hung in the Royal Academy when completed. The engravers, Dickinson and Watson, were enquiring about making an engraving of her portrait by Angelica Kauffman, which was in the same style. She was also booked by Anne Seymour Damer who wished to create a terracotta bust of her, having nearly completed one of Lady Melbourne whose little boy (? William Lamb, her 2nd son, by Lord Egremont) was being painted by miniature painter Richard Cosway. [2]

Anne Damer was probably known to the Duke and Duchess. She was the daughter of General Conway who had gone into politics after a career in the Army, retiring as its top General. He was a much esteemed, close friend of the Duke's father, who left him £5,000 in his will. Her cousin and guardian, when her parents were abroad, was Horace Walpole, Earl of Orford. On his death in 1797, he left her a life tenancy in his home, Strawberry Hill. Her neighbour there was the actress Mary Berry. Her half sister was the wife of the Duke of Richmond of Goodwood in Sussex. The latter was a good friend of the Duke and Duchess and lover of Bess Foster. The latter three spent time together at Goodwood in the 1790s.

In 1776, Anne Damer's husband, having squandered a huge inheritance of £30,000, committed suicide in the Bedford Arms, Covent Garden. They had separated two years before that and Anne was trying to develop a career as a sculptor. It is typical of the Duchess to assist up and coming talent whenever she could. Not too dis-similar may have been the case of James Barry. Was this further support for a distressed artist? It is clear that she was a patron of both arts and artists by this time (1780). After Richard Cosway moved to part of Schomberg House, Pall Mall, in 1784, he held musical parties and receptions attended by the Duchess and the Prince of Wales, for whom he did commissions.

Meanwhile at the end of that month (March 1780) the Duke and Duchess went north to Derby for an election meeting, stopping off at Milton, the home of Lord and Lady Fitzwilliam, where they found Lady Fitzwilliam and the

Duke's brother, Richard. Presumably Richard was heading to Derby too. The Fitzwilliams lived at Milton Hall, near Peterborough (where the descendants still reside) and were good friends of the Duke and Duchess. 4th Earl Fitzwilliam was a prominent Whig politician serving as Lord President of the Council and Lord Lieutenant of Ireland. In 1782 he succeeded to the Watson-Wentworth estate in Yorkshire, which included Wentworth Woodhouse. Thereafter the Duke and Duchess went there regularly, presumably for the shooting on its 80,000 acre estate.

Refurbishment work at Devonshire House was reaching completion, the Duchess advising her mother '*I am got into my rooms but without half my furniture*'. [3] She celebrated by having a play at the House. It must have been doing the rounds, as it had previously been held at Lady Melbourne's London home, Melbourne House. The play was a success '*my rooms every body said were beautiful for they were the lightest and the most brilliant thing you ever saw which is not customary in the present stile (sic) of furniture – I had full room for every body and as the theatre was raised it had a very good effect*'. [4] She was writing to her mother who had just gone to Bath with her father who wished to take the waters for his gout. The Duchess of Portland, The Duke's sister, gave birth to a son at about the same time. On 27th August she celebrated her 30th birthday.

The Gordon Riots

In the first week of June 1780, the Gordon Riots started, with Georgiana impatient to move Charlotte away. Premises in Brampton were being considered Taking advantage of chronic indecision about the legality of troops firing on the mob, London began to burn. On the 7th the Orders to fire were given to the soldiers as the Court of Kings Bench was set alight along with Lord Mansfield's home. The previous day, gin poured down the streets as distilleries were destroyed and Newgate Prison was sacked. There were more problems on the 7th, so much so, that the streets ran with gin and the water supply of Lincolns Inn became alcoholic. The mob was beaten by the 9th, but the death toll was enormous. Killed or wounded were counted at 458 people at least, with another count being c. 700 and at least 280 killed and as many wounded. [5]

It would appear that the Duchess arranged for Charlotte to stay at Brocket Hall with the Melbournes during the riots, returning a few days after it was all over. [6] This seems to indicate that Charlotte may have been staying at Devonshire House, which was probably the case as the Duchess was quite fond of her. Lady Spencer was also staying and a month after the Duke and the Duchess left for Plymouth in late July 1780, she picked up Charlotte and took her home with her. Lady Spencer wrote to her daughter with a note written by

Charlotte: *'She looks very well but is not the pen of a ready writer as you will see by what follows – her name she bragg'd she could write without help which she has accordingly done'*. [7]

The cause of the rioting was the proposed increased emancipation for Catholics, which the Whigs supported and which made them targets for attack. The Duchess's correspondence refers to the Riots and she initially was *'frightened'* for the Duke's safety. On 5th June 1780 she wrote to her mother that there was *'a violent mob at Moorfields and I have heard that 500 of the guards are gone down there'*. On 7th, she reported that *'Minchin's hampshire regiment and the Queens are encamped in high* (Hyde) *Park*. She was more upbeat by the 8th: *'I was thro' the parks to day, in hyde park there are encamp'd the hertfordshire, the hampshire, the queens and royal irish and in St. James's park the other hampshire and some regular regiment – two troop of Mr. Fitzroy's are to patrol up and down Piccadilly and as the Duke don't like having the soldiers here again (as there is no need) the depot of guards for this part of town will be at Ld Melbourne's. I stay in town as there is no manner of danger and that they think Chiswick is damp ... the Duke does nothing but regret his regiment being gone to Portsmouth'*. [8]

During the riots the Duke was *'in garrison at Ld Rockinghams till five which alarmed me not a little but now Ld R's is the safest place as he has plenty of guards'*. Wraxall records that *'The Edinburgh Reviewer (Sir James Mackintosh) ... writes: "During the riots, twenty gentlemen remained there nightly on guard at the Marquis of Rockingham's house, armed with muskets and heavy pistols in their belts. Among them were Mr. Thomas Grenville, General Fitzpatrick and Mr. Fox"'*. It will be noted that all three were members of the Devonshire House circle and that they were accompanying the Duke. [9]

The Duchess understandably, was not too happy being left at Devonshire House while the Duke was defending someone else's home. Lord Mansfield's house had been reduced to ashes and Sir George Saville's house in Leicester Square had been plundered by the mob. The King's Bench Prison, the Fleet Prison and Fleet Market had all been set alight as had many more properties. Lord North, the Prime Minister, found a baying mob outside 10 Downing Street on 7th June 1780. A Col. North with twenty grenadiers were upstairs ready to fire into the street causing the mob to discreetly move away, allowing Lord North and others to return to their wine. [10]

Devonshire House was considered a prime target, despite the soldiers camped in Green Park across the street. The Duchess *'yielding to her fears, did not venture to remain in it after dusk for a considerable time. She took refuge at Lord Clermont's residence in Berkeley Square, where she deemed herself safe from attack and lay down for successive nights on a sofa or a small tent-bed placed in the drawing room. Many other persons of both sexes of the highest rank either quitted their own dwellings or sent their most valuable effects and jewels into the country'.* [11]

Large numbers of the dead were thrown into the River Thames, especially on Blackfriars Bridge where the army had opened fire on the mob. They had done so also at the King's Bench Prison and the Bank (of England) particularly.

If Wraxhall was correct in his comments on the length of stay of the Duchess with the Clermont's, where was the Duke sleeping and why was he detained following the end of the rioting nearly a week after it started? Wraxhall also makes it very clear that in his view, initial operations to restore order were under the direct control of the King. Is this why there was a lack of direction by Ministers and the Army Chiefs in the riot's initial stages? Finally, the thought of a turkey-shoot by Grenadier Guards into the mob at the Prime Minister's front door is a powerful one indeed, let alone its consequences. As for the bodies floating away down the Thames, that would send its own message.

Nonetheless, this experience for the Duke may have had an important consequence for him in 1789 in Paris, when he thought he had made the right decision to leave his two illegitimate daughters there in what turned out to be the beginning of the Revolution.

Back to Normality

The annual mustering together of the county militias saw the Duke heading for Portsmouth in July. Much of his spare time seems to have been spent hunting with like-minded officers. No doubt the Duke and Duchess's evenings would be spent as in previous years with a heavy programme of socialising over dinner, cards and supper. They appear to have rented Admiral Keppel's house *'in the High Street, it is a very good one'.* (In 1778 – 1779, Lord Richard had a spell in the Navy and served under Admiral Keppel. In 1780 Richard was returned to the House of Commons as MP for Derbyshire in place of his uncle, Lord George Augustus. [12] Soon after their arrival, the Duchess went off in *'a little boat'* to Spithead to see the *'West India fleet'* arrive but had got out of bed too late to see it. The East India fleet was also there, ready to sail on that night's tide or the following day.

The end of July saw news arriving from Lady Spencer announcing that Lord Duncannon (the future Earl of Bessborough) had proposed to the Duchess's sister. Harriet pondered over the fact that she found him grave and herself giddy. Her mother pondered over the inadequacy of his finances. He was only able to offer £2,000 p.a. for them to live on, with an additional £500 p.a. for Harriet's pin money. However she (Lady Spencer) thought that *'his character will give her a better chance of happiness than a much larger fortune if they like each other as much as I think they do, but if she should take a turn for dissipation and extravagance I shudder to think what wretchedness it may occasion'.*

It will be clear where this letter was leading and she continued: '*I think of this most seriously my Dearest Georgiana and let your affection for her prompt you to avoid with the utmost care leading her into the smallest degree into your way of life or set of company – let me rather hope if she does give him the preference she seems strongly inclin'd to do, that she may be a means of leading you out of dissipation fully and noise instead of you carrying her into it'.*

The Duchess replied in an upbeat tone with reservations on the finances. However perhaps Harriet agreed to the proposal knowing that all was not what it should be. Although she bore him four children, the 1780s saw her starting a liaison with Richard Sheridan and then, later, with Lord Granville Leveson – Gower and having two children by him. [13] The marriage took place on Harriet's 19th birthday, 27th November 1780. By 1782 Duncannon was making advances on Lady Elizabeth Villiers. Lady Spencer's aspirations for Harriet's future must have been shattered by all of this, let alone her continual worry about the Duchess.

The Duke did not remain with his regiment as long as in other years. He had developed a very bad cold and by early September had set off for Derbyshire, taking Dr. Gisbourne with him. [14] The following February (1781), the Duke and Duchess set off to Hardwick from Mansfield – probably from Sir William Boothby's house, Mansfield Woodhouse. They had picked a particularly bad night, with a heavy storm which affected the east of the country right down to London. It was particularly dark, raining and blowing '*dreadfully'*. It took two hours to cover seven miles. A tree blew down on the Duke of Portland's estate, grazing the coat of one of the Duke of Portland's staff, who was unhurt. At least Hardwick was nice and warm when the party reached there. The beds (and presumably the linen) was taken prior to the visit from Chatsworth and returned back there after the visit ended.

The Duke as usual threw himself into hunting straight away. Quite literally too as it turned out, as he suffered a bad fall which left him badly bruised and in much pain. Fortunately no bones were broken. He was in a great deal of pain the following day (Tuesday 13th February 1781), but by Friday he was mounting his horse again despite the pain. The Duchess had also had a new horse in her stable, making three very quiet horses she was most content with.

The Monday after the Duke's fall, they went into mourning for Lady Cowper, the Duchess's grandmother, who had died of breast cancer. The following day they did the same for the Queen of Portugal. The Duchess received a letter from her mother sent that day. She wrote that she was going to Lady Buckingham's, Harriet to Burlington House, her brother George to Charles Street, Mayfair (the Lucan's), also in London *'and your father to the Ale House'*. Clearly there was a limit to his tolerance of his wife's standards of probity. [15]

George, Lord Althorp, had his eye on his wedding on 6th March 1781 to Lady Lavinia Bingham, the daughter of the 1st Earl of Lucan. He appears to have ordered a scarlet coat for the day. This time it was the Duchess whose standards were offended. *'I don't like my brother's scarlet at all. I have just sent to order my wedding gown, which shall be bijou'*. The Duke's order for a new coat had been sent as well. We can take it that it wasn't scarlet.

Lord Althorp became an M.P. and supported Pitt from 1794 to 1801 when Pitt went out of office. He was appointed a member of the Privy Council in 1794 and held the position of Lord Privy Seal from July – December that year until he became Lord of the Admiralty, a position he held until 1801. He was later Secretary of State for the Home Department, 1806 – 07. His papers while Lord of the Admiralty (First Sea Lord) may be viewed in the British Library. [16]

The Complete Peerage has this to say of him *'For him, more distinctly perhaps than for any other English Administrator, may be claimed the title of organiser of victory. It was under his rule that the battle of St. Vincent and Camperdown were fought and won ... and it was still more directly by him that Nelson was singled out for independent command and sent to the Mediterranean to win the battle of the Nile'*. Like his father, he was an avid collector of rare books and his papers in the British Library include letters from booksellers abroad advising him on purchases. His collection was reputed to be the finest in Europe extending to 40,000 books. The collection was purchased by Manchester University for £250,000 in 1892 to form the Rylands Library. [17] He became 2nd Earl Spencer in 1783. The current Earl is the brother of the late Diana, Princess of Wales.

The trip to Hardwick seems to have been a quiet one, the guests being a few local friends. The thoughts of Hardwick being warm and comfortable were soon banished. The Sunday after they arrived they found the chapel so intensely cold they had to abandon the thoughts of prayers there. The visit was short and at the end of the month they returned to London for George Spencer's wedding.

There are no further letters in the Duke's series at Chatsworth until July 1781, by which time the Duke would have been looking forward to rejoining his regiment (see below). However during this period the issue of further debts incurred by the Duchess had surfaced. On 6th August, the Duchess of Portland, writing to her husband, advised him that she was having difficulty getting hold of John Heaton *'who is searching for money for 'G'*. She hoped that this disappointment for her brother would not spill over to them for she had heard her uncle, Lord Frederick, talk of calling in £5,000 he had lent the Duke'. [18] Matters would have to be a lot worse for that sort of a rift to occur in the closed ranks of the Cavendish family.

The Plymouth Review, 1781

In the last week of July 1781, the Duke and Duchess set off for Plymouth, where the County Militias were to muster for the Annual Review. They stopped off at Wilton for a social gathering there. Wilton still remains in the same family, the Earls of Pembroke. Heading on for Plymouth, they dined at Sherbourne and slept at Axminster, although they were not too enamoured the following morning. *'The people of Axminster began ringing their bells at 6 this morning, in honour to us as a compliment you may easily image we could have dispens'd with as the church was close to our windows'*. They arrived at Plympton House, which they had taken for the duration of the Review. After the experience of the mud previously, the Duke was still having none of it this year, although it was seven miles or so from the barracks. The Duke was keen to start to exercise the men in drill, shooting practice etc., prior to the actual Review itself on 21st August.

Their doctor (Dr. Moore) arrived the following day, bringing with him *'a beautiful gold enamell'd etui that Obyrne had received for me from a french Ly (Lady)'*. It was believed the Lady's name was Martin. An etui is a small ornamental case usually carried in a pocket, handbag etc. She could keep hairpins or a few sovereigns etc. in it. Several other visitors to Plymouth, primarily to socialise with the Devonshires, stayed with Mr. Parker of Saltram House (now National Trust owned). These included Charles Fox, Lord Robert Spencer, Lady Clermont and Mr. Crawford. There is little mention of the Jerseys or the Melbournes at this time, although Lord Egremont turned up for an overnight stay only. Cards were the usual distraction in the evening. The previous February, the Duchess had written to her mother about Lord Robert Spencer for she must have taken a shine to him: *'For one cannot help loving the poor Brute'*. [19]

For social trips during the day when military matters allowed, the party went to Mount Edgecumbe, across the estuary. Trips up the Tamar were arranged together with one to the Eddystone Lighthouse, built in 1759. The weather turned rough and all were seasick except the Duke, the expedition having to return before they got to the lighthouse, (since re-erected on Plymouth Hoe). There was alarm that our fleet had been forced back to home waters (at Torbay) and it was anticipated that the French could attack literally at any time, as part of the French-Spanish combined fleet.

The Duke and Duchess received an invitation to visit the home fleet in Torbay and they went on 27th August. Between Brixham and Totnes *'we met 300 french prisoners that were conducted by 50 cornish militia men to the Mill (military) Prison at Plymouth. It was very painfull to see them – most of them however seem'd of so low an order of beings that the being imprison'd had no effect of them, but every now and then a man rather better drest (sic) who made a civil bow to the carriage touch'd one very much'*.

Off Brixham, they dined on the HMS Royal George, a 200-gun ship, with Sir John Lockhart Ross, the Rear Admiral. *'The whole fleet of 21 sail of the line were in it* (Torbay) *to day and form'd in order of battle in a crescent, the first rates without the 2ⁿᵈ within – I never saw so fine a sight – it is rather a damper to the ideas it would naturally give one that this fine fleet and the one triumphant fleet of England had been oblig'd to sculk along the french coast to avoid even being seen by the combined fleet'*. The problem for the Royal Navy was that it had insufficient resources to take on the combined fleet. [20]

There was a more immediate problem for the Duchess. On returning to the quayside she *'was to go out of the boat first when one of the sailors gave way and I tumbled in with Capt. Jervis and 3 sailors after me – the ale house at Brixam* (sic) *was so full* (no doubt with Jack Tars) *I could not get any room to change myself and I was oblig'd to come quite wet to Totnes …'*. [21] No doubt the future Admiral Jervis (Lord St. Vincent) remembered that event throughout his illustrious career. It may also point towards the Duchess travelling with her maid and a trunk of spare clothes wherever she went.

The following April, Jervis, captain of the HMS Foudroyant, captured the French ship *Pégase*. He was wounded in the engagement and invested as a Knight of the Bath as a result of his success. The *Royal George*, the largest warship in the world when launched, was the flagship of Rear Admiral John Lockhart Ross until December 1781. On 29ᵗʰ August 1782, a year and two days after the Duke and Duchess's visit, *Royal George* foundered whilst being keeled over for repairs at Spithead. Some 900 people, including perhaps as many as 300 women and 60 children went down with her. During salvage operations in 1834 – 36, the divers investigated why fishermen's nets were being snagged nearby and found the HMS Mary Rose. [22]

Coincidentally in 1781, Dr. Samuel Johnson said that he had not observed *'that men of great fortunes enjoy any thing extraordinary that makes happiness, What has the Duke of Bedford? What has the Duke of Devonshire?'* [23] The answer was his time with the Militia at the Annual Review. In 1782, he was getting up at 7 a.m. every other day (in 1782) to be out with his men. His wife wrote each year to her mother telling her of his enthusiasm in the camp. There can be little doubt that he did enjoy the job. Admittedly he took his comforts with him, eventually exchanging his tent and camp accommodation for a more civil existence in a hired house nearby. Quite frequently in London apparently, he might be on his way home at 7 a.m. after a night's play at his club, let alone getting up and driving at that time to the camp. The Duke's expenses at Plympton were £1,540. [24]

Coincidentally the Dukes of Bedford made their money at another copper mine just up river on the Tamar from Plymouth – Devon Great Consols near Tavistock, which opened in 1844. It also was a major source of arsenic and was at one point described as having enough of it to wipe out every living thing on the planet. Much of it was exported from nearby Morwellham Quay. This indeed was fabulously rich with shares fetching up to £1,000 each at one point.

Whilst the Duke was at Plymouth, his sister-in-law, Harriet, gave birth to her son, John William Ponsonby, later 4th Earl of Bessborough, in September, 1781. He had blue eyes like the Duchess. Lady Spencer wrote to the latter commenting on her christening presents. They *were magnificent and beautiful – only too fine in my opinion'*. No doubt she was considering the cost and continuing debt. [25] Harriet had celebrated her 20th birthday on the previous 16th June.

For a diversion, on 4th September 1781, the Duchess launched HMS Anson, a third rate, 64-gun ship of the line. She (the ship) seems to have proved herself against the French and Dutch but was wrecked off Loe Bar near Porthleven in Cornwall on 29th December 1807. Both her anchors failed as she sought shelter from a gale and she was driven broadside onto a lee shore where she was caught on rocks. Her main mast fell which enabled some of the crew to get off her to safety. Estimates vary how many men were lost, between 60 and 190.

The wreck resulted in two developments however. It was usual to bury drowned seamen without a coffin or shroud close to where they were found and often in unmarked and unconsecrated ground. Quite often the bodies were not immediately buried either. A local solicitor, Thomas Grylls, was appalled by this following the wrecking of the *Anson* and drafted a Bill which the local M.P. introduced before Parliament. It was enacted as the Burial of Drowned Persons Act, 1808. A monument to those lost was erected by the entrance to Porthleven Harbour. Additionally, a Henry Trengrouse witnessed the wreck and developed a rocket to shoot lines onto ships to take the men off in cradles. It was an early form of the breeches buoy. Two weeks after the launch, the Duchess sat for her portrait to James Nixon. Although he spent most of his working life in London, the Duchess was still in Plymouth. [26]

Lord Richard's Death

On 7th September 1781 the Duke's brother, Lord Richard, died of bowel disease in Naples. The Duke first heard of it on 5th October, when he opened a letter whilst still in bed at Plympton. There was no measure of preparation in it for the delivery of the bad news. It was in the first line of the letter. Its effect was profound and the Duke was initially hysterical. The Duchess managed to get hold of the letter and hid it *'as the detail is very affecting …'*. It was during the evening that day that the Duke first had an opportunity of telling his youngest brother George, which seemed to steady the Duke somewhat. [27]

Lord Richard's body was brought back to England for burial, by sea by his man-servant, despite the latter's aversion to the sea. Later, a substantial gratuity of £500 was sent by the Duke to his brother's doctor, Dr. Drummond. In September 1782 Georgiana advised her mother that he (the doctor) was dead. It was from a fall from a horse lent to him by Mr. Beckford of Fonthill in Sussex. The news was conveyed by his father, Sir William Drummond, to his first wife Lady Hamilton (presumably Dr. Drummond's mother) and the shock of it killed her. Horace Walpole wrote: 'All the papers say that Lord Richard Cavendish is dead ; I was scarce aquainted (sic) with him, nor heard any thing but good of him'. [28]

Much of Lord Richard's income was drawn from rentals of land left to him by his father for his lifetime, with a reversion after his death of the income back to the estate. A smaller amount per annum was transferred to his younger brother, George. The total income was £5,680 plus an amount under his grandmother's will (Countess Katherine Burlington) which amounted to c. £1,000 p.a. The total coming back into the estate was of the order of £4-5,000 p.a. With the death of the Duke's paternal grandmother, Dorothy in 1777, when the payment of £2,500 p.a. ceased, the Duke's net income rose by £6,500 - £7,500 p.a. or thereabouts.

Lord Richard was buried in the family vault at All Saints Church (now the Cathedral), Derby. Following the death of his brother, the Duke spent more time at cards, playing with his wife, Mr. Parker and Lord Northington. He was playing seven or eight rubbers and winning hardly any. The stakes grew too with 'near two hundred (pounds) sometimes depending on a rubber and I am overhead (i.e. losing) to Mr. P. but the D (Duke) who knows of it will save me from jail and I generally play fast asleep'. She also commented that Lord Richard had left all he could to the Duke of Portland – presumably with his sister in mind.

Two years' later, in 1783, Lord Spencer (the Duke's father-in-law) died. Under the terms of the Duke's marriage settlement of 1774, upon the Earl's death he was to receive £10,000. [29] Presumably the Duke then continuing to pay the interest thereon to the Duchess.

7

1782-83 Enter Bess Foster

The previous year had ended with the Duchess suffering from *'this tormenting sick headache'*, even forcing her to bed early on Christmas Day. She later called it a *'nervous headache'*. At the beginning of 1782, a play, Ode to Hope, written by the Duchess, was playing in London. Walpole described it as being *'easily and prettily expressed, though it does not express much.'* It is possible that the play was underwritten by the Duke, for Walpole seems to suggest this happened the following April with a comedy, written by a *'poor Irish clergyman'* named Stratford.

The acerbic Walpole wrote: *'The Duke of Devonshire has got his comedy and I am sorely afraid the poor man's madness will be a jest instead of a matter of compassion; but I shall at least endeavour to make them pay for laughing at a man that ought to be respected. He (the Duke) cannot bear the name of Johnson, for his acrimony against Milton; in short he is a whig to the marrow'.* Well, Walpole got the last bit right. As for the Duke not liking Dr Samuel Johnson, the two got on very well together when they met at Chatsworth a few years later and it is known that the Duke's exemplary manners are unlikely to have shown a display of anything less in public to the philosopher. [1]

In May 1782, the Duke and Duchess set off for Bath spending a night at Maidenhead Bridge and the following night at Midgham House, six miles east of Newbury, Berkshire, where they stayed with her uncle, William Poyntz. Coincidentally, his grand daughter was later to marry the 4th Earl Spencer.

The main reason for going to Bath was her health and just over a week after arriving she was feeling much better. *'The waters agree beyond belief with me. I am sure neither bathing or drinking* (she was taking up to three glasses of mineral water a day) *has heated me the least and my appetite is voracious'.* This may not have been the only reason for improvement in her health for she complained that Bath was the *'dullest of all places'*. In other words, there was little company for them to socialise with – or as her father would have said, less racketing.

Shortly after their arrival she wrote to her mother *'I hope Bath will do me good for it ought, it is amazingly disagreeable. I am surprised at the Duke's bearing as much as he does but he is so good natured he bears everything well.'* On their first morning there they walked about town calling on various people including Lady Elizabeth Foster. Of the surviving Chatsworth correspondence this is the first reference to her. A couple of days' later all three, plus Lord Frederick, were at a play where Mrs. Siddens *'acted charmingly'*.

Foreman suggests that Georgiana may have been pregnant and suffered a miscarriage, hence the trip to Bath. There is however no evidence to prove this. She had been suffering from at least a *'nervous headache'* over the previous Christmas which sheds no light on the matter. One could understand the quieter social life if she had been pregnant whilst at Bath but there is no evidence to support that either. On the other hand a quiet spell taking the waters might have been tried to try and improve the chance of conceiving and one suspects this sort of thing might have been tried periodically. The cost of the Bath vacation was £568. [2]

By 1st June the Duke was showing the first signs of influenza, preventing them from going to Court for the Royal Birthday – no doubt to the Duke's relief, one wonders. Within days, the Duke had blisters on his lips. Bess Foster had caught it together with others amongst their friends. On Georgiana's birthday (the 7th) she thought she was catching it, but was much better on the 8th. Soon the town's theatres were shut as it spread to the actors. This was part of a national epidemic, at least in the south of England and the home fleet at Portsmouth was badly affected by it. Lady Melbourne wrote to Georgiana describing the *'fever'*. Lord Melbourne had it and *'is at present quite ill and nobody escapes'*.

Lady Elizabeth Foster appears to have wasted no time ingratiating herself with the Duke and Duchess. The latter wrote to her mother on 8th June: *'she delights me by her enthusiasm about you'*. She had also told them about her losing custody of her children at about that date. By the end of July, the three of them were at Plympton for the Annual Review of the county militias. Bess Foster had separated from her husband in 1781. Her husband took custody of their children and deprived his wife of any access to them until his death in October 1796. She had moved to Bath in January 1782 and was living with her sister Mary (who was also separated) on an allowance of £300 pa from her wealthy father plus a little extra from her husband. [3] If Bess thought that befriending the Devonshires might change her fortunes and assist in the recovery of her children, the latter at least was unsuccessful.

There is a suspicion in Georgiana's correspondence to her mother that there may have been less socialising this year, even less card play. The Duke was spending evenings reading to his wife and Bess: '*the D. read to us the best parts of Hamlet, Midsummer Night's Dream, the tempest and I after supper read Queen Catherine and Wolsey's speech*'. He read Rousseau's *Confessions* with enthusiasm, to Lady Spencer's disgust.

Commander Williamson of the (? *HMS*) *Belisle* called on a Sunday and mentioned that seven ships of the line plus three frigates '*were going to try and find Ld Howe, they imagine here that he is gone after the Dutch*'. There was a belief that the combined French/Spanish fleet had left the English coast and more upbeat news that the Navy was being run better, especially with regard to ship building, under the Duchess's brother. [4] Her correspondence with her mother is peppered with details about the fleet, while her mother knew before most of Lord Howe's relief of Gibraltar and that news had travelled overland through France.

Also in May 1782 (on 30th May), a son was born to Georgiana's brother, George. He was baptised John Charles Spencer on the 7th July at Wimbledon Park. However, all was not well. Lady Spencer referred to the baby as '*the poor little animal*' and to his '*poor diminutive (sic) carcase*'. [5] Just prior to this, The Duchess had written to her mother about Lavinia Spencer's mother, Lady Lucan: '*How as the incorrigible Lady L. behaved?*' and '*I must know how Ly Lucan received her grandson whether as a blessing or a missfortune*' Despite an apparent faulty start, John did well academically and in politics, where he was much respected. [6]

With the fleet at sea, the army took on some of the responsibility for defending Plymouth. The defences were weak on the Cornish side of the River Tamar. This stretched the deployment of the regiments into November. With the refurbishment of the formal rooms at Chatsworth (see below) precluding a return there, the Duke, Duchess and Bess went to Bristol. The Spencers had gone there to see if the waters at Hot Wells would help the Earl's condition.

Having been civil in correspondence to her daughter about Bess Foster, Lady Spencer now wrote to say that she hoped that the former would not be travelling to Bristol too. The Earl, she maintained, would not be up to seeing unknown visitors in his condition. The Duchess refused to accept this. During their stay at Bristol, the Derbyshire Regiment walked through on its march from Plymouth to Derby. Bess went too, keeping a low profile but in some pain. She left for Nice in late-December. It was hoped the better weather would be good for her health. The cost of the time in Plymouth (and presumably Bristol) was £1,747. [7]

However before Bess left, she would have been aware that the Duchess was pregnant and at least by early December, probably a little earlier. It would appear that from Hot Wells, they went back to Devonshire House. Although there was *'a good many people'* there on 1ˢᵗ January, she was soon taking it easier, with a good many letters from her mother labouring the point. Her mother wished that she would go to Wimbledon or at least *'shut your doors for some time'*. Bess was to be away until July 1784. She went initially to Paris and then made her way to Italy via Nice before returning via Lausanne in Switzerland (staying with Gibbon) and Paris again. She took Charlotte Williams with her, who came back fluent in French and Italian.

Having gone to Bath in May 1782 and then on to Plymouth for the militia duty, the time spent there with the Derbyshire Militia was extended because of the need to reinforce the garrison in case of a French/Spanish landing. The Duke liked to go to Chatsworth in the autumn for the hunting and he did his best to find opportunities to do the same at Plymouth. Being able to hire dogs must have been a blessing to him. Leaving there for Bristol to see the in-laws not only gave his wife the chance to see her parents (and especially her sick father) but points to the fact that the refurbishment of the family rooms at Chatsworth precluded a visit there. The family's arrival in Derbyshire was delayed until the following autumn, i.e. 1783.

Lady Spencer had other problems closer to home for the Earl's health was becoming a matter for concern. In May 1783, they travelled to Buxton to take the waters. She found the place *'some 50 degrees more dreary and dismal than my memory had represented it'*, a view Mrs. Delaney had had some time before. However change was on the way and the new hotel complex was rising. It was sufficiently developed for her to describe it as being *'very magnificent indeed and the plantations on the top of the surrounding hills which are began and I am told are to be continued are a glorious work and will in time be as beneficial as beautiful'*. No doubt an opinion shared by John Heaton as he watched the Duke's tree plantations and their cash crop gaining height and girth. [8]

8

Meddling and Maternity 1783-84

Refurbishment at Chatsworth

A couple of months earlier, while they were at Hardwick, the Duke planned to meet John Carr, his architect for the Buxton developments, on 4th March 1781. However it appears that he was elsewhere but must have sent word for Carr to sort out a serious problem. One of the beams above the Hall (now The Painted Hall) ceiling at Chatsworth had failed and was poking through. Carr gave orders for the beam to be made secure. However that was only the beginning of his problems.

Carr also ordered the removal of the slate off the main roof and adjacent offices of the Kitchen wing attached to the north side of the main house. The kitchen roof was in a bad way (although the nature of the decay – rot or worm – is not identified in his surviving report) [1] and timber for the roof replacement was ordered, probably from Hardwick. By September it was clear that the House roof was *'found to be in a very infirm state'*. There is a hint that it could have been wet rot caused by inferior slate, but one would have expected the evidence for that to have been obvious from leakage through the ceilings below. House in this context is thought to be the central building in the annexe housing the Bake House, Wash House, Dairy etc. The main house roof is flat and covered with lead, not slate.

By November 1781 it was clear that there were also problems with the Stable roof, which is surprising as it was relatively new, the Stables having been built in 1758-63. However, here again, it could relate to the additional Stables in the annexe, although they are of the same date. Also in that month, Carr was asked if he could examine whether a new Music Room could be made between the Chapel and the Drawing Room (by merging three smaller rooms) together with unspecified *'many other alterations and improvements which were laid before His Grace'*. Work on refurbishment was in fact well under way during the second half of 1782 when Francois Hervé was paid for work to that date on Anglo – French-style furniture. At Chatsworth, work on the principal rooms of the first floor of the South and West fronts was also well under way with French and other craftsmen at work.

Early in 1783, the Duchess was pregnant and her thoughts turned to a refurbishment at Chatsworth, including the creation of a Nursery. Carr ordered a chaise for 22nd February 1783 and went back to Chatsworth with his nephew. He met Monsieur Gaubert (a French craftsman living in London and managing the work on a daily basis) there and spent a fortnight determining *'the manner of fitting up and furnishing the rooms as Her Grace had directed'*. At the beginning of April, work began on removing the walls of the *'old bed chambers and dressing rooms and the Music Room formed properly'*.

The Duchess was involved with the nursery work but perhaps being present when work on the principal rooms on the South Front was discussed, felt that she was involved with this too. If so, she was wrong and it was to have far reaching circumstances.

Minded that the baby was due in July, Carr had several meetings with the Duchess and Gaubert in London in May and June. This included the furniture (made and carved to order), chimney pieces etc. While there, he ordered the Music Room (now the Blue Drawing Room) fireplace from Mailes. Also in May, Lady Spencer, then staying at Buxton as noted above, took a trip down to Chatsworth. She had little to do at Buxton and it is not clear whether she was just going to thank Alex Barker, the Steward, for the food and small beer he was sending her or not. She could well have been asked by the Duchess to check out how work was proceeding on the new Nursery etc.

She found that several rooms were about finished other than the furnishing. However she also found that Mrs. Graves, the housekeeper, was *'in the utmost distress about the house, which she fears will never be finished for your coming down this year'*. Mrs. Graves had told her (Lady Spencer) that when Gaubert was not there, the work progressed only slowly. Clearly she wanted it to be finished before the Duke and Duchess came with the expected baby. Lady Spencer recommended that the clerk of works – Gaubert – be instructed to ensure it was ready … *'tell him if his workmen are not all out of the House in July, it will never do, for the House will require a great deal of airing and cleaning when they are gone and the smell of paint, if they stay to the last, will be intolerable'*.

Lady Spencer went on to describe various rooms: '*The room between the Drawing Room and the Chappel* (sic)) *will be a very handsome one – the Gallery* (now the Library) *does not look well now, but it is not finish'd and may look better when there is furniture in it – the ceiling of the* (Painted) *Hall is almost finished and seems very well done – I look'd at the Nursery's which are a very Comfortable nest of rooms …*'. [2] Here was an example of the Duchess helping young artists.

In 1781, one of the ceiling joists in the Hall had poked through the ceiling. It resulted in major restoration work of the ceiling and damage to the paintwork. Two boys, the sons of one of the Duke's miners at the Ecton copper mine were being sponsored by the Duke/Duchess at the Royal Academy. The oldest, Thomas Hardy, must have been doing particularly well, for he was released after four years into a six year scholarship about the beginning of 1783 to paint the new plasterwork and was almost finished when Lady Spencer commented that it seemed very well done. Hardy was then asked to do further refurbishment in the Chapel. While at Chatsworth, the Duchess commissioned him to paint a Chatsworth pageboy, which survives in the boy's family. She also asked him to paint Little G with a dog, which is still part of the Devonshire Collection.

Lady Spencer wrote this about Mrs. Graves, the Housekeeper: … '*whose looks I like mightily – she seems civil attentive and diffident of herself*'. A few days after arrival, by contrast, the baby's nursery maid was sacked for being drunk and dirty: '*she made the bed stink of wine and strong drink whenever she came near it*'. It appears the baby was sleeping at least in the same room as her mother or close to it so that she could breast feed her in the night. [3] This new nursery was for the first family baby in nearly thirty years. It was situated on the bay on the North Front on the first floor. Although they were not here that frequently, Little G and her younger sister, Haryo slept together in a four post bed with cotton chintz pattern hangings.

It was unusual for aristocratic women to breast feed (the Duchess referred to it as 'suckling'), preferring a wet nurse instead. It was sufficiently unusual for the Ramblers Magazine [4] to state: '*Her Grace deserves commendation for this, but it is rather a reflection on the sex, that females in high life should generally be such strangers to the duty of a mother as to render one instance to the contrary so singular a phenomenon*'.

At the beginning of July 1783, Carr returned to Chatsworth to check on progress. However he found that Gaubert had '*paid no regard to the method we had settled of fitting up the House*'. He stopped the painting contractor, Reinagle, from proceeding and advised John Heaton of the problem. This was on 2nd July, ten days before the birth of the baby. Gaubert was clearly not there, possibly distracted by the Duchess's demands on his time. Carr eventually caught up with him mid-month, remonstrating about the work and possibly because he had not stopped the work. Carr then went on to London for a meeting with the Duke and John Heaton. He was directed to return *'immediately to Chatsworth and discharge the workmen and put the House in order'*.

This occurred on 4th August and Carr stayed for ten days, leaving the work in the hands of his assistant William Atkinson who stayed for 46 days in order to *'get the furniture replaced and things taken account of'*. The unwanted furniture etc. was sent to Devonshire House. There would appear to have been a lot of it and it took 19 days to pack it all up. The family would appear to have arrived with the bulk of the work done, around 1st September.

What is not clear is whether the work undertaken by Gaubert followed fresh and differing instructions from the Duchess. It seems strange that he would simply ignore the instructions of his employers which could only have one conclusion. One wonders whether there is a link between this event and the cost of it affecting John Heaton's judgement the following month (September) when he advised the Duke of rumours of an affair between the Prince of Wales and the Duchess. It certainly upset her and that might well have been Heaton's intention. If so, it appears to have worked for she wrote to her mother expressing her intentions to be wary of him in the future (see below). Some evidence that the Duchess had authorised the work may be drawn from a note by Carr [5] indicating that in late October *'more silk found and sent to London to Mr. Wilson and also several polished grates, a marble chimney piece etc.'*. The design and colour of the silk (? curtains) would no doubt have been chosen by the Duchess and differed from that in the originally agreed plan (otherwise it would have been used).

Some six weeks after it was decided to dismiss Gaubert, the Duke confided to the Duchess that he felt Heaton had a hold over him. She held the opinion that the Duke had a reasonable grasp of his affairs. He replied *'I do not look enough into my own affairs'*. The Duchess had responded that she thought it a pity that he did not and his reply was *'If I found out that Heaton was ever so great a rascal I should be mad to quarrel with him for it w'd quite ruin us'*. This would explain why the Duke agreed to the dismissal of Gaubert and his men, overruling his wife's changes and causing her embarrassment [6] and did not object to Heaton's comments about the Duchess and the Prince of Wales. This embarrassment stung the Duchess when they eventually reached Chatsworth in September 1783 (see below).

The Duchess's opinion about Heaton was bolstered after a discussion with the Duchess of Portland, her sister-n-law. It appears that Lord George (the Duke's younger brother) and his wife had taken occupation of Burlington House,

Piccadilly, (as stated by the Duchess). Heaton clearly did not act impartially in the negotiations according to her, and after seeing the correspondence on the matter from Heaton to the Portlands. In fact the Portlands would appear to have left Burlington House in 1782 when inventories were drawn up of the wine cellar, household furniture, the state of the building and the plate.

It was claimed that Heaton was acting preferentially towards the '*Georges*' because Lord George was first in line to the succession of the Dukedom in the absence of the Duke not having a legitimate son. There is some evidence to suggest that Heaton asserted himself at the expense of appearing to show vanity and possibly arrogance, even when it may not necessarily be the case. The Duchess of Portland claimed Heaton was jealous of Lord Commissioner Hotham's trusteeship over the former Burlington estates. If Heaton's concern was from a view that Hotham was not exercising proper control, he was later to be proved correct, regarding both the Yorkshire and Irish estates and also probably the home farm and land at Chiswick. [7]

As far as Burlington House was concerned, Heaton was hindered by the Duke not wishing to upset his sister, who refused to leave '*for ever*'. Lord George eventually purchased the property from the 6th Duke for £70,000 in 1815 but by then both the Duke and Duchess of Portland had passed away.

The hurt the Duchess must have felt over the Gaubert affair surfaced again unexpectedly on the family's arrival at Chatsworth. She found '*to my great displeasure*' that John Carr, the architect, was telling the Georges all about what had gone on concerning Gaubert and '*the expense of it etc. tho the Duke had wished the contrary – this exposed me all day long to the Georges finding fault with everything*'. The Duchess knew however that she held the best card: '*the idea of my having a son prevents many schemes that might be thout* (thought) *of against me*'. [8]

'*The Duke stopped Carr's mouth the next day*', she later wrote, '*but I am too late as all the country seems to know that things are sending back etc*'. (i.e. furniture and other furnishings were being sent to Devonshire House). Nonetheless the work on their private apartments (on the South Front first floor from the Chapel, right across the front to the Gallery (now the Library) on the East Front) found favour despite it not being her re-design and the Drawing Room '*is the prettyest and most comfortable room I ever saw*'. [9]. The Duchess seems to have considered extending the refurbishment of private rooms facing the West Front but nothing seems to have become of this at that time.

Despite a bad start, with Lady George Cavendish finding continual fault making the Duchess angry, there was soon a reconciliation here too, the catalyst being baby Georgiana. '*She* (Lady George) *is very good to me and really a very good natured little thing*'. This is more than she could say for Lord George:

'*he will never be popular because he will not give anything up … to the ideas of others*'. From her description, he appears to have been stingy, unable to make up his mind etc. Notwithstanding the above comment re his wife, the Duchess wrote: '*God knows it wd* (would) *have been better for me and my Dr* (dear) *D of D had it been otherwise*' (that Lord George's character was so different to his sister-in-law and his brother). (10)

The Duchess had further problems with debt as well as the refurbishment work at Chatsworth. Clearly the Duke did not wish to confront his wife over the Chatsworth improvements. It seems that he did not wish to confront her over anything else either because in 1784 and again in 1787 he was loathe to do so over massive accumulations of debt, in both cases the amounts being far more important than the Duchess's embarrassment and loss of face over room furnishings. Despite the Duke telling his wife that Heaton was to be '*subservient to me*', (11) clearly Heaton felt no qualms in going right up to the line, but not crossing it. Moreover, having control of so much of the Duke's landed property and its income generation, his duty to the Duke would rightly take priority.

This did not prevent her spreading malicious gossip about Heaton. Malicious in the sense that she did not mention that the dispute over the Chatsworth furnishings (which involved carving new furniture and employing expensive painters for the room decorations) was of her own making. Additionally, she was suggesting that Heaton was stealing.

The Ecton copper mine profits had been drawn off into a separate account but it is inconceivable that the strict accounting system of records of all income streams did not apply to this. Its only difference was that there was probably no independent check on it.

With more unjustified comments the Duchess made to Bess Foster: '*he tries to keep Canis* (the Duke, because of his love of dogs; Bess was Racky because of her cough and the Duchess was Mrs Rat) *(I think) out of money and he sinks I suspect some of the produce of a copper mine he has the care of … and I may be mistaken in my suspicion and I never utter them only watch him for Canis's sake*'. This is nonsense, for she would never have access to the accounting records to make any judgement of substance. (12) Her action in this way probably reflects that she was seriously in debt again. She had mentioned her anxieties over this to Charles Fox, but he had sought a disclosure of the full facts and she was not prepared to do this ahead of telling the Duke, which she feared to do. (13) Creditors must have been pressing John Heaton for she wrote to her mother '*I have some how or other lately began an opening to the Duke about the state of my affairs as I find from Heaton's letters it is necessary. He* (the Duke) *has been very kind about it*'. (14)

A month later, she wrote on the subject again to her mother (but not telling her the amount owed): '*you cannot conceve* (sic) *how good he has been and he knows everything*'. In another letter to Bess Foster, in Rome, of the same date (8th March 1784) she said the debt was '*many, many' many thousands*' ... '*I told him with fear*' ... '*every year of my life I have cost him immense sums, a mind he could not trust in – and how do you think he has received the avowal – with the utmost generosity, goodness and kindness – his whole care has been that I may not vex myself and you would think he was the offender, not me*'. [15]

This situation was neither salutary or an end of the matter. Two years later her debts had risen over that period to between £30 – 40,000. As will be seen below, her view then of Heaton changed completely. His view of her went unrecorded.

Partying at Chiswick

The Duchess's expenditure was not all gambling debts. In fact the celebrations for the Duke's 35th birthday give an example of where the money was going. Unless her letters purposely only show low levels of losses, the high levels of debt had to come from other sources.

The reason why Mons. Gaubert was missing at Chatsworth in May 1783 was because of the Duchess's demands upon his time at Chiswick, as well as other work in London. On 25th May the Duke and Duchess held a breakfast to celebrate the Duke's 35th birthday. Gaubert was responsible for (no doubt with other work) decorating the gardens. The trees and shrubberies were hung with festoons of flowers, with sashes of roses, intermingled with oranges and myrtle. Guests began to arrive at about 1 p.m. and amongst them were the Prince of Wales, the Duc de Chartres, attended by the Duc de Fitzjames '*and most of the foreign nobility*' plus Lords Carlisle, Althorp, Jersey, Melbourne, Duncannon, Herbert; Cols. Fitzpatrick and St. Leger; and Ladies Melbourne, Duncannon and many others (friends of the Duchess). The refreshment consisted of tea, coffee, chocolate, fruits of all sorts, ices, etc., until 4 p.m. when the guests returned to town. [16]

With external work at Chatsworth reaching an end, this party may well have given the Duchess the idea to take a look at Chiswick as a socialising venue instead of Devonshire House. The following year the Duke undertook some minor changes to the garden, a prelude to significant alterations to the house which commenced in 1788.

The End of an Era and a New One

Lady Spencer had gone to Chatsworth and reported on the state of the refurbishment there in 1783 while staying at Buxton, where her husband was taking the waters. To her, Buxton was dreary. For such a prodigious letter writer Lady Spencer was also unimpressed with mail deliveries from London to Buxton limited to Thursdays, Saturdays and Tuesdays. Alex Barker, the Chatsworth Steward, was sending '*excellent mutton and small beer and Mr. Treviss (the gardener's name is that I think) very good garden stuff which is the more acceptible (sic) as not a cabbage an onion or a bunch of parsley is to be got at this place*'. [17]

This seems to suggest that they were not having the food provided at the Buxton Hall Inn. So whether they were staying there is not clear nor what alternative would have suited them. No other inn was situated next to the bath with priority over the bathing. A range of quality accommodation was not available until the completion of the Duke's development three years later. The supply of Chatsworth provisions was maintained until they left and would have made the stay more tolerable.

Barker's instructions would have been at the command of John Heaton, no doubt instigated by the Duchess, but it was the Duke who the Countess thanked through a letter to her daughter, rather than directly. Equally it is probable that her suggested instruction to Gaubert to complete the Chatsworth work before the baby arrived came through the Duchess to Heaton rather than through the Duke. Either way, the Duke's lack of involvement in his own affairs was to change shortly. In fact 1783 saw several changes, directly and indirectly. By August, Buxton Crescent was being roofed and renovation work on the Chatsworth formal rooms was finished.

Yet despite the sumptuous nature of the refurbished private quarters at Chatsworth, the state rooms and other parts of the house seen by visitors failed to impress them. Mrs. Cust, on her visit in October 1775, had described the house as '*not well furnished*' (see Chapter 4). Dr. Johnson was not impressed by the furniture in 1784 (see above). Johnson felt that of all the Duke's possessions, what he liked best was his horse, Atlas, at 15 hands 1½ inches high. [18] As late as 1811, a visitor, Louis Simond, wrote '*...The apartments have nothing remarkable; gobelin tapestry, old, faded and in wretched taste; and numerous pictures still worse. It is inconceivable that a person of so cultivated a taste as the last Duchess should have been able to bear the sight of these daubs*'. [19] The 6th Duke was to change this negativity.

A Daughter For The Duchess

Springtime 1783 had seen the Duchess proposing financial support to Bess and if it could be arranged, the schooling of her second son in England at Devonshire expense. Bess's boys were living in Ireland with their father and this was a ruse to get at least one of them back in England with just his holidays spent with his father. It did not succeed. At this stage, the Duchess was suggesting that she would look for a house for Bess near to Devonshire House, rather than living in the latter *'The summers you shall pass at B. A.* (Bolton Abbey), *Chatsworth or in some other scheme, the autumn hunting with Canis and the winters in London'.* [20] This did not succeed either, Bess Foster moving in with the Duke and Duchess. Meanwhile the Earl's precarious state of health staggered on as attention turned towards the Duchess's pregnancy and it coming to term. The jinx of previous miscarriages of her mother and herself was not happening this time. This was at least a partial success, but marred by the birth of a girl, Georgiana, known as Little G, and not the required heir.

Bess wrote from Marseilles on 1st June 1783 confirming that she was ready to return to England *'to nurse and attend you in your confinement'.* It will be remembered that she had taken Charlotte Williams (the Duke's illegitimate daughter) with her *'I took Charlotte with me and she was in high airs ... I have promised her if she is good she shall dine there with me.* [21]

The birth was on 12th July, but Bess had not been recalled. With her at the time were her mother, the Duchess of Portland (the Duke's sister) and Dr. Denman, with the Duke at the door. She wrote to Bess: *'I had a very hard time of it towards the end'.* She clearly thought that her baby was stillborn and took expressions of anxiety from her mother to mean the same. A gusty cry dispelled that notion. Bess's absence was probably the doing of Lady Spencer. The birth was celebrated by the Duchess with her customary financial exuberance: *'her cradle, robes, baskets etc. are I am afraid foolishly magnificent – they are covered with the finest lace'.* The Duchess could not be faulted in taking on her responsibilities as a mother. Walpole had it completely wrong when he speculated: *'she (Lady Chewton) will be a more staid nurse than the Duchess of Devonshire, who probably will stuff her poor babe into her knotting bag when she wants to play at macao, and forget it'.* [22]

Her sister Harriet had given birth on 6th July to a boy. (See Chapter 23, Lady Duncannon, for more on this birth). How the Duke must have felt the irony. The Cavendish family had seen no problem in giving birth to sons, let alone conception. As this was his second child including Charlotte, the latter would appear to him to lie with his wife. However, both of these children were girls – his sister, Dorothy, Duchess of Portland, already had four boys (and a girl) and his younger brother, Lord George Cavendish, had had a son (William) in January of that year (his wife was to bear him another three boys and a girl to match Dorothy).

Later that decade the Duke was to have yet another girl, Caroline, in 1785 by Bess Foster, in the same year as he had Harriet (Haryo) by the Duchess. Three years later he did have a son, Augustus, by Bess. His much wanted heir, William, kept him waiting until May 1790. Children by three women at least proved to him than conceiving was not an issue as far as he was concerned. There was a joint christening at Wimbledon on 9th August. For a christening gown, the Duchess had ordered one to be made of lace in Brussels. Her own dress was a lace habit, trimmed with Brussels lace, with an apron to suit, the whole outfit being in white.

The baby was christened Georgiana Dorothy Cavendish (known as Little G) after her mother and the Duke's sister, who were the godmothers with Earl Spencer, the godfather. Harriet's child was christened Frederick Cavendish Ponsonby. The Duchess was his godmother and the Duke of Portland and Lord Bessborough his godfathers. Everything comes in threes and family friend Lady Lincoln also had a baby in the first week of August. Meanwhile, the Duke would have been thinking ahead. By the end of the month they were on their way to Chatsworth. The refurbishment was ready for him and Chesterfield Races were the week after his arrival. On 8th July 1783, Lady Louisa Conolly writing about the Duke's sister, the Duchess of Portland, said she was '*just as pleasant and delightful as usual, but has got into the way of keeping such late hours that she says it knocks her up*'. It is highly likely that her brother and sister-in-law were responsible for that, given the date just prior to Georgina Dorothy's birth. [23]

September marked another annual aristocratic ritual they inflicted on themselves: the two public days at Chatsworth. In 1793, thirty nine people sat down to a free meal at the first one; the second one was quieter. A couple of days before the first one, a large party staying at Chatsworth went with the Duchess, but not the Duke, to Buxton (? another pointer to him not liking the place). She wrote to her mother: '*I never saw anything so magnificent as The Crescent – tho' it must half ruin one, my spirit makes me delight in the Duke's doing it.*' The roof was being placed that month, so essentially the external appearance would have been apparent. It had taken three years to reach this stage and the internal work and fitting out would take another three.

Success At Buxton, Sadness At Bath

Although The Crescent at Bath existed, it was virtually a curved terrace of houses. Buxton was arguably Britain's first purpose built inland holiday resort. The Buxton complex included two hotels, several apartments, shops, new mineral bath development including facilities for taking the waters, an Assembly room, colonnaded walkways under cover etc. It must have been a breath taking experience to see it rising in such a small village (when one considers that the joint annual income of a married couple with both working and of a working class background would probably be c. £30-£40, this development was to cost £67,000). Another comparison puts the last comment into perspective: in the period that The Crescent was being built (1780-86), the Duchess incurred debts which were similar in amount to the construction costs. It is ironic that she noted this cost *'must half ruin one'*. Taking both costs into account, it shows the magnitude of Devonshire financial resources that it could cope with both sets of expense together.

Following seven weeks at Chatsworth, on 22nd October 1783 the family moved from there to Hardwick. For once, the Duchess was happy with life in the country: *'the D. talks of my going to town but I shall try not'*. It followed on from a Public Day on 20th October which was becoming a popular event. *'Many staid [presumably for dinner] … we never had such public days and we have had 4 sets of people this summer who were staunch enemys before'*. Quite a few guests were also staying there, including General Smith, Messrs. Crawford, Grenville and General Mordaunt, who had *'been here all summer'* (and was probably related to the Duchess's maternal grandmother), and Sir William (? was he known as Harry) Hunloke. All the men rode horses to Hardwick while the Duchess and her baby went by coach. [24] It was unusual to have a Chatsworth Public Day in October.

On the 24th, Lady Spencer wrote from Bath about the Earl's deteriorating health. The latter's descendant, Earl Charles Spencer writes that the Earl had a stroke in 1781 and had been in ill health the year before. He died on the 29th October. Lady Spencer went from Bath to Holywell House at St. Albans, which she preferred to Althorp. From now on she would need to learn to live on £4,000 p.a. [25] Amid the Duchess's distress for her personal loss and her feelings for her mother, the Duke would appear to be ill too with a stomach complaint at about the same time. The symptoms must have been uncomfortable for him to write to Erasmus Darwin at Derby seeking advice on cutting down on alcohol and its side effects.

One cannot help wondering whether the Duke's decision to reduce his alcohol intake was also induced by the death of Earl Spencer. Although the latter was older, he was still under 50 years old, a gout sufferer possibly brought on through drink (like the Duke) who had been ill from one thing and another for a long time. Whether the Duke had the strength of character to permanently reduce his intake is not known. He does not seem to have shaken off the complaint and went to Bath for Christmas, hiring a house in The Crescent amid rumours of smallpox and measles there (which proved to be no worse than normal).

At the end of the year the town was suffering from the weather's icy grip: *'it was 16 beyond freezing. A 60 yr old gentleman said he could not remember such cold weather'* wrote the Duchess to her mother. After taking the waters for a fortnight, the Duke wrote to Bess Foster in Italy to say he was feeling better for having done so. However comparing with the previous time he was there eighteen months previous, *'then I had the Rat and Bess and good health and fine weather and now I have none of them'*. The Duchess had written to her, just prior to the Duke, saying *'Canis has some fever but better on the whole - he talks forever of you'*. [26]

At least their house was comfortable, *'house is delightful – magnificent drawing rooms and parlours'* wrote the Duchess to her mother. The Duke's uncle Frederick was there (he often went with them on their travels). The Duke's improvement saw a dinner party on January 2nd and afterwards they all went to a ball except the Duchess, claiming tiredness of company *'as I am grown unust* (sic) *to it'*. [27] If this was true, she soon found the remedy, throwing herself into the April 1784 election. Was the latter a backlash from the death of her father? Whatever it was, the election was to be distasteful to the Duke both from its result and possibly the costs of it incurred by his wife.

The Duchess's letters seem to reflect her miserable mood probably induced by her debts, so perhaps her description of Bath needs to be seen in that context. She wrote to her mother: *'Bath is the most hateful of the places for scandalous ill nature owing to the swarm of old maids, old Cats and old Bachelors that live in it. Our neighbour Mrs. Grenville is at the head of the slandering tribe'*. [28]

9

Complications 1784-85

Charlotte

For a distraction from her miserable state of mind, the Duchess started to think about the future of the Duke's daughter, Charlotte. Having been abroad with Bess Foster for a considerable time, she (the Duchess) may have felt the desire to consider what would be necessary to re-assert her control once she (Charlotte) was back. It was the intention to place her in a school (Mrs. Belvoir's) in London, where Lord Thanet's daughter Elizabeth (aged 15) and Caroline (aged 12) were being educated along with other girls the Duchess knew. She was also going to ask the Duke if he would give her the surname Cavendish. If she did, the Duke did not agree.

It was expected that at age 17, Charlotte would spend the summer at Chatsworth with the ultimate intention – and with whatever sum the Duke would give her – that she would wed the son of a local squire. This would have the double advantage of having her near to hand and out of London *'for which I fear the poor little thing has too much susceptibility'*. In the end, at the age of c. 18 or 19, in September 1793, she married the nephew of John Heaton, Charles. [1] In a letter from Naples, part of which is missing, Bess Foster appears to be advising the Duchess that *'you must not yet tell her* (Charlotte) *her birth'* and seems to be saying that Charlotte's ideas/mind were filled with contempt of others [detail missing] recommending that on her return the two *'consult together and try what we can do'*. Miss Lloyd, who was at Chatsworth at the time of the second Public Day, 27th September 1784 and presumably met Charlotte then, wrote to Lady Spencer *'I don't like this Charlotte much, I feel there is something bad about her…'*. [2]

Bess Foster was not keen to come back to England, notwithstanding that she knew the Duke wanted that above anything else. She wrote to the Duchess at the end of June 1784 *'I w'd give the world you had come to me instead of my going to you'*. [3] Bess arrived back with Charlotte in July. By early-August, the three were together at Chatsworth, along with Charlotte. The Duke and Duchess had come from Newmarket, which had given the Duchess an opportunity to see her mother. Bess had gone abroad with the idea of enabling her to get over a persistent cough. But it had returned, forcing her to remain indoors. The Duke and Duchess rode amongst the timber plantations, they walked after dinner and even went fishing in a little pond one evening. The catch was 23 brace and a half of perch, with Charlotte catching 27 of them and the Duchess nearly slapping Little G in the face with one catch while still on the rod.

Charlotte was being taught at home (Devonshire House, from 1786 at least) so presumably her teacher, Mrs. Moreau, also travelled with the family for the lengthy stays away (in 1787 they were at Bath for ten weeks and 12 weeks the following year) unless Charlotte remained in London as she became older. In 1788 she was still only 14 but had a companion, Miss Vigoureaux (probably the one who was left £500, along with her sister, in the 6th Duke's will). The latter's father worked for the Duke, but his position is not clear. His family may well have been related to the Spencers.

Charlotte's education cost c. £175 p.a. and her other costs, noted as sundries in the accounts, were around £40 p.a. – presumably clothing etc. The Duchess encouraged her to join dances with guest etc. and presumably either paid for the dresses she would need unless she fitted into the Duchess's cast-offs. [4]. Foreman states that the Duke and Bess Foster had determined by 1785 to have the latter's daughter Caroline and Charlotte educated in Paris. If so, the Duchess may have prevented this at that time unless there was some problem over Caroline. [5]

1784

The early part of 1784 saw the family at Bath, returning to London in mid-March. The Duchess went out to the Opera on the 18th to see the Reine de Golconda, which included a March she had written. The next night she was out again after dinner. Her letter to her mother included a sketch of her appearance: *'my hair very rough, a flatish cap and a handkerchief up to my chin'*. (see p.23 of illustrations).

Back To Chatsworth, 1784

In early August 1784, following a diversion to Newmarket, staying at the house the Duke rented there, he went with the Duchess and Bess Foster to Chatsworth.

It was the time of year for the Derby Races yet again with the Duchess taking to the dance floor at the Ball, slipping from a minuet with old Lord Ferrers to country dancing with the other younger steward, Mr. Bateman. She was dressed in an *'English night gown of muslin with small silver sprigs'*. As in previous years, she stayed with Mrs. Gisburn and the latter's uncle this time. A large group returned to Chatsworth for a party at the end of it all. [6]

At the end of the same month, August, they went off to the Chesterfield Races, going daily from Chatsworth. It appears that the Duchess developed a swelling on her face so much so that she felt she could not go to the races. The Duke bumped into Erasmus Darwin while there and brought him back to Chatsworth where, no doubt, he enlightened conversation and checked out the Duchess's face. Whether he was there on the 4th September to experience the Devonshire equivalent of a fishing trip isn't clear.

The men rode horseback into the River Derwent (below the house) to arrange large nets to trap the fish. To preserve gentility, the ladies piled into the *'great open carriage'* which presumably also went into the river. The outcome isn't known but it seems it was followed by yet another pond fishing trip a few days later to *'the pond in the garden'*. The Duchess would probably have enjoyed fishing the series of ponds just north of the house which were removed by the 4th Duke just prior to his death.

The 6th September 1784 was a Public Day at Chatsworth and an unexpected visitor was Dr. Samuel Johnson, who was staying with Dr. Taylor at The Mansion in Church Street, Ashbourne and had been ill with asthma. While at Chatsworth he *'met young Mr. Burke, who led me very commodiously into conversation with the Duke and Duchess. We had a very good morning. The dinner was Public.'* This was not the first time that the Duchess had met him but it's unclear if the Duke had. Wraxhall noted that Johnson had seen her, probably in the early years of the Duchess's marriage *'in the first bloom of her youth, hanging on the sentences that fell from Johnson's lips and contending for the nearest place to his chair. All the cynic moroseness of the philosopher and the moralist seemed to dissolve under so flattering an approach …'* although he appeared oblivious of it. [7]

The Duke and Johnson retired from the others to converse under the lime trees in the garden, both indicating that they had enjoyed it. At the dinner, the Duke and Duchess had the opportunity to experience Johnson's bizarre eating habit. Even Boswell described him as being *'well-known for his slovenliness and roughness at the table'*. [8] The Duchess wrote that *'Ly Eliz and me where* (sic) *very sorry to leave him the public day – he din'd here and does not shine quite so much in eating as in conversing for he eat much and nastily'*. [9] The trees that Johnson and the Duke sat under are thought to be still there, above the Canal Pond.

Johnson's views on the improvements just completed at Chatsworth do not seem to have been recorded or the reason for a third Public Day (it was traditionally two days annually, a fortnight apart and on a Monday), although the third one was also on a Monday (4th October 1784). The Duke and Duchess would have been pleased to have had time with Dr. Johnson. Three months later, on 13th December 1784, he died aged 75 years. The tranquillity of autumn life at Chatsworth and the presence of Bess Foster also had another effect. The Duchess became pregnant in November.

There was concern about Bess's hacking and persistent cough. It had prevented her from attending the Derby Races Ball in August, confining her to the house. It was agreed that she would go south to France on 2nd December and head for a warmer climate. The attention of the Duke of Dorset may have been another attraction from his point of view, but Bess avoided him. The love between the Duke (of Devonshire) and Bess expressed itself in a profound way. In fact as they waved their farewells at Dover, the Duchess was not the only one carrying the Duke's child. Both women had conceived in November. If Bess was wondering if she was pregnant, the Duchess had no idea and probably the Duke too.

Although the end of the year probably saw the Duke still oblivious to this, there had been several milestones earlier in the year. The main one of course would have been the completion of the work on the main domestic rooms of the family at Chatsworth. Other events were the Duke reaching 20 years of his Dukedom and 10 years of marriage (and still no sign of an heir); his uncle John had reached 50 years of age and his brother George was now 30. The roof was now on at The Crescent in Buxton and plans for improvements to the gardens at Chiswick were progressing.

Bess being pregnant makes it difficult to assess the true nature of his feelings for both ladies during this year. However he did do one thing which might have been evidence of his intention to placate the Duchess after the refurbishment problems at Chatsworth the previous year. During their time at Chatsworth in 1784, it was the Duchess, not the Duke who was seeing to further work there. John Carr's invoice for work done makes it clear that she went around the House with him discussing many things and gave directions for a new water closet to be made and *'and the maids room to be fitted up, the laundry maids to have another room, the wash floor to be raised and proper boilers and wash tubs to be made which were much wanted'*.

However, a major disappointment would be the sight of Bess's boat sailing away from Dover on that 2nd December, not knowing when she would be coming back again. It was to torment him the following year, 1785. She had been in England for five short months. As a distraction of some sort, it appears he set off in mid-February from Devonshire House to hunt with the Quorn. [10]

Problems of Passion

A widespread outbreak of smallpox at the beginning of 1785 caused alarm in the family as Little G had not been inoculated. The Duchess wanted to go to town (London) because she needed to see Dr. Denman and Dr. Warren about her nerves. She had thought of going to Chiswick but it was thought to be damp there and the Duke wasn't happy about it. The Duke's reasoning was clear: The Duchess had stayed there previously when the old Jacobean house was considered to be damp one winter and had caught '*a putrid disorder*' while there. [11]

They clearly did not wish to expose Little G to anything of that nature A couple of years later, their neighbour, the 4th Duke of Rutland (he owned Haddon Hall, near Chatsworth), caught putrid fever and died of it, aged 33 years, on 24th October 1787. [12] He left a wife aged 31 years and six children. She was the daughter of the 4th Duke of Beaufort and did not remarry.

This may have highlighted in the Duke's mind the need for improvements which followed, although the nature of the work is not clear. The Duchess spent months trying to get her mother to come to stay but she was having none of it. She eventually lost her patience, writing to the Duchess in mid-April 1785: '*the very idea of all your squabbles, explanations etc. imports me into a fever ... Lady Pembroke will I dare say see the necessity of your acting the part you do – but I will have done with this disagreeable subject.*' [13] So that was that.

However she relented somewhat stating that she would be prepared to go to Chiswick or have Little G stay with her. The problem was that Lady Spencer knew that her daughter had no self-control; said one thing and did another. One Monday, 14th February 1785, the Duchess wrote to her mother: '*the balls do not affect me – I am never out after twelve*'. Two days later in a separate letter she told her mother she had arrived home at 3 a.m. that morning from a ball at Lady Lucan's (the house of her brother George's mother-in-law). Eventually Lady Spencer gave way, agreeing to look after Little G at Chiswick as her daughter's pregnancy came close to term.

In the Spring of 1785, Bess's Journal includes the comment about the Duke: '*love so lately given and proven to the Duke of D – e*'. Later, she wrote '*...so totally did I love him*'. There is no doubt that the three of them felt the same way for the other two although the Duke did not express himself as much as the women but his love for both was deep-seated.

Meanwhile, the Duke had found himself with a problem of his own. He had quite obviously fallen for Bess Foster and she was abroad with no return date set. Indeed, there were even suggestions that she might not return. Chapman relates a good account of where Bess was (and was not), living the lie at least to the Duchess about where she was and of course hiding any knowledge that she too was expecting the Duke's baby. Meanwhile the Duchess was '*so big she can hardly waddle and she thinks she shall have twins and if that should happen intends to make you a present of one of them'*. (14)

Before this letter had reached Bess, she had given birth to a girl (on 13th August). This particular comment from the Duke would seem to suggest that the Duchess did not know of Bess's pregnancy. However two letters of the previous May would seem to point in a different direction. On 16th May the Duke wrote to Bess indicating that he was prepared to tell the Duchess: '*I am certain that if she did* [know] *she could not think you had been to blame about it, particularly after I had explained to her how the thing happened'*. Six days later, Lady Spencer wrote to the Duchess: '*things it will be supposed could not have gone such lengths without your perceiving it and some I suppose will say without encouraging it'*.

Persuasive in content, the dates are too close for the Duke to have had a reply. Did the Duchess know before the Duke realised? Alternatively, if this second quote relates to the Duke's feelings for Bess, then Lady Spencer was close to the bone. Bess had her baby in a town called Vietri, about 20 miles/ 32 km west of Salerno, south of Naples. She was called Caroline St. Jules and would appear to have been fostered in the south of France until 1789, when she was united with her mother in Paris. (15)

If the Duchess did not know of Bess's situation, Bess certainly knew of the Duke's. He had written to her to tell her '*I hope you are not out of humour with, or forgetful of C-s* (Canis), *who loves you as much if not more than ever'*. By August, his reticence at being too familiar in mail prone to be opened was subsumed by a change in the familiar normality of his character. With an element of forward planning borne out of a bubbling release of passion, he had made a decision of the heart: '*I have some thoughts if I have time of going to Bolton* [Abbey] *to shoot the moors and to prepare the place for you against next summer, for I intend to take you there whether you like it or not, let the consequence be what it will, do don't talk any more nonsense about not returning to England.'* (16)

In an earlier letter, the Duke responded to a comment Bess had written about him flirting. He responded sharply: '*you are much mistaken in what you say in your letter … about my flirtations, for I have had none and don't desire to have any'*. (17) It was to be another year before he saw her again, with no passionate escape to a hideaway at Bolton Abbey at Wharfedale in the Yorkshire Dales.

The 1784 Election

The Duchess, her sister and Lady Melbourne did their best to promote the fortunes of C.J. Fox in the Westminster election. The Duke was at York with John Heaton where they were assisting Lord John Cavendish, the Duke's uncle, to retain his seat. However it was to be an uphill and unsuccessful struggle, despite him being the Chancellor of the Exchequer in the previous administration, or perhaps because of it. The Duchess is well known for trading kisses for votes with itinerant tradesmen on the streets, along with her companions. As discussed in Chapter 22, this was probably because she had no money to use instead and was unable to ask the Duke to assist her as he was away in York and would probably have not allowed her to do it anyway.

Satirists and the Tory press tried to use such activity to their advantage but it turned out to be a powerful vote winner for Fox. It may have failed, not because of voters saw little value in an aristocratic kiss or held little esteem for the magnetic personality of the Duchess, but because of the unexpected illness of Lady Spencer. Along with her sister, the Duchess ordered her bags to be packed and her coach made ready as they left for their mother's.

The Duchess's absence saw a swing to the Tory candidate, Mr Wray, and the Duchess of Portland, acting as agent for her husband, the Prime Minister in the previous administration, wrote to her sister-in-law: '*There are a great many votes you can command and no one else and now if you can only stop at people's doors will be quite sufficient and really your presence is quite expected*'. Even the Duke of Portland earnestly wrote to her: '*Everyone is convinced that your exertions have produced the very material alteration which has happened in Fox's favour*'. The Duchess returned in time to stem the tide. The latter was decidedly on the turn across the country, sweeping Pitt into power, but Fox was to be victorious, emphasising the potent effect of the Duchess's popularity and personality.

A jubilant procession paraded through the streets to Devonshire House, trailing a banner with the words 'Sacred To Female Patriotism'. Bringing up the rear were the two Duchesses, each in a coach and six. Even if the women did not have a vote they had probably never been such a blatant example of how the pulling power of the fair sex could be manipulated for mass political gain in a British election.

However the manipulation had gone too far and the Duchess was stung by the ferocity of the campaign against her, both in and beyond the press. She had learnt the hard way and never took part in subsequent elections. [29]

Babies

Before the end of 1785 there was to be another birth and another girl in the family when the Duchess's sister, Harriett, gave birth to Caroline Ponsonby on 13th November. Caroline was later to become the wife of William Lamb who later became 2nd Viscount Melbourne. Bess's baby was named Caroline Rosalie Adelaide St. Jules after an 'old friend' in France who looked after the child in 1786 when Bess returned to England. Bess's Caroline was to become the wife of George Lamb, William's brother.

It wasn't just Bess that the Duke had in his mind in June 1785. The Duchess wrote to Bess to say that she was in the Duke's room and he was dressing for the House of Lords. It was rare for her to mention his going there. [18] The beginning of August 1785 saw the family at Devonshire House with the Duchess eight months pregnant, hopefully with the heir. She was not too well and was *'blooded'* on the 3rd. It seems to have done the trick, for the next day as Lady Spencer moved to Chiswick with a *'very fretful'* Little G, she observed that her daughter's (the Duchess's) *'cold was much better'*. The following day she had the Duke for company at *'the new house'*. In the evening she *'drove round the farm with the Duke in his phaeton'*. [19]

Meanwhile, it was August and at Devonshire House parties were in full swing. Lady Spencer had returned there and clearly was not too amused. For several nights she avoided the *'posse of people coming in'* and retired early. On 18th she took a walk to the Panthian with Lord Frederick Cavendish *'to look at the ballon* (sic) *suspended there – a wonderful sight'*. Nonetheless, she *'retired early to my room as there were a great many people here'*. [20]

The Duke however was not there. From Chiswick he had gone to Chatsworth for the Derby Races leaving his wife at Devonshire House, probably with her mother, no doubt hoping that she would keep her daughter in check. It is worth noting that the Duke had done little to alleviate the Duchess's stress over her level of debt and pressure from creditors during the pregnancy. Nor was the Duchess leading a quiet life at Devonshire House in the final weeks before the birth. In June she had written to Bess telling her that she had *'left off my play and extravagance'*. It clearly was only a temporary relapse. [21]

The Duke and the Duchess's second child was born on 29th August 1785. It was another girl, to be called Haryo, her christening being on the 1st October, when she was named Henrietta Elizabeth, to be known as Harriet, after her maternal aunt. The following day, Lady Spencer recorded in her diary that both mother and daughter were *'nastily unwell'*. Two days later they were both *'very well'*. However on the 5th October the Duchess started with a stomach complaint with which she swayed from being seriously unwell and in considerable pain with violent wretching to being much better and then being unwell again. These cycles lasted for a full month before she started to recover. Laudanum eased the pain at night and made her sleep. [22]

1785: Other Events

On the 19th August, the Duchess was *'gaining strength everyday'*. It would appear that the Duke had gone away, leaving a sick wife. Regular doses of laudanum were having no effect but the Duchess's recovery coincided with the Duke's return on 20th August 1785. The following day, as the Duchess had a further relapse, the Duke held a party. It was no quiet affair, perhaps arranged before the extent of the Duchess's illness was appreciated. The guest of honour was the Prince of Wales and the number of other guests was considerable. They included not only the Prince's favourites but most of the Duke's too, although Bess Foster, decamped in Italy to have the Duke's other baby, was absent.

Amongst the ladies present were Ladies Salisbury, Essex, Southampton, Payne and Mrs. St. John, as Lady Spencer recalled in her diary, *'plus a shoal of men'*. She did not bother to record the names of any of them! No doubt she retired as early as she could. The Duchess continued to fluctuate between health and ill health until the end of the second week of September. However she seems to have rallied for the christening. On the 5th *'all the house was in a bustle'* noted Lady Spencer the day before the event. [23] Lady Duncannon came with her children from Roehampton; the Bishop of Peterborough officiated, with Lady Betty Ponsonby, Lady Duncannon, Lord Bessborough and Lord George Cavendish (the Duke's brother) being the 'sponsors' – the godparents in modern parlance. *'There were foreigners and other Company in the Evening and the whole was very magnificent and pretty'* recorded Lady Spencer. The latter did not stay at Devonshire House, returning to Holywell House. Her removal had nothing to do with the revelry; she had a more personal and emotive reason for leaving: her pet dog, Mouton, had died. She ended her day *'bathing for the first time in my warm bath'*. [24]

The ill health of the Duchess is a reminder that in the days prior to the discovery of penicillin, the treatments available were sometimes strange to us now. Shortly after Lady Spencer lost Wimbledon Park by fire, she was struck by a terrible pain in her face for many hours. Eventually *'I tried snuff within the mouth and [?] drops without which* [improved] *it entirely in a most wonderful manner'*. [25]

The main problem about the smallpox outbreak at the beginning of 1785 was that Little G had not been inoculated. Although there are some years in between, the Duke of Newcastle wrote in his diary about an epidemic of the disease in August 1833. He added that inoculation gave protection against it. [26] An earlier outbreak in Edensor village, Chatsworth, had seen those affected recovering, as they had been inoculated.

On 15th December Lady Spencer went to the theatre to see a play, *'The Duchess'*, with Lord Jersey and Lord Frederick Cavendish. Neither of the men could get a seat, the place was so full. The heat was excessive *'but it all went off very well and people seemed much pleased'*. [27] The play's subject was the Duchess, but the Duke's thoughts about it seem not to have survived.

Lady Spencer may well have been glad to see the end of 1785. Following the death of her soul mate husband (Earl Spencer) she had had to shoulder more of the responsibility for her own affairs. In March 1785, a huge fire had consumed Wimbledon Park, although most of the paintings, books and furniture were saved (and nobody was hurt). She had two *'sad sleepless nights ... for a place I was so partial* to'. [28] The house had come down from Sarah, Duchess of Marlborough in 1744 with 200 acres. The grounds had been subsequently been re-designed by Lancelot 'Capability' Brown. His work had been a success and the house and gardens were subsequently renowned for their beauty. The surviving servants' quarters were used thereafter until a new house was built by Henry Holland in 1798 – 1801 for the family. Part of the Park is now the home of the All England Tennis Club.

Unfortunately for her, everything came in threes and in 1786 the Duke announced he would seek a separation from the Duchess (see below) because of the huge amount of her debts. No doubt she experienced more sleepless nights as a result.

10

Upheaval 1786-90

A Nightmare Set to Run

The new year, 1786, saw little change in the Duke's emotions. He was clearly thinking that he could, may be ought, to go to Italy to be with Bess Foster, but for some reason he did not go. The Duchess must have sensed that she was walking on thin ice and planned a summer away from London. Yet by March, she was gambling again. [1] There was talk of the three of them meeting in Spa, but that fell through in June. It may be because of a re-occurrence of the gout that the Duke did not go. He was certainly suffering from it in August when they went off to Chatsworth, the Duchess caring for her patient.

However events were about to take a different turn as Bess Foster returned to England. Since the initial meeting at Bath in 1782, she had only spent nine months with the Duke and Duchess in four years. She went to see her mother initially. Was this diversion because the Duchess had discovered that Bess had given birth to her husband's child and was unsure of what reception she would receive? Clouds have silver linings and this allowed Lady Spencer an opportunity to journey to Chatsworth. She arrived there on 2nd September 1786. At some point her daughter Harriet, Lady Duncannon, joined her sister there with her husband, Bess Foster eventually going too. It was at this point that the Duchess advised the Duke of her gambling and the claim of Martindale.

Foreman states [2] that when Georgiana told the Duke that she owed Martindale £100,000 'without hesitation, the Duke demanded a separation' in early October 1786. She also states that 'over the next two years Foster encouraged the Duke to separate from the Duchess, while remaining the latter's closest confidante'. [3] This appears at odds to her comment 'if Georgiana was publicly separated *from the Duke, Bess Foster would not be able to stay at Devonshire House without scandal, nor would the Devonshire House circle tolerate her usurpation of Georgiana's role at Chatsworth'.* [4]

There was however someone else who was directly interested in a separation: Lord George Henry Cavendish (heir presumptive to the Dukedom) and as has been seen above (see under 1783), he had a close interest what happened to the estate if there was no heir to the 5th Duke; he also had the ear of John Heaton. It was certainly in his interests to be alarmed at the potential serious harm to the family fortune which the Duchess was already inflicting on the Duke. Most of the estate consisted of settled lands, which meant that the Duke enjoyed the income from them but could not sell them. Yet the huge Buxton programme of development at The Crescent was not settled and the copper mine monies were clearly vulnerable also.

The Duke also knew that without his wife, there would be no heir and therefore over a short time his position changed. It shows the tolerance of the Duke, let alone questions of his judgement, unless he was clearing the decks for what he had hoped was a new beginning with her. If so it is against a background (as mentioned above) of the Duke drawing closer to Bess Foster. It also points to the ends the Duke was prepared to go to have his heir. It would appear that Richard Sheridan may well have interceded on the Duchess's behalf, negotiating *'her release from Martindale'* and *'was even successful in the delicate diplomacy needed to prevent a domestic crisis at Devonshire House'.* [5] It seems a little strange that within a few days of the Duke being told of the Martindale debt, they set off together for Buxton, to take the waters (see section on Buxton below). Maybe the intervention by Richard Sheridan had had a positive outcome.

Now, the Duchess needed friends where she could find them and suddenly her view of Heaton changed. ' *I must tell you that I am vastly pleased with Heaton – his appearance at first is against him – tiresome on ordinary subjects – with some degree of insolence – but he has a comprehensive laborious active mind and a spirit of order and regularity in the arrangement of business very pleasing – he has just finished extricating the Duke of Portland from distress and even by useful speculations gives him the prospect of affluence – I hope and think he will be as successful with us as our case is not so desperate as theirs was'.* [6]

The demand for a separation occurred prior to 5th October 1786. [7] By the 9th there may have been some resolution with the separation moving to being conditional as Lady Spencer wrote to Caroline Howe. *'I hope both she and the Duke will persevere in this present resolution of an absolute reform and of her not going to Town. Nothing else can save them and I believe by all I here* (sic) *it might now be done with good effect'.* The violent spasms caused by the Duchess's anxiety over her money problems had also abated and she was '*calmer and better*' by the 9th, the Duke having '*behaved with great temper* (i.e. calmness) *and tenderness to her*'.

Lady Spencer left on 15th October or thereabouts and the Duke and Duchess went to Buxton and then on to Hardwick with the intention of going back to Buxton. Although a plan for the Duchess's immediate future had not been determined by the Duke, it was his intention that she should stay away from London that winter.

Lady Spencer offered to take in her daughter and grandchildren, and suggested they went to Londesbrough. The option of the Duchess going to Althorp was repugnant to her as well as to Lavinia Spencer (sister-in- law to the Duchess). There was talk of the need for trust to be re-established of course; whatever the Duke decided was going to take time to reach a satisfactory conclusion.

The whole issue was taking its toll on the health of the Duke, Duchess and equally importantly on John Heaton who was suffering with his nerves, ending up with all three of them seeking relief at Buxton at the same time. With the threat of financial ruin hanging over them, it was left to Heaton to see what could be done. His being ill brought no quick answers. By 21st December he had at least been able to tell the Duke that despite being distressing (in terms of effect on the estate as well as emotionally) it was not ruin. [8]

The pattern of the Duchess's letters to her mother of conflicting comments must have again left her mother shaking her head with frustration. In the same letter of 21st December, the Duke is described as being ill with head and stomach complaints. Within a week she was describing him as looking '*so well these last two months*' – perhaps an indirect reference to the effect Bess Foster had had on him rather than a question of his health and the effect she (the Duchess) had inflicted. [9]

Despite the apparent contrition and the need for the building of trust mentioned above, it was short lived. Keeping her from town (London) was one thing but on the pretence of meeting her mother at Newmarket (Lady Spencer was staying with her brother at North Creek, near Burnham in Norfolk), she appears to have lost £6,000 on the horses the following February. [10] However she was in denial over any additional losses in letters to her mother shortly afterwards.

By May she was out socialising in London every night, telling Thomas Coutts one thing and doing another. '*I am under a sacred promise with regard to playing Faro and insurance in the lottery, which no temptation can make me break*' she wrote to him from Cheltenham. It was just after a breakfast party at Chiswick in honour of the Polignacs from France, who were long-standing friends. Not only was there dancing in the dining room and supper in the hall, there was a Faro table '*in my room*'. [11]

No wonder the Duke let the issue of separation run on as well as the pressure on her from creditors (less Martindale). However it was having little effect. The problem for her bankers – both Coutts and Denne & Co. - was that the Duchess was an obvious liability but they were afraid of a negative reaction from the Duke if they upset her. So long as the Duke held out hope of an heir, this nightmare was set to run and run. And it did.

Gleeson [12] points out the parallel situation of Lady Duncannon, the Duchess's sister. One can only reflect upon the disappointment both of them inflicted on their mother. Incapable of having any influence over either of her daughters, she sought solace in staying away from them, turning to her religious beliefs, her charitable work and staying out of the way as much as she could, hence time in Norfolk.

Bess returned to England in September 1786. A short time later, the Duke commissioned Sir Joshua Reynolds to paint her portrait. She sat for him a total of seven times between April and May 1787. It was finished later that year and cost 50 guineas (£52.50). [13] The Duke's ardour for her continued upon her return and she conceived again in c. August 1787.

In the Devonshire House Inventory of 1811, following the Duke's death, there is no mention of this painting, which makes one wonder whether he had initially given it to Bess. It is known that there was a painting of her in her bedroom at Devonshire House in 1802, [14] but one can only speculate whether it was the Reynolds. However, if it was not, would the Duchess go to see an inferior one in Bess's bedroom, when there was the lovely Reynold's of her in the house?

Today, that painting is on display at Chatsworth. It is *one of the simplest and one of the most penetrating he ever painted ... The sitter was, perhaps, too intelligent ever to fit well into English Society, a quality which Reynold's captures*. Five years later, upon the Duchess's return from exile in Europe, she (the Duchess) found in her bedroom an unfinished Reynold's painting the Duke had bought from the late painter's estate, showing Lady Spencer and the Duchess as a child. Perhaps paintings were used by the Duke as an instrument to express his pleasure. [15] The Reynold's portrait of Bess seems to have captured a mischievous look and smile, so patently missing on the 1819 pencil and chalk portrait of her by Lawrence. Here the pleasure of 1787 seems to have been replaced by sadness, given away by her eyes. She was still an attractive woman and one is struck by the portrait, but drawn back to her eyes.

Now, we can only speculate on Bess's level of intelligence, mentioned by Kitson. Even if the Duke's passion for her diminished in a physical sense, he could well have continued to appreciate her company from the level of the conversation between them. This would certainly offer an explanation for the Duke's ongoing interest in her. The Reynolds painting remains a tangible reminder of the Duke's passion for a woman he loved. Yet it retains a secret: when Bess, as the last Duchess of Devonshire until 1891, left these shores a final time for Italy, did she leave this painting at Devonshire House, as one last physical link to the man she had married, but had lost years before in the bed of the Duke of Richmond? Alternatively, did Bess leave it to the 6th Duke on her death?

The Devonshires at Buxton

In October 1786 the Duke and Duchess were unwell and the cause was persistent. One wonders whether there was any connection with the cause of the stomach-related illness she had suffered a year previous, although it may well have been the stress of the Martindale debt and of course, the demand for a separation. Lady Spencer left Chatsworth around 15th October 1786. The Duke had asked her if she would go and live with them. However the shadow of Bess Foster prevented that. In fact correspondence between her (Lady Spencer) and her friend Caroline Howe maintains a commentary about where Bess Foster was and what she was doing. It affected where and when Lady Spencer did what. *'I should have the greatest hopes of everything with regard to her getting soon right if it was not for one insurmountable obstacle so every idea of comfort that sticks close to her and I have too much reason to fear guides everything.'*

Lady Spencer remained implacably of this view: *'if I could once get her and the Duke to taste and enjoy a little solid and agreeable* (sic) *Society, they have such good understandings that I am sure they would be delighted with it but that is one of the Circumstances that the obstacle I mentioned make absolutely impracticable for that obstacle is itself the bane of all Society'.* Lady Spencer seems never to have changed this view until 1792-93. [16]

The family went to Buxton so that the Duchess could take the waters there which it was hoped would clear up the affliction, staying at the Buxton Hall Inn. This was the inn adjacent to the mineral bath. Additional baths were going to open to coincide with the opening of The Crescent.

Staying at the Hall Inn points to their own apartment not being ready. On 14th August 1786, William Gould, the Hartington Collector of Rents, wrote in his diary: *'Slept in the Crescent at Hannah Hodgsons the town being full of genteel Company and scarce a bed to be got for a stranger'* On the 17th, he was in the St. Ann's Hotel, kept by James Hall, so clearly parts of the development were finished. They were at Chatsworth on the 22st October with Lord John and at Buxton the night after. [17]

On their next visit two months later, just prior to Christmas Day, The Crescent was open for business. [18] Heaton had allowed for an apartment for the Duke in the new development. It was situated beneath the family coat of arms in the middle of the front façade. The Duke and Duchess found it better than they had expected. [19] Nonetheless, the Duke had not been too pleased about going to Buxton. As mentioned above, he thought that the seasonal fogs there were *'unwholesome'* but went for the Duchess's benefit and his own on other occasions where he had rheumatism etc.

The two hotels there, the St. Ann's and the Great Hotel (to the left and right respectively when viewed from the front) had the practice from the beginning of serving the principal guests their dinner in their own rooms. The Duke and Duchess preferred this arrangement as it allowed them the chance to be on their own when they felt like it and not have to spend the evening (or part of it) in the company of other guests. The Heatons were there for instance on that first visit and others they knew were: Dr. Denman, Mr. Shaw Stuart and *'his new marryd wife'*, Lady Maxwell and her daughters plus a few more. They were pleased to find that Lady Warren had left (presumably the doctor's wife). After their meal they played cards together and on their own, or with others in their party.

The day after their arrival the Duchess bathed in the mineral waters – the practice was to hire the Ladies Bath and bathe naked – and drink two glasses of the water. She complained in a letter to her mother of being in *'a good deal of pain'*. John Heaton was probably taking the waters too, the Duchess writing that *'he seems to me to have suffered much in his nerves'* On her trip to Buxton in October 1786 she rose in the morning at 9 a.m. and went into the cold bath (cold bath bathing was fashionable at the time). She walked a great deal and rode her horse a lot. It *'carrys me with ye greatest safety'*. In the evenings *'we played as usual'*. [20]

The Duke and Duchess returned to the Bath at Buxton in mid-December, possibly from Hardwick. Records survive showing who bathed on each day and although the Duchess records bathing prior to Christmas Day, the daily records do not record her taking a bath until January 1st when she went almost daily until 22nd January 1787. The Duke bathed on 20th and 21st December only. John Heaton tried the waters on 27th and went 11 times during the four weeks they were there in January 1787. His wife was not as keen, bathing in the first and third weeks only. The baths were open on Christmas Day. [21]

As an alternative to cards, for entertainment there was the Undress (casual dress) Ball on Monday and Friday evenings, with the Dress Ball on a Wednesday. There was a Card Room and billiard tables were available. Extra dining facilities were added later at each hotel together with a Coffee Room. As an alternative, there was the theatre at the rear of The Crescent where plays were held on several nights per week. Divine Service was held at the Great Hotel until the St. John's Church was opened in 1812 (the large date stone at the east end is dated 1811 but the completion of the building (including the roof) dragged on into 1812).

The dances, or Balls, were held in the Assembly Room adjacent to the Great Hotel. This together with the Card and Coffee Rooms were run by the estate as a separate business to the hotels, which were rented out. Despite the private apartment being more comfortable than the Duke and Duchess had expected with '*a decent parlour and good bedrooms*', they hardly used it and it was eventually used, along with other private rooms available for hire, as the basis of a third hotel, The Central.

The Crescent was built with a colonnaded front, enabling guests to reach the Assembly Room (or Ballroom) and the baths without getting wet. There were several upmarket shops off the colonnade including Mr. Moore's lending library, post office and newsagents. The Manchester – London coaches initially stopped here with London being up to 3 – 4 days away. The 'poor people' were excluded from the main baths and the Assembly Rooms while the gardens opposite the Buxton Hall Inn were for guests only. A charity bath was built later behind The Crescent and guests were surcharged a shilling (1s.0d.) to provide for this.

The Dress Ball could be quite a spectacular sight when '*ladies of the first fashion*' were present, their lovely and expensive dresses making a significant contribution to the elegance the ladies made to the evening's dancing. To many eyes, even the frocks they wore on the Undress evenings would have been an improvement on many of the garments used at the Dress Ball, purchased from shallower pockets. These were usually the wives and eligible daughters of the aristocracy and the first of a new breed of the *nouveaux riche*, buoyed up on fortunes prized out of the new pickings from industry, commerce or occasionally from a good run of prize ships captured at sea etc.

In between the two trips to Buxton, the Duke went shooting at Welbeck Abbey on the 7th November, staying at Hardwick. William Gould met him there. He was not only a Collector of Rents (basically the estate manager) for Hartington and Buxton, he held a similar position for the Duke of Portland, both ducal estates being under the control of John Heaton and therefore very much run on the same lines. Gould recorded that '*His* Grace (i.e. Duke of Devonshire) *was very free and conversant and asked me a number of questions on several subjects*'. Clearly no shyness here. [22] The Duke returned the following day with the Duchess and Bess Foster.

The Duke had taken his keeper and groomsman with him and although he went shooting on the Portland Estate, he was only there for a week, although his servants remained there waiting for him for the following two weeks. It is not clear whether he was ill again or not but he had virtually no success with the gun all week. Perhaps the prospect of potential financial ruin was behind it all.

Complexities of Calmness

The last week of January 1787, the Duke and Duchess left Buxton, probably for London. They dined at Lady Clermont's on 1ˢᵗ February with the Duchess's sister Harriet and Caroline Howe. The latter found the Duchess '*looking vastly well*'. The waters and rest at Buxton would have appeared to have done their trick. The latter was thinking that with the Duke they would shortly stay for a couple of weeks with her mother (quite possibly at Althorp). They appear to have been at Devonshire House with Bess Foster, Lord George Cavendish and Sir William Boothby of Mansfield Woodhouse. Bess Foster planned to spend the time the Duke and Duchess would be away with her mother. Harriet meanwhile was pregnant. [23]

Bess Foster was ill again in April 1787. By late June, Lady Spencer was planning to go from Althorp to the Duke and Duchess at Chiswick '*till Harriet wants me*'. Her pregnancy came to term in late July or beginning of August with the birth of William Ponsonby. [24] It was probably the latter as on 30ᵗʰ July the Duke was still deciding whether to go to Yorkshire for the grouse shooting (probably Bolton Abbey) or to go to Chatsworth. [25] In the end, the Duke decided to do both, going to Bolton Abbey in mid-August with the Duchess and Bess Foster, staying in the Abbey '*…our habitation being the gateway of the priory filled up so the room we live in is like the Isle* (sic) *of a chapel and supported on gothick arches – we found Ld George and Mr. Collins and a good supper*'. [26] It is probable that Bess conceived Augustus while they were there, as he was born on 26ᵗʰ May 1788`. They returned to Chatsworth in time for Derby Races, with Bess Foster going on from Derby to London ahead of the arrival of Lady Spencer.

Mentioned above, the Duke of Rutland, who owned Haddon Hall, adjacent to Chatsworth, died of putrid fever in October1787. The following mid-December, Lady Walpole was also in great danger because of the disease but recovered. [27] In February 1788, Haryo was inoculated, probably against smallpox. The recovery would take 6 – 8 weeks but the protection was considered reliable and worth it.

The Duke's dithering was a characteristic of his – he does not often seem to have done anything spontaneously. Early September saw him off to Chesterfield Races, with the Duchess, his brother George and Uncle John. A little later, guests included Lord and Lady Melbourne and Richard Sheridan. Lady Spencer arrived on 5ᵗʰ September.

The threat of separation had been replaced with the Duke being '*remarkably attentive and kind to me which adds greatly to my satisfaction in being here*' wrote Lady Spencer. '*Ld and Lady George with their lovely boys are here for some time and very pleasant* (sic) *because it seems an unaffected cordiality subsists among them all without the least jealousy about the children who are all four, charming children. Little G is much grown and improved and Harriet is one of the most comical little animals that ever you saw. It is hardly possible to look at her without laughing'.* A year later at Chatsworth, Lady Spencer, continuing her almost daily correspondence with Caroline Howe wrote: *'Little Harriet carried all her dolls to the Duke that he might play with them as he was not well. He is much better.'* The effect of the dolls is unrecorded. [28]

Whilst at Bath in July 1787, the Duke wrote to his brother-in-law Earl Spencer to advise that they (the Duchess and himself) would be unable to meet him and Mr. Bingham (? The Earl's father-in-law) who were going to Chatsworth for the shooting. The Duke advised the Earl that he had written to his steward (Fletcher) to *'have everything ready'* for them. *'You had better make an inn of Chatsworth in your way and if you will let Fletcher know when you will be there he will send the keeper with my pointers to the Moors, and you need not be at the trouble of sending your own, unless you chuse* (sic) *it'*. [29]

Looking back now at the number of people who turned up at Chatsworth (apparently not always by arrangement) seeking board and lodgings – and not necessarily people known to them, but of the same circle – Chatsworth looks as though it was some aristocratic inn and clearly the Duke thought of it like that too. However this way of moving around the nation was quite common at the time. Dinner with close friends was one thing but for the rest *'we are always ready to jump out of our skins with joy when our dinner company goes away'*! [30]

The pleasant atmosphere at Chatsworth was interrupted for Lady Spencer with news of the intended arrival of Bess Foster, resulting in her deciding it was time to leave, if tinged with regret. However Bess Foster was too ill to travel. Nonetheless she (Lady Spencer) left on 16th October. They were reunited at Brocket Hall as a result of Lady Melbourne urging Lady Spencer to join them all there as the Duke and Duchess travelled to Devonshire House. She set off on 21st November. It was a short reunion, as the Devonshires continued their journey south. It was their intention to go on to Bath but on the 26th November (or thereabouts), the Duchess had a miscarriage. This was clearly a surprise to Lady Spencer. She speculated whether her daughter might yet have another child, although for her daughter's sake she hoped it was out of the question *'after all that passed with the last'* (i.e. Haryo's birth). [31] A little prior to this, the Duke and Duchess lost another close friend, Sir William Boothby. [32]

A Boy For The Duke

Early in 1788 another child was on the way: Bess Foster was pregnant again. The baby, a boy, was christened Augustus Clifford and brought up as the Duke's child, but there was initially some speculation as to whether the father was in fact the Duke of Richmond. [33] Despite that speculation, paintings of Augustus later in life, as an adult, show that he looked very much like the Duke.

The Duchess had intended going abroad with Bess Foster, but her (the Duchess's) mother did not approve unless the Duke went too. Bess Foster left Dover for France on 21st February 1788. The Duchess started organising small parties at Devonshire House *'as the Duke likes it'*. In the absence of Bess Foster, she was starting to take advantage of the opportunity to improve her relationship with the Duke still further. Foreman states however: *'she was mistaken if she hoped for any rekindling of love between them – neither would ever be in love with the other'*. [34]

The quotation from a letter she wrote to Bess Foster as support for this comment is less than convincing. There can be no denying the patience, understanding and care the Duke often displayed to his wife, especially when her careless spending seriously challenged Cavendish finances. Yet one wonders whether his deep rooted shyness affected his ability to show his love and feelings for those nearest to him in a demonstrative manner, whether it be his wife, Bess Foster or his children. Certainly Lady Spencer thought they were in love nearly a decade later. [35]

There was, nonetheless, perhaps another reason for Foreman's comment: it appears that the Duchess may have ended a possible affair with the Duke of Dorset in 1788 with the emergence of Charles Grey on the scene. Closer to home was the prospect of Bess Foster's affair with the Duke of Richmond (see above). Her baby was born in Rouen on 26th May 1788 and was put out to foster parents. James Hare went to see him in 1789, indicating that he was in Normandy, so it is probably that he was being fostered in Rouen (see below). Bess Foster returned to England in c. July of that year. [36]

Bess named her baby Augustus William James Clifford. The Duke was of course Baron Clifford. All three Christian names were Cavendish too: the 1st Duke's oldest son was called James, Augustus was the name of one of the Duke's uncles and William had been the name of all five Dukes (but only because of James's untimely death). If the 5th Duke's father still holds the position of the youngest death of a Prime Minister, his son, Augustus, holds the record of the longest serving Black Rod since the reform of Parliament in 1832. He served from 25th July 1832 – 31st March 1877. [37]

Respite For Lady Spencer

From Lady Spencer's point of view, Bess Foster's time abroad gave her a respite from having to put up with the *'obstacle'* as she called Bess Foster, depriving her of the close relationship she would have preferred with her daughter. She remained resolute over this despite something of a charm offensive from the Duke and Duchess. She made her stance clear just before Bess Foster arrived back in England in a letter to the Duchess:

'*You know how anxious I am to make you happy and to show my regard and gratitude to the Duke for the constant tenor of his behaviour to me ... I always avoid naming Lady E.F. and if any body is injudicious enough to mention her to me I endeavour to give such answers as will show them I am determined not to enter into the subject – my behaviour was not premeditated – it arose at Chatsworth from my own feelings at scenes I was unfortunate to be witness to and finding I have so little power to command myself when I am deeply affected – I thought it better to avoid all opportunities acting in a manner that might distress us all – I certainly mean to behave civilly to Lady E.F. whenever I meet her and hope of late especially I have done so.*

'*I never wished to avoid speaking to the Duke on any subject and if ever he should mention this, I shall as on all other listen candidly to him and tell him truly if he chooses I should, what my sentiments are.*' Her resolution was clear – avoid Bess Foster whenever possible. On the other hand the Duke's plan to go abroad (? to Spa) in the summer of 1788 for four – six weeks were postponed with the arrival of Bess .

By early 1788, the measure of calmness continued to exist between the Duke and Duchess. Lady Spencer went up to Devonshire House in mid-February and found them alone. They (the Duke and Duchess) went out to a function at Gloucester House in Piccadilly, the home of Prince William, 1st Duke of Gloucester and 1st Duke of Edinburgh and Princess Maria (nee Walpole). They returned home early and '*I supped with them*'. At the end of March, Lady Spencer went up to Chiswick with the Duchess, who '*went on to town to see the children and bought the Duke back with her ... the evening past very pleasantly*''.

A fortnight later Lady Spencer went back to London, this time to Devonshire House where she found just her daughters, Georgiana and Harriet (Lady Duncannon). They read two sermons on the love of God. The next night the reading was lighter and the three of them sat reading the Spy and other papers with articles written by the Duchess until 2 am. [38]

By the end of the month (April) the Duke and Duchess were back at Chiswick where Lady Spencer joined them and her grandchildren. '*We did not dine till long after 6 so that I got but a short walk in the evening but the birds and especially the nightingales sung delightfully.*' Playing whist at home kept the Duchess's weakness under control, although there was a scare while Lady Spencer was there. Presumably the Duke had agreed to his wife going up to town to play (gamble).

The Duke and his mother-in-law '*drew the great piece of water several times – we drove out after dinner – and had some conversations on serious subjects in the evening after which we read our respective books and waited not without some anxiety for the Dss [Duchess] return from the play till after two o'clock – when the Duke sent a chaise to Town to know of any accident had happened but he met her near Chiswick she had been delayed by a great crowd and other circumstances.'*

These trips to Chiswick were presumably part of the process of emptying the Jacobean house ahead of its demolition.

Back To Buxton

The Duke would no doubt have been glad that they were shortly leaving for Buxton, although how long it had been planned is not known. It is likely to have been to try and enable the Duchess to shake off the continual cycle of ill health and the *'headaches'* from which she always seems to have been afflicted. As they generally put her into bed, she may well have been a regular migraine sufferer, possibly brought on by the stress of debt.

On their first visit to The Crescent in Buxton they found that their personal apartment allowed them to eat in their own room allowing a measure of privacy from other guests booked into either the St. Ann's or the Great Hotel. They repeated this in 1788 for their guests – or at least Lady Spencer, who had her own apartment which she found *'clean and looking very comfortable'*. Also with them was Lord Cremorne. Having arrived at 11 p.m. on the 19th May, they left on 22nd, both the Duke and Duchess riding horse back to Chatsworth. The month had started off *'excessively hot'* but with an easterly wind which on occasions blew *'intensely cold.'* The hot weather lasted until 28th; four full weeks of sun.

There had clearly been some talk at Buxton about the Duchess going abroad, which had left Lady Spencer with a *'wretched night'* at the thought of it (see above). Fortunately for her nothing came of it, but the family did return to Buxton again a little later. In the meantime, they relaxed in the sun at Chatsworth, even fishing in the evening of their first full day there. The following day, a Saturday, the Duke went fishing. Lady Spencer wrote *'the Dss [Duchess] and I were in the boat the whole morning, rowing above the River [Derwent} while they were putting in the nets – the views of the park were beautiful and I never enjoyed anything more'*. However the enjoyment was spoilt by the Duchess having to retire early to bed with a *'sick head ach* (sic)'. The 8th May 1788 had been Lady Spencer's 51st birthday. In her diary she reflected that *'it is a long period to have lived'* and determined to run the rest of her life quietly, moderately and getting the most out of it. Clearly the morning on the river was a good start. Another part of the plan was spending more time tending to those worse off than she was.

At the end of the month they went back to Buxton for a full week and with plenty of company. The Duchess wanted to see Lady Derby who had nearly lost the use of her wrists and was hoping for improvement with a course of hydropathy for which Buxton became a major national centre. Lady Parnell was there *'a good old Irish relation'* of Lady Spencer's mother. Also there was the Dean of St. Asaph with the Shipley family and the Duke's 'auditor' or agent, John Heaton with his wife and niece. Sir William FitzHerbert was also part of their party (no mention of his wife). Dr. Denman was on hand and he advised Lady Spencer to use the mineral bath.

Lady Spencer found the water colder than she had expected initially but once accustomed to it, very pleasant and she *'felt a proper glow after I came out.'* She spent the rest of her time having guests for dinner, strolling with the Duke and John Heaton; with the Duchess on another occasion; reading and writing and generally enjoying the sun and air in one of the highest communities in England (it had not developed beyond a village then). One evening, no doubt missing her own children, the Duchess took three children of other guests to a play at the theatre, conveniently situated across the garden at the rear of The Crescent. On the Sunday during their stay, Lady Spencer, the Duchess and Mrs. Shipley went to St. Ann's Church in what is now Upper Buxton. Lady Spencer described it as being a *'shabby little place'*. In 1812 St. John's Church was consecrated to the rear of The Crescent.

She left Buxton with the Duke and Duchess for Holywell House, St. Albans, the Duchess having had a headache all day on arrival. The latter seems to have stayed there with the children, the Duke going on to London, returning a couple of weeks later, but not staying long, returning again within the week. On 23rd August 1788, the Duchess returned with Charlotte Williams. The Duke and Lord Frederick Cavendish arrived at Holywell two days later. Whether they met Charlotte is not recorded. The two men played cards with the Duke's mother-in-law until 2 a.m. when the Duke left (at 3 a.m.) for Chatsworth, presumably for the shooting and Races. The previous month (July 1788) Lord Frederick had made the Duchess happy (and presumably the Duke too) by telling him that he thought the Duchess's *'conduct about money was grown very good'*. A few days later, Lady George Cavendish would have also given the Duke good news when she speculated that before long the Duchess would be pregnant again. Fifteen months later, she was proved correct. [39]

It comes as no surprise that the Duchess liked Frederick the best of the Cavendish uncles describing him as the pleasantest of the uncles and of men in general. She found Lord George Augustus as being very kind but Lord John as *'disagreeable ... he finds fault with everything and tells the Duke'*.

Whether Lord John had just upset the Duchess isn't clear, but the following November during the celebrations of the centenary of the Glorious Revolution, she wrote: *'I never saw Lord John kinder'*, so maybe he did have a better side to him. [40] Charlotte's visit may have been spoilt somewhat as the Duchess '*was obliged to go to bed early with a bad head ach (sic)*' on the day of their arrival. [41]

They returned to town early in November to meet Bess Foster. Plans to send Little G to Welbeck Abbey were changed because of smallpox around there. A previous illness (affecting Mrs. Smith, Little G's governess) had delayed their departure to Chatsworth, presumably resulting in their missing Derby Races. With none of today's antibiotics, illness was always treated seriously. [42]

Centenary of the Glorious Revolution

Before the return to London, there was another and important date on the calendar.

In 1668, the 4th Earl of Devonshire and others met at an inn at Whittington, near Chesterfield, to plot the overthrow of King James, a Catholic. An invitation was subsequently sent to William of Orange, who was married to Mary Stuart, to take the throne. William accepted and arrived at Brixham in Torbay on 5th November 1688 with a force of 10,000 men, declaring: '*The Protestant religion and the liberties of England we will maintain*'. The King fled and his actions earned the Earl his Dukedom on 12th May 1694. [43]

A great celebration of this was held 100 years later at Whittington and Chesterfield. Proceedings commenced with Divine Service at 11am before proceeding to what is now known as Revolution House. One cannot help feeling that the Duchess was in the thick of the arrangements. Blue and orange were the colours of the day. The Duchess had earlier complained to her mother that no orange ribbon was to be obtained in London. John Heaton's wife had to make do with yellow. [44]

The procession was led by local 'clubs' each accompanied by a band, there being nine in all. There were some 2,000 people involved in this section alone. This was followed by the Duke's coach-and-six bedecked in orange. In front of his coach were his household (presumably led by the Steward, Mr Fletcher). Behind his coach, came a group of his attendants. There were nearly 70 coaches, chaises etc (plus attendants to each) behind the Duke's coach, followed by about 500 gentlemen on horseback and behind them their servants also on horseback, plus civic dignities bringing up the rear. The whole procession was over a mile in length.

It proceeded from Whittington to Chesterfield and did a circuit of the main streets.

At 6pm there was a firework display 'during which the people were regaled with liquor'. This was followed by a Ball at which were present the Duke and Duchess, Lady Elizabeth Foster, the Earl of Stamford, Lords George and John Cavendish, the Earl of Danby and his brother, Lord Francis Osbourne, Sir Harry

Hunloke and his wife, Sir Francis Molyneaux, 'and many other persons of distinction'. Thousands lined the route to watch, the total estimated to exceed 40,000 and *'few solemnities of a national kind exceeded it'.*

The employees of the Ecton Mine were also given a party that day, broken up into groups in the local village inns, there being no other way of accommodating up to 500 people. It cost £22. There was something else to celebrate there: the starting of the Duke's new state-of-the-art steam winding engine supplied by Boulton and Watt to the mine. [45]

11

The Birth Of The Heir 1790

Family Matters Abroad: Paris 1789

The decision by the Duke to go abroad with both the Duchess and Bess Foster in the summer of 1789 would have involved a significant amount of planning. They were taking Charlotte Williams to join Caroline St. Jules in Paris before going on to Spa where the Duchess hoped to recover her health. It is not clear whether the Duchess knew about Caroline. Little G and Harriet were staying behind with Selina Trimmer under the care of their grandmother, Lady Spencer. There would have been a number of staff too, although enough would be left to cope with family members wishing to stay at Devonshire House and handling estate and security issues at the property etc.

In addition, arrangements would have been made for their reception in Paris, with audiences with the King and Queen expected. There would be wagon loads of clothes, plate, possessions of servants etc. The Duchess had other arrangements to make: She asked her brother to lend her £400 - £500 before she went, imploring him not to mention it to her husband or mother. [1] They left on 19th June 1789, bound for Dover. The wind there was favourable for a quick crossing which must have created some apprehension about the roughness of the sea. It is not clear whether they took their own coaches with them or whether these were hired in France: probably both.

They left at 6 a.m., possibly sleeping on board ship. The voyage to Calais took a quick three hours but they arrived 'very sick and tired'. They stayed there to recover until 3 p.m. (which may also point to having to wait for coaches, horses, etc. if not pre-ordered). Leaving for Paris, they reached Boulogne, arriving to find their preferred inn full. The alternative was described as being 'wretched'. There were to be two more nights on the way and they also had to endure a severe thunderstorm, which frightened the horses to the point that they broke the pole, the shaft between the horses and the coach.

They reached Paris on the 23rd, having been met on the way at Chantilly, the Duchess describing the inn at Clermont as 'vile'. If her mood en route had been dented by the experience, she and Bess quickly embraced Parisian society and a heavy round of socialising. On the 27ᵗʰ, the French Revolution started.

On 25ᵗʰ June, the Duke stayed behind while the Duchess and Bess set off for Versailles for an informal meeting at the Palace. The Duke was dining with his friend the Duke of Dorset, then the Ambassador. The following day the Duke dined at the Embassy. Bess stayed in, too tired to stir while the Duchess went socialising again. The Duke may have been waiting for arrangements to be made for him to receive a formal presentation to the King. The Duchess proudly wrote: *'think of him in a drest coat, his hair finely drest and a hat and black feather before 12 and whats more liking it.* [2] This suggests that the Duke had some State business with which he had been entrusted.

It therefore may be too simplistic to think that this detour was simply to place Charlotte in Paris to continue her education. For one thing, she was joined by Caroline St. Jules, which seems an odd arrangement, if a convenient way of keeping attention from the latter and the question of her paternity. One thinks that there could be little doubt that Bess would have been keen to be reunited with her new son, Augustus Clifford, but it is unclear as to whether he came to Paris or whether in the light of the Revolution it was felt it more prudent for him to stay away.

The two girls were placed with a Monsieur and Madame Nagel. The Duchess, writing to her mother, referred to Caroline as *'luckily there is only one other pensioner. Mme. De St. Jules, a young lady from the provinces and as she is very young, Mme Nagel will attend entirely to poor little Charlotte.'* Of the latter, she continued *'there is much difficulty with her to be sure, unconquerable faults (with much good) to all appearance – but I don't despair – and entire change was the only chance'.* It appears that the teenager's manners needed improving (this sounds like symptoms of adolescence). Although not telling her mother, it would appear that there is a possibility that the Duchess knew the identity of Caroline. A copy of a letter (held in private hands) survives written in French from the Duchess to her French banker. In it, she states: *'... If there are riots you will remember our two little ones who are at Monsieur Nagel's 10 rue de la Madeleine'.* [3] The intensity of the revolt in Paris continued to worsen and on or about 10ᵗʰ July, the Duke left for Spa, arriving in Mons on the 12ᵗʰ. The Bastille fell on the 14ᵗʰ, the day they reached Brussels at 4 a.m.

On hearing of developments of the revolt into a full bodied open revolution in Paris, the Duke broke down in tears when he realised that he had left his two daughters in mortal danger. His judgement had probably been influenced by his experience of the Gordon Riots where he had been involved as a Militia Colonel. However the difference was that in London the King and the Executive retained the loyalty of the military. Although procrastination over the order to fire had prevailed for far too long, when it came, the determination was ruthless. The Downing Street mob dissolved when they saw the Guards with rifles trained on the street in upstairs windows. Elsewhere, gin-crazed looters and arsonists were mown down in the hundreds. The act of throwing the bodies into the River Thames showed pointedly that no mercy was intended or would be given (see also above under 1780).

Paris showed what the opposite to this could result in. Fortunately, both girls spoke French; indeed for Caroline it was probably her first language. However, Charlotte was English, in the care of an aristocrat and Caroline could be seen as the relation of a French one. It was a dangerous situation, especially if Charlotte had been at Versailles. A servant was sent by '*express*', i.e. the equivalent of a fast English fly coach, back to Paris with a message for the Duke of Dorset to place them in a convent or get them to safety.

As a favour to Thomas Coutts, whose two daughters were in Paris on their arrival, the Duchess had gained them introductions into Parisian society and they too were still there, to be whisked from sight and into a convent. Appeasing her banker, admittedly at his request, had nonetheless placed even more responsibility on the Duke and, perhaps more so, on his wife. In fact Coutts wrote to the Duchess claiming that she had put (and left) his daughters in danger, an allegation she strongly denied. In fact James Hare had been to see them more than once. The girls were not apprehensive of any danger, more worried about the prospect of dullness that forthcoming winter! They were staying at Penthémont for their education. Hare wrote that their education might not be the best, '*but anything is better than living in the Strand with that tiresome idiot, Mrs. Coutts*'. [4]

Before leaving England, it would appear that it was the Duke's intention to be away a couple of months, with Lady Spencer expecting to hear their plans to return in mid-August, giving them about four weeks in Spa. The Duchess was clear that she was expecting her health to improve from being there. [5] The prospect of the Duke of Dorset and James Hare being able to get Charlotte and Caroline out of Paris caused them to stay on in Spa. The two girls, with Augustus Clifford conspicuous by his absence, had arrived by 10th September, probably at least a few days prior to that, as that was the date Caroline Howe wrote to Lady Spencer to tell her the news. [6]

Where had Caroline been prior to coming to Paris and for that matter where was Augustus? James Hare, working for a while in the Paris Embassy of Great Britain, seems to have known the answer and indeed had been to see them on behalf of Bess Foster. A letter he wrote to her while she was at Spa appears to reveal it. Referring to Caroline he wrote: '*I was very much struck with her at Sorèze, but much more in Paris*'. Early that month he had written to the Duchess stating that '*she is the prettiest child I ever saw*', whilst chastising the Duchess for not taking her (Caroline) immediately into her care. Sorèze is a large village in Tarn Department, Midi-Pyrenees Region. This is probably where the aged Comte St. Jules lived. It was a long way for Hare to go to check all was well with her on behalf of Bess Foster.

He did not state specifically where Augustus was, but described him as being *'the little Norman'* so he appears to have been in Normandy, probably at Rouen. Hare had been to see him: *'I found him perfectly well. He promises to be a giant. He is uncommonly shy (how happens this)* [it is likely he knew the Duke was his father, so this was a tease] *and would not take much notice of me'*. It appears that the lady looking after him did not know who his mother was. [7] James Hare had recognised one thing about Augustus: he grew up to be a very tall man, as did his half brother, the Marquis of Hartington. No doubt Bess Foster wished to reclaim him and take him to England. First of all she needed to have Caroline accepted within the Devonshire family. That occurred almost a year later and from an unexpected opportunity (see below).

Having left Paris to avoid one revolution, while at Spa they found themselves in the middle of another, involving the overthrow of the Prince of Liege. This was a bloodless event compared to Paris, however. The stay in Spa continued for longer than planned. The Duke was enjoying the time there immensely. He was getting up at 7 – 8 a.m., getting exercise, given up suppers and getting to bed earlier. There was in fact virtually nobody there to socialise with in any event. The Duchess's headaches had stopped at the beginning of September.

Pregnant Again

By early October 1789 they had all left Spa and reached Brussels, staying at the Hotel due Prince de Galles by 11th October. [8] Having had two children, the Duchess would have recognised the early signs of pregnancy. She had her suspicious whilst at Spa. Having confirmed her belief that she was pregnant to the Duke, he decided not to risk a miscarriage. It was inconceivable that they could go on to Paris until the rebellion was over and security restored, so they hired a house in Brussels. Yet even here there was sufficient unrest to drive them out of town for a short time. Moreover, there was sufficient unrest in the country to prevent the children coming over from London, either with or without their grandmother (and Selina Trimmer).

Lady Spencer moved to Devonshire House from Tunbridge Wells with the two girls and Miss Trimmer. These months saw the beginning of a close friendship between Lady Spencer and Selina Trimmer. The latter was to become very close to the family and later a useful source of information on happenings in the family for Lady Spencer. It had been the latter's intention to be at the forthcoming birth of her daughter-in-law's baby but she reduced the time away to accompanying her son George to the Mayor's Feast in St. Albans – a measure of her confidence in the new governess, leaving her behind to look after the children.

The truth of the matter however was that Lady Spencer was experiencing a wonderful time with her grand-daughters. Although it must have cut across her normal routine she was in the event having great fun with them. The girls were having a great time with their grandmother too: *'I do not know how I shall ever* (sic) *with them, and Dr. little G: who is the most affectionate little creature in the world burst into tears yesterday upon somebody's saying that when the party here broke up we should probably all go different ways'*. [9] A little later Lady Spencer also wrote reflectively: *'I grow so abominably fond of these sweet Children that I know not how I shall part from them and I am sure if you could see all Georgiana's little coaxing ways with me you would not wonder at me. Her evening reading is Robinson Crusoe and she is all impatience just at present for we are on the brink of finding Friday, one of the Constant employments at Tea and at Breakfast time is to try to Puzzle her in the multiplication table which is now very difficult as she is grown by this method very perfect in it'*. [10]

Meanwhile, in Brussels, although the city was quiet, there was open rebellion continuing in the country. As James Hare pointed out, they had the distinction of being in three revolutions in three months. It was not the only movement of the hand of fate at that time. The Duke's regime at Spa (including taking the waters) had made him feel better and healthy for the first time in years and his spirits were high (wrote the Duchess to her mother). The last week of August saw the final day of her period. The Duke was content and happy to wait for the two girls from Paris and they had arrived by the 10th, with the Duke intent on staying a little longer. By the time he was ready to leave Spa, the Duchess was recognising the first signs of pregnancy. He left for Brussels and if the Duchess confirmed this while there, he would go no further, not wishing to risk a miscarriage on the voyage home.

Because Lady Spencer had wanted to leave Tunbridge Wells for Lavinia's lying in (ahead of the birth of another boy) towards the end of September, the Duke's original intention was to spend only four weeks or so in Spa. Everything had changed as he waited for the girls from Paris. In fact he pre-empted their removal because Charlotte had become 'dangerously ill' and Mme Nagel and the other two children had also become ill following the redecoration (painting) of the house. (Clearly there was something causing this in the paint and the Duke had had experience of this in England). Had they left in late August, it begs the question would the Duchess have conceived? Would there have been opportunity? Would conditions have been right anyway as they lurched along bumpy roads, worried about their safety and potential arrest and then possibly facing a rough crossing to England?

After 15 years of marriage and various miscarriages, one wonders whether waiting for the girls may well have made all the difference to her state of mind and increased state of relaxation and health thereby assisting conception. The pregnancy was to make all the difference to history: Much of what the visitor sees at Chatsworth was touched by the hand of the 6th Duke – the North Wing, the garden, the Emperor Fountain, the additions to the fine art and book collection and the alterations to some of the rooms (e.g. the Library created out of The Gallery on the first floor) are all his work. It just might be that two girls in France had critically influenced events too, let alone a soldier who was a lousy shot (unless he was just trying to assert himself, see below).

In November, their stay was rudely interrupted by the Patriot Army and they were advised to leave Brussels. They went to Lille, where they stayed for a few weeks. The Duchess described the inn as *'stinking'*, although they were eating well. To make matters worse there were plenty of English people there, but only two whom they knew – Mr. & Mrs. Storer. (11)

It would appear that this journey followed on from another in the previous month, October, when they appear to have gone to Liege and returned to Brussels just prior to the end of that month. On the way back, they drove into a dangerous situation when they were stopped by rebels (the Duchess referred to them as 'Volunteers'). They ordered one of the postillions to get down from the carriage and one of the men fired a pistol at the coach *'luckily without effect and from Ly Elizabeth placing herself before the coach window, I did not know the danger till it was over - for to add to our embarrassing situation, the Duke had walked on and our servants were not up with us.'* Not only were the rebels clearly restricting their movement and security, she was also unwell: *'the least exercise more than usual lays me quite up, by giving me very alarming pains in my back and the Duke seems very anxious indeed for my doing well'*. (12)

At the end of the year there was a fatal accident at Chiswick House involving two men. In Brussels the Duke was preparing to leave for England. Chiswick may well have been on the Duke's itinerary for work there was continuing. (13) There had also been another death affecting the family: Charlotte William's mother had passed away. *'...we have been at last obliged to tell Charlotte of her poor mother's death and she is so nervous and was really so fond of her that it has hurt her and shattered her nerves sadly'*. (14)

The Duke returns to England

Gleeson states that the Duke came back to London in 1790 to prevent scandal to the family name owing to the pending divorce of Lord Duncannon (his cousin) and Harriet (his sister-in-law). (15) This seems most unlikely: it cuts across the very character of the Duke to stir himself and undertake such an arduous and unsafe journey for this reason alone. The divorce proceedings had been initiated in June 1789 and there would have been plenty of time for the Duke to have asked Lord Frederick (Duke's uncle) or Lord George Henry (his brother) to intervene on his behalf. He could even have written setting out what is claimed to be the reason for Lord Duncannon changing his mind (the distress it would cause his aged father).

The trip to England was to alleviate stress on the Duchess. There was a more pressing need much closer to home than the divorce which forced the Duke to stir himself and set off for England. While they had been away (since June 1789) virtually every letter the Duchess sent to her mother (2 – 3 per week) state how she was missing her children. She had expected to see them in September 1789 when she would have been back in London. The decision to see out the pregnancy in Brussels brought expectation of the children, accompanied by their grandmother, Lady Spencer, travelling to join them.

The Duke went to England to bring back the three of them and presumably his sister-in-law, Harriet, at the Duchess's request (or at least organise their journey). Gleeson makes it clear that Harriet would do anything for her sister, but she was unwell, despite a determination to go. She also recognised that it would put pressing creditors (she had gambling debt problems like her sister) at a respectable distance. The Duke delayed his return (initially by two weeks) in the hope that she would recover sufficiently to travel with him.

It appears that the Duke realised that he could not afford to break his journey if Harriet's condition worsened, as it would expose his children to potential danger from rebellious troops. He needed Lord Duncannon to accompany his wife. He too had problems with creditors, but he had little appetite to be with Harriet and it would seem the divorce (filed with the Doctors Commons where divorce cases were held) was likely to be heard soon. The Duke, it appears, convinced Duncannon that to suspend the divorce until after the death of his father was the better course of action. Staying with the Duke until after the birth would also reduce his expenses significantly. If Harriet's condition deteriorated, the Duke could continue on to Brussels leaving Harriet in safe hands. In the event, the Duke left without his daughters.

Some of this is conjecture, but it seems to be plausible. The Devonshire House accounts include a payment of 15 guineas (£15. 15s. 0d) to Captain Baxter on 12th March 1790 *'for the ladies'*, [16] relating to the ferry costs to Calais for the whole party. Their arrival in Brussels would have reduced the Duchess's stress level more than anything else, including Harriet's divorce case. The arrival of her sister and Selina Trimmer would have completed her contentment. In February 1790 Lady Spencer had a *'craion picture'* completed of Little G by John Russell. He was Britain's leading pastellist. It was described by Lady Spencer as being *'finished by Russel. It is drawn in the cap she wore while she had his* [? the Duke's] *cold and which I thought became her much'*. [17] Russell drew Haryo in the same year, also wearing the same cap which suggests that it was also commissioned by Lady Spencer. [18]

The Duke appears to have only rented one house in Brussels, Lille (when they were obliged to leave Brussels for security reasons) and Plassy near Paris in May 1790. A total compliment of c. 25 – 30 people seems likely, plus a few more who went to Brussels in May or direct to Plassy for the birth (see below). [19] The Duke arrived back in Brussels on 17th February 1790, so he would have probably left London on 13th. He seems to have been alone. In the event, Lady Spencer did not make the journey with the children. It appears likely that the reason was the presence of Bess Foster with the Duke and Duchess. Amongst those making the journey were Mr. Crofts, the Duchess's doctor (who stayed for just over a week before returning to England).

The Duke also called for saddle horses, and a couple (or so) grooms literally went for the ride. The passage from Dover was on 12th March 1790 and they arrived in Brussels on 17th March. Lord and Lady Duncannon left a few days after the two children, either on 25th or 26th March 1790. [20] Larger premises were rented from Lord Torrington on the edge of The Park. Harriet was not the only one who was not well: Selina Trimmer, with whom the Duke and Duchess were delighted with her manners and success with the two girls, was also giving cause for concern. *'If she gets through the spring well here, I will answer for Spa setting her up'* wrote the Duchess purposefully in a long letter to her mother, the day after the Duke returned from London. [21] In fact she wrote enthusiastically to her mother about the children with the Duke's comments on them. *'[the Duke is quite delighted with the improvements of the children. … G's playing is very very good and that Harryo reads like a clergyman'*. [22]

As the Duchess became closer to the end of her pregnancy, Lady Spencer made arrangements to leave for Brussels, arriving early in May. The Duke seems to have run his life as close as he could to life in England – doing some hunting with Lord Duncannon and presumably socialising as much as his wife's condition permitted. It is clear that for some reason (probably continuing unrest, as Ann Scafe wrote in her diary (see below) that there was continuing unrest in the neighbourhood) the Duke intended leaving Brussels for the birth.

The Hague was recommended but there was some issue there between the Duke and the Embassy. This is a little intriguing as early in 1790 the envoy to The Hague was Alleyne FitzHerbert, later Lord St. Helens, the younger brother of William, the Duke's lifelong friend from Tissington in Derbyshire. Alleyne was engaged to Bess Foster's younger sister, Louisa, but he died unmarried. William died the following year, 1791. Lady Spencer's journey was documented by Ann Scafe, her maid. [23]

They left Holywell House on 1st May 1790 and for some reason stayed at Devonshire House until the 4th when they left at 3 a.m. arriving in Dover at noon. The packet boat was ready to sail and slipped its moorings as soon as they and their luggage was on board. She filled her sails with a *'fair wind and an exceeding fine day we had a charming passage*', reaching Calais and getting inside the town gate before it was shut for the night (at 8 p.m.). Unfortunately, Lady Spencer had had a violent headache all day and her travelling bed had to be put up in her cabin during the passage. The weather held and they reached Brussels in the evening of the 6th, having endured a *'miserable lodging'* en route.

A Baby in Paris

The Duke had heard that all was quiet in Paris and having allowed time for his mother-in-law to recover from the journey, they set off on the 9th May for Paris, arriving on the 12th. They lodged at The Hotel University. Lady Spencer went off looking for somewhere where they could rent a house large enough for the party and found one four miles away at Passey, close to the Bois de Boulogne, belonging to the Duc d'Arenberg and conveniently empty. Time was pressing: the arrangements being concluded apparently on the 19th.

Early the following morning the nurse alerted Lady Spencer that the Duchess was clearly getting close to the birth. She immediately sent two housemaids to prepare the house for their arrival. This was cutting it a bit too fine. As soon as the Duchess had a little breakfast, she was put into the carriage with her mother and the latter's maid Ann Scafe and then driven *'gentley'* (sic) to Passey. It was late at night before everybody and their baggage were installed there.

When Lady Spencer had left England for Brussels, it would appear that Dr. Croft and Mrs. Barthno, a nurse, had travelled with her and they were also at Passey. The Duchess may have gone into labour before everybody had arrived at the house, and the Marquis was born *'a little after one o'clock in the morn'* (i.e. 21st May 1790). At the bedside were Lady Spencer, Bess Foster, Mrs. Barthno, two ladies on the Duchess's staff and Dr. Croft. As soon as the baby cried the Duke came into the room. As Ann Scafe (who was also present) wrote: *'there never was a more welcome child'*.

It had been agreed to have two independent witnesses, the Dowager Duchess d'Arenberg and Lord Robert Fitzgerald, Secretary to Lord Gower, the Ambassador. Lady Spencer sent them both a note that birth was imminent, but Lord Robert's servant thought that the note was of little significance and did not pass it over until the following morning. The Dowager Duchess arrived just in the nick of time. This record of the birth of the Duke's son was to prove vital in 1811 following the death of the Duke. The latter's brother Lord George Henry raised the question of succession, but ceded his claim on reading Ann Scafe's diary. The Arenbergs were the wealthiest and most influential family in the Austrian Netherlands but the Dowager's daughter in law, married to the 6th Duke d'Arenberg, was French and co-incidentally, also pregnant.

There had been talk of the baby being switched. This could have been subsequent gossip founded mistakenly on the fact that Bess Foster had had the

Duke's child, Caroline, at the same time as the Duchess had Haryo. With Bess Foster being conveniently abroad with the Duke and Duchess while the latter was pregnant, had Bess Foster been pregnant too? Luckily, the number of independent witnesses identified alongside the events recorded by Ann Scafe was sufficient to quell any threat to the 6th Duke.

On 30th May 1790 the Duchess took her son to the Royal Palace at St. Cloud to show him to the Queen of France. However the christening was postponed because Little G was very ill. Soon after the birth of the Marquis, the household was struck by illness which affected Haryo initially. It must have been serious, for her grandmother (Lady Spencer) wrote to Caroline Howe: '*I was really afraid we should have lost her, but I think she is now recovering fast*'. [24] It was another fortnight before she had largely recovered, by which time her mother and sister were both ill.

By 19th July, at least two of Lady Spencer's servants were ill with '*putrid sore throats*'. They had probably picked the complaint up through having waiting constantly in the ante-chamber while Lady Spencer spent day and night (literally) attending first, Harriet, then the Duchess and Little G. [25] Although the Duchess had seen the Queen of France on the 30th May, by the 3rd June she (the Duchess) was ill: '*the Duchess had above 20 motions yesterday and was very ill last night … Mr. Croft (i.e. the doctor) and I up with her greatest part of the night but thank God she is so much better in every respect this evening that we are quite in spirits about her*'. [26] Whether she passed her problem on to Little G is not clear, especially as the Marquis continued in good health. However as her mother picked up, Little G was complaining of feeling unwell.

By the 7th June she was shivering and suffering from a violent headache, followed by a severe fever. Ten days later, matters were significantly worse. Her grandmother had been at her bedside throughout: '*Our dear lovely child is still alive my Dear Howey, but I fear there is no hope left, it is useless to say what I have gone through these last 10 days, and what I have still to go through I dread to think … the Dutchess* (sic) *fainted several times yesterday and was very ill with only suspecting that I thought her (Little G) worse … we all have reason to believe everything has been done for her that could be done … 8 o'clock the dear little thing has just waked with less delirium but her flesh is burning hot, her pulse quick and low and her breath rather short. Mr. Croft says while life is in her he will not despair*'. [27]

The following day there was some improvement including Little G's delirium which had reduced her father one night to loud sobbing. The recovery was rapid over the next day or so. Dr. Croft was attributed with saving her life. However Little G had a serious relapse on 21st June. By early July, the Duke was seeking an alternative opinion from England leading to Dr. Pitcairn leaving for France on 12th July.

Selina Trimmer, writing on behalf of Lady Spencer to Caroline Howe explained the delirium experienced by Little G and the effect of it. One minute she would not suffer to have Selina in her room and then screamed continuously to have her back only to reproach her with allegations of ill treatment, all of it a nonsense of course. Her grandmother found that she would hardly ever leave the bedside with Little G demanding that she (Little G) should sleep with her head on her grandmother's shoulder. The latter was also subject to violent rages until after well over a month of this treatment her calmness broke, reducing her to tears *'most violently'*. Despite being at the centre of the storm for weeks, Lady Spencer avoided catching the illness. [28]

By the time Dr. Pitcairn arrived, he found the patient recovering again, this time making a full recovery. The treatment was largely small doses of laudanum, sometimes with an additive, such as musk. With the patients returning towards good health, the Duke turned his attention to returning to home. They had left on 19th June the previous year. In the party was Caroline St Jules who landed in England a day prior to her sixth birthday. [29]

On 20th June her recovery was sufficient to allow the Duke to write to Lord Spencer asking if he would be a godfather (alongside the Duke of Portland and Lady Rachel Walpole, the Duke's aunt as godmother). He had not written earlier thanking them for their congratulations on the Duchess being brought to bed in case he then had to write with *'disagreeable news'* as he put it. Lady Spencer was well, he wrote, although it was clear that she had unstintingly had her work cut out attending her granddaughter. [30]

The christening was postponed as was the return to England but the Marquis was baptised in France by the Ambassador's chaplain when he was six weeks' old. However Ann Scafe remarked in her diary that *'we have to leave Passy very soon'*. They set off slowly (out of regard for Little G *'who still remains low'* on 10th August 1790 taking a route via Chantilly and had a *'very good passage'* from Calais once the *'carriages and baggage'*; was put on board on the 15th. The Marquis was eventually christened William George Spencer Cavendish on his 1st birthday, 21st May 1791, at St. George's Church, Hanover Square, London. It was followed by a large family party at Devonshire House.

According to the Wikipedia entry for St. George's Church, it was a very fashionable place of worship at the time. Their child could very conveniently have been christened at Devonshire House. However the use of St. George's points to the desire to make a statement that the Cavendish dynasty had been protected by the Duchess's birth of a son, albeit at long last. In terms of 'fashion ability', the church would have been enhanced following this christening. The church in the song 'Get Me To The Church On Time' in the musical 'My Fair Lady' is apparently St. Georges.

Later, the Duchess, writing to her brother, recorded that *'I really believe we owed much of our safety* (in France) *to the good offices of La Fayette'*. [31]

12

Weary of Errors, 1790-93

Lull Before The Storm

The 1790s was to be the last complete decade of the Duke and Duchess's marriage. It was a defining one too. By mid-summer 1791 the Duchess was pregnant again, but it was not the Duke's child. Banished abroad, she was accompanied by her sister, mother and Bess Foster. It was nearly two years before she returned. Her return saw a much chastened Duchess, a more loving Duke, not only with his wife, but with three growing children.

Steering clear of London society, the Duke filled the gap, giving the Duchess work to do, chiefly at the house they liked most, Chiswick. For one reason or another, the Duchess hardly went to Chatsworth or Hardwick and probably never to Londesbrough. It was a decade in which the Duke lost not only his sister but two of his uncles and when the Duchess's brother brought glory to Britain as First Sea Lord at the expense of the French. He gave teeth to the Navy, the threat of which thwarted the success of French invasion designs in Ireland and India (or at least the Middle East).

Her life was marred by a life-threatening disease resulting in the near total loss of sight to one eye, a disfigurement she bore with typical fortitude. After twenty plus years of marriage, the vicissitudes of life saw the Duke continually affected by gout, the Duchess affected by her headaches (? migraines), both she and Little G experiencing life-threatening illness and the Duke's sister Dorothy losing her life to an ovarian cyst as large as a man's head (see Chapter 13).

Within a month of their return from France, the Duchess was trying to find some way of ending the deadlock of the frostiness of her mother towards Bess Foster. They had after all, all been under the same roof for nearly three months at Passey. The Duchess found her mother implacable on the subject (and on a different matter), as were her creditors. The anticipated resolution to her debt problem following the birth of a son had not occurred, affecting her mood: '*I shall put up with content with all the misery I am likely to encounter – for kind as he* (the Duke) *seems inclined to be to me, I fear the Duke must be wearryd* (sic) *of errors. His health is indifferent, his nerves are shook and quiet and gentle society is now of consequence to him*'. He was probably still getting over Little G's illness.

However the rest of this letter to her mother includes an interesting revelation: '*...was I absolutely discover'd in an intrigue* (i.e. an affair) *you cd* (could) *not be more uneasy than at the possibility of yr son-in-law having an attachment, which except the attachment of friendship and esteem is other ways false, and some time or other I can prove it to you ...*'. [1] Surely this is indicating that the relationship between the Duke and Bess Foster had lost its ardour, at least in a physical sense.

It certainly may have had an impact on events the following summer. Why did the Duchess choose to make the observation? What was the big deal for her mother if they (the Duke and Bess Foster) were only friends? This letter was preceded by another the day previous. Despite the fact that he did not give any indication about a separation or not over her debts, he made it clear to his wife that if at any time she had any uneasiness about Bess living with them, then he would be far from wishing her (Bess) to continue living there. [2]

The Duke's lack of good health seems to have persisted for at least a couple of months. For some time he had been seized with a sudden rheumatic spasm, which lasted for several hours. Beyond that, he was well. Whether this was just a bad attack of cramp or not is not clear. That autumn, the two girls were also unwell, with whooping cough. Their mother took them to Compton Place, Eastbourne, the home of Lord George Cavendish (the Duke's brother), so that they could have the benefit of sea air.

Early in 1791, the Duke's immediate relations, particularly his sister Dorothy, had turned against the Duchess. Dorothy felt slighted over something the Duchess had said and the latter felt that she was in bad odour with them all (except Lady George Cavendish). [3] Moreover, the Duchess's sister Harriet was also far from well. She had caught a cough which possibly had caused a blood vessel to burst in her head, resulting in the loss of use of her left arm and leg. Bessborough speculates that it might have been TB. [4]

During 1791 and probably at least by the Spring, the Duchess had an affair with Charles Grey, a 27 year-old Northumberland M.P. He became 2nd Earl Grey and later, as Prime Minister, brought in the Parliamentary Reform Bill. They had a child (see below) through this relationship, born on 20th February 1792, which would point to conception being mid-May 1791, whilst the Duchess was in London. Earl Grey tea is named after him.

Sowing The Wind, Reaping The Wild Wind

Because of the serious nature of Harriet's illness and no doubt remembering her assistance in leaving England to accompany the Duchess during her pregnancy in 1789 – 90, the Duke, according to Foreman, arranged for two houses to be rented in Bath, one for the Duncannons and one for the Duchess and children. It took a week to travel from London to Bath, because of the state of Harriet's health. Also in the party were Lord Duncannon (Harriet's husband), Selina Trimmer, Bess Foster and Lady Spencer. They were to stay at Marlborough Buildings, a street situated adjacent to the far end of The Crescent from the town centre.

By the end of June, Lord Duncannon had found a small house in Queen's Parade, halving the distance to the Baths and probably also cheaper. The total cost of the stay in Bath was £1,666. [5]

Lady Spencer also found accommodation elsewhere, which of course would be away from the disliked Lady Bess Foster. Grey followed the Duchess to Bath, but Lady Spencer ordered her daughter not to see him. There is some conjecture as to whether she did or not, but if she did, it was without her mother's knowledge.

Presumably Lady Spencer was unaware of her daughter's condition when the Duke joined the party in July. He was there by the 19th, when Lady Spencer reported to Caroline Howe that the Duchess had slipped down a few stairs and hurt her side the previous Sunday. It was nearly 10pm, but the Duke would not allow her to go to bed until she had been seen by the doctor, as it had affected her breathing. The doctor blooded her and she recovered. The Duke stayed until August when he appears to have gone to Chatsworth for the usual calendar of race meetings. By September, the Duchess was unable to conceal her pregnancy. Harriet's condition deteriorated and Dr. Warren was called. He suggested that she should go abroad for the winter, recommending Lisbon. However, the two sisters persuaded him to suggest Devon or Cornwall, where hopefully, the birth could be kept secret and from the Duke.

Both Foreman and Gleeson state that the Duke received an anonymous letter suggesting that he called upon his wife. Neither give a date or reference. If this is so, it could have been after his return to London and therefore in September, or at the beginning of October. He went unannounced to Bath, staying with his mother-in-law and clearly finding his wife pregnant again. Stung by the revelation that the child was Grey's, with his usual procrastination his decision on his wife's future was considered, arbitrary and given by the 11th October: She was to go abroad and the child put to adoption immediately after birth. She was to go direct and not to return to London. [6]

In his uneasy but deliberate way, following the birth of his son, the Duke was moving closer to the Duchess: Bess was no longer an item in his life if the Duchess's word is to be accepted. He had paid for a month's rent at Bath for Harriet and the Duchess (in all probability) and no doubt there would have been other signals. Now he realised that at the time of his son's christening, his wife was having an affair with Grey and quite possibly was even pregnant.

His wife now faced an indeterminate exile without her children and told to wait until allowed to return. The alternative would have been a public separation before a baying media mob and no access to her children. This was a difficult moment for Bess. On the one hand there was not much point in staying behind unless the Duke wanted her to. Here was her opportunity to cement a relationship with him if he wished it. Bess had returned to London and had still not reached a decision to go when the rest boarded the boat for France. Here they waited in Rouen, where her son Augustus was presumably still being fostered, a fact possibly only known in the party by the Duchess, if at all. A week later, they had reached St Germain, 15 miles from Paris, which Lady Spencer had *a thousand reasons to wish to avoid*. Her daughter's debts (this could well have been Harriet as well as the Duchess) and the pregnancy would have been high on her list.

There was still no indication of when the rest would arrive. Gleeson states that the Duchess left with the Duke having made no financial arrangements for her. [7] If that was the case, it surely was to change. In fact, their Steward for the journey, Townsend, probably Earl Spencer's Steward, was delayed, like Bess Foster and the two Carolines. Bess because the two girls had developed a cold (unless this was a cover) and Townsend possibly because he was waiting for items he was to take with him. A further delay was bad weather at Dover. Bess and the children reached the Duchess and the others at about the time they left Paris. Townsend caught up with them all a few days later in early December. He arrived *with all the fine packets he was charged with*. One wonders if this included financial arrangements, i.e. cash and bonds drawn on an English bank.

Exile Abroad

Prior to the birth of the baby, the Duchess made out a draft will. In it she refers to her rings, jewellery and Vatican Prints. The latter survive at Chatsworth. When she died in 1806, the Prints were being held by a London bookseller as security for a debt for books she had purchased. [8] They are a poignant reminder of this time in her life.

Dr. Warren had announced that Harriet should winter in the South of France. The party consisted of Harriet and her husband, Lord Duncannon, the Duchess, Lady Spencer and Lady Bess Foster together with Caroline Ponsonby and Caroline St. Jules, Bess's daughter, Dr. Nott and several servants. They were in

Lyons on 9th December [9] and had their first view of the Mediterranean Sea at Marseilles on 28th December. However their journey nearly ended at the Loire with a close shave with a disaster. They crossed the river at Nevers, some 130 miles /200 kms south of Paris.

As Harriet's chaise was pulled off the ferry, it slipped off the hard standing into *'a sort of quick sand'*. One side sunk into the silt, although Harriet remained out of danger with the servants and local boatmen at hand. Horse power failed to draw the chaise out, with Harriet still inside. She was forced to remain there until more powerful oxen were found and brought to the quayside. The Duchess and her mother were some way behind and had a safe crossing oblivious of the earlier drama, although they both found the ferry *'very frightful'*.

With Harriet far from well, it was an experience she could have managed without. It was with some difficulty that they were able to get her upright onto crutches. Her left leg had to be forced to lift it forward and her right leg then had to be drawn down, all of which was quite painful. She was unable to stand upright even when supported by the crutches.

They had left Lyon on 18th December, having been delayed by snow, intense cold, high winds and rising river levels. They journeyed on by river, down the Rhone to Avignon. It took four days to make the trip, with two boats: one for the passengers and one for all the carriages. The cabin was made of planks *'that do not join cover'd with straw and sail cloth'*. Straw and tapestry substituted for carpet. A modicum of privacy was met by tapestry hanging from the ceiling, although they at least slept ashore each evening. Not only was the river smoother, it was safer. They had to pay in places for the Gendarmerie Nationale to protect them from robbery and danger.

Having reached Marseilles, they then moved on to Toulon and were just east of there at Hyères on 7th of January. Here they initially heard that there was no house available in Nice (their objective) large enough for them. It was a place that Harriet remembered fondly from her childhood. Here it was resolved the party split up, with the Duncannons, their daughter Caroline and Lady Spencer heading for Nice, arriving there on 10th February. [10] It had been a difficult journey because of the state of the roads and risk of robbery. The roads, at best were unmaintained since the revolution and many had been destroyed by flood waters in the mountainous areas. Robbers were now endemic, especially on quiet stretches of the roads.

The same day, the Duchess, plus Bess and her daughter Caroline, set off for Aix-en-Provence to meet the Comte St. Jules, with whom Caroline St Jules had spent much of the first years of her life. He was delayed and they must have gone part way to meet him. Bess wished to meet the Comte again, although the reasons need to be regarded with suspicion, given the need for a plausible cover story to have the Duchess away from the party for the birth. A week or so before the latter, they had still to reach Nimes because of the intolerable state of the roads, as the Duchess described it. It would appear therefore that the baby was born in Nimes, the Comte having travelled up from Sorèze (see above chapter). The Duchess gave birth to a baby girl on 20th February 1792.

She was named Eliza Courtney and somehow (details not known) was taken to England by a wet nurse where she was adopted by the 1st Earl Grey and his wife. Eliza was visited by the Duchess with her two girls when the Greys were in London and on occasion she did lessons with the girls at Chiswick. She married Gen. Robert Ellice, had two sons and a number of daughters, one of whom was named Georgiana and who married Hugh Horatio Seymour in 1846. Eliza died a widow at Norwood in 1859, aged 67 years. The Duchess kept in touch with her other three children via mail, writing to Little G from Aix on the 15th January. She must have sent to her previously some spar samples and coral, which Little G had liked. (11)

The Duchess did not rest for long after the birth for they soon returned to Toulon, reaching there on 3rd March where they were joined by Louis Rossi (Bess's servant) with a carriage to take them on towards Nice. She described Toulon as being '*so full we are in the Garret*', quickly moving on to Frejus. She described Aix as being quiet, which is at odds with Bessborough who states that there were riots at both Aix and Toulon, but gives no reference. (12) It is likely that the Duchess's pregnancy was only known by her mother, sister, Bess Foster and Dr Nott.

Bessborough also seems to contradict himself on another point: He states '*Although Georgiana had been abroad for some months, the Duke's anger still continued unabated. Harriet, writing to Lady Melbourne from Nice in March, spoke of the persecution of her sister by the Duke. Bess, writing to the same correspondent went so far as to describe the Duke as 'a brute and a beast' and said she had no patience with him*'. However, he goes on to state that in another letter to Lady Melbourne in April, Harriet mentions that the Duke never wrote to Georgiana and seldom to Lady Elizabeth. (13) However the Duke did write to Lady Spencer that April stating that the Duchess should remain with her sister and if she came home so should the Duchess. If her doctor recommended that she (Harriet) stayed abroad, he (the Duke) would go out to join them that summer. (14)

For the moment then, the Duke was still unhappy but was extending an olive branch. It was, to be fair, only a few weeks after the birth of the baby. Lord Duncannon was considering a return to England, but the Duke rejected a suggestion that his wife be permitted to return for a short while (to see her children) and then go back to Harriet. We do not know how serious was the

Duke's intention to go abroad to visit his wife that summer. Duncannon could have returned to England the way that he had come, but in the end the party decided on an alternative plan.

This was to take a felucca and sail to Genoa and then proceed by road from the port north to Geneva. It took the whole of May before they arrived. There seems to be three possible reasons why they did this – to go some way with Duncannon (? in case the Duke changed his mind), or to travel to Lausanne to consult Dr. Tissot, an eminent physician, neurologist and expert on migraines, who lived there. The third reason was that the route would be safer for Duncannon, although longer. They were in Geneva by the 29th May.

In the Devonshire Collection is a terracotta statue of Jean Jacques Rousseau. Its provenance is that it was acquired by the Duchess in 1792 but there is no documentation to support this. The sculptor was Jean-Francois Hess of Geneva. It is a particularly fine piece, Hess using Rousseau's little known death mask in its execution. Both the Duke and Duchess were enthusiastic about Rousseau (although Lady Spencer was not). Perhaps the Duchess acquired it for the Duke whilst she was at Lausanne, although no expenses are recorded in the Chatsworth or Devonshire House Accounts and there are no surviving records indicating its purchase for the Duke's personal account.

The main issue is how would the Duchess have paid for it. She would have had insufficient funds and it is unlikely that her mother had enough either. This situation arose again in 1803 when Bess Foster was in Paris and wished to bring home an expensive two-volume book on Egyptian archaeology. She wrote to the Duke asking for his leave to buy it. In other words, he would pay for it through his bank from London. [15] It is persuasive to think that this is what happened regarding the Rousseau statue. If so, it is also persuasive that this is how the reconciliation began, with a letter from the Duchess asking the Duke if he would like the statue and if so, if he would arrange for the payment. Unfortunately the Duke's bank account for this period cannot be located.

As will be seen below, by early May 1792, the Duchess had reasons for thinking that she would soon be heading home. This suggests that something had occurred prior to May and the statue may well have been the catalyst for it. Using their joint interest in something (in this case Rousseau) to smooth the waters was a technique the Duke used once the Duchess was home. Remembering his problems with his wife over the 1783 Chatsworth refurbishment, he gave her the job of organising the furbishing of the two wings at Chiswick. He knew she would relish it. Whatever happened regarding the statue, it remains at Chatsworth as a reminder of a difficult period in the life of the couple and possibly how a resolution of it began.

Previous writers emphasize the interest developed by the Duchess, while staying north of Lausanne at Yverdun, in botany and mineralogy. This may indicate a pastime developed whilst undertaking treatment from Dr. Tissot. See under 1793 below for more detail on him. The Duke's plans to go abroad to meet the Duchess that summer did not materialise. In a letter to the latter in September 1792, Lady Sutherland wrote that Miss Lloyd and Caroline Howe *'think he is idle about setting out having a multitude of things to settle.'* [16]

The two socialite ladies, a generation older than the Duchess, were correct, although they would not know the extent of the Duke's problems in Ireland. Moreover, he was now a much more 'hands on' Duke. With the retirement of his agent for the former Burlington estates in 1791, significant areas of miss-management had been discovered in Yorkshire and particularly in Ireland. Additional to this were the failure of the Ecton Copper Mine in 1791 and the loss of c. £25,000 in annual income.

The year 1792 saw the discovery of most of the very serious problems facing the Irish Estate and towards the end of the year, the development of a complex management plan. The latter probably could not have been completed if he had gone abroad.

Charlotte Williams

In July 1792, Charlotte Williams returned to Devonshire House from Paris. She accompanied the husband of Mrs. Smith, Little G and Harriet's Governess. He had gone there to fetch his father's little girl, his *'fruit d'amour'* as he had told Miss Lloyd. Charlotte had been ill and spitting blood, wrote James Hare to the Duchess, who had heard it from the Duke. The latter was unsure what to do with her. This was probably because it was felt that her manner was prejudicial to the two girls – the reason why she had gone to Paris in the summer of 1789. John Heaton had offered to take her in and the Duke took the offer up. In an undated letter, but considered to be late 1792, Hare wrote to the Duchess to tell her that Charlotte had married Heaton's nephew, Charles. [17] Thereafter there is no mention of her in the Duchess's surviving correspondence and no mention of her being involved in any social occasions, both at Devonshire House or elsewhere. Had the Duchess had her way and married Charlotte off to one of the minor aristocratic families in Derbyshire, no doubt she would have continued to have had the benefit of that connection.

Moving On: Switzerland And Italy

Having arrived in Geneva at the end of May 1792, the party went on to Lausanne, hoping to stay/see Edward Gibbon who lived there. Although he moved back to England to comfort Lord Sheffield, whose wife had died, he was still at home on 2nd September. He may have delayed his journey to England: some years previously, he had proposed marriage to Bess Foster, but had been rejected. Needing quite a big house to get everybody plus the servants into, they settled in Yverdun to the north. They appear to have stayed at Ouchy (near Lausanne), on the shore of Lake Geneva, at least from 7th June to early August.

At the end of August, Sir Charles Blagden arrived in Lausanne and met the Duchess and her sister while they were out riding. On 2nd September, he had a long conversation with Gibbon, author of the 'Decline and Fall of the Roman Empire', about recent discoveries of a geographical nature, chemistry and experiments on nerves. The Duchess told him that she was *'quite wild'* on studies of that nature. That day, he was at the Duchess's house, attending a lecture given by a Mr Struve on mineralogy.

Blagden, the Secretary of the Royal Society, importantly stated that *'The Duchess told me that now she came to town with very different ideas from her former ones, to see the men of science and eminence'*. It is now recognised that she took a significant interest in mineralogy and other scientific matters. It is quite possible that he and the Duchess were acquainted as he had been an assistant to the scientist Henry Cavendish in 1783 and she maintained contact with him, contrary to the Duke.

Meanwhile the Duke had left it with his wife to decide whether to go on to Italy or stay in Switzerland until the middle of October *'for the chance of his going there'* or to follow her mother to Italy or to return to England. However, he thought it best if they did not return home, one of the reasons being the danger of the journey. He had in mind seeing her the following April *'somewhere'* and going on to Spa, hopefully with Lady Spencer and Harriet too. [18]

However, events in Switzerland went in a different direction. Lord Duncannon, returned to London in June 1792. Lady Spencer and Harriet were still at Lausanne at the end of August. Blagden noted in his diary that the Duchess was ill on the 6th September. It could have been this or continuing treatment from Dr. Tissot, which caused them to leave for Italy with Caroline Ponsonby, leaving the Duchess and Bess Foster behind. By early November, the latter two were also south of the Alps, her mother and sister heading for Florence with the intention of waiting for them at Pisa. [19]

The inevitable flow of letters continued, even whilst both parties were moving south wards towards Pisa. Lord Duncannon lost his father on the 11th March 1793, succeeding to the title of 3rd Earl of Bessborough. He rejoined his wife, now Countess Bessborough, and the others there and they all journeyed on to Rome and Naples after spending time at the baths in Lucca for Harriet's benefit. The Duchess continued extending her collection of minerals and other geological specimens, constrained however with very little money to spend on their acquisition. Whilst in Rome, the Duchess met Richard Westmacott, who had arrived there from England in January 1793, on either 22nd February or 22nd March. A little later, the Duchess wrote to him, thanking him for some drawings and inviting him to dinner. Some of his drawings still survive at Chatsworth. [20]

The following May, 1793, the Duke wrote and asked his wife to return home However, for some reason it was late July before they set off. Prior to the Duke writing to the Duchess, she must have had an inkling that her exile was soon to end. On 4th May 1793, she wrote to Thomas Coutts *I believe I shall set out for England early in June*. [21]

Also in May, of course, was the 3rd birthday of the Marquis of Hartington. Despite the absence of his wife, the Duke appears to have celebrated it, with at least two nights of dancing etc. as well as whatever else the Duke provided for his friends. The band for two nights cost three guineas. One may be certain that in the absence of the Duchess, there was a significant saving on the cost of the music, let alone celebrations as a whole, as provided by the Duke. [22]

At this time, rumours were circulating in London that the Duke had separated from his wife, yet more worry for Thomas Coutts. Having just prized £5,610 from the Duke, he was still owed £15,800. The Duchess responded that *'he is very kind in his letters to me, kind in sending me money here, but alas no notice of the great circumstances with regard to my affairs'*. So we also know that the Duke was paying his wife's costs. Coutts had been trying to get in touch with the Duke, but was getting no response, although the mail may not have got passed on by John Heaton.

The Duke had paid another pressing jeweller named Jeffries, and Coutts advised her *'There are a great many Bills of yr Grace's and Lady Duncannons unpaid and waiting for money – I believe should the Duke hear of them the effect must be very prejudicial to you'*. In October 1792, two of the Duchess's creditors took legal action against her in her absence, although the amounts were small. [23] Yet another good reason for staying south of the Alps. If it wasn't baying creditors north of the English Channel, it was baying French troops south of it. The French had declared war on Britain on 21st January 1793.

On 3rd July 1793 the Duke received a DCL (Doctor of Civil Law) from Oxford University. [24]

Returning Home

At the beginning of August 1793, the Duchess and Bess reached Bologna and left the Apennines for the Po Valley and on to Parma, Piacenza and Milan. Here they stayed for two days *'working and preparing our boats'*. It was also too hot to do much on 6th August, with the temperature soaring to 92° F. Worried that *'the Milanese was infested by a band of robbers, it caused us some alarm and obliged us to some precautions'*. This would appear to have seen them heading for Sesto (now Sesto Calende) at the southern end of Lake Maggiore. Here they boarded a boat and sailed north to Magadino, a two day trip, with all their baggage and their carriages, de-wheeled for the trip. Magadino is in Switzerland. The Duchess wrote *'from the moment we entered the mountains of Switzerland, we travelled without fear and felt perfectly secure.'* [25] By the 10th they had reached Magadino opposite Locarno, moving on into the Ticino Valley. Reaching Bellinzona on the 11th, they stayed until the 13th.

The Duchess seemed captivated with Ticino. Although they left on 13th for Pollegio, they spent the day in Bellinzona, not leaving until early evening. (Modern spellings are used for towns and villages. Sometimes the Duchess must have been making a guess at the name). Although it is only some 15 miles/24km, it took four hours. The transport was a form of chair suspended between two horses and with 3 – 4 guides for both the Duchess and Bess. Although they could have ridden horse-back, they found the woman's saddle *'very bad'*. [26]

Their carriages were not too far away, but for some reason were not used. They were delighted with the beautiful scenery as they travelled along the banks of the River Ticino, and found a *'decent inn'* in Pollegio with *'excellent butter and good fish from the river, and a rare and good bird the name I have forgot'*. A violent thunder and lightning storm followed their arrival. Their room was *'as neat as any Inn in England'*. Continuing north to Airolo, they abandoned the chairs for the use of the maids and took to horse-back, crossing the St. Gothard Pass and then descending to Altdorf. Although the day after Pollegio was another four mile meander (to Giomico), the next three days (with stops overnight at Airolo, Wassen and Altdorf) saw them covering 20 – 25 miles a day/ 30 – 40 km.

The carriages were not de-wheeled and presumably were used by some of the servants when possible. In more difficult areas, the carriages were carried (there was snow in the area of the Pass), with ropes passing underneath them. The Duchess, writing to her mother, reported *'immense'* amounts of commercial traffic using the route, which was open all year round. She said the road was better than *'ye high road'*, presumably the Furka and Grimsel Passes road. It was 15 feet wide and paved with granite; [27] a road you felt safe on.

The inns were all to her liking too: *'clean beds, excellent fish, cheese and butter, very good water and decent guide people'*. Unfortunately Bess was ill, spitting *'a great deal of blood'* but Caroline and the Duchess were well and clearly enjoyed the trip. Another experience awaited them at Altdorf. The journey from there was being rowed to Lucerne on a flat bottomed boat, taking seven hours to get there on Lake Lucerne. Townsend and Mason, their servants, were left behind to await the arrival of the carriages. Bess was better in Lucerne, (reached on

17th August), where they awaited for Townsend to go to Lausanne and return. It had taken them ten days (to complete a trip achievable today within the day) from Milan and over two weeks from Florence. There was no mad dash to England however. [28]

Bess's condition, though better, was clearly of concern; she was in need of medical attention. Instead of going from Lucerne to Basle, they took a detour to the west, to Berne. From here Bess went with Townsend to Avenches, west of Berne. The Duchess advised her mother that on 21st August, Bess was setting off 'to *Avenches to meet Tissot'* , [29] and if necessary to go on to Lausanne. Here we have the reason why she had gone there in 1784 and in May 1793. Here was probably why they had all gone north from Genoa to Geneva so far out of their way, and on to Lausanne, staying with Edward Gibbon. She was seeing Dr. Tissot again.

He is described as having written on the '*diseases of the poor, on masturbation, on the diseases of the men of letters and of rich people and nervous diseases'* [30]. He was recognised in his day as '*the classic authority on migraine* (which may point to the Duchess seeing him too in May that year) *and arguably wrote the greatest medical best-seller of the 18th Century'*. In April 1787 Napoleon Bonaparte wrote to him, complimenting him for spending his '*days in treating humanity'* and advising him that his reputation '*had reached even into the mountains of Corsica'* as well as telling him the respect he (Napoleon) had for his works. Tissot died in 1797.

In the meantime, the Duchess found other company with whom she went to Grindlewald. Although Bess had gone on to Lausanne, she caught up with them, all of them arriving in the village at about the same time. Reflecting on Bess and the doctor, the Duchess wrote to her mother to tell her that she had not had a headache since she had left Rome. [31]

It took another month before they sailed from Ostend. Their route took them to Basle, Freiburg, Mannheim and across to Maastricht before heading for familiar surroundings in Brussels reached on 13th September 1793. Sailing conditions were not good with high winds and fog. On top of this they had been recommended not to leave Bruges because of the proximity of French troops. Having reached Ostend, any anxiety of finding French troops or a vessel was soon lifted: '*C. Bowyer of ye Amphitude has taken upon him to give us a convoy as Adl. Machelside is off Nieuport. Lord Wicklow will escort us in his little yacht, in which he carrys home Cl. Gascoyne and another wounded officer – and Sir John Peters ye Consul and his wife have begd to go with us; at one time they thought Ostend might be attacked tonight but now they say there is no danger ...'* [32]

In fact the French had broken out of Dunkirk and moved away, following the battle for Dunkirk (the Battle of Hondschook) on 6-8th of the month, defeating the hereditary Prince of Orange at Menin on 13th September 1793, capturing 40 guns and driving the Dutch towards Bruges and Ghent, just as the Duchess and her party reached there. However on the 16th, the day they reached Ostend, the French, under Houchard, were routed by Beaulieu at Courtrai. Ostend was not attacked, but there may have been skirmishes nearby. [33]

The Duchess then left a relatively calm Ostend for a sea that was anything but calm. This however is what Foreman has to say on the departure, quoting the above letter as her reference: '*There was not a single space on any of the boats leaving the port. Fortunately, in the midst of the general panic, Georgiana came across a friend, Lord Wicklow, just as he was heading for his pleasure boat. Eyeing their baggage and servants rather doubtfully he nevertheless squeezed them onto his little yacht. As the men cut the moorings some English refugees rushed up and begged to be allowed on. Georgiana was distraught at being forced to leave them behind but there was nothing they could do. The boat pulled away from the stragglers, and she watched them standing forlornly on the quayside as the city burned behind them*'. [34] With Ostend the port of entry for the British Army, it would have been well defended and the French had insufficient resources to take it and burn it, as the Duchess arrived there.

Despite all the rigour of travel they had made it so close to the Channel and safety at Dover: Ignoring safety concerns they pressed on to find the weather their last tribulation. It was to be no joke either, having to contend with being tossed about in fog for several hours on a passage that took 22 hours. With no small amount of fortitude the Duchess wrote to her mother from Dover: '*I am so agitated and tird* (sic) *I cannot sleep, eat or rest. I have not slept since Ostend*'. [35]

As the returning party rumbled towards Brussels from Maastricht, the Duchess reflected on times ahead. She hoped she would return impressed with a '*very deep humility*' and a wish of atonement by doing more for others. In terms of her relationship with the Duke, she intended '*perfect acquiescence in all his intentions and wishes. I hope likewise to make use of ye very great good fortune that has attended me – by increased prudence and care.*' [36] To what extent she achieved this is not clear. She failed where controlling her expenditure was concerned however, probably doubling her debt (or close to it) in the remaining thirteen years of her life.

The Duchess had paid a heavy price for her fling with Charles Grey. Principally one suspects from her separation from her three Devonshire children. The girls had been without her for long periods between the summer of 1789 to mid-September 1793. Her son would not know her at all. Lingering emotions for Grey were to be dashed in 1794 when he married Mary Elizabeth Ponsonby without even letting her know. Ironically one of Grey's children, Rev. Francis, married the Duke's grand-daughter, Lady Elizabeth Howard, the daughter of Little G. Grey had 16 children with his wife and apparently yet more affairs.

The Duke appears not to have mentioned the pregnancy to anyone. She had gone abroad supporting her sister was the line the Duke took. He did not mention her to close friends and they appear not to have raised it with him. It appears that after a respectable absence of six months he decided that enough was enough. The children were under the watchful eye of Mrs. Smith and Selina Trimmer looked after their education. On her return, the Duchess wrote to her mother telling her that *'the Duke seems very fond of her* (Miss Trimmer) *and sent to wake her last night when the express came.'*

Nonetheless the children would be telling their father that they (the girls at least) were wanting their mother. In May 1793 he therefore wrote asking the Duchess to return home. There can be little doubt that he was missing his wife and possibly Bess too, despite an apparent cooling of his ardour for her prior to her departure. *'There never was anything equal to ye attention I have met with from him – to the generosity and kindness'* wrote the Duchess. He had bought her a new, light blue coach with silver springs (how she would have appreciated that in Rome for a more comfortable journey). [37]

As mentioned above, James Hare reported that during the summer, Devonshire House was looking dirty. By September there had been a transformation, the Duchess finding it *'very neat'*. Her bedroom held *'every comfort'* and there was a *'very pretty new bed in the Duke's room'*. Despite lack of sleep on the ship during its 22 hour passage to Dover and the subsequent journey to Dartford where the family was reunited, they did not stay there, the Duke having arranged for a fast express to carry them on to Devonshire House, where joyous servants were lined up to meet her.

The Duke had *'bought my picture (rather yours) with the child at Sir Joshua's sale'*. This is thought to relate to a preliminary sketch for the unfinished painting of Lady Spencer and the infant Georgiana, now in the National Portrait Gallery. [38] In a further effort to please, he had given her a miniature of her mother, which he kept in his personal drawer. *'I never saw anything so kind as he is …'* she wrote. His enthusiasm for her arrival was mirrored by the servants. They were *'mad with joy, and when the news came at night of my coming, Mrs. Brown went round and carryd (sic) them all wine.'* [39]

Whilst the Duchess was away, during April – June 1793 in fact, the Duke spent £428. 9s. 6d changing the upholstery at Devonshire House. No further detail is given, but was this indicating that the Duke was anticipating his wife's return? Early in the following year, the Duke was contemplating redecorating Devonshire House and wallpapering it, presumably for the first time. [40] In fact the Duke seems to have managed well enough during the exile. Had he chosen to divorce his wife, the consequences for her must have been very clear, especially as she knew only too well the consequences Bess Foster had suffered following her divorce. She never saw her children for 14 years.

Meanwhile, her son by the Duke, Augustus Clifford, had been living in Somerset with foster parents for some time. He must have left there at least by November 1796, when he started at Harrow School. It is known that he had initially frequently visited Devonshire House and he lived there in the Harrow School holidays. What is not clear is when the illegitimate children became acquainted with their parents and for that matter, appreciated their relationship with each other. It is also unclear when the Duchess was told of their existence. In 1797, Bess Foster was reunited with her two boys, Augustus and Frederick, following the death of their father, when they went up to Oxford. They too would regard Devonshire House their home in future, although Augustus joined the Horse Guards in 1799 and moved on from the Guards to the Diplomatic Service in the USA.

13

Building Bridges 1793-95

Reconciliation and Escape from London

While the Duchess had been away, the Duke had not completed the furnishing of his two new wings at Chiswick. He was awaiting the return of his wife and the opportunity of pleasing her by involving her in the selection of furniture, carpets and curtains etc. However it was a while before the Duchess could turn her attention to this project. Initially she spent much of the day with her children including dining with them. Dinner was at 7 p.m., presumably too late for the children. She had supper with the Duke and remained up with him until 2 – 3 a.m., complaining that she hardly had time to get sufficient sleep.

The Duke did recover his health, his regular visitors at Devonshire House while he was ill being John Crawford, James Hare and Messrs. James and Greville. At the end of November, the family went off to Bath. For the Duchess it must have been a difficult and emotional time. On the face of it, it appears like an own goal for the Duke. Having gone to so much trouble to please his wife on her return, it is likely that there was a more compelling reason. Just prior to their departure, she wrote to her mother to say the Duke was in good spirits. It was for Little G's benefit that they felt the need to go to restore her to good health. It also got the Duchess away from town. She was reluctant to engage in Society and hardly ventured out for a month. Bath was a convenient excuse to be away from London, with the expectation of going afterwards to Hardwick. [1] There may well have been another reason: see below.

Although the Duke had left Devonshire House for Bath, the affairs in the Irish Estate continued to require much attention. It was even necessary for John Heaton and William Bowman, who had come especially from Ireland, to interrupt the Duke's stay at the spa just prior to Christmas. At the end of the year, Little G's health was much better, but the Duchess was reluctant to return to town with the Duke, contemplating staying on. [2] It was while the Duchess was there that she went to Bristol to see Dr. Thomas Beddows. (See the Introduction for more on this important pointer to the Duchess's interests in science).

It would appear that with the Duchess returning to England and home, the Duke refocused his attention on Chiswick, only to find a major outbreak of dry rot, making the house beyond habitation.

Francis, 5th Duke of Bedford, was as passionate about hunting as the Duke and his kennels acknowledged to be amongst the best in the country. These were at Oakley House, near Bedford, and a major remodelling of the house had only recently been completed in 1792. It had been entrusted to Henry Holland, the fashionable architect who had married the daughter of Capability Brown. It conveniently had three major bedrooms and the Duke and Duchess, together with Bess, would, no doubt, have appreciated its Louis XVI interior.

Francis offered, with the only exception of personal servants, all of the family's needs, including wine. Hunting at Hardwick could wait. The family returned to London in January 1794, filling two carriages, with the Marquis, for some reason, following on three days later. However, the Duchess still did not venture out other than to call on the Duchess of Gordon and to go to the opera. However, about ten days after getting to London, she met Lucas, the Duke of Bedford's steward at Oakley (at the request of the Duke of Bedford).

The Duchess wrote to her mother: '*the duke* (of Bedford) *has new furnished the house lately with paper and canvas ... it is very pretty and consists of a very handsome dining room, drawing room, kennels, stables, etc. – we shall have very good room for the children and I hope bring few servants – in short I am very much pleased with it indeed*'. The Duchess found Oakley '*so exceedingly pleasant*'. [3]

However the 5th Duke died aged 36 years in 1802 from a difficult hernia operation. He lived at Woburn Abbey, which is still the family's home. The Duchess clearly liked the young Duke of Bedford. She rather wished that he was ten years' younger, with marriage to Little G in mind. No doubt the latter had her own views on her mother's aspirations; she had no time for him. She was now 10 years of age. The 5th Duke of Bedford was succeeded by his brother.

The return to London from Bath may have been because of the Duke being required in the House of Lords, as the Duchess wrote to her mother saying that she thought the Duke would support the war. She was also worried that the Duke's thoughts of hunting at Oakley may be dashed by a recall to militia duty. The French were threatening an invasion but the logistics and military adventures in Flanders kept them occupied. [4] However a jittery Government would have kept the Duke on his parliamentary toes in 1794 as it suspended Habeas Corpus and brought in The Seditious Meetings Act (banning meetings of 50 or more) as well as The Treasonable Practices Act. As Watson subtly puts it: '*criticism of the constitution had carried* (Pitt) *to the Cabinet* (10 years before) *but now it would bear a poor wretch away to Botany Bay'.* [5] Even freedom of speech was clearly under attack.

However the Duke's expectations regarding hunting seem to have been dashed and a couple of months after going to Oakley, he was not enjoying his stay as he had hoped. The weather was exceptionally cold and icy but he had another problem, which if not worrying his doctor (Warren) was certainly worrying his wife; he was spitting blood and was experiencing pain in his heart and stomach. Writing to her mother (who was now returning to England) she told her that she was *'quite frightened and vexed about him'.*

The renewed closeness in her relationship with the Duke was continuing. He had asked her to oversee the work at Chiswick where dry rot in the new wings development had to be dealt with before making them habitable. She was expecting to spend some time there and living quarters were created for her in the servants' rooms. The main quarters in the Jacobean house had been demolished in 1788. The Duchess would have been glad about this, it not only kept her away from London, she would have relished the work.

The use of French style furnishings had been embraced at Chatsworth in 1782-83. These included furniture designed by Francois Hervé from mid-1782. The French carvers continued their work at Carlton House for the Prince of Wales, working under Henry Holland. Surviving French-style furniture at Chiswick is similar to the designs of Hervé. The payments for furniture there in early 1795 and early 1796, amounting to £4,740, would appear to suggest that it was ordered following the 1794 visit to Oakley, where the Duchess expressed her pleasure with the Louis XVI interior. Some of the Chiswick furniture was purchased and returned there following the Attic Sale at Chatsworth in 2010.

This additional responsibility given to the Duchess did not end with the work at Chiswick. In June 1794, the family went to stay at Chatsworth. The following month, the architect, John Carr, was invited to stay there while consulting with the Duchess over a new dairy. This interest in a new dairy may have come as a result of the Duchess – and maybe the Duke – taking the Duke of Bedford in mid-April to Althorp, then the home of her brother, George. He had been particularly interested in the library and the dairy. [6] *'I have been making some useful alterations'*, she wrote to her mother. The same letter includes a line or so which she deleted prior to ending it. The deleted words can however be still read: *'we shall have 4 excellent water closets which were badly wanted'.* However there would appear to have been one in existence in c. 1787 when Miss Lloyd, the socialite friend of the family, wrote to a friend stating that her room was *'near the Water Closet, so I am quite at my ease'.* For some reason the introduction of more water-flushed toilets was delayed, although it took another near three decades before they were installed in the Duke's hotels and inns at Buxton. [7]

The previous March, the Duchess was telling Thomas Coutts that alterations were planned for the gardens at Devonshire House too. [8] This was quite a change for the Duke, some twenty years after his marriage. She wrote: '*It* (the garden) *is much out of order as we propose some alterations*'. The Duke had learnt the value of involving his wife on such matters, especially as she was still spending much of her time at home, rather than socialising every night or at least many of them. More to the point, she was spending much of her time away from London, which may point to this being part of any conditions made by the Duke for her return to the family.

Above, it is mentioned that the Duke was contemplating redecorating Devonshire House in early 1794. Whether his wife was involved in this is not clear, but despite her reluctance to stay in London, it is likely that she rose to the challenge, but Oakley and Chatsworth may have delayed matters.

The Duke had also increased her allowance by another £700 a year. While staying at Billing House, Lord John's home, she and the Duke had slept together, which was not usual in those times, but does point to a growing closeness. A guide to Chatsworth dated 1793 mentions that the Duke and Duchess shared the same bedroom, albeit with their own bed. The house was regarded as being short of good bedrooms. Her letters do not reveal him agreeing to settle her debts. However, Thomas Coutts wrote to her in April 1795 advising that her account was £199 in the black. The Duke must either have paid it off, or at least taken the debt over. It may well have been the latter for the Duchess wrote to Coutts in January of that year asking him to give the Duke a little time to pay interest which was due, stating that the Duke would explain the reason '*shortly*'. A further, undated, letter the Duchess wrote to Coutts (considered to be early January 1795) stated: '*I think all may and will soon be settled*'. [9]

The Duke's reconciliation with his wife was mirrored with improved relations with the Cavendish family in general. They, no doubt, had been urged to do so by the Duke, especially the protectiveness of his sister, the Duchess of Portland. '*I am very good friends with the Dss of Portland*'; … '*I was glad you have seen the Dss of Portland and do not wonder at its giving you a headache*'. [10]

Oakley was convenient for the Duke with the Derbyshire Militia being camped at nearby Bedford. However his illness prevented him from reviewing his troops. It seems rather bizarre now that his son (then not quite four years old) substituted for him. '*Hartington has been reviewing the Derbyshire Militia now at Bedford – you cannot think how pretty it was to see his little figure in Regimentals, standing in the midst of the field – and taking off his hat as they saluted him – his little forelocks blowing about by the wind – of his own accord he desired to give the soldiers bread and cheese and ale*'. [11] This must have been his baptism in public duty.

Illness and Deaths, 1794

The Duke's discomfort had started after he had gone on a 20 mile/32km very fast horse ride at Oakley. Within the previous five years, he had been experiencing a shortage of breath. It generally lasted for about three weeks at a time but he was free of it when lying down. On occasions he also experienced shortage of breath associated with violent pain around the pit of his stomach which was controllable by medicine. However since that horse ride, every time he took a little more exercise than normal, he coughed up a small amount of blood (about a small teaspoonful) in the night or on waking up. Moreover he was experiencing pain which went from his chest through to his back.

Having put up with this through the summer and no doubt aware of his wife's agitated state of mind about it (like her mother, she could become very agitated with ill-health), despite Dr. Warren's lack of concern, the Duke asked Dr. Erasmus Darwin for his opinion in the following October. The doctor replied from nearby Derby that the blood was a symptom of gout or in those who had slight bilious or hepatic complaints, as in the Duke's case. He was advised to avoid violent exercise (no more long runs on horseback at speed) and too much food or wine at night. More uniformity in his hours of meals and the quantity of drink was recommended (not the amount, but keeping to a similar amount daily). [12]

The Duke may have been jolted into writing by the unexpected death of three members of his family. On 2nd May 1794, Lord George Augustus, the Duke's uncle died in his carriage whilst travelling from home, Holker Hall in Cumbria, to London. Towards the end of the same month, May 1794, the Duchess recorded that 'young Lord George' had 'lost a lovely child ten days ago of water on its head'. Infant mortality was significantly higher at this time compared to today.

The Cavendish family were buried at that time in the Cavendish vault at All Saints Church, Derby (now the cathedral), along with close family, such as the 2nd and 3rd Earls of Bessborough. The vault does not contain the remains of a child who died in 1794.

The Duchess's brother (Earl Spencer) and his wife, Lavinia, lost two infants: Richard, born 18/10/1789, died 20/1/1791, and Lady Harriet who died before her first birthday. Their daughter, Georgiana Charlotte, died on 21/2/1823 aged 28 years, eleven days after giving birth to a daughter, May, who died when two months old. Despite many women having a large number of births, death from puerperal fever contracted during birth was a continual danger. [13] The 2nd Earl Spencer became Lord Privy Seal for several months in 1794 before becoming First Sea Lord in December 1794, a position he held until February 1801. Lavinia apparently had strong opinions on political and other matters and by 1794 had grown very large and used a stick when walking. A generation earlier, Lady Spencer had lost a baby, Charlotte, in 1766, a year after her birth. [14]

It is not clear who the Duchess was referring to. *'Young Lord George'* indicates Lord George Cavendish but both *The Complete Peerage* and *Burke's Peerage* have no entry of a child dying in 1794. The same applies to her brother, George, (but she would not have referred to him in this manner in any event) and to Lord Bessborough.

If this was not enough, on 3ʳᵈ June, the Duke lost his sister, Dorothy, Duchess of Portland, aged 43 years. She died from an ovarian cyst, the size of a man's head, which was blocking the passage from her bowel. George Canning, the future Prime Minister wrote: *'…such virtues she had in as great a degree as perhaps she could have them without detracting from the femininity of her character. Mrs. Crewe (the society hostess) must be seriously afflicted, and most lastingly, be her loss, for she valued the Dss. of P., I think, beyond any person of her own sex in the world.'* (15)

Shortly after the funeral of his sister, the Duke took his family to Chatsworth. Calling in John Carr regarding the proposed dairy (see above) focussed minds on something new. The dairy would presumably have been in the two ground floor rooms either side of the large entrance lobby at the rear of the central block of the north wing extension to the main house, later removed by the 6ᵗʰ Duke. They are marked as 'Dairy' and 'Dairy Scullery' on a surviving plan. Perhaps trying to keep the children occupied as much as anything, on 1st July there was a fete with the milkmaids dancing *'on the green'* with a bigger event a few days later on the 12ᵗʰ for Little G's 11ᵗʰ birthday.

Children from the Duchess's Edensor school, including 11 specially clothed for the event, formed a procession carrying flags, garlands and nosegays (small posies of scented flowers). Accompanied by Morris Dancers, they all marched through the park and to the House garden to the Green House which was decorated with flowers *'and G's cipher in flowers and there they dined'*. Little G was presented with a basket of 11 little presents covered over with flowers. However the best treat was still to come. At a ball that night, the children were allowed to stop up until 1 a.m. It backfired as Little G was still *'languid'* as a result four days later. (16)

They knew that this visit would not be a long one, despite it probably being the Duchess's first visit to Chatsworth since late 1788. There is no intervening correspondence from there written by the Duchess and a lot of the time she was abroad. The minds of the family were focussed upon the expected arrival before too long of Lady Spencer and her daughter, Harriet, who was now enjoying better health.

Avoiding the French, they had arrived in the Austrian Netherlands (now Holland) by late July and proceeded to Helvoetsluis. However, bad weather kept them there until at least 12ᵗʰ August 1794. Earlier that month, the family returned to London, the children separately and at a slower rate. The Duchess then went on to Harwich for the reunion. The Duke had had no enthusiasm for Derby races and had the best of excuses to avoid them. The Countess's and Harriet's arrival helped to draw some measure of closure on sadness. [17]

Holidays

At the beginning of November 1794, the Duchess advised Thomas Coutts that her sister had gone to West Teignmouth in Devon and that she anticipated joining her a month later with the Duke. She certainly went there to join her sister but without the Duke, who arrived there in the last week of April 1795. The family then went off exploring the area together, eventually returning to London on 12th May. Despite enjoying these days out: *'we had a charming walk with Papa and Mama to all manner of places'*, ominously, the Duchess's bad headaches seem to have been unrelenting. [18]

However, they appear to have been staying at Stonehouse from Mid-April and from there the Duchess made visits to Saltram House at Plymouth, Ivybridge and Exeter: *'The Duke takes us out all day and we return so tired we seldom can write'*, she eventually informed her mother. A different diversion was a trip out to Eddystone Lighthouse where the Duke reached the building by climbing up 'perpendicular ladders over the sea'. [19]

After celebrating the Marquis's 5th birthday, the Duchess went to Chiswick once more. *'The house will be very pretty indeed'* suggests that it may not have been entirely furnished. The drawing room in the east wing was finished, including the hanging of paintings. It would seem that the Duchess had arranged the hanging, which was unusual in a male-dominated world at that time.

The successful trip to Devon saw a further trip to the seaside by the beginning of September 1795, this time taking accommodation at Bognor, the Duchess bathing in the sea shortly after her arrival. Her headaches were still a problem. A lucky escape occurred shortly before leaving for Bognor when the horse fell whilst pulling the Duchess and five children. The open carriage overturned but fortunately nobody was hurt. [20]

Shortly after their arrival, they all headed off to Goodwood again so that the Duke could shoot with the Duke of Richmond. The regime there was different than in the Devonshire household: *'The hours are terribly early and regular, dinner at 4'* (7 pm usually for the Devonshires) and *'supper*[at] *10' – the duke of R has always a great deal to show one; and as he is never tir'd of riding he makes one ride morning and eve'g: sometimes too there was chemistry of the eve'g'*.

They were persuaded by the Duke of Richmond to stay longer with some sailing in his yacht to Portsmouth. On another trip, there was a diversion into the South Downs part of the estate for a review of the Horse Artillery firing their cannons amidst the hills where the sound echoed back and forth. They all then drove to the Chichester River, down which they sailed for five miles to a bathing lodge, where they relaxed, riding around the grounds before dining and spending the night. All on a fine and a very hot day. In fact the good weather lasted the whole of September, with the holiday continuing until the third week of October when the Devonshires returned to London via various family houses and Bess returned to Goodwood.

The family appear to have gone to Chiswick for Christmas. A few days later (it isn't clear if they were still there), the Duke had a rude awakening from his slumbers on 7th January 1796. At 2 a.m. a message was received from the Prince of Wales requesting his presence at the impending birth of his child (a daughter). The Duke was obliged to go to Carlton House in formal dress and await the birth, to which, along with the Duke of Leeds, he would be a witness. However the birth did not occur until 10 a.m. whereupon he returned to his bed. Unfortunately, Princess Charlotte was to die during birth of her own child in 1817, owing to complications. [21]

14

Family Life, 1796-98

Relations with Lady Elizabeth Foster and Lady Jersey

As has been seen above (see 1788), the Duke's longing for Bess Foster had paled probably following her affair with the Duke of Richmond whilst abroad. Later in 1790, the Duchess had written to her mother to tell her that the Duke's view was that Bess stayed at the Duchess's pleasure [1]

In 1795, the Duke, Duchess and Bess had gone to stay at Goodwood, the home of the Richmonds, whilst on vacation at Bognor in Sussex. The 3rd Duke of Richmond was apparently effectively living separately from his wife, who, in any event, may have been in ill-health prior to her death on 5th November 1796. On leaving Bognor on 25th October 1795 to return to London, (the Duke appears to have already gone on ahead), the Duchess and Bess went via Roehampton to see Harriet, the Duchess's sister. From there, Bess returned to Goodwood.

She must have been confident that it would not jeopardise her position in the Devonshire household. It also points to the fact that she would have been unlikely to have gone there had her relationship with the Duke been a strong one. The very fact that she had gone there on her own would have done little to improve her image with some of Georgian Society. When the Duke had banished the Duchess to the Continent in 1791, he (at least initially) had not only stopped the Duchess's allowance, but Bess's too.

He was no doubt upset that the latter knew about the Duchess's affair with Grey and the pregnancy which had resulted from it. In April 1792, the Duke would not allow the Duchess to return home, if only for a month to see her children, although he gave Bess *'leave to do as she liked'*. [2] Foreman, quoting comment at the time, also confirms that the Duke was *'now less smitten'* with Bess. Bess did not return to London until January 1796. On the 20th March 1798, Bess Foster received a letter from her father, the Earl of Bristol. He wrote: *'As to the Duke of Richmond, I do not suppose he has any interest, else he could refuse you nothing'*. [3]

Previous writers have suggested that the two women had a relationship which was closer than their individual relationship with the Duke. Here we see why Bess had the need for a close relationship with the Duchess: her continuing stay within the Devonshire fold relied upon it. Moreover, after the Duchess returned from Italy in 1793, her relationship with the Duke grew mutually stronger. Her position as the leading socialite was forsaken. As she said to her mother '*I have become a retired person*'. [4] She avoided staying at Devonshire House, both the Duke and his wife preferring Chiswick, which was no doubt smaller, cosier and quieter. As has been noted above, even Chatsworth was forsaken for several years, at least by the Duchess.

In part, the quieter life adopted by the Duchess may have been influenced by the resumption of her many and often severe headaches. There was also another aspect to all this: they had a growing family of three children, who took an increasing part of family life. The Duchess had been stung by her absence from her children. Hartington did not know who she was at all. By the time she was 13 years old (in 1796), Little G was accompanying her parents to balls (and possibly Haryo too). It is also clear that at least Little G was spending much time with her father as well as her mother (the latter even as a teacher) and this too probably extended to the younger sister. On one occasion Little G stayed up with her father to well after supper time while her mother was at the opera. [5] The parents were getting older and family life took on increasing importance for both of them.

In the immediate years after the Duke's marriage, Lord and Lady Jersey were regular guests at social occasions organised by the Duke and Duchess. Following the Duke's very public affair with Lady Jersey in 1778 at Coxheath Military Camp, the Duchess was initially stoical about her on-going relationship with one who had been a close friend. Eventually, the Duchess found it difficult to continue that closeness and the Jerseys seem to have been on fewer guest lists.

Lady Jersey had however begun a relationship with the Prince of Wales. In 1794 she was one of his Ladies in Waiting along with Lady Cholmondeley and Lady Caernarvon. In the position of the Prince's Master of the Household was Lord Jersey. Both Lord and Lady Jersey seem to have been throwing their weight around (at least in the perception of the Duchess and her mother). Lady Jersey had accompanied the Princess when she came to England to be introduced to the Prince as his future bride, despite his well-known lack of enthusiasm for it. [6]

Eventually the tide of public opinion turned against the Jerseys. Lady Spencer wrote to the Duchess to remind her that it was Lady Jersey who had 'dropped' both the former and her sister Harriet. [7] However it appears that the Duchess had kept and continued to keep her contacts. A children's ball had been organised for early April 1796 at Devonshire House. Two of the Jersey children had been invited and were expected. However they had caught chicken pox and would therefore not be going. Lady Georgiana Cavendish (Little G) wrote to Selina Trimmer to say that Lady Jersey *'looked very handsome'* [8] when the bad news was passed to the Duchess.

A Martyr to Adversity: a Brush with Death

At the beginning of April 1795, the Duchess was experiencing problems with her eyesight and a month later, bad headaches. She had been a migraine sufferer for much of her adult life but before long her complaint developed into something much worse. [9]

The series of headaches continued into the following year, although at the beginning of April she appears to have been 'quite well', hosting a supper after going to the opera. [10] By early summer her eyesight deteriorated and she wrote to Thomas Coutts: …*'I make use of a person who is in habits of writing for my sister as my eyes do not permit my writing so much'*. The envelope is endorsed in small print: *'excuse the writing my eyes are so bad"*. [11] In June, she wrote of her *'vile head'*. [12]

During mid-July 1796, the Duchess was proposing to take her children to Worthing to join her mother who was already there. The Duchess was expecting to join her for three weeks ahead of going to Chatsworth for the Derby races. The problem with her eyes may have been initially the result of an inflammation. [13] It is now believed that the Duchess was suffering from C.S.T. (Cavernous Sinus Thrombosis). It used to cause thrombosis of the jugular veins if the patient had not already died of septicaemia first. In view of the Duchess's *'survival against long odds, it* (C.S.T) *must have been of the non-infective variety'*. The disease has disappeared thanks to antibiotics. [14]

The vacation to Worthing was cancelled as the inflammation worsened and the Duchess's right eye swelled in size to the size of a fist. (To be more precise, perhaps a lady's fist as the description was that of Lady Spencer). Dr. Warren, the family's usual doctor, was called in and he consulted John G. Gunning, Surgeon to St. George's Hospital and Senior Surgeon-Extraordinary to the King, together with two others, including J. W. Phipps, who later treated the King for a cataract in 1805. Despite their combined expertise, the treatment seems to have been pretty desperate. To increase the blood flow to the head (to counter-act the inflammation) they squeezed her neck, almost strangling her in the process. Laudanum, as usual, gave some relief. Horace Walpole, in letter to Miss Mary Berry on 9th August, wrote: *'They have saved her eyes by almost strangling her with a handkerchief and forcing all the blood into her head, and then bleeding her with leeches'*. [15]

The Duke summoned his mother-in-law on 1st August 1796. At that time it was unclear whether the Duchess would lose her eyesight, the Duke warning that if she did, it would *'much alter the outward appearance of it'*. [16] Horrified,

Lady Spencer sped as fast as the horses could get her to Devonshire House where she remained for nearly two weeks before going to Holywell.

On 4th August she (Lady Spencer) wrote to Selina Trimmer, telling her of the Duchess's conditions. It is the only account of what she was suffering to survive: '*Every attempt was made to lower this inflammation so as to prevent any ulceration but this has been in vain, a small ulcer has formed on top of the cornea and has burst and as far as that reaches the injury is not to be recovered – if the inflammation should increase, the ulcer form again, and again burst, it would destroy the whole substance of the eye, which would then sink. But the inflammation is so much abated, the eye so much less swelled and the discharge so much diminished, that there is the greatest reason to hope that it will in some degree recover an imperfect sight and a very tolerable appearance. The eyelids are still much swelled and scarred with the leeches and the little opening between them is always filled with a thick white matter. The eye itself to those who see it, (for I cannot), is still more horrible ...*'. The Duchess was very lucky to survive. In a life in which she seems to have been a martyr to adversity, here she fortunately beat the odds. She lost some of her sight and her left eyelid drooped a little. Apparently she considered using an eye patch but did not pursue the idea.

During her illness she was also supported by Bess Foster, who presumably came back from Worthing with Lady Spencer. The children remained with Selina Trimmer at Worthing. On the 4th, the surgeons were hoping that the worst might be over and on the 6th, the Duchess got up from her bed for dinner (of boiled or roast chicken and artichoke). Continuing to see the better side of Bess Foster, Lady Spencer wrote to Selina to say that '*Lady Eliz is a most tender nurse*'. [17]

In November 1798, Louisa Ponsonby (a relative of the Duchess) was staying at Chatsworth. She wrote: '*...the Duchess looks amazing handsome when she is dressed. Notwithstanding her eye which I fear quite gone. It disfigures her less than one coud (sic) have conceived possible but still it is a sad thing; I never saw any more patiens* (patience) *as she is about it*'. Much has been repeated concerning the loss of sight in the Duchess's right eye. Indeed, the comments above are clear in their indication that the Duchess had lost the sight in that eye. The reality would appear to be different however. The Duchess makes it clear that some sight remained: '*I owe him all the sight remaining of my unfortunate eye.*' [18] Joseph Farrington confirmed in 1799 that as a result of this illness, the Duchess was blind in the eye affected. She wore a curl of hair over it. [19]

From Holywell, Lady Spencer started sending carp, helping to maintain a diet of lighter food. Writing to her daughter, Harriet, who was still at Devonshire House, she warned of the impending arrival: '*I shall send a carp to Town by tomorrows coach, so if it does not arrive at Dev. House by 12 o'clock they had better send to the Green Man and still in Oxford Street for it*'. [20] She (the

Duchess) received splendid news on 25th August 1796. She was tolerably free from pain by then, had more use of her eye and less inflammation.

She had been cheered by her brother, being very proud of his position as First Sea Lord who had called with good news. Almost all the merchant fleets had arrived home safe in convoys protected by the Navy. One had consisted of 290 ships laden with corn and naval stores (with the escort ships, what a sight that must have been). Another convoy of 170 vessels had come in from the West Indies with yet a further one from the Leeward Islands (possibly Antigua, where the North Leeward Islands fleet had a base) laden with sugar and other cargo while two other convoys had arrived from the Mediterranean. The feel-good factor was marred by a dose of laudanum *'which has made her stupid'* wrote her mother. [21]

Much has been repeated concerning the loss of sight in the Duchess's right eye. Indeed, the comments above are clear in their indication that the she had lost the sight in that eye. The reality would appear to be different, however. On 15th September 1801, she wrote a letter to Thomas Coutts. She was writing an important letter to him relating to a plan to pay off her debts. She wrote: *'My eyes are still weak but I cannot trust this to my little writer, who however, is one of the best little men, brought up in the village of Chatsworth, but by deformity from a fall when young, oblig'd to support himself by sedentary labour … I owe him all my sight remaining of my unfortunate eye'*

Not for the first time, she writes a letter where she states something contrary to what she has already written, for she goes on to add (concerning an occulist to whom she owes £400): *'I owe him all the sight remaining of my unfortunate eye, but I owe him the greatest gratitude for his uncommon generous attachment and the highest esteem for his good qualities'*. [22] The common feature here is that she is telling Coutts that some degree of sight remained in her eye. For clarity, the affected eye was what we would now call the left eye. See page 8 of the illustrations.

By mid-September, the children were back from Worthing and the family went to Chiswick, including Lady Spencer who wrote: *'This place is very delightful'*. [23] Making good use of the completed wings, several family visits there were made during the rest of the year. The previous January, Selina Trimmer described it as being: *'The complete happiness of my life, not only on my own account, but for the great good it does the dear children'*. [24] The Duke's redevelopment of the site around the Italianate villa was clearly regarded as a success.

In mid-August, the children had gone out walking on the South Downs. In a letter to Lady Spencer, her grandmother, just prior to her 11th birthday, Harriet mentioned seeing *'many traps for the wheatears'*. She also mentioned making a batter pudding with the flour she had got at Heydown Hill (now High Down Hill where there was a windmill). Maybe this is the area where the bird traps had been placed.

Prior to the Duchess's illness, Lady Spencer had hired houses at Worthing for herself and for the Duchess. It was a popular venue for nearby were the Prince of Wales, Duke of Marlborough (related to Lady Spencer through her marriage), Lord and Lady Jersey and others. With their holiday unexpectedly interrupted, they were to return to Sussex the following year. For one reason or another, the delights of Chatsworth were being neglected, although perhaps not by the Duke and his shooting companions, for he certainly went there in 1797 (prior to mid-August) when he moved on to Bolton Abbey in Yorkshire. In November, 1796, Augustus Clifford entered Harrow School, leaving in 1799. [25]

At the end of 1796, the Duke took his family to Chiswick for Christmas, but it was marred by the death of Lord John Cavendish on 18th December. Lady Spencer went to North Creek, Burnham in Norfolk, to be with her brother, Charles Poyntz. [26] Much more time was being spent at Chiswick rather than Devonshire House and this continued. In early 1797 when at least the Duchess found she had to leave there, the children remained behind. By the end of January, Dr. Croft surprised the Duchess by telling her that she had miscarried, despite her quieter lifestyle. Early in February, Lady Spencer wrote to her daughter to remind her of plans made the previous year for change in the garden and to send for Samuel Lapidge. Maybe he was otherwise engaged for the work was not done until later that year (see below). [27]

It is not clear how quickly the Duchess returned to her usual pace following the illness in 1796. An undated letter of 1797 refers to the return of headaches, but she was back in the swing of things by May, when she wrote to the Royal Academy asking if she could see the exhibition on Sunday 28th May. An excuse had been made to resist this, but her sister intervened on the Duchess's behalf and the R.A. Council agreed to it. She went the following Sunday with a party of sixteen people, including her sister and Lord Bessborough together with Bess Foster. [28]

A bombshell landed in the lap of John Heaton in June 1797 with the discovery that his son-in-law, a Mr. Ellis, had *gone off forever* leaving behind his wife, 7 children and debts in excess of £30,000. [29]

The family went to Bognor for the summer months, spending some time with the Duke of Richmond at Goodwood. His wife had died late in 1796. Presumably Bess Foster was there too, with a clear field as a result. The Duke remained behind, or at least had his eye on the annual trip to Chatsworth for the shooting and the races. He was not in Bognor at the end of July when seven year old Hartington wrote to him about his watch. He had heard of a proposed watch tax: '[I] do not know what to do about mine – I have not got any money and cannot pay it myself. I shall be very much obliged to you if you will pay it for me if not I must give my watch away. I care not much about it but all I know the matter is that I cannot pay taxes without money. Pray answer my letter soon'. [30] That would have produced a wry smile. The Bognor trip cost £1,411. [31]

Illness prevented the Duke's trip to Chatsworth (and maybe a planned stay at Bognor/Goodwood). He was much better by early August and had a few days at Chatsworth, going to Bolton Abbey on 11th August. [32] With his departure, the Duchess went to Chiswick: '*I had so much to do about the house and the garden and the dairy*'. [33] It will be recalled (above) that she had been interested in her brother's new dairy at Althorp and had refurbished the Chatsworth dairy as a result. Now she had Chiswick's dairy in her sights.

From the Duke's point of view, all this work about the houses his wife was engaged on presumably met with much approval and kept her from the distraction of dissipation, as her mother would have put it. Nonetheless it continued to be very much an activity usually undertaken by men, not their wives. Women ran the household and that was usually the limit of it.

In November 1797 the family had gone to Hardwick for Christmas. During the last two weeks of December, the gallery there was re-hung with paintings sent up from London, including four packing cases full which arrived on the 29th. They were mainly paintings of children with animals (plus some tapestries). [34]

Also just prior to Christmas, the parish church for Hardwick, Auld Hucknall, four miles away was '*fitted up*'. It has a Cavendish Chapel, which may have been in need of repair. Was this another project of the Duchess? Both this and the hanging of the gallery paintings following on from the hanging at Chiswick may be pointers to the Duchess keeping herself busy sooner than might have been expected after her illness.

On 14th November 1797, the servants had a dance in the hall at Hardwick '*in honour of my cousin's birthday*'. A 94-year old woman at the dance remarked that this was the first one to be held there since the 3rd Duke's days (i.e. since before 1755). [35] Early in December, Hartington had a feverish cold and had become very deaf as a result. It was an affliction he suffered as an adult and one wonders if this could have been the beginning of it.

There was such a gathering there – Lady Spencer arrived on 2nd December with Ann Scafe (and a parcel of brown trout caught at Holywell). Lord George Henry was there with his large family, but the intention was that only his two oldest children stayed for Christmas. Perhaps this was just as well as a Ball was held there on 16th December with more than 15 couples attending. The house was so full that the Duke's daughters had to sleep in their grandmother's room.

An example of the Duke's humour surfaced when he dictated a letter to Caroline Ponsonby, which made Haryo laugh: it was a '*history of all the animals in this house*'. The one person missing was Bess Foster who was at Goodwood with the Duke of Richmond.

During the stay at Hardwick, 34 sheep and 7 oxen were slaughtered and sent from Chatsworth together with 30 loads of flour. The meat weighed 3 tons 7 cwt. [36]

This lovely portrait was painted by Sir Joshua Reynolds, c. 1775 – 76. Following her marriage in 1774, the Duchess soon influenced fashionable society. Married to one of the richest men in the country and with a most engaging personality, she became a phenomenon. Portrayed here with ostrich feathers of moderate length, she was soon leading a fashion of much longer feathers up to 4ft/1.3m long, until the Queen banned them from her Palace assemblies. It is perhaps one of Reynold's most sensitive portraits, bringing to life the enigmatic and captivating personality of one of Georgian England's beauties

The vibrancy of the Duchess was captured by the young artist
Richard Cosway in 1786

The 5th Duke of Devonshire, painted in 1768 by Pompeo Batoni. The Duke was then 19 years old and in Italy on his Grand Tour

Left: Portrait of the Marquis of Hartington by Sir Martin Archer Shee

Bottom Left: Lady Georgiana Cavendish, painted by Elizabeth Royal, copying John Russell's painting of 1790

Bottom Right: Lady Harriet, Georgiana's younger sister, also by Royal

This painting of Lady Elizabeth Foster by Reynolds was commissioned by the Duke in 1787, following Bess's return from Continental travels and the birth of Caroline St Jules. The island on the bottom right corner may portray one of those visible from Vietri, near Salerno, where the birth took place in 1785. The painting was probably given to Bess by the Duke, who was passionately in love with her at the time. His passion faded when she embraced other lovers, although he married her in 1809

The Duchess's mother Lady Spencer who was painted by Thomas Gainsborough in 1780-81. She tried to maintain a steadying influence on her daughters, often without much success. Her husband squandered much of the family fortune and the Duchess inherited his inability to control expenditure

Above: Sir Augustus William James Clifford, the 5th Duke's illegitimate son by Bess Foster, born in 1788 in Rouen, Normandy. His half – brother, the 6th Duke, then Lord Chamberlain, appointed him to the position of Black Rod in the new Parliament in 1832. He died in office in 1877, the second longest holder of the office since Medieval times. Engraving by William Giller after Frederick Richard

Left: Caroline St Jules, the Duke's illegitimate daughter by Bess, as a young girl. The painter of this miniature is unknown, but the date is probably after she came to England in August 1790, aged six

Caroline Ponsonby, the niece of the Duchess, painted by Thomas Phillips. She was schooled at Devonshire House. On 3rd June 1805, she married William Lamb, later Lord Melbourne, who became the Prime Minister around the same time as Augustus Clifford became Black Rod. Known as Caro, she had a very public, but short lived, affair with Lord Byron

Possibly the last known image of the Duchess, painted by Henry Edridge, c.1800 – 1805. The artist has avoided painting her left eye, leading to the conclusion that this is her damaged eye. The Duchess is wearing a turban and portrays her preference for white muslin dresses

Thomas Hardy also painted this portrait of the Duchess's oldest daughter, Georgiana, when she was five years old. She was known as Little G in the family and later as G as an adult. Under the 6th Duke, when he was abroad, G was entrusted with the houses, allowing family and guests to stay and even recuperate in them

Opposite page: The Duke and Duchess supported young artists. These included Richard Cosway, see his painting of the Duchess p.2. The Duke paid for a scholarship to the Royal Academy for two of the sons of one of his miners, Thomas and William Hardy. Thomas restored Laguerre's Painted Hall ceiling at Chatsworth in 1783 after a joist failed and came through it. He also did restoration work in the Chapel. At the time, he had only completed four years of a six-year scholarship

The west front of Chatsworth, familiar to the Duchess. It was drawn by Sir Francis Chantrey in c. 1818. The trees hide the domestic offices replaced by the 6th Duke with the current North wing. See below

The Kitchen Annexe, as it was known, occupying much of the site of the current North Wing. This is taken from measurements made in 1818 by Jeffry Wyatt. Some assumptions have been necessary, but the basic detail is largely correct. At the left, northern, end a curtain wall curved around to meet the lodge. At the right end, the building reached the main house at the east (rear) side of the bow in the North Front. The front of the bow is indicated where the line of the eaves ends. Above the columns of the middle building was a balustrade.

The left hand building was a stable block with a poultry yard separating it from the Steward's Offices and some bedrooms on the first floor with a dairy and other domestic offices on the ground floor. The right hand building housed the Kitchen, with a coal yard between it and the Steward's Offices. Right of the Kitchen were a corridor to the main house and the Servants' Dining Room.

Hardwick Hall, to the east of Chatsworth, built by the Duke's ancestor, Bess of Hardwick, eight generations preceding the 5th Duke

Devonshire House, Piccadilly, London, from Green Park, one of the finest houses in the capital, although the exterior was drab looking. Taken from Thornbury's *Old and New London*, 1873 – 74 and altered to give more accuracy, except for the external double staircase to the first floor entrance, which is not shown

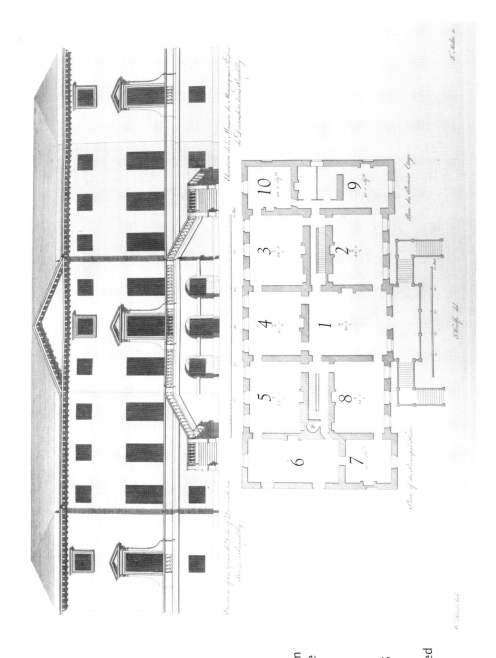

Devonshire House in
1767 from *Vertruvius
Britannicus* showing the
Entrance Front and a plan
of the formal rooms. The
rooms were:
1 The Saloon;
2 The Dining Room;
3 Drawing Room;
4 Middle Drawing Room;
5 Drawing Room;
6 Library;
7 Room later incorporated
in Room 8; Ballroom;
9 Ante Room;
10 Duchess's Room

Burlington House, Chiswick, painted by Jacques Rigaud. This portrays the Jacobean house and the 3rd Earl of Burlington's Palladian villa. The latter was built in the 1730s to house the Earl's art collection. The house to the right was owned by a neighbour, Lady Mary Coke. The 6th Duke bought it for £7,050 on 12th June 1812 and demolished it

The Earl's grandson, the 5th Duke of Devonshire, added two wings from 1788 probably designed by John White. It was not ready to receive its Anglo-French furniture until 1794-95

One of the fronts of Burlington House, Piccadilly, London. Occupied for many years by the Duke's sister the Duchess of Portland and her husband. It was sold in 1815 by the 6th Duke to his uncle, Lord George Cavendish, for £70,000

Spencer House, St James's Place, today, viewed from Green Park. Built by 1st Earl Spencer, the Duchess's father, it remains arguably the finest neo-Classical house in London. Unfortunately, it is now hemmed in by more recent development, but retains its exquisite interior. It is open at certain times to the public

Edensor village as the Duke and Duchess would have known it. In the middle is the Duchess's Charity School overlooked by the church. She opened the school to commemorate the birth of her oldest daughter, Georgiana. Both buildings have now gone, the church being replaced in 1868

Edensor village in the days of the 5th Duke and Duchess, showing the many properties they also knew and which were demolished by their son, the 6th Duke. This plan of 1785 also shows the outline of the current roads for identification purposes

The site of Devonshire House today. The building on the left is the current Devonshire House. Underneath it is Green Park tube station but it is not in the cellars of the old house, which were further away from Piccadilly. The building on the right is The Ritz Hotel

The former gates to Devonshire House, Piccadilly were moved across the street to the end of Broadwalk, which crosses the Green Park to the Canada Gates and Buckingham Palace. They are now called the Devonshire Gates

Brooks's Club, St James's Street, where the Duke spent many hours, but perhaps rather less than is often claimed

Marlborough Buildings, the street adjacent to The Crescent, Bath, where the Duke discovered that the Duchess was pregnant with Charles Grey's child in 1791

The Hanover Street Church, Mayfair, London where the Marquis of Hartington was christened on 21st May 1791

Two examples of the collection of Anglo-French furniture at Chatsworth delivered in 1783. Both are attributed to Francois Hervé. Top: A giltwood confidante. Bottom: A pair of Marquises and footstools

Buxton Crescent, which opened for business in 1786. It is arguably Britain's first purpose built inland holiday resort

The Square, Buxton, up-market residential accommodation funded from copper mine revenues, with its collanade. It was built next to the Bath in 1806. It is not a square building however. A neighbour would not sell the land necessary to make it a square!

The Hall Hotel, Buxton, which opened for business in 1572. An early guest was Mary, Queen of Scots. The Duke and Duchess stayed here when they came to take the water and use the mineral bath prior to the opening of The Crescent

St John's Church, Buxton, which was probably built as a memorial to the Duchess. It opened in 1812 and Pevsner's Buildings of England states that the tower had no equal at the time. The date stone shows 1811, but the roof was incomplete at the end of that year

The Palladian villa at Chiswick House today

The neo-Classical bridge built by the Duke in 1774. The Duke initiated a number of schemes in years when there was a significant anniversary. He was married in 1774. Supporting the view that this happened here are the four pedestals at the end of the walls either side of the bridge. In a large oval on each of the three visible sides of each pedestal are 12 acorns

15

1798-1800

Diversions, 1798

1798 saw a ramping up of unrest in Ireland. It had followed much unrest in the previous couple of years fuelled by an anticipated invasion by the French. Some 1,400 French troops had landed in Cardigan Bay on 22nd February 1797, but soon surrendered at Fishguard to Lord Cawdor and the Castlemain Yeomanry, supported by local volunteers armed with scythes and pitchforks. A more significant force had landed in Bantry Bay in Ireland the year later but a pincer movement by British troops had defeated them before the Irish could rise in support. Nine French ships full of troops had been engaged by Sir John Borlase Warren and five had been taken on 12th October 1798. Had all these extra troops landed, a more difficult position would have faced the British forces.

However a general rebellion of the United Irishmen had already erupted with much civil unrest followed by open warfare in 1798, with the British army meting out significant retribution, especially at the Battle of Vinegar Hill, not far from the Devonshire estate. The Duke's lands remained untouched owing to his policy of alleviating poverty and his political stance supporting Catholic emancipation. Effective French support for the Irish however needed naval supremacy and by 1798, under the direction of the Duchess's brother as First Sea Lord, and the brilliance of the Royal Navy's commanders – Howe, Jervis and Nelson etc– the Royal Navy had the upper hand.

One of Earl Spencer's first initiatives following his appointment as First Sea Lord in 1794 was to increase the size of the Navy by 15,000 men. Five thousand were to be recruited from the merchant service and another ten thousand raised from the parishes of England and Wales. [1] This formula was already used to raise men for the Militia.

In February 1797, Sir John Jervis had captured four Spanish ships of the line at Cape St. Vincent and the Dutch had lost 15 ships at Camperdown off Texel on 11th October 1797. However at the beginning of 1798, the French still controlled the Mediterranean Sea. H.M.S. Lion had captured a further Spanish ship off Cartagena in July 1798 and Nelson was sent to blockade the French fleet at Toulon. However it had left port and Nelson chased it to Egypt. The Duchess was very proud of her brother and regularly went to the Admiralty to see him and pick up the latest news. The French had disembarked a 40,000 invasion army with designs of drawing British forces to protect India and thereby reducing capability nearer home. Seventeen French ships of the line and frigates were anchored off Alexandria at Aboukir Bay. In a pincer movement, Nelson destroyed four, captured nine with four escaping, leaving troops trapped between (British) ships and sand. It became known as the Battle of the Nile.

Earl Spencer's reorganisation and strengthening of the Navy was paramount in giving the Navy the opportunity of asserting itself, culminating in the Battle of Trafalgar in 1805. Pressures in Ireland eased resulting from more tolerance, the Act of Union in 1800 (enacted 1st January 1801) and eventually Catholic emancipation – plus Earl Spencer's stronger Royal Navy keeping the French at bay. It would be naïve to suggest that these solutions solved the problems of Ireland but they were part of the beginning of an endeavour to provide a solution.

The Duchess sent Nelson china on two occasions via her brother. On the day of Little G's marriage, 21st March 1801, British forces engaged the French army at the Battle of Alexandra. Although outnumbered 3:2, the British were victorious, which led to the surrender of the French garrison at Alexandra on 2nd September 1801. This of course followed on from the naval battle at nearby Aboukir Bay in 1798.

Coping with Sickness

In 1797 the Duke's trip to Chatsworth for the local races was reduced to a few days because of illness. In 1798 he missed it altogether with a complaint in his bowels. [2] However he was able to go at the beginning of September and the family stayed there until just prior to Christmas. For more detail on this trip, together with a description of the food they consumed etc, see Chapter 24. A month after they arrived, the Duke was described as being *very lame and when he is getting well again, he relapses into the gout, we got him however on horseback yesterday*. [3] Guests included the Duchess's sister Harriet and her family. Lady Spencer was conspicuous by her absence.

At an unknown date, but probably c. the end of August, prior to the trip to Chatsworth, Haryo went to Astley's Circus in London, describing her attire in a letter to her sister: *'It was a chip hat with a wreath of grapes, which looks very small and pretty, a white gown, gold chain and my Lilack cross. Lady Liz (Bess Foster) went with us of course and mama staid with papa'.*

It seems probable that having returned to London, the family spent Christmas at Chiswick and were still there in January. Around the beginning of April 1799, the Duchess took the girls to visit *'old Mrs. Grey and little Elizza* (sic)'. [4] The Duke's on-going problem with gout had returned and he was very lame and uncomfortable. Early in May, the Duchess consulted Sir Walter Farquhar, Physician in Ordinary to the Prince of Wales, about Little G who had developed a *'yellowness and languor'* from biliousness. He recommended that she went to Cheltenham – a place the Duke loathed. That meant the Duchess or maybe her mother going instead – but not immediately, the former regarded the place too damp even in June.

The Duchess had her own reasons for not wishing to leave Chiswick. She had developed a deep fascination with mineralogy when in Switzerland in 1792. Her friend, White Watson, an early geologist/mineralogist from Bakewell, the town close to Chatsworth, was spending nine weeks arranging her mineral collection at Chiswick. The Duchess had pain in her eye and had had the *'vessels of my eye blooded'* to relieve it. [5] In 1798, she had complained of having been in pain for two days and one wonders if this was the same complaint. She was feeling pleased with herself nonetheless as the Duke of Bedford had a problem he wanted her to sort out for him and he was clearly going to pay her for it. His postillion (coachman) had run over a man who was seeking compensation. He wanted the Duchess to assess what was justified (and basically was the man telling the truth). [6]

At the beginning of July 1798, Hartington started his school life at Harrow. A month later he was home again as the school holidays began. He seems to have settled in well and quickly too. There is an indication that upon such occasions a coach was sent to collect him. The Duchess, writing to her mother in October 1798, said he *'is the delight of his Father'*, which must relate to something favourable emanating from Harrow. [7] With the completion of work at Chiswick, the family took to using it regularly and at the expense of Chatsworth. Other than using it on the way to Castle Howard, it appears to have been hardly used at all. In fact no note of the Duchess staying there after the 1801-02 Christmas visit has been seen and it was October 1810 before the Duke went again.

The thought of being able to go away with Little G to Cheltenham must have been a compelling one for Lady Spencer and they set off on 11th July 1799. She had relished her time with her Devonshire grand daughters in 1789-90, when the Duke and Duchess were abroad. They stopped off at Windsor, where Lady Spencer wanted to look up a friend, Lady Finiss. While there, a knock at the door revealed the Queen and her five daughters wanting to join the conversation.

It was an event the Queen recalled at Little G's later Court Presentation. (Lady Finiss was one of five daughters of Thomas, 1st Earl Pomfret and Governess to the Princesses). [8] From there, their coach rumbled on to Cheltenham via Oxford, where they found a *'good inn'* for the night. The Duchess had written to her mother that day, coincidentally, reflecting on how she thought Little G would conduct herself: *'She has an elegance* (sic) *of taste in her mind that makes her, young as she is* (she was 16 years old the next day), *capable of appreciating all the superior charm of your society'.* [9]

From the Duchess's point of view, the meeting was useful, for her mind was focussing on the upcoming Presentation in 1800: *'it is pleasant in itself and is an opening to the only thing I want from their Majesties – the giving some mark of civility to my child when she comes out'.* That was going to keep her guessing for another year. They returned five weeks later with much commotion at Devonshire House. Bess Foster had been given a dose of laudanum by mistake (and would have been insensible until it wore off) and a maid was having spasms, *'and her screams were heard far and near'.* [10]

Shortly after grandmother and grand-daughter returned from Cheltenham, Hartington became unwell. Forever cautious (perhaps even over-sensitive) where illness was concerned, the Duchess rented a house in Margate and despatched him there with his *'Lizzy'*, Bess Foster, early in September. She set out herself nearly two weeks later, staying overnight in *'a very good inn'* at Rochester. She reached Margate the next day in time for a late dinner at the Cock Inn. After Hartington's second dip in the sea, she wrote to her mother to say he was 'visibly mended'. Whilst there, the Duchess was also ill, but they returned, presumably all recovered in November 1799. The Devonshire House accountant met the account for the trip. It was £993. 8s. 2d. [11]

The Duchess had gone down with a bowel complaint, while Hartington had a stomach problem, although she felt it had been picked up from his eating hot bread on a dry blanket on damp ground. But then *'I am always fretting about him … he is dearer to me than I can confess',* she wrote to her mother, adding a note that his schooling would have to wait. [12]

There was no apparent problem about the Duke, which must have been something of a relief. For quite some time in the early part of the year he had been laid low, was depressed with it and in need of the Duchess's attention. The nature of the complaint was not disclosed, but it came back twice. Probably it was gout or his stomach complaint.

Little G's Court Presentation and Birthday Ball

The Duchess was preoccupied by her daughter's Court presentation for at least a month and it had been in her mind for some time. In fact it had been at the back of her mind since at least July 1799. [13] The event appears to have been held on 22nd May 1800 (or the day before).

Little G's dress was of white crepe, trimmed with *'blond and silk cords and tassels'*. She wore a diamond necklace and earrings with a large chain of diamonds on her hair, the latter also augmented by three white feathers, perhaps symbolic of the family friendship with the Prince of Wales. Her day got underway with introductions at Devonshire House, starting with *'the maids and there* (sic) *friends and she behaved so kindly and so gracefully that several of the old women cried for joy'*. The servants' hall was crowded with staff and family friends.

Both Little G and her mother went off to the Palace by chair, the former's with four footmen and her mother's with two, and via St. James Street. Once at the Palace, the Duchess of Marlborough and Lady C. Beauclerk (Spencer family relatives) escorted her around. She had clearly been groomed in her deportment and it caused comment relating to her elegance. Even the King and Queen were delighted to see her, the King reflecting on where the time had gone since Lady Spencer had been married and here he was talking to her granddaughter, nearly 45 years' later.

The event did the Duchess good too, Haryo noting that she and her sister-in-law, Lavinia, had gone to the opera that night and *'mama looked better than I ever saw her today and is very happy'*. [14] Little G had not only caught the eye of the King: she had turned the head of both Lord Morpeth and the Duke of Bedford.

Lord Morpeth's name started cropping up as a dancing partner, although both he and the Duke of Bedford were initially shy at making an approach in case they were rejected. Bedford was almost 35 years old and Little G did not like him when she stayed at Oakley in 1794 (see above). On the other hand, George Howard (Lord Morpeth) was closer to home. His grandfather (the 4th Earl of Carlisle) had married Lady Frances Spencer and his father (the 5th Earl) had married Lady Margaret Leveson-Gower. She was the sister of Granville Leveson-Gower.

Therefore Lord Morpeth's uncle, Granville, was known to Little G. He was having a long affair with her aunt, the Duchess's sister, Harriet, and later had a child by her in 1801 and another in 1804. This relationship became even closer and stranger, for Granville went on to marry Little G's younger sister, Haryo (see Chapter 23, Affairs and Mistresses). The bizarre nature of Little G's relationship with Granville was that on his marriage to her sister, in 1809, Little G's husband's uncle became her brother-in-law. George was younger than the Duke of Bedford by eight years and was 27 years old. George Howard was educated at Eton and Christ Church, Oxford. He, like the Duke, had an honorary Doctor of Civil Law degree from Oxford University (awarded in 1799). In 1825 he became 6th Earl of Carlisle. Their house was Castle Howard,

Yorkshire and her marriage to George Howard was not to be long delayed; it was on 21st March 1801.

In the meantime, Little G's 17th birthday was coming up and the Duchess, with her usual over-the-top style, was organising a party. However there was more to it than just her own ball. The Duchess had re-engaged her social life, presenting Little G. Within a few days of the latter's coming out, the Duchess wrote to her mother: 'I am very busy in my new life and it does pretty well with me – she is so adored – it is said that they are glad that at least a civil Duke's daughter is come out – this is a little cut at the Bentincks' (and another family, name not clear). At home, there were balls coming up to celebrate the Duchess's birthday, another for Little G's birthday, and then one at the Duchess of Gordon's and yet another given by Lady Louisa Manners. All with a new dress for Little G; whether there was an inference of 'me too' was not recorded. [15]

The Duchess's party was on 11th June and at Devonshire House. The children (and some of their friends) had made 1,100 artificial roses, the organisation and decoration being done by the Duchess, helped by Louis Vigoureaux (recently retired on £150 p.a. pension). There were two sittings for dinner, with places for 400 at each sitting. Mindful of the expense, she was hoping the cost would be around £400, although much had been supplied from Chiswick and at a saving. Here was another example of the Duchess's concept of cost. Others would appear to have told her it could be nearer £1,000, a figure she felt was way over the top. The cost was £1,013. 18s. 10d., and this excluded anything for the produce etc brought from Chiswick. [16]

Haryo liked the ball but found it too hot and overcrowded. She put the number of people at 1,800, but may have misunderstood the quantity being 800. She had opened the dancing with Frederick Ponsonby, probably in his military uniform. She found she was 'very much frightened indeed' by the experience, forced upon her as Little G's gown *'had not come home'*. At one point she and Caroline St Jules were stuck in a doorway for half an hour unable to move 'without any possibility of getting in or out of the crowd'. She wrote to her grandmother (Lady Spencer): *'I hate a crowd. I like a childrens ball as twice as well as a grown up one and dear little Chiswick better than either of them'*. [17] The children went to bed at 5am, as Little G took to the floor for a final time. Haryo never lost her passion for Chiswick and ended her days there.

The Duchess described her decorations for this ball and it gives a good impression of the extraordinary lengths she went to in order to impress her guests, let alone her husband. The columns supporting the pediment of the Palladian entrance front were adorned with evergreens and artificial roses. On the staircase up to the entrance were wreathes of natural flowers in glasses (to keep the flowers fresh and therefore presumably holding water), which were suspended from banisters.

There was a terrace at the top of the twin set of steps up to the entrance hall, or The Saloon as it was known, for which she *'hired a canvas room, with openings opposite the* (entrance) *hall windows, which I took out in their frames – I hung the canvas room with fishing nets and these I stuck full of boughs – and flowers, artificial and fresh.'*…

I place'd fine exotics in pots on a bench and hid the bench and pots with a railing of canvas covered with trellice paper. I plac'ed two orange trees from Chiswick and (? pasted) *trellice paper on their boxes'*. There was a bower lit *'with roses holding 18 wax candles – the effect was like magic'*. There were several of these, consisting of wooden hoops with the candles (probably in glasses), suspended from the hoops by *'invisible string'*. One had 29 candles and all were bound with flowers. `

The basic plan of the ground floor of Devonshire House consisted of a large reception or entrance hall in the middle of the Entrance Front also known as The Saloon, with another large room behind it (The Middle Drawing Room). Either side of this were two very large rooms, separated by a staircase on each side of the Saloon. For the ball, the two rooms at the front of the house were for card playing (the room on the right of Saloon) and for socialising (the room on the left, otherwise known as The Ballroom, although there may have been little room for either until the dining areas were cleared – see below). The two large rooms at the rear, also known as the Red and the Green Drawing Rooms, were used to seat most of the 400 diners of each of two sittings. The Saloon and the Middle Drawing Room behind it were also used for dancing. [18]

There was a large forecourt in front of the house, which fronted Piccadilly and Green Park, with a large brick wall for security. It must have been chaotic in the street as several hundred carriages converged on the entrance gates. One wonders if it was large enough to accommodate them all. Today, Green Park underground station occupies the forecourt site. It is said that the booking hall is in the old house cellars.

The Derby Mercury newspaper reported that the more youthful turned left on reaching the top of the wide entrance staircase, with older people turning right where the large expanse of space was divided into four card rooms. The tented room, at the top of the steps, was used for refreshments. The paper described it as being 'lined all round with real flowers and orange and lemon trees etc brought … from Chiswick; at one end the flowers and wreaths formed a grotto and two boxes were made, from which the company could be seen through the windows in the dancing and card rooms. What a difference that must have been: one full of vitality, movement and grace and the other of quiet studious attention and contemplation. The windows in the tented room were venetian blinds, which allowed an inflow of air. It made the room cool and refreshing and was chiefly made for the dancers to retire to and hopefully cool down in. One wonders if Haryo and Caroline found this little oasis.

The Derby Mercury reported that the Prince of Wales and his younger brothers were all present and each table was presided over by the Duchess (the Royal table) and her family and friends (all women, including Little G and her aunt Harriet). All were served dinner on plate. Having let the opening of the dancing to her younger sister, Little G was reported as closing the dancing with the final flourish at 5am. It was 7am *before all the company departed, dazzled by all the splendour of the scene*. Having returned to the limelight, the duchess set a new benchmark for party giving. [19]

The Duchess was described as being *plainly and elegantly dressed in white and chains of pearls, with a new fashionable head dress, which was much admired, consisting of lace, pearls and feathers. Lady Bessborough and Lady Elizabeth Foster were the same. The ladies were generally dressed in white and silver with a profusion of diamonds. There were a few slate coloured crapes, richly embroidered with silver, which were very beautiful'.*

On 12th July 1800, Lady Georgiana Devonshire celebrated her 17th birthday. Her parents celebrated it rather differently on the 5th with the Duchess's Public Breakfast at Chiswick with 900 guests. They started to arrive at 3 p.m. and were largely all there by 4.30 p.m. From 2 p.m. – 3 p.m., the roads from London were continually enveloped in dust. Curricles, chaises, coaches with four and six horses, out riders etc. passed in a continual cavalcade. At least 400 carriages were making their way to Chiswick.

They proceeded to the South Front and a winding double flight of stone staircases. At the bottom of each were several lemon and orange trees, loaded with fruit. The staircase was lined with shrubbery and natural flowers. Beyond the staircase was the Portico, supported with six fluted Corinthian pillars below a pediment and dome, allowing light into an octagonal saloon hung with old master portraits and other paintings. On the left was the Green Room where 14 were seated. In the gallery were three more richly ornamented tables for 19, 28 and 14. The Duke's dressing room had been converted into a dining room for 30, the Duchess's dressing room accommodated 20. The house's *breakfast room* holding another 20 (the house dining room in the west wing).

Outside on the lawn (on the right-hand side) were swings and see-saws for the young at heart and a marquee containing 28 tables, decorated like the others but with the additional ornament of the arms of the Prince of Wales, who spent much of his time directing his regimental band from Guildford, consisting of 24 men in full uniform. The Lord Mayor brought the band of the West London Militia and there were four bands of Savoyards. Music and the scent of rows of orange and lemon trees pervaded the grounds. A second marquee had been erected further on, opposite the Italian-style Garden, with another 28 tables and with '*an excellent band, organ etc.*'

In the Temple was arranged a table for 30, hosted by the Duchess of Devonshire and Little G. Amongst the guests at this table was the Prince of Wales, the Duke of Bedford and Richard Sheridan etc. At the entrance of this Temple was another table for twelve. Presumably the Duke hosted this table (he is not mentioned in either of two newspaper articles. Across the Garden was yet another marquee for 24, amongst whom were Lord and Lady Cholmondeley.

No-one sat down to eat until the Prince of Wales arrived. Available were cold meats, pies, jellies and 'fruits of every kind', all washed down by wine. Amongst the music played was the Overture of Coserara (?Costera), the Overture of Figaro and Sir Charles Grey's Troop, '*a favourite march composed by one of the Band*'. One wonders what the Duke thought of that, especially as Grey was there.

A ball commenced at 6 p.m. for three hours, opened by Lady Georgiana Devonshire partnered by Mr. Byng. She was followed onto the floor by the ten-year old Marquis of Hartington and Miss Ord and Lady Georgina Gordon and Lord Mark Kerr. For the men looking for something less energetic, there was a cricket match with Messrs. Bexall, Raye and Graham, the outrunners at Lords Cricket Ground.

Some of the guests had arrived by barge, embarking at Westminster Bridge and travelling up from the river on the new canal extension to Chiswick, a distance of 17 miles (11 km), the barges being rowed there in about an hour. Both the King's Barge and the Admiralty Barge were used, along with the City Barge carrying the Lord Mayor and 40 of the guests. Mr. Shepherd, the Water Bailiff, presented the Lord Mayor with a sturgeon taken near Putney, which was '*seven feet (nearly 2m) in length, 3 feet (1m) in circumference and weighed 170 lb (77 kg)*. [20]

At 7 p.m., the Duchess, accompanied by her sister, the Countess of Bessborough, plus her children, Harriet and Lord Hartington, distributed 5s. 0d. (25p) and a quarter loaf to 170 '*poor persons of the neighbourhood*'. In 1800 a 4lb loaf in London cost 1s. 3¼d. The total cost was £681 excluding the cost of the Lord Mayor's Band and the hire of the tent frames. [21]

The Bessboroughs and Debt

Towards the end of 1799, the crisis, which had been getting worse, concerning Lord Bessborough's debts – let alone those of his wife, the Duchess's sister – reaching tipping point. His debts, according to the Duchess were c. £93,000, although Gleeson's figure of £101,000 may well be nearer the mark. [22] It had been agreed to establish a trust to help advance the money needed to clear the debt. The Duke and Lord Frederick put in £10,000 each with further monies coming from the Duke of Bedford and Lord Fitzwilliam.

The security would be provided through the Bessborough houses at Roehampton and London, which would be rented out. Additional savings would come from staff no longer needed at these houses and a sale of some heirlooms – paintings, marbles etc.

There appears to have been at least a couple of problems: Lord Bessborough changing his mind and he and his wife needing at least £10,000 p.a. to live on, and realistically a need for it to be under £5,000 p.a. It was being mooted that they live somewhere quiet for a while such as Devonshire or Hardwick. John Heaton was providing legal advice etc. until he appears to have withdrawn his professional services. The main trustee was to have been the Duke of Bedford.

While all this was being considered in January 1800, the Duchess borrowed £6,000 from the Duke of Bedford, of which £1,700 was still due when she died in 1806. At that time, she owed Lord Bessborough £1,725, which may be a pointer to his finances being in a better state. [23] The Bedford loan was at 5% interest. The Duchess had promised the Duke that she would not borrow with interest payments as her mother had reminded her the previous May: *'It is now five years and a half since you promised the Duke you would not borrow no money nor buy any article till you had the money in hand to pay for it ...You let a mistaken good nature reign over you with so despotic a sway that it is become an absolute vice ... Open your eyes my beloved child to see the impropriety of your conduct in reflecting so little on the most solemn promises and making light of such sacred engagements'*. [24] However good intentioned, the Duchess seems to have lacked the ability to make a promise with the intention of keeping to it. The Duke of Bedford ended his close friendship with her because of this.

The Bessboroughs moved to Hardwick towards the end of 1801. They did not like it there: there was little social life, Harriet was separated from Leveson Gower, her lover and of course this was not a comfortable home. It could be very cold, it was not the elegant and airy home they were used to. Consequently, it appears that they did not stay there very long, moving on to Chatsworth and Brocket Hall. Come summer, they joined the Devonshires at Ramsgate. A sale of part of the Collection occurred in 1801 consisting of 92 paintings which raised £9,450. These included Poussin's Venus and Adonis and Salvatore Rossa's Jason Poisoning the Dragon. There was a further sale of antiquities to raise even more funds necessary to make some impact on the debt. [25] Importantly for the Duchess, it provided the idea for something similar for herself but it is not clear whether it found favour with the Duke. One wonders whether this was washing too much linen in public for him.

16

Re-engaging The Social Scene, 1800-02

Little G's Engagement and Marriage

Following the Court presentation, Lord Morpeth joined the family for a couple of weeks from the fourth week of October 1800, possibly at Chatsworth and spent most of his time with Little G.

If they were getting closer, neither gave any sign of it. Both of her parents grew more and more preoccupied with what might be, but the Duchess felt that while he *'would make a woman happy ... he is rather too cold for her'*; on the other hand, the Duke liked him.

As the end of the year drew ever nearer, the Duke was troubled by gout. James Hare even offered to accompany him to Bath, but so long as Morpeth remained with them at Chatsworth (having left them early in November and returned), the Duke would not go. By the second week of December, the Duke and Hare were both of the opinion that there was no doubt of his intention. The house was full, with 23 sitting down to dinner on 12th December (plus children). They were getting through 15 sheep and 2 oxen per week according to the Duchess with the poorer cuts going to local poor people. The one thing they could not get enough of however were eggs. In fact from 27th September 1800 to the end of the year they ate their way through 20 oxen, 115 sheep and 11 lambs. The weight of meat was 15 tons 5½ cwt, costing the house account £794 (from the Home Farm account). There must have been more guests than just the Duke and Bess staying after Christmas because from 1st January to 2nd February 1801, they consumed another 8 oxen, 54 sheep and 1 lamb. This weighed 4¾ tons and cost £266. 16s. 6d. The cost of travel and carriage of goods from London/ Chiswick to Chatsworth was £263. [1]

On the 15th, Morpeth proposed but a quick response was not forthcoming. In fact, she said something which hurt and unsettled him on the 17th and he talked of leaving. '... *the misery this caused her let her into the secret of her own heart*' and the following day she accepted him. The Duke settled on his daughter the interest (at 5%) on £30,000, (£1,500) p.a. The Earl of Carlisle was bound to give his son £5,500 p.a. giving the couple an initial income of £7,000 p.a. However '*she is not expensive*' wrote the Duchess to her mother. [2]

The Duke's gout failed to improve over the next month which caused a predicament. With a wedding to organise, the Duchess needed to be in London. In the end, Bess Foster offered to stay with the Duke until he was well enough to travel. She wrote to tell the Duke of Richmond '*I am aware how much it may renew old stories*' she told him [3] '*and he has been uneasy about, but I have told him how little I mind if it does so and have made him consent to my staying.*' She also made it clear that it gave her a chance to repay the Duke for his kindness over the years to her. Richmond had not taken up the opportunity to marry her since the death of his wife.

If this was a ruse to push her lover a long a little, it failed. Moreover the Duke was probably long past another passionate relationship with Bess, even if a physical relationship continued (which is unknown), and probably with anyone else. He was happy with his family life and now had the prospect of a son-in-law. However by mid-January 1801, his gout became worse, moving from his feet to his shoulder and elbow. He was confined to bed with no indication of when he would be able to leave it.

For month after month, illness had struck first one and then another member of the family. It was a constant worry for the Duchess particularly. What was unexpected was the sudden news for Bess Foster that her mother had died on 19th December. Bess did not even know she was ill. She suffered from '*dreadful convulsions*' as a result. She was treated with laudanum to calm her down, although she wrote to the Duke of Richmond that '*calm alas is not a sensation easily to be attained by a heart like mine*'. [4]

A few days later in another letter to the Duke of Richmond, Bess Foster tried another approach, suggesting that in '*a little time and I shall probably leave this dear country forever ... Caroline (St. Jules) will obtain protection from the Dss and Georgiana than I could give her*'. No mention of the Duke of course who was already looking after and 'protecting' her quite adequately. [5] The flow of letters to the Duke of Richmond by Bess Foster did nothing to push him towards matrimony. In fact he did not remarry and died on 29th December 1806. He had had a military career and gained the rank of Field Marshall in 1792. He had no legitimate children, but did have three through his housekeeper. [6]

It was just as well that Dr. Denman was with them with both the Duke and Bess Foster needing his attention, for the Duchess was taken ill on New Year's Day. *'Georgiana alarm'd us all sadly … she was taken with a violent spasm in the stomach from some physick disagreeing with her and how terrible indeed was the alarm.'* It would have been left to others in the house to celebrate the Act of Union of Great Britain and Ireland that day (1st January 1801). [7] In the event, Haryo was also taken ill on the return to London of her mother and sister and was left at Chatsworth in the first week of February. [8]

In January 1801 the Duke and Duchess received many letters from well-wishers, but one had an unexpected tone. It came from Lady Jersey, who did not name Little G, in the letter, just wishing the Duke and Duchess joy, and then *'a most violent encursion into Morpeth as she calls him'*. In a letter to her mother, the Duchess noted: *'I have always observ'd her affection of indifference about Georgiana – and the comparative fuss she makes about Harrriett' (sic)*. She was not stating that Lady Jersey wrote ill about Lord Morpeth just the opposite, but she noted: *'where she finds her affection for him upon long acquaintance cannot be full of very favourable recollections to him'*. A very cool response went back to Lady Jersey.

The correspondence between the Duchess and her mother shows the former being confident that the Duke would pay Little G £1,500 p.a., the arrangement being for life. However the payment was for interest on £18,000 at 4%. [9] These monies were paid annually to Lord Morpeth. Additionally, early in April 1801, Lord Morpeth received £2,000 from the Duke and his new wife received £1,850 from him, paid from his personal bank account. [10] The Duke also paid a further sum personally of £7,979 in 1810. No detail has been uncovered relating to why he did this. This means that the couple received the interest on £18,000, plus cash of £11,829.

Table 1
Payments to Daughters:

	Little G	Haryo [13]	Caroline [11]
Lifetime	£11,829 x £18,000 +	£2,000 x £10,000 +	£2,000 x £28,000 +
Death of Duke	£20,000 +[12]	£30,000 +	Nil

x = cash (some to husband); + interest on this sum (5%)

Does the additional cash sum to Little G reflect pressure from his wife, who passed away before the other two married, or later pressure on his cash flow?

Wedding Preparations

Before the Duchess left Chatsworth for London with Little G, it would have been necessary for her to clear the expense of the trousseau with the Duke. Her own had cost her father c. £3,500, so she would have had a bench-mark figure to work on. It is likely that something of the order of £3,000 - £3,500 was agreed. It seems reasonable that her shopping list would probably have been similar to her own of 1774, although there had been some inflation since then.

For a compulsive spender, this must have been like giving a child the candy jar as she headed for Nunn and Barber (Lacemen and Haberdashers) of York Street, Covent Garden. For this 18th century top-drawer dressmaker, it must have been like the boat coming in. The list of purchases seems endless. The total cost was £3,368. 9s. 6d. for over 900 items in all. The Devonshire House accounts for 1801 seems to have wrapped the total cost of the wedding into one sum: £4,912. 12s. 3d of which Nunn and Barber were paid their main invoice plus another £44. Other costs were therefore £1,500. 1s. 3d. [14]

The Duchess suggested that the Duke offer the couple Londesbrough as a home which the Duke is likely to have done, but in the event, they lived at Castle Howard with his parents despite Londesbrough only being 20 miles/32 km away. [15]

The wedding was fixed for Saturday 14th March 1801. In the event, it had to be postponed a week, much to the anger of the bridegroom. All that is known is that it was down to 'Heaton's delay'. Presumably difficulties concerning the marriage settlement were the cause. Lady Spencer declined to attend. This does not appear to have been because of any objection to the marriage, although she did not go out of her way to meet Lord Morpeth after the announcement. This was notwithstanding some serious prodding to do so by the Duchess. Lady Spencer referred to 'hurt of her heart' despite her affection for her granddaughter. Their marriage was to last over 58 years and she had six girls (all with Georgiana as one of their names) and six boys (all with George as one of their names). [16]

The wedding took place at Devonshire House at 8.30 pm. It was performed by Rev. Coombe of Curzon Street Chapel, in the presence of the Duke and Duchess, Earls and Countesses of Spencer, Bessborough, Carlisle, and Lord and Lady George Cavendish. It was a quiet affair, with the bride and groom leaving for Chiswick House at 10pm for three weeks. The bride was simply dressed in a Cambrick (sic) muslin robe. It contrasted with her diamond necklace and ear-rings. The former had cost 1,000 guineas (£1,050). [17]

The comment above that this was a quiet affair is a presumption. However, if the diamonds were paid out of the Duke's private account, the total cost of around £1,300 for them would have meant a lot of expenditure available for a large event, paid out of the Devonshire House account (see above). However, surely the Morning Post would have carried details of it. It contrasts vividly with the 500 guests at her grandmother Spencer's wedding. Little G's wedding cost of £4,913 would appear to have been: trousseau - £3,368; diamond necklace.- £1,050, ear-rings say £250; marriage licence £21; to the vicar, say £50, other items - £174 (e.g. flowers etc).

The Duke is likely to have been pleased with his son-in-law. He is described as being a *'quiet liberal, and an intensely Christian gentleman'*. Lord Morpeth entered politics and did much to support Catholic emancipation. His life was based principally in London, where he had a house in Grosvenor Place for which he purchased Old Master and contemporary English paintings. [18] Little G's bedroom at Castle Howard is largely as she left it (she died in 1858, a few months after her brother, the 6th Duke). Lord Morpeth succeeded as the 6th Earl of Carlisle in 1825.

The London Social Scene c. 1800

It has been seen above that the Duchess re-engaged the London social scene in 1800 following the presentation of Little G at the coming-out ceremony at the Palace, before the King and Queen. The members of the upper end of the aristocracy were known as the 'fashionables' by 1800. If you were part of that set, you generally held at least one party in the Season. The larger your house and deeper your pocket, the more people you could invite with an elite who could invite 300 or more.

Other than for the Devonshires, who picked up the mantle of leadership of the bon ton (i.e. as the Fashionables) effortlessly in 1800, effectively after a 11-year gap, the ton helped to establish some sort of pecking order. It also gave mothers an opportunity to steer daughters and maybe a son towards a good matrimonial match.

Not only did the Devonshires have two priceless assets for partying in Devonshire House and Chiswick House, the Duchess was an asset in her own right. Her friendship with the Prince of Wales (he remained particularly close to her in a non-physical relationship) and his brother and sister-in-law, the Duke and Duchess of York, bolstered her position. It produced a clamour to have her on your guest list as well as have you on hers. Although the Duke attended some events, he left others to his wife. Gout was a cause (but not necessarily exclusively) of this and there would be others where, initially at least, the Duchess would have wanted to accompany Haryo as she stepped into the limelight after her presentation. Presumably, Brooks's Club would have allowed him a quieter night.

Most of the younger element of such gatherings were of course unable to host them because of the expense and that was accepted. However for many others, membership of the ton would have depended upon the ability to host them. There must have been some, like the Duke, who would have been happy to get by without it. Lady Spencer was one. In her case cost may not have been too much of a problem, but it was for her children, Earl Spencer [19] and the Bessboroughs, where pockets were shallower. Being members of the Fashionables brought a merry-go-round of countless extravagance and expense; alright if you had deep enough pockets.

From the Duchess's point of view, having a different theme became important, introducing a new style of dancing, more flowers and lights and French dances for example. Only she would go so far as to have French guests only one supposes, but it certainly showed her sensitivity to their position as basically, refugees. Such changes kept her at the forefront of the pecking order, one step ahead of the other fashionables intent on keeping up.

In 1800 the Duchess hit the ground running, inviting 800 to Devonshire House and 900 to Chiswick a few weeks later. At the beginning of June, the Duchess informed her mother: *'I am very busy with my new life and it does pretty well with me'*. Having the Devonshires on your guest list was quite a coup, although the Duke clearly had a limit to the number he felt it enjoyable to attend. This was not an affliction initially affecting his wife, although she is not reported in the Morning Post as attending more than the odd social event in 1801 and only a couple of so a month thereafter. She probably found two all night parties per month enough. She did also go to evening functions at Ranelagh and Vauxhall Gardens, Kennington however, but these ended before midnight. (Ranelagh is now the home of the Chelsea Flower Show). The Duke went to very few. However it was necessary for the Devonshires to be in London and in 1802, the return from Chatsworth had to be put back a month twice, because of the Duke's gout. They eventually rolled into Piccadilly in the first week of March *'to the great joy of the fashionable world, who now regard the Season as commenced'*. [20]

However the joy was short lived for within a week or so the Duchess was inconsolable following the unexpected death of the Duke of Bedford. However her mother had some hard hitting advice: keep that up and people will be asking why. After a few days with her mother at Holywell, St. Albans, she returned to the action after passing her time with a few short stays at Chiswick with Haryo. By mid-summer many of the 'Fashionables' were thinking of their summer break in the country. The early departures were off by mid-July and although some parties continued, the Season ended by the end of July. For those going to the Sussex or Kent coast, there were enough friends and acquaintances around to keep the socialising going. For those off to the family country seat, it was a time to re-engage with local friends from nearby plus the family especially where close members lived elsewhere. [21]

London then became rather quiet for those left behind. In September 1803, Haryo wrote to her sister: *'my principal occupation is lamenting. I scarcely know one person now in town excepting Mr. North whom I see now and then in the streets'*. [22]

It was of course not just how many were on the guest list, it was the quality of the people there too. The Duchess could usually rely on the Prince of Wales as noted above. Most balls started late in the evening and went on until 6.30 – 7.30 a.m. At the Marchioness of Abercorn's ball in 1801, 174 sat down to supper and the ball wound up *'at the early hour of half after four'*. [23] However the Duchess found her age was catching her up. At 44 years old she complained that the life tired her. It was becoming *'so totally without interest to me except when I see my children and Ca* (Canis, the Duke) *happy and so being fatiguing – for we are habitually so late that I get up late'*. A week or so later she wrote: *'our hours are so late that really I am never up'*. [24]

The Duchess also had other events which she called Public Breakfasts, which started at 4 p.m. at Chiswick and ended by early evening at 7 p.m., sometimes enabling them to return to Devonshire House. She seems to have had three of these a year. Set in the exquisite surroundings of Chiswick House and its very fine gardens, they were very popular. It was not unusual for there to be a total of twenty balls/routs etc. week in, week out. Ever sensitive to the French refugee community, in 1802 she handed the guest list to a French friend and asked him to invite who he liked. This is likely to have been the Duc de Orleans of the French royal family, or his younger brother, the Duc de Montpensier.

Compared to her good planning (usually handling it all herself with trusted Louis Vigoureaux), the same year, 1802, the Duke of Cumberland (brother of the Prince of Wales) showed how not to do it, even though he had five friends (all men) organising it. The first problem was inviting all the members of the Union Club, for 1,500 lapsed members suddenly paid overdue subscriptions. This swelled the guest list to 3,000!

His masked ball was at Cumberland House on the 31st May 1802. The queue of carriages (two lines abreast) stretched the length of Bond Street, Piccadilly and Pall Mall. Some guests waited in line for three hours and it was 3 a.m. before they had all arrived. This aristocratic rush hour became a feature of the London street scene. Each carriage kicked up dust. Imagine what up to 400 did! Many, in their masked costumes, got out of their carriages and walked through the crowds of onlookers. The ball began to break up at 5 a.m., not only without a taste but even a sight of supper for many. Most managed to get away by 7.30, some not until 10 a.m. There was mass confusion and it was raining.

In the crush, most people did not realise the existence of, or could not get to, a second staircase, there being so many guests. A large crashing sound from the ball room caused some panic, thinking that the staircase was giving way. A reporter wrote that *'twenty ladies might be seen fainting at the same moment in the same room. The females of firmer nerves were all the time busily employed in taking the diamonds from their head-dresses and putting them and their other valuable ornaments in their pockets. Thus all the labour of the toilette were lost in a moment, and all the economy of beauty deranged. The dresses, which upon an average cost from thirty to forty guineas, were torn to pieces and wigs of the most exquisite taste and fancy forced from their foundations'* leaving so many *'bareheaded beauties'* all likely neither to forgive or forget.

The mass confusion inside was matched by even more outside. *'A great proportion of the carriages were broken, 3 horses were killed and several servants sustained fractures. A milk woman fainted in the street from the pressure of the crowd and was nearly killed.'* The Prince's supper room on the other hand *'was an exception to the general confusion and disorder'*. There was no mention of the Duke and Duchess being there, but the reporter said: *'Everybody was there'*. [25] That would definitely include the Devonshires.

For the general populace, such events were beyond them of course. They were restricted to being curious bystanders, seeking glimpses of the rich and the famous, politicians, a general or naval commander etc. as they passed by. Some events were open to others who could afford the entrance fee or could participate without cost. Vauxhall and Ranelagh Gardens attracted huge crowds of several, sometimes many, thousands. Usually they would have a patron who would pick up any costs above admission and catering receipts. The Prince of Wales and Duchess of Devonshire featured in this role regularly. They were popular for organisers because they attracted crowds in their own right, additional to the attraction itself.

The gala to celebrate the peace with France in 1802 was one example. Held at Ranelagh on 10th May, it was under the patronage of the Duchess of Devonshire and the Marchionesses of Townsend and Salisbury. It was a music concert with fireworks. Three months later on 12th August, the Prince of Wales celebrated his birthday at Vauxhall Gardens. In the crowd of some 12,000 participants were the Duchess and Lady Melbourne with a large party. [26]

These were eclipsed however with another event which started at Ranelagh Gardens on 28th June, also in 1802. This one was of historic proportions. It was to be an ascent of a hot air balloon by a Frenchman, M. Garnerin and a Capt. Sowden R.N. (who paid 100 guineas to be on board). This was not the first balloon ascent in London, but it turned out to be the most spectacular event London had ever seen. The Duchesses of Devonshire and Gordon were amongst the patrons. [27] The balloon was about 30ft/9.14m in diameter and 45ft/13.72m in height.

Despite a stiff breeze it rose into the air at 5 p.m. In the crowd were the Duchess, the Morpeths and his father, Lord Carlisle, Haryo and the Marquis of Hartington. Refreshments followed for members of the Pic-Nic Society. The road to Ranelagh was completely blocked by carriages. Caught by the wind, the balloon drifted down to and over Westminster Abbey and then kept to a line between the river, Strand, Fleet Street and St. Paul's Cathedral. This was the first time that a balloon had crossed the heart of the capital. The finest spectacle of the whole attraction was seen by the highest number of spectators ever in this country and of course none were paying for it (other than those at Ranelagh).

The balloon was airborne for nearly 45 minutes and came down 4 miles/6.5 km north of Colchester, having been brought down because of increasing wind speed. Its anchor eventually caught in a hedge near a house. The inhabitants were so frightened by the experience that they threatened to fire on the balloonists! The Duchess's experience of the event was marred by her continuing problem with her finances. The costs were £3,000 including £500 to M. Garnerin and the receipts only £2,000, leaving the patrons to find the difference. [28] On the other hand, the cost of the Duchess's Public Breakfasts etc. would have been done with the Duke's full support for they were paid for out of the Devonshire House accounts. This first for London would have appealed to the Duchess. The son of the Dowager Duchess d'Arenberg, the independent witness to the birth of the Marquis of Hartington, sponsored the first ever manned gas-filled balloon flight in 1783 from Arenberg Castle in the Austrian Netherlands. [29]

The dress wear for the girls living at Devonshire House, principally Haryo, Caroline St. Jules, Corisande Grammont and probably Caroline Ponsonby was a *'white cambric muslin dress trimmed with either lace or muslin with a montem bonnet of willow or muslin, plus Nankeen shoes and open-docked silk stockings'*.

With such competition between events on six nights of the week, with up to ten or so in any one night, the pressure to hold them on a Sunday grew. In May 1805, the 5th Ladies Sunday Concert was held at the Marchioness of Stafford's home, notwithstanding *'the interference of the Bishop of London'*. The event was very popular and there were a great number present. The music was described as being *'mostly of a sacred and very sublime description'*.

Public events could equally be as distasteful as was the Duke of Cumberland's Assembly. Although a little before 1800, George Canning's description of his first masquerade on 17th April 1785 is worth quoting. He went to socialite Mrs Crewe's Masquerade in a domino and found it enjoyable. Upon leaving, he was persuaded to go to the Publick (sic) Masquerade at the Haymarket, *'which I found at least as dull and disgusting as the other had been pleasant and lively ... but when at about ½ past 4 o'clock the gentlemen began to get quarrelsome and the ladies drunk and sick, I whipped my domino into my pocket and walked home to the Temple to my bed'.* [(30)]

Life at Home

In May 1800, Augustus Clifford left home for a final time. He had left Harrow in 1799 and went on a European tour before he entered the Navy in May 1800. He saw action in the Leeward Islands (at St. Lucia and Tobago) in 1803 and in Egypt in 1807. In fact he was frequently mentioned in gazettes between 1807 – 1815 for his courage. Nelson had good words to say about him but one perhaps needs to bear in mind that he was a neighbour of the Duke and Duchess (see below 1803) and the Duchess was an admirer of him, sending him wine coolers and china to celebrate his victories, via her brother, Nelson's boss, the First Sea Lord.

Augustus last saw service at sea in 1831, but still rose to the rank of Admiral of the Red in 1864. He was also a politician, eventually becoming Gentleman Usher of the Black Rod in 1832 when his half-brother, the 6th Duke, was Lord Chamberlain. He first entered the House of Commons in 1818. He shared an interest in and was a patron of the arts, an interest he shared with the 6th Duke. He married Lady Elizabeth Townsend, the daughter of John Townsend and Georgiana Poyntz, on 21st October 1813 (the latter a relative of the Duchess), and both her parents were close friends of the Duke and Duchess. He died on the 8th February 1877, a little before his 90th birthday. [(31)]

With the Duke's gout keeping him and Bess Foster at Chatsworth in early 1801 it would have given him little comfort to learn that his uncle Frederick was equally indisposed at Twickenham Park, let alone his daughter left ill at Chatsworth with him. The Duke was back in London by the end of February but the gout was still troubling him. The Duchess, Little G and Lord Morpeth (and perhaps others in the 'family' i.e. the other girls at Devonshire House) left the Duke behind along with the wedding preparations to go to Drury Lane on 24th February on the opening night of a new play *'Deaf and Dumb'* which opened to a good review. [(32)] It was a month prior to the wedding.

After the post-wedding private suppers and daytime visits, the Duchess did not pursue too many balls, routs and other parties, spending her time alternatively at Chiswick and Devonshire House, with a Public Breakfast at Chiswick on 20th June 1801 for 40 guests. The guest list did not appear to include the Jerseys. The Duchess had another two shortly afterwards on the 4th and 11th July. Reports in the Morning Post, including even the date of the last event, differ from the Chiswick Accountant's records.

The latter paid for 427 bottles of wine and spirits (including 180 bottles of port) for these events. Cricket was played in the park and music provided by the Coldstream Guards (first event); Mr. Jones's Dancing Music (second and third) and the Princes of Wales Band at the third. The Morning Post reported that the Prince's younger brother, the Duke of York, was present, not the Prince of Wales, at the June event and his band was there in full (? military) uniform. The Prince and Princess of Orange were also at the June event. In the first quarter of 1801, subscriptions to White's Club started (10 guineas per annum). Payments (£75 per quarter) ceased to Little G and payments to Caroline St. Jules (£25 per quarter) started. Haryo's payment was lifted from £50 per quarter to £75. [33]

By the end of August, the family was planning to go to Chatsworth and then in October, after Hart had gone to school, to journey north to Castle Howard. However the Duke's gout remained persistent and seems to have resulted in plans for Chatsworth to be dropped. The Duke seems to have resumed playing at (?) Brooks's and White's Clubs during the year, but clearly his gout would have influenced his nights out.

If plans for Chatsworth did not materialise, the family did get away and to Derbyshire and Hardwick for a few days, despite the Duke's lameness. They left on 2nd September 1801 and arrived the day after, with the Bessboroughs reaching there the next day, followed by Lady Spencer and Selina Trimmer. The Duchess, writing a new diary she soon dispensed with, added a note that her eyes were troubling her. [34]

This could only have been a short stay for on 7th October they left London again. This may have been to head for Castle Howard. However, they reached Hardwick on 9th with Haryo unwell. Whatever the reason, the stay there was extended for nearly two weeks, eventually reaching Castle Howard (north-east of York) on the 22nd, for a reunion with Little G. The stay was intended to last for about ten days and they then left and went back to Hardwick, where Lady Spencer had been invited to go in their absence. The servants had been left there when the family went north. [35]

Filed with letters for late 1801, but undated, is a long letter sent by the Duchess to the Duke relating to Hart's character and disposition. For quite a lot of the detail, one could be forgiven for thinking that she was writing about his father rather than an eleven-year old. She wrote that he had habits 'of reserve, seclusion and timidity'. She wished to continue her practice of his living with girls when not at school, primarily because boys of his age tended to not submit to the will of a woman. He sulked if he did not get his own way. Contrary to his mother, he had, she judged, a 'reserve of disposition', partly from deafness and for not being used to 'manly exercise, which makes him prefer keeping out of the way or with the servants'.

She was concerned that '*he should not perceive of his situation so as to think exertion on his part useless*': shades of his father, one thinks. '*Idleness destroying the labours of his mind in which he has already learnt*'. The six weeks of school holidays was when he let go the shackles of restraint observed at school '*and to which he looks for indulgence in the various things I think most pernicious*'. Nonetheless he had his good points: '*...you can find no boy who is less like Hart, to the flattery and sevility* (sic) *of the most ignorant and irregular set of servants*'.

The Duchess drew an analogy between the Duke and his brothers growing up with hunting, riding etc. She then added, subtly, something she would have had in her mind since the trip to Castle Howard, when even Haryo was aware of the benefits of eating at regular and reasonable hours, far removed from the Cavendish nocturnal lifestyle: '*Pray reflect on the house before we are up from 8 (when he rises) to 12 or 1. What can he do? This time with a person to lead him to it would be spent in riding, walking, swimming or some other game which would make him a match for other boys at his return to school and prevent his keeping out of the way and getting unpopular. When we are about* (i.e. when we are up), *you could be sure of riding with him if he had a horse and was taught*'. [36]

It is likely that the Duke intended that his heir would be able to ride before too long. He had himself taught, or had someone teach, his older son, Augustus Clifford, to ride as a young man and he was only two years' older than Hart. In fact the Duke started to teach him (Hart) to ride in his 1802 summer holidays at the latest.

It is uncertain whether they remained in Derbyshire for the remainder of the year. There appears to be no notice of them being in any late-year parties, but then Morning Post entries for the Devonshires in 1801 regarding party-going are infrequent. That changed in 1802. The family spent Christmas at Chatsworth. On the guest list were: Lord and Lady Bessborough and family, Lady Spencer, Dowager Lady Bradford, Lady Bess Foster, the Morpeths, George Leveson Gower, Lord Cowper, Lord Ossulston, a Miss Fleming and others. An open house was kept.

Although the Duke's birthday was on 14th December, it was celebrated on 4th January 1802 with an invitation sent out to all the neighbouring nobility and gentry. Although it was anticipated that the family would return to London later that month, gout detained him until March. It also detained Lord Bessborough until February. [37] This illness deprived the Duke and his brother-in-law the opportunity of joining the others in skating, presumably on the nearby ponds. Corisande Grammont and Caroline St. Jules skated in disguise only to find someone sweeping the ice in a carter's frock. Lord Duncannon (the Bessborough's oldest son) avoided detection for some time! Corisande lived at Devonshire House and was brought up with the Cavendish girls. She was the daughter of Antoine, Duc de Grammont and his wife Louise, the daughter of Armand, the Duc de Polignac. The latter family were close friends of the Devonshires. [38]

Those speculating that the Duchess's return to London at the beginning of March 1802 would see her throwing herself into the party scene were to be disappointed however. Prolonged mourning, (too long according to Lady Spencer) for the sudden death from a rupture following surgery of the Duke of Bedford, followed by very bad headaches, saw the Duchess taking it easy at Chiswick. *'I lead a life in London about as quiet as the country'* she wrote to her mother at the end of March.

In fact, she appears to have been rather careful about her party going, keeping to 2 – 3 per month, with other events confined to evening gatherings at Ranelagh and Vauxhall Gardens which allowed her to get home before midnight. She may have invited people back for a quieter supper, which finished earlier, but this was probably all dictated by those fearful headaches. There was also another distraction. Little G had a baby son on 18th April 1802, named George, born at Berkeley Square, the first grandchild for the ducal couple. Following her mother's experience, it would appear to have been a difficult birth. [39]

The Duchess threw a party at Chiswick towards the end of June 1802, but that appears to be the only one in the whole season. More notable was that the Duke went to at least two parties; those given in late May and early June respectively by the Portuguese Ambassador and the King. He was probably at another too, given between these two by the King's son, the Duke of Cumberland. So although the Duchess was engaged in the social partying round, she had yet to ratchet up engagement with it. That was to happen in 1803.

17

Two Beauties In Town & Relaxing Ramsgate, 1803

Haryo: From Adolescence to Dazzling Beauty

Haryo, having reached the season in which her 18th birthday fell (the date was 25th August), was presented at Court by the Duchess, Earl Spencer and Countess Bessborough on 28th April 1803. The Duke does not appear to have been there, which may be a usual feature for fathers, as Earl Bessborough was not mentioned as being there either by the Morning Post (see below). The Devonshire servants involved *'all had splendid new liveries for the occasion'*. No additional detail survives of the presentation in the Devonshire Collection Archives.

Harriet, Countess of Bessborough, was also at Court that day for the first time in twelve years, to present her daughter, Lady Caroline Ponsonby, Haryo's cousin, to the King and Queen. The Duchess had also been there on 24th March 1803 in order to present *'the young and beautiful'* Duchess of St. Albans on the occurrence of her marriage. The Duchess's dress *'was white, superbly embroidered in silver with a profusion of diamonds'*. On this occasion, the Duchess was accompanied by Little G. [1]. Little G *'was very prettily drest'* (sic) according to the Duchess.

The Morning Post described Lady Caroline Ponsonby as being *'lovely ... we think the young lady bids fair to rival her mother, not only in her beautiful person, but in her elegant and unaffected manners'*. There was no such compliment for Haryo. However a year later, this changed following a ball given by a Mr. M. P. Andrew and in the presence of the Prince of Wales and her mother. The same newspaper reported: *'The grace and activity displayed by Lady Harriet*

Cavendish was unusually admired. Her ladyship's elegance of person attracted the eye while her dazzling beauty overpowered the senses'. (2)

As Haryo's appearance flowered to match her older sister, so there developed a maturity in her opinions and manner. She recognised this herself in a letter to Little G towards the end of 1803. There were clearly times when her mother failed to appreciate that her daughter was maturing in her thoughts and that she was deliberately trying to act in a manner that reflected that growing maturity. An example of her mother's misjudgement occurred over the relationship between Haryo's cousin, Lord Duncannon (John William Ponsonby) and one of the Jersey's daughters, Elizabeth Villiers. He had told his sister, Caroline, that *'he was undecided and unhappy'* and hinted to her that he was entangled in this affair with the Jerseys and wished extremely to *'get off from it'*.

Despite this, the Duchess *'gave me* (i.e. Haryo) *a most furious lecture about trying to get D. to love her and not Lady V'.* Haryo was actually undecided whether she wanted Duncannon or not. In fact Duncannon side-stepped Lady Jersey's clutches by leaving Ramsgate for London, later moving on with his parents to Paris. He married Lady Maria Fane, the daughter of the Earl of Westmorland, in 1805 (see below) (3) but not before he wandered through the arms of several other eligible young ladies; let alone his friendship (if nothing else) with Haryo.

Meanwhile, Duncannon's mother, Harriet, the Duchess's sister, was still in the throws of an affair with Lord Granville Leveson-Gower. In fact she had a second child by him in 1804, which she managed to keep from her husband. In the early days of the Duchess's parties following Little G's presentation, Granville was on the guest list. At the fifth party given by the Duchess in 1803 on 15th June, Haryo led off the dancing with the Marquis of Lorne and on the second set, was partnered by Granville. By November, the Duchess was being accompanied to balls etc. by Haryo. At the Duchess of St. Alban's Ball in July, Haryo was at her first ball (other than those of her mother's) where Granville was also reported as being present. Whether they also danced with each other was not reported. Other than opening dance partners (usually the younger guests), partners were not usually divulged. Anonymity prevented disclosure of unwanted pursuit, liaisons, difficulties with progressive dances etc., let alone taking up valuable column inches. It is therefore not known whether the first seeds of their eventual relationship (and marriage) were being sown at these events.

There is a slight amount of evidence which could suggest that the Duke had a crush on his cousin, the lovely Duchess of St. Albans. He attended this party too and even stayed all night long. It was so unusual, that the Morning Post noted that the Duke had *'not been known to pass an evening in a similar way for many years'*. It is not suggested that anything came of this other than a mild flirtation, the family not giving a second thought to them. [4]

Haryo was clearly an accomplished dancer, both traditional and new French dances, even leading the dancing off where she was a guest, rather than on home soil. She was equally accomplished with a guitar and also at billiards. Her grandmother and her father must have been particularly pleased about the latter: *'I have dazzled all beholders with my skill at billiards and making cannons and strikes at a great rate'*. [5]

She refers to her growing maturity, whilst staying at Roehampton, the Bessborough's home with her mother, in a letter to Little G: *'Oh! Time has changed me … it really has in some things and sobered a great many foolish ideas'*. The adolescent girl was becoming a lady, a point clearly recognised by Lord Granville Leveson-Gower. [6] One wonders whether the Duchess was content with the latter partnering her daughter, as Haryo emerged into adult social life, knowing that he had a stable relationship with her sister, Harriet Bessborough. What the Duchess could not have foreseen was the love that eventually developed between them. The Duchess's death in 1806 robbed Haryo of her mother's guidance on this.

Many years later, Haryo's grandson, the Earl of Bessborough described his grandmother as having a *'downright manner, mordant wit and caustic tongue, was apt to intimidate those who did not know her well'*. She ended her days living at Chiswick. Haryo's wit was recognised by her mother in September 1804 in a letter to her mother: *'she is however a dear girl and has an uncommon kind of true feeling, a little conceded by indolence and wit. G tells me she is the delight and admiration of C.H. (Castle Howard)'*. [7]

The Visit of Madame Juliette Recamier to London

Paris had its equivalent of London's bon ton. In fact London followed its counterpart, being ever watchful for changes of fashion. The head of the Paris social scene was 24-year old Madame Recamier, the wife of a rich French banker.

On 24th April 1802, the Morning Post announced that, with the peace agreement between the two countries (it was not signed until 29th April 1802), Madame Recamier would be visiting London, having been invited by the Duchess of Devonshire. This in the event, was probably untrue, for upon arrival, the former booked into Durant's Hotel in Albemarle Street. The Devonshire sense of good manners would have seen her being offered accommodation at Devonshire House had she been invited by the Duchess to visit London. Within a week or so, she had rented Mr. & Mrs. Duff's house in Grafton Street, the Duffs having moved to Curzon Street in Mayfair.

The visit is interesting, not least because of the reaction to it including the

Duchess's, plus some comments by the latter which must be ambiguous and certainly misleading, with even more from Haryo's grandson and the reaction to her manner of dress at the time, which may now be judged from surviving portraits and a terracotta bust.

Her initial London social life went unreported until she accompanied Lady Melbourne to the latter's box at the opera on 8th May. Bessborough [8] wrote that her appearance there caused such a sensation that she had to leave through a side door before the end of the performance. His comments are not supported by any reference and although the Morning Post reported the visit, it makes no mention of any disturbance. It did report at length on a disturbance the following day when it was Madame Recamier's intention of going for a promenade in Kensington Gardens. She may have been there the previous Sunday (2nd May), as this intention was reported in the Morning Post, indicating that her *'house is the headquarters of the beau monde and one of the most beautiful of women'* and that she would be *'dressed in the highest Parisian style'*.

What unfolded was possibly a result of that earlier visit and an exhibition of the latest Parisian style, perhaps not so well known because of the recent war. The paper avoided any detail of the new style, but a letter to the editor gave the game away, with a reference to *'nakedly dressed'*. It would appear to be a term which had more exposure than the state of her dress. However, she had bared her shoulders in public and it caused a sensation on the 9th May. Contemporary paintings of her and a terracotta bust, now in the Getty Museum, record her similarly dressed. She was strikingly attractive and was painted by Baron Gerard in 1802, sitting on a couch in a low cut, off-the-shoulder dress. If her dress in London was anything similar, it is no wonder she caused a sensation; a riot might have been a more appropriate expression, the exposure of her cleavage in a public place being of greater interest than her shoulders.

It would appear that Madame Recamier had gone out the week before, as someone now unknown, accompanied by another woman and by *'two gentlemen'* imitated her on the 9th. The women were dressed *'in high Parisian costume, with pockets outside, aprons of bizarre fancy and tremendous veils'*. There was a great commotion and they were forced back to their carriage. Shortly afterwards, Madame Recamier arrived, also with a female friend (it could have been her mother, who had come with her from Paris) and two gentlemen. Both ladies were dressed in white, with white veils and light violet-coloured parasols.

The crowd *'pressed on all sides upon her, men kneeled down before her to peep up under her veil ... after a turn and a half they left the garden. The situation outside was no less painful. Grooms and footmen with the most insolent curiosity crowded around them. Gentlemen on horseback left the ride and rode up to join the admiring mob. Their servant could not penetrate the crowd to apprise them of the place where their carriage was waiting'.* Despite a *'terrible fright',* she was at the Marchioness of Salisbury's party that night.

In an endeavour to pour oil on water, the Morning Post blithely reported the French dresses were in a modest and simple style and that the men trying to peep behind her veil or maybe lifting her hem a little were *'Italian corset makers, men milliners and shoemakers'* thinking of *'blonde and Brussels lace instead of paying homage to a shrine of beauty'.*

The visitors were invited to several other parties, but there is no mention of a visit to Devonshire House. On 14ᵗʰ May there was a subscription masquerade at Martindales in Bond Street in honour of the peace. A temporary building had been erected there, 300ft/ 91m long and 60ft/ 18m in width. It had been fitted out to resemble a greenhouse with 22 wagon loads of lilac and other shrubs. The walls were adorned with roses etc.

Madame Recamier found there the Prince of Wales, accompanied by Mrs. Fitzherbert, the Duchess of Devonshire, Haryo, and even Lord Nelson. It is possible therefore, that she was introduced to the Prince and Duchess, although towards the end of that year the latter wrote to Bess Foster (then enjoying the Madame's company in Paris) to say that they never met. A similar thing happened with Lord Nelson too shortly after his death.

Probably with a quieter life in mind, Madame Recamier left just over a week later for Bath, a couple of days before her husband arrived from Paris. The Duchess wasted no time in adopting the nakedness of bare shoulders, but was stopped by the Duke, who must have felt that this was inappropriate for a Duchess: *'I was obliged to drape all of me with only naked arms to the shoulder'.* Presumably that rule applied to Haryo too. [9]

It is quite reasonable to assume that we can ascribe the date of May 1802 when women of rank bared their shoulders in public on the streets of London. In the true spirit of *entente cordiale*, we allowed the first lady to be a French visitor. In the true spirit of English reserve, many men of rank may well appear to have been unimpressed. As for everyone else …

Foreman [10] quotes the Morning Herald of 4ᵗʰ April 1803 regarding female dress a year later. The paper refers to the Marchioness of Townsend's late 'rout' in *'… full dress : The Duchess of Devonshire has given the same precautionary hint and the decorous example will, it is hoped, run the whole line of female fashion'.* The Morning Post also reported on this event, and although the Marchioness was there it was actually given by the Ladies Townsend, the two oldest daughters of the Earl of Leicester. The Post reported on ladies present being extremely well, as richly, dressed, dripping in rubies and diamonds, others in gold and silver muslin dresses. Just how many husbands or fathers went this far in funding such excess would be interesting to know. [11]

The Morning Herald report probably relates to a move to stamp out ladies appearing with bare shoulders, rather than appearing in more expensive dresses. It is more convincing given the reference to 'full dress' which the Townsend girls had requested to their guests to wear in their invitations. However there was little point in holding back the tide. Change was on its way: In 1805, the Morning Post reported on fashion changes for the new season: *the dresses continue to be made very short waisted and very low over the bosom and back'.* [12]

Heading For Ramsgate

On 25th May 1802, the Duchess's book 'Le Passage du Mont St. Gothard' was published in the form of a long poem. It was published by appropriately named Prosper & Co., Booksellers, of 1 Wardour Street, a street in an area indelibly associated with publishing to this day. The price was 7s. 0d. (35p). It had been translated into French by M. L'Abbe Deville. By the end of August 1802, the Duchess told her mother that it had already seen three editions. She presumably meant three printings. In 1803 it was published in Italian and in 1805 in German. Coleridge wrote of it:

'O Lady, nursed in pomp and pleasure
Where learned you that heroic measure' [13]

In 1816 Bess Foster, who had been on the trip over the St. Gothard in 1793, published a special edition illustrated with her own drawings. It marked a decade after the Duchess's death.

Perhaps the Duchess was also finding the hosting of such large parties too much, despite her usual ebullient frame of mind. The Duke allowed her to choose what it was she wanted to do, but in any event, to some extent the birth of little George had meant that she had missed the boat for 1802. By June, a number of people had already left town or were about to leave. She really favoured Chiswick as Devonshire House tended to be *'very hot and fatiguing and more limited to numbers'.*

She also had the following year in mind when she felt smaller parties would be more appropriate following Haryo's presentation at Court. Although she was not to know it then, this was rather fortuitous. She caught the changed mood of society rather early on following Bonaparte's unilateral declaration of war that summer. The Duchess wrote in mid-June to her mother about her next party giving her a free hand to invite who she wanted, but it was rather late and only a few days ahead of the event, which was on 16th June 1802. It cost £742. [14]

Shortly after this, thoughts turned towards the summer holidays at Ramsgate.

Many 'fashionables' would be heading for Margate, including the Jerseys, which suited the Devonshires very well. However there were some initial distractions before they headed off, primarily the balloon flights of Frenchman, M. Garnerin (see above), Peace Parties and the Prince of Wales' birthday party in mid-August at Vauxhall Gardens, which the Morning Post stated had attracted a crowd estimated at 12,000. The Duke, however, was not there, confined to his home/ bed by gout and the Prince of Wales went round to see him.

On 24th August 1802, the cavalcade set off for Kent. There were six carriages, plus a sociable coach and a curricle. At Ramsgate they had hired two adjacent houses at Chatham Place, one for themselves and other for the Bessboroughs. More boarding houses had opened up than previously and all were full, the average price being 50/- (£2. 50) per week exclusive of tea and wine. This holiday was intended to restore their health and it seems to have worked. The Duchess bathed regularly in the sea and had a warm seawater bath every other day. Within days the Duke had a regime of getting up between 8 – 10 a.m. (almost unheard of). He and Col. Crawford were using the hot baths every other day. Daily walks along the pier or/and the promenade helped too.

The Morning Post even sent a reporter there for the duration of their stay, with regular reports appearing throughout September. After a month there, the Duchess wrote to her mother: '*I have no time and if you was to know the kind of gayety the Duke's returning health gives him you would not wonder*'. (15)

Some years previously, while at Plymouth, the Duke had wanted to take a boat out to reach the Eddystone Lighthouse. The first trip encountered bad weather, but a second trip was more successful, climbing up vertical ladders over the sea to gain access. This time he wanted to take a boat out to the Goodwin Sands. The scourge of shipping to this day, the Sands are exposed at low tide. What better than to take a party out for lunch there? Like the first trip to the Eddystone Lighthouse, the weather was poor and most of the guests turned back at the pier.

The Duke not being one to do things by halves, had ordered two sailing boats in case of any accident with one of them. A particular concern would have been being caught by a rising tide pushing the boat onto the Sands in the event of the wind not assisting a withdrawal. Undaunted, the Duke set off with Miss Manners, Mr. & Mrs. Duff (the latter described in glowing terms re her beauty in one Morning Post article) and a Mr. Robinson (plus servants of course). After a few miles, the horizon cleared and it turned out to be a lovely day. They landed on the Sands, had a meal and set off just prior to the tide turning. The pier at Ramsgate was covered with spectators as the boats rode the tide into the harbour under billowing sails. Everybody who went, or wished they had gone as planned, was reunited at a '*grand dinner and supper*' that evening.

Perhaps the Duchess had had enough excitement some three weeks previous to the Duke's expedition. She had taken the curricle (a lightweight, sprung and open carriage) along the road from Ramsgate to Pegwell Bay. The weather had been good and she was clearly taking the sea air. However, the horses were startled by the arms of a windmill and they bolted off the road, heading for the top of the nearby cliffs, with no fence etc. to restrain them.

It is not too clear what happened next, but the postillion kept his seat and a footman seems to have restrained the coach until some labourers came along and lent a hand for which they were well paid by a grateful Duchess. With the coming of November, the Devonshires returned to London and Bess Foster took the boat to France and Paris. It was the first time in 15 years that the two women had been apart in a situation where they could not be reunited within a few hours.

Coming the other way were the Duke and Duchess de Grammont (the parents of Corise who lived at Devonshire House). It had taken them 7 days to make the journey. It seems strange today to realise that the Devonshires (and plenty more people) considered it necessary to spend a fortune and several weeks in sea air, bathing in cold or hot seawater and regular walks on the prom or pier. Their health would have been much better with life in more daylight hours (and less nocturnal activity), exercise, less port and more beer (it tended to be alcoholically weak) and perhaps a more varied diet, all of which cost nothing or very little. One dietary change introduced on the recommendation of their doctor, Sir William Farquhar, was the local oyster, which tended to be larger than usual. He also recommended it to William Pitt. [16]

One aspect of their stay reflected on by the Duchess in a long poem to her mother was the public appeal of the couple from the general population. They were the nearest most people would ever see to royalty. The Duchess's diamond studded dresses of finest muslin or silk, the latest style of coach emblazoned with the Cavendish coat of arms, liveried staff, etc., were all symbolic of their status. Accompanying them would be some of the most attractive women in the Kingdom with their own finery, if not the diamonds. This helps to explain the crowds watching the Duke's return from the Goodwin Sands, with the Duchess and Bess Foster waiting to go on board for a meal at the quayside, together with family, probably some of their friends and more servants of course. [17]

Soon, most of the crowd would board a sailing ship of their own for the return trip to London, their boarding house holiday over for another year. They would have their memories of what they had seen, and for the lucky few, such as the labourers restraining the Duchess's frightened horses close to the cliff edge, the ring of a guinea or two extra in their pocket. You could buy 100 or so pints of beer for a guinea.

At least Ramsgate saw the couple returning to London in good health after perhaps a diffident year. It had seen the birth of grandson George and the Duchess would have enjoyed being a patron of balloonist Mr. Garnerin with his several ascents over London. As Christmas approached, the Duchess became depressed and stressed with both Little G and Haryo's proposed departure for Paris, with Lord Morpeth, to join Bess Foster. This was in early January and the family are likely to have spent Christmas at Chiswick as a result.

The Duke was perhaps a bit more sanguine. Under the Act of Union, he had lost his control over seats he held in his Irish boroughs. However it was not all bad, for he had been compensated for his loss to the tune of £32,219!

18

Partying, Paris and Pain, 1803

Recurring Ill-health, a Poor Start to the Year

The Duke and Duchess must have returned from Ramsgate buoyed up by their newly found good health, but it was not to last. In fact the next six months saw recurring ill health. Before a month had passed, the Duchess was hoping to cut down on late night events: '*I cannot get to bed early here* (Devonshire House) *when I am tired*'. By the end of the year, she was continually complaining of headaches, a condition which persisted until May 1803 at least. [1] It has been noted above that prior to Christmas the Duchess had become depressed and stressed with both her daughters leaving for France in January. Early in 1803 the Duke was suffering from gout again. In a letter to Bess Foster, the Duchess wrote: '*he would stay at home in an evening if I could get any pleasant parties, but now that I am not well, it is rather difficult*'. Her difficulties quickly worsened for a few days later, she wrote again '*I am confined to the house with a swelled face which always makes me low*'. [2]

To make matters worse, a flu epidemic was sweeping the country and claimed the life of Lady Caroline Fitzroy and Miss Harriet Lamb. The Duchess postponed a 'grand ball' in consequence of the death of the latter, which may suggest that she was related to the Melbourne family. [3] Lady Spencer also caught it and it would appear that in March 1803, the Duchess had it too, it having been reported that she was 'indisposed' some three weeks after her mother's illness. The Duke of Richmond was dangerously ill with it and one of the upper servants in Lord Melbourne's family died. [4] With the whole house affected with it on the 14th February the paper reported that the Duchess was holding no more parties until her mother was better. In fact there were reports of only ten parties held by the Duchess at Devonshire House in the first five months of the year and most of these were described as being small. Two more were held by the Duke.

The declaration of war on France on 17th May 1803 resulted in many people cancelling their parties from July, although the Queen, the Duchess and Lady Heathcote continued, for a while at least. In May, the Duchess was nursing the Duke and confined to home. He was suffering *'from the gravel and dare not go out even to Brookes'.* [5] As a result, Devonshire House saw only two small parties being reported in the paper on the 3rd and 10th. With the party season in full swing, a total of 52 were noted by the Morning Post for the week (Monday – Saturday) commencing 23rd May. Of the Duchess's two parties on the 3rd and 10th, there were only 63 guests, including the Prince of Wales at the first and only a 'select' number at the second. [6]

The Duke and Duchess were getting on well together too. In January the Duchess wrote to Bess Foster stating: *'It is impossible to tell you how sincerely, affectionately and de tutte tutto* (interpreted as 'everything') *is Car* (Duke) …' If matters were fine domestically, a sense of apprehension descended nationally after the declaration of war. Bonaparte started to mobilise a large fleet of small vessels for an invasion. The French were waiting for calm weather and sabre rattling that they only needed 16 hours to cross and land. The Duchess summed up the mood: *'I think the times very bad yet I believe they will find it difficult to land'.* [7]

What made matters worse was the lack of a government showing leadership following Pitt's resignation. Although the Whigs were trying to form an administration, nothing was being achieved. The King's health did not help matters, with the Prince of Wales concerned about Regency matters. Although the activity amongst the Whigs involved the Duchess acting as a facilitator, (according to Foreman), the extent of her influence from November 1802 until mid-1803 was probably much less than is alluded to by Foreman. The problems outlined above make it clear that the latter's comment *'Georgiana spent the next few months,* (i.e. from November 1802), *consolidating her contacts in each of the factions by holding political dinners almost every night'* appears very doubtful. [8]

It is certain that if this had been the case, the importance of the Devonshire House circle would have aroused comment in the Morning Post (London's highest circulation newspaper) as the search for a new administration to replace Addington dragged on. The Duchess was simply not in a position to do this or even have parties of any size prior to June (when she hit the ground running) let alone have significant influence on Whig party strategy: she was either too ill or looking after ill people. In fact it is worth repeating what she wrote to

Bess Foster at the end of November: '*I am well now as you will see but the life tiresome, so totally without interest to me except when I see my children and Car happy and so being fatiguing for we are habitually so late that I get up very late*'. Hardly the words of one so infatuated with Whig politics that she is throwing dinner parties virtually every night. A week later she wrote again complaining of rheumatism or lumbago in her side being so bad. This of course was additional to the headaches. [9]

Surprisingly, during December 1802, the Duchess wrote again to Bess Foster, this time trying to place a completely different spin on events at Devonshire House, despite her on-going ill health. She was clearly enjoying (or at least saying she was) the company of three old friends: Miss Lloyd, Mrs. Howe (her mother's indefatigable letter correspondent) and Lord Clermont. Despite advancing years, Miss Lloyd was described as being '*gay and coquettish*' and the company of all three was compared favourably to that of the younger set that lived in the house. These had grown in number to include the Duke's children (by both his wife and Bess Foster), the latter's two boys, Selina Trimmer on occasions, Corisande Grammont and Caroline Ponsonby.

The letter continues '... *I wish I was in the country ... I dare not move whilst I keep d of d* (the Duke) *from Brookes and d. house is very pleasant I feel for we have every night a society in which there is often some of the cleverest and first people of all parties. A little whist, chess and a very good music ... it is like a large house in the country and I seldom go out except now and then to the play*'. In fact the Duchess had deliberately switched the venue from one of the large public rooms to the Red Room, because it was much smaller. Guest lists shrank in extent and she found she could get to bed earlier. However, these parties were not to last long and there is nothing to suggest that they were political parties: they were social gatherings of friends. [10]

The conviviality and perhaps the bringing together of different Whig factions seem to have been subsumed by ill health and depression. By mid-January the Duke was back at Brooks's tables. Perhaps this letter had another purpose. Bess's letters portray an active social life in Paris. Was the Duchess trying to create the impression of the same at Devonshire House, when in fact she was ill?

Paris

After Ramsgate, Bess Foster sailed to France, where she stayed for several months. She became a regular visitor to Madame Recamier. In the company of Lord Pembroke, she asked to see the terracotta bust of her: '*her bust was brought in and flowers put around it, the bust is beautiful but has the fault of nakedness to an unnecessary degree – it is a great pity – I really like her and think her situation a most trying one*'. The nakedness, as noted above, referred to the naked shoulders. Madame Recamier was also using her maiden name at this time – Madame Bernard.

Bess was also socialising with another member of the Devonshire House inner circle, then in Paris – Lady Caroline Gordon. The latter was to have married the 5th Duke of Bedford, confidant of and money lender to the Duchess, who had died during the year (see above). Whilst in Paris she met the 5th Duke's brother (now the 6th Duke) and married him in 1803. She also took advantage of the latest Paris fashion, not entirely to Bess's approval. (Bess described her thus: *'Lady C.G. puts on her veils very well and very prettily – a sable narrow trimming to the white spence* (r) *is also very much worn – the gowns are all round breasted, short waists very often white sleives* (sic) *to a coloured gown, of patent lace – or embroidered muslin – generally they lace behind their gowns, but many don't, I think it looks too girlish – embroidery or lace up the middle of the gown'.* [11]

In the first week of the new year, the Morpeths left London for Dover, accompanied by the Duchess and Haryo, who went to see them off. They booked into Wright's Hotel on 2nd January 1803, expecting their ship, the 'Countess of Elgin' under Capt. Sampson, to leave the next day. However the weather conditions kept them there until the 5th. Lord Morpeth became agitated by the delay, which increased the Duchess's stress level, as she was worried the ship would leave in less than the best conditions just to please him. They boarded before 6 a.m. (when they left, before dawn).

The Duchess was impressed by the packet boat. It had been fitted out for the Duke of Dorset. The cabin was decorated in white and gold, with yellow satin furnishings, but Little G remained on deck, more interested in seeing the sun rise. They were detained for four hours (presumably on the French side) and the passage took twelve hours in all. The Duchess waited in Dover for word from Capt. Sampson that the Morpeths had landed safely and arrived back at Devonshire House on the 8th.

The Monday night had seen a party on the eve of departure, given by the Duke, with the Prince of Wales and the French Ambassador present. The ship departed with the Duchess weeping and with a bad headache, but she returned feeling much better and expecting her mother, who was coming to stay, within a couple of days. [12]

The four hour delay may have been waiting to hire a coach or horses. Whatever, their arrival in Paris saw them soon into a schedule of social visits and parties. Bess reported to the Duchess that Lord Morpeth *'is disposed I think to be amus'd and to like things and tonight will be a very good place to begin with'*. It was a ball (hostess's name illegible) and she was right. Amongst those they went to see was Madame Recamier. At the beginning of February, Lord Morpeth was presented to Bonaparte, but the latter did not converse with him. At the same time, Bess indicated that she was contemplating returning to England.

It will be recalled above that at the Battle of the Nile in 1798, Nelson successfully burnt or captured a French Naval Battle Group. Surrounded by sand and sea, with the Royal Navy maintaining a blockade, the disembarked French troops did manage to turn their attention to some cultural activity of lasting significance. They undertook a survey of Egyptian archaeology. In 1802, there must have been much national pride with the publication of a two volume book describing what is now seen as the foundation of modern archaeology. [13]

At the beginning of 1803, Bess Foster wrote to the Duke asking for his leave allowing her to buy a copy. In the event, the Duke wrote back declining, but only because the Duchess had bought a copy, which survives (both volumes) in the Devonshire Collection. Such a request suggested a book at a high price and thinking of the Duchess and her debt problem, he enquired how much it would have cost.

It appears that Bess Foster had her eye on some furniture she would have liked to have purchased. The Duke wrote back: '*With respect to furniture, I of course have no wish for any, and the Duchess says you had better bring plans of furniture only, that might be executed here, or otherwise we might have duplicates of things that we have already and the house* (i.e. Devonshire House) *is very much overstocked with furniture in general*'. [14] The overstock probably relates to the furniture sent there from Chatsworth in 1783. With the eventual sale of Devonshire House, it would be interesting to know how much of the rejected 1783 furniture was to be returned to Chatsworth.

By the end of February 1803, the Duke confirmed to Bess that he would pay her costs of returning to England. A payment to her appears in the Duke's personal bank account for £200, dated 29th March 1803, which presumably relates to this. A payment to her of £150 on 22nd September 1802 probably relates to her costs of getting to Paris. [15] She must also have asked for his views on her returning. He played the question down the middle of the wicket: '*I am perfectly convinced that I shall approve of whatever conduct your own judgement directs you to pursue, and shall rejoice for you at any event that is likely to contribute to your happiness for you may depend upon it that the love and friendship that I have so long had for you are firmly fixed and unalterable*'.

It would appear that equally firmly fixed and unalterable was Bess's negative opinion of the displaying of cleavage, short or no sleeves and bare shoulders. She considered that Madame Recamier was in '*a dangerous situation and I fear will not continue as insonciante* (sic)' – meaning her showing a casual lack of concern about her appearance. After the presentation of the Duchess of St. Albans to the King and Queen on 24th March 1803, the Duchess wrote to Bess

Foster regarding Little G's dress, noting: *'you would have approved of her sleeves – everybodys are short and many much more so than hers'*. [16]

Bess arrived back at Dover on 24th April. For those remaining in Paris when war was declared less than a month later, the situation became immediately more serious as they were declared prisoners of war by the First Consul (Bonaparte). These included James Hare. The day before war was declared, the Morning Post reported that *'a large group of fashionables were leaving Paris for London today including the Duke of Bedford and the Earl of Thanet'*. [17] They presumably left France after the declaration but possibly oblivious of how close a call was their leaving.

James Hare managed to obtain a release from detention and returned to England within a few months. However his health had not improved and it would appear that it was unlikely to as he was being treated with mercury. Bess Foster wrote to the Duchess in September from Devonshire House (the latter would appear to have been out of London - ? in Tonbridge) wishing that Hare would see Sir Walter Farquhar. It was an illness from which he never recovered. [18]

The Cholmondeley family had returned to England a little earlier, but somehow or other, the family plate had been left behind in France. It appears that it had been stopped, falling foul of some exportation ban. However they had been offered a service of Sevres instead. [19]

Another event in April was the death of Sir William Hamilton on the 6th. Upon his return from Italy (he was the British Envoy in Naples) he rented a property in Clarges Street at 23, Piccadilly and was a near neighbour of the Devonshires. He had lived in Italy in a *ménage a trois* with his wife (who was twenty years younger) and Lord Nelson, although of course the latter was at sea for much of his time. They had met Nelson in Naples on 22nd September 1798. Sir William died aged 78 years and his body was taken to Milford Haven, Pembrokeshire, for burial.

Emma Hamilton had given birth to Nelson's daughter, Horatia, on 31st January 1802 and in the autumn of that year, Nelson purchased Merton Place at Wimbledon. When Nelson left for Malta in May 1803, Emma was pregnant, but the baby died when a few weeks old, in early 1804. Emma's entry on Wikipedia states that the threesome went to live at Merton Place, but the Morning Post stated after Sir William's death that Emma *'remains in town, at her house in Piccadilly'*. [20] Exactly two and a half years later, after this report, on 21st October 1805, Nelson was also dead, below deck on HMS Victory, off Trafalgar. The Duchess was passionate about Nelson's naval successes.

Party Time, 1803

With illness being a pre-occupation for the Duchess in the first five months of

1803, she was clearly ready to return to the action and as already noted above, she hit the ground running. At the beginning of June there was an Installation Ball of epic proportions (see below). Her first ball of the year was on 15th and over the course of the following three weeks she held two more, plus two public breakfasts, one at Devonshire House and the other at Chiswick. If that was not enough, during June/July she attended six other events, including one at the Palace. Contrary to previous form, the Duke attended three of them.

The Duchess had attended the Queen's Drawing Room event on 28th April and both she and the Duchess of St. Albans had good reason for remembering it. The former (Duchess of Devonshire) lost a diamond ear-ring and the Duchess of St. Albans lost a '*magnificent diamond sprig of much value*'. Could there have been a light fingered visitor there that day? The next day Sir Walter Farquhar gave a grand dinner to c.100 guests. Most of the Duke's household and family were there and the known guest list reads like a list of his patients. [21]

There can be little doubt that not only the Duchess of St Albans but also the Duchess wore diamonds of great value. A perusal of the expenditure of the latter gives much weight to this and also to the extent that her expenditure was out of control. She was clearly determined to have the best and be the best dressed where diamonds were concerned. It needs to be clear that the expenditure detailed below relates only to accounts outstanding at her death and not necessarily to all jewellery suppliers or accounts paid.

Table 2

Examples of the Duchesses Jewellery Purchases

4/1799 – 4/1801	Rundell, Bridge & Co., Ludgate Hill	£1,323
1801	Cripps & Francillon, Norfolk Street	£869
1801	Wakelin & Gerrard, Panton Street	£149
11/1804 – 2/1806	Anthony Calvert, Hatfield Street	£2,519
1805	Flower & Mainwaring	£2,278
TotaL		£7,138

Using the equivalent of average earnings, this is today c. £6.5 to £7 million

On 1st June, the Installation Ball was held at Ranelagh. It was '*one of the most magnificent fetes ever witnessed in this country.*' [22] It was all ticket and the newspaper reported that the string of carriages extended to Pimlico (the following day it said Piccadilly). It was given by the newly installed Knights of the Bath. A temporary room had been put up extending to 160ft x 80ft /49m x 25m. Eight chandeliers hung from the roof with 300 lamps on each one. It was built over and around trees which were also hung with lights. The paper stated that there were 40,000 lamps in all, which must have made it rather hot.

'*The furnishings left you dreaming you were in some Fairy Temple*', wrote the reporter. There was a new ballet, singing and dancing, with 1,200 sitting for supper at 1 a.m. and with another 7 – 800 more in boxes. The total present was c.2,500. '*Green pease* (sic) *in profusion, though they are very dear … Grapes and cherries, at a Guinea a pound were in plenty. There were also strawberries at three shillings a thumb* (16 strawberries) … *One of the grandest scenes ever seen in this country*'. The Duchess (no mention of the Duke being there) spent the evening with the Prince of Wales' party. When the dancing started, she walked up and down for half an hour or so on the Prince's arm.

During a *pas de deux*, between the ballet's writer and '*a young lady named Adams*', the latter was '*dressed in one of the most superb dresses we have ever seen on the stage*'. The Duchess of York (Prince of Wales' sister-in-law) spoke to her in flattering terms, she was so captivated by her. Unfortunately after the event (it broke up at 6 a.m.) a carriage ran over a post and one servant behind the carriage was thrown over a wheel and was killed with another having his leg broken, itself a life threatening injury at that time.

On 15th June, the Duchess held her First Ball. The Morning Post announced it in its customary style, knowing the continuing fascination of its readership: '*This elegant and very accomplished leader of the haut ton gave on Wednesday night a splendid ball at Devonshire House*'. As usual, it was held in the main entrance hall and the drawing room behind it (the middle drawing room). The large folding doors between the two rooms were removed as in 1802, and the orchestra occupied that position – playing into each room. There were a selection of English dances for the hall and French dances for the drawing room. The hall was decorated with artificial flowers '*in the form of festoons, wreaths and garlands among which were placed a vast number of richly cut glass lustres. The floor was chalked, the centrepiece the family arms encircled by a very elegant mantle*'.

The drawing room walls were draped with azure blue silk formed into flutes. At 11.30 p.m. Haryo with the Marquis of Lorne led off the dancing, changing to Lord George Leveson-Gower for the second dance. Others dancing this one included Caroline Ponsonby and Caroline St. Jules. Supper was at 2.30 a.m., using up all the remaining floor space to seat the 400 guests. Dessert was a selection of fruits from the Chiswick hot houses. From 4 a.m. there was a final two hours of dancing, finishing as usual with reels and strathspeys.

Heading the guest list was the Prince of Wales and Mrs. Fitzherbert plus the Portuguese Ambassador. There were 2 dukes and 5 duchesses (excluding the hosts) and including the Duke and Duchess of St. Albans. Additionally, there were 5 marquises, 13 earls (including Jersey, Carlisle, Cholmondeley), 17 countesses (including Jersey and Harriet Bessborough, but not her husband), 4 viscounts and 6 viscountesses (including the Morpeths), 24 lords and 55 ladies. [23]

When Bess Foster returned from Paris, she brought with her the latest in French society dancing. The Duchess must have embraced this immediately, especially getting the young ladies of the household and their immediate friends to practice the new dances. They were called the French Cotillions and were introduced at this Ball. The Cotillion was already known as a dance and so this new introduction must have involved some new type of formation. It was a forerunner of the quadrille, with the dancers in a square, dancing various patterns or figures. Despite the artificial flowers noted above, most of the flowers had been grown at Chiswick. The Post reported that the fragrance was delicious. [24]

Perhaps not surprisingly, the Duchess was reported as attending only one party in June – the Duchess of Gordon's Rout. Despite several of the Devonshire/ Cavendish household being present, the Duke was not there. A week later on 22nd June the front door opened to welcome guests to the Duchess's second Ball, which was given less column inches in the Morning Post. *'Amongst the most beautiful young ladies … were Lady Louisa Corry, Lady A. M. Stanhope, Miss Manners, Lady Sarah Saville and Lady Augusta Fane. The Duchess of St. Albans and Countess of Conynham shone the brightest of the married dames'*. No mention of the beauty from within the Devonshire household, but an interesting reference to their young friends. There were 150 guests at this event. The Duchess of Gordon was the major sponsor of Robert Burns and raised the Gordon Highlanders along with her husband and son. [25]

On 30th June, there was a Public Breakfast followed by a concert at Devonshire House, with a second Public Breakfast, this time at Chiswick on 4th July. The latter would have ended early in the evening, which is just as well for the Duke and Duchess went on to Lady Hunloke's Rout. The latter gave another party on 13th July and both the Duke and Duchess of Devonshire were again present. Perhaps an additional attraction (Lady Hunloke was a Derbyshire neighbour) for the Duke was the Duchess of St. Albans although no impropriety is inferred.

In the midst of all this activity was a further ball by the Duchess at Devonshire House on 7th July followed by the Duchess of St. Albans' Ball, attended unsurprisingly by both the Duke and Duchess. The Devonshire House Ball was reported as being more elegant than those held previously there this season. There was a greater profusion of flowers and no less than three bands. It commenced at 11 p.m., the Prince of Wales arriving a little later. The dancing was led off by Haryo and Earl Cooper (? Cowper).

The new French dances started at 1 a.m., followed by supper an hour later. The latter was described as being a very costly one, all served on plate and the fruit dessert being superior to any seen this season. The Milanese Minstrels played during supper in the ballroom (the Hall). Clearly the Duchess intended ending the season on a high note. Following the resumption of dancing at 3 a.m., Lady Sara Fane called for *'O'er Bogle wi' my love'*. The fiddlers set to with gusto and the same dance was continued for an hour.

On 24th June, Little G gave birth to a daughter, Caroline Georgiana (Caroline's grandson became the 9th Duke of Devonshire) and it appears that the two Public Breakfasts were delayed until she (Little G) could be present. She was as much a party goer as her mother. From 29th April to 26th May, she attended six parties and in June prior to the birth she attended four more. It would appear that she was unable to attend the Queen's Drawing Room gathering in the afternoon of 9th June and Lady Heathcote's Rout that night, probably because she was indisposed. Her husband, Lord Morpeth, did attend both events. [26] There is no indication that the Morpeths or the Carlisles gave parties of their own but then Little G could never compete with her mother and all her friends are likely to have been on her mother's guest list in any event.

On Friday 16th July 1803, the Duke and Duchess went to the West India Docks with a party of 70, including the Prince of Wales. They boarded *'3 elegant pleasure boats with streamers flying and sailed down river to Woolwich'* after inspecting the Docks, which had opened the previous August and is now the site of Canary Wharf. Julius Angerstein was waiting (along with their carriages) at Woolwich, from where they proceeded to his house, Woodlands, on Blackheath, near Greenwich, for dinner. They all left at 11 p.m. and went back to town for supper at Devonshire House. Unknown to them, there they found Lord Duncannon, James Hare, and Mr. Foster (Forster), who had been given an exit visa to leave France (Boulogne), apparently sent to them by Bonaparte.

The Duke, with a large party, left for a stay at Chiswick the following Monday, 15th July, and that week, Lord Duncannon and Mr. Foster (sic) were presented to the King and Queen, at the latter's Levée by the Earl of Bessborough, Duncannon's father. [27] They were accompanied by the Duchess and her sister-in-law, Lady George Cavendish. A further report mentions Mr. Foster (not Forster) being at the Levée, which suggests that he was Bess Foster's son.

The partying was not over the Duchess however. The Morning Post reported her intention of being at Vauxhall Gardens (with c.100 in her party), with supper in the Pavilion on 22nd July, after going to the Royal Amphitheatre to see a production of 'The Invasion'. This was two days after she had been at the Marchioness of Hertford's Rout, with the Prince of Wales. The Duchess had taken Caroline St. Jules with her. That same week, a book, 'Twelve French

Country Dances', was published. It was adapted for the piano and dedicated to the Duchess. (28)

Over the next few months, the family appears to have alternated their time between Devonshire House and Chiswick, with both the Duke and Duchess being ill for much of the time. Early in September the Duke fell off a swing at Chiswick, which did not help matters. The Duchess had organised a party for 21st August whilst they were at Chiswick. She had a headache so painful that she could not attend it.

A month later she was much more seriously ill with a gallstone 'of amazing size', which had formed without any prior symptoms. Her sister Harriet was sent for from Roehampton, together with her mother. For several days the pain continued unrelenting, with Harriet staying up all night, every night, by her sister's bedside. By 21st September 1803 there was some improvement, but Harriet was still sitting up at night. In March 1805, the complaint returned (see below). (29) The Prince of Wales wrote enquiring after her condition from Brighton on the 17th.

This gallstone indicates the beginning of a liver complaint which eventually claimed her life. The return of gallstones in 1805 plus yellow jaundice were all symptoms of the same problem: probably a blockage or infection either in her liver, gall bladder or at least in that region. This could explain why the five doctors at her post mortem could not agree on the specific cause of death – identifying where infection had originated.

This prevented any autumnal holiday by the sea. It is not even clear if a planned trip to Castle Howard in August materialised. Devonshire House and its 3 acre garden adjoined Berkeley Street where a building caught fire on 8th September 1803. Haryo, writing to Little G, confirmed that the family had returned to Devonshire House from Chiswick at that time and wrote that it was *'opposite our windows. It was quite dreadful and if it had been a windy night, Devonshire House would have been in the greatest danger'*. Showing how careful one has to be with newspaper reports, the Morning Post stated that the Prince of Wales went around to Devonshire House whilst the fire raged. He didn't: he was in Brighton on holiday and wrote asking if all was safe.

A month later, Lady Spencer, in bed at Holywell, St. Albans, awoke about 5 a.m. because of a commotion in the courtyard. A maid poked her head through the curtains to find that 5 or 10 men had come for her fire engine as the White Hart was on fire. The fire had started in a baggage wagon parked up by some soldiers. It quickly destroyed stables and other rooms on either side of the inn courtyard, together with nine horses. 'No *lives were lost and nobody much hurt*', she wrote to Selina Trimmer. Unfortunately *'the devastation is great tho' the shell of the house is safe but almost all the furniture is destroyed by the injudicious haste with which it was torn down and flung into the street'*. A new post chaise was also destroyed and two ladies only rescued by breaking down the top of the door and dragging them through it.

Lady Spencer formed a bucket chain from the women to hand empty pails down one side of the hill to the river, while the men handled the full ones up the other side of the road to keep the fire engine topped up. She kept the women at it for three hours and wrote that *'the proof that I was of some use was that from the moment I left off, not a woman could be prevailed upon to touch a bucket any longer!'* [30] Lady Spencer was 66 years old at the time.

On 21ˢᵗ October 1803, Lord Frederick Cavendish died at Twickenham Park. He was almost the last of a race of men of measured self assurance, a belief in bringing the good out of people in a selfless, almost passive, way. Men who did great things not necessarily from ambition. As the Duchess wrote: *'a peculiar stamp of character which was a blessing to the country whilst they retained any influence'*. She felt Lord Fitzwilliam still possessed these qualities. The Morning Post described Lord Frederick as a *'gentleman of the most amiable manners, respected for his virtues and his talents'*. [31] As soon as the funeral was out of the way, the Duke decided it was time for a change and he set his sights on Bath.

Lord Fitzwilliam was a relative and regular visitor to the Devonshires. He lived, in the country, at Milton, in Northamptonshire and had a London house in Grosvenor Square. Under Lord Frederick's will, the main beneficiary was Lord George Henry, the Duke's younger brother. Some £39,846 lent by Lord Frederick to the Duke now passed to Lord George. It would appear to have been paid back in 1809, less monies George owed the Duke. [32]

A Change of Scene: Bath

Despite the death of Lord Frederick, a music party followed by supper which was planned for two days later was not cancelled. It was probably the Duchess's last for that year, for on 12ᵗʰ November, they arrived in Bath. Both Duke and Duchess were in good health and spirit. It was as though the anticipation of it had done the trick. Despite a late start, party life in London/Chiswick had been a great success – until the ton left for coast or country. Was it possible to have a winter mini-season in Bath?

Haryo did not think so. She had become bored to death at home and she felt the prospects in Bath to be not much better. To be fair, there had been many visits there which the Duchess had not particularly enjoyed and the Duke too, although they would have remembered 1782 when they met Bess Foster there. They had initially booked into the White Hart, whilst, according to the Morning Post, three houses were being prepared for them. At least the hotel suited the Duke. Writing to Selina Trimmer, Haryo wrote: *'I believe he thinks Chatsworth and Chiswick much inferior to this Hotel'*. A week after arrival, they were still there, with Haryo telling Little G: '*We are still in this Hotel – Papa thinking it, I believe, Paradise regained'*. Of the three houses, the third was actually for the Bessboroughs who were delayed as their second son was ill. They were at the end of Poulteney Street, where it opened '*on every side to beautiful hills and fields and a walk of two miles along the side of a canal'*. [33]

Haryo's grumpy attitude continued initially in Bath. She found the pump room '*more bustling, vulgar and noisy than any place I ever was in …'*, she wrote to Selina. A little later, she was no better: '*Bath does not increase in charms and if it does not improve wonderfully upon acquaintance, I shall be as happy to leave it as I was sorry to come to it …It is quite melancholy to see the quantities of lame and sick people that are wheeled and carried all about town and it is impossible to walk a hundred yards without meeting some dreadful object'*. [34]

Shortly after arrival there was another person ill in Bath: Bess Foster. Their time together in Paris had not changed Haryo's view of her. Her letters being caustic about Bess: '*Mama, in an hotel, as everywhere else, kinder, more indulgent and more unlike the lady or the dog* (i.e. Bess and her dog, Sidney) *than I can express'*. At least the Duke was on better form: '*Papa is at this moment relating a flirtation he had with a very pretty housemaid here'*. [35]

Haryo mellowed as her mother organised their social life, attending balls etc. The Bath concerts began on 7th December with the Duchess present and over Christmas, she decided to give her own concert under the direction of Mr. Rauzini. Haryo managed to write another light-hearted swipe, this time the subject being the marriage of John Heaton, following the death of his first wife: '*I think the bride must be either as deaf as a post or a patient, else how will she bear the sleepy monotony and never ending hum of her spouse's voice. Do you remember his giving the young French lady a short history of the nature of fens, marshes and damp grounds?'*. [36] Oh dear!

19

Alliances and Marriages 1804-05

1804: A Better Start To The Year

The much smaller parties which the Duchess turned to in late 1803 were repeated the following year but on a much greater scale. The Morning Post recorded 23 events at Devonshire House or Chiswick (principally the former) and the bulk of these were small (the word used at the time was 'select') ones. Additionally, the Post observed that she was to be seen at 14 parties given by others and there were probably more. At least on home ground the Duchess's intention to get to bed earlier was maintained. It would be easier to leave the events of others in favour of an earlier night.

Initially, however, they remained in Bath, possibly longer than intended with Lord Morpeth indisposed because of gout. The Duchess had four generations with her, from her mother to her grandson. By the time they returned to London in late February, the Duchess was well and walking before breakfast. Hartington had gone back early in February to return to Harrow. Payments at Bath from the Devonshire House account book [1] were (from 19th November 1803-27th February 1804) £3,586.13s.8d: an incredible amount of this, provisions and liquor, cost £1,848.

Within a day or so of returning, both the Duke and Duchess attended a Ball at St. James's Palace on the 26th along with 600 others. The whole family attended, including Lord Morpeth. [2] All were in 'perfect health', according to the Morning Post. However in mid-January, one of the Duchess's chairmen named Hoy was found to be raving mad at Devonshire House. He remained like that for 3-4 days before passing away.

March saw the party season underway. On the 14th, the Countess of Cholmondeley's Rout saw the Duchess there with Haryo and Lord Morpeth (Little G perhaps unwell – she was seven months pregnant). Some 600 invitations had been sent out and most recipients were present. It included Granville Leveson Gower and the Jerseys, the latter by now keeping a rather low profile. A week later, the Duchess was at the Countess of Perth's Ball with Haryo taking the floor as part of the first group of dancers with the Hon. Mr. Murray. There were over 300 present with the Duke giving both events a miss.

In between the two, the Duchess had her own party for 50 or so after the Opera, with food served in the opulent Saloon. She was still sticking to small events where she could. '*Her Grace looked as lovely and as interesting as usual*', purred the Morning Post. Haryo caught the eye of the reporter, who wrote that she '*appeared healthy and blooming, like the Goddess Hebe*'. The same edition also noted the presence of 1,000-1,200 vessels at Boulogne, although they were mostly small craft. The threat of invasion remained potent however. [3] At the end of the month, the family went off to Chiswick at Easter for five days. If the threat of invasion was potent, the desire to continue partying was permanent.

With the parties in full swing, in mid-April Haryo was in the first dancing session with Lord Ossulston. Non-dancers on the dance floor caused the dancing to stop and the music to cease. Rescue came from the Duchess who had the Devonshire House dancers on the floor dancing French Cortillions led by Haryo, and Lord Ossulston. The Morning Post announced further admiration of Haryo's appearance. [4]

In May the Duchess held the first of three musical subscription concerts, on the 10th, with the other two following over the next two weeks. It would appear that there was an entrance fee and over 350 people attended the first one. It started at 9.30pm and concluded at 2am. It would have given many a unique opportunity of seeing inside Devonshire House. Unfortunately the Duchess missed much of it. Little G was about to go into labour, with a second granddaughter born at 10am on the 11th May. She was called Georgiana and was christened at Chiswick House at the end of June. The grandparents (sponsors, in those days) were the Prince of Wales, Haryo and Lady Cawdor. The event was in the West Wing Drawing Room, at 5pm, with dinner afterwards. From 7-8pm guests (there were c. 50) promenaded on the lawn and in the garden with music provided by the Milanese Minstrels, a favourite group of the Duchess.

Little G wore a dress of Brussels lace upon white satin, with a cap of the same. According to the Morning Post it cost 500 guineas. If true, it would appear that she had developed the same expensive tastes as her mother. A good dancing dress could be purchased for 40-50 guineas at that time. [5]

Another significant Devonshire House expense was the wine/beer cellar. Ignoring the wage to the cellar-man, and incidentals, such as corks etc., the bill for the year was £1,737.17s.9d., of this (incurred in the 2nd and 4th quarters of the year only) were wine: £1,278.00 and malt (for beer making) £363.00. However, there was a contribution within the wine bill for the wine spent within the Steward's Room, where they paid for their own wine. Other entertainment costs included boxes at Drury Lane Theatre (£105 p.a.) and The Opera House (£157.10s.0d). A different social event happened in mid-July when the Duchess held a water-trip to Richmond, organised for her by Lord Ossulston. It included the Duchess, the Bessboroughs, Morpeths, Lords Ossulston and Duncannon, Messrs Clifford, Lamb (presumably William), Forster (sic), Hill, Corise and Caroline St. Jules. The Duke did not go. A procession of carriages left Devonshire House about 3pm for the Privy Gardens and the Whitehall Stairs, where the Admiralty barge was moored, followed by another carrying the Duke of York's military band, who played until they landed at Richmond, at 6.30pm after being rowed there.

Twenty-seven people sat down for a two-course meal at the Castle Inn. At 9.30pm they re-embarked and continued to Chiswick where carriages met them and took the party back to Devonshire House, arriving at 11.30pm. There supper was served and they were joined by 'many foreigners of first-rate distinction'. The week before, the Scarsdale Legion of Volunteers, comprising of nine companies of men, mustered at Hardwick Hall, where they were all regaled with the Duke's hospitality. This might explain why he missed the Richmond trip but more likely it was because he was secretly expecting visitors (see below) [6]

The birth of Georgiana came a couple of months after the death of the Duke's close friend James Hare on the 7th March. It will be recalled from above he had been ill and treated with mercury. A week later, the Duchess wrote to her mother saying that the Duke was still 'extremely distressed'. Devonshire House had been closed to visitors, with only Little G and Countess Bessborough admitted. [7]

The Duke had been touched by the attention that James Hare had received from his niece, a Miss Jolliffe. He had settled £100 p.a. on her to enable her to marry a Mr. Humphy (writing not clear) in September 1804 and had 'a very nice home in Bristol. It is in the Duke's name as well as mine. I write to beg you if you can, to recommend a couple of pupils ... he means to take two at present, which with his little preferment (presumably the £100) will enable them to do very well for the present. [8]

Clearly by September 1804, Hartington was reasonably proficient at horse riding, if a little reckless, as he came off when he tried to go too fast between two carriages and the wheel of one of them caught his leg. He was kept from Harrow on medical advice for a while. He went to Hastings to recouperate, with Bess Foster, and her daughter Caroline St. Jules, probably to stay with the Bessboroughs there. They appear to have gone for a month. This was at least the second time that she had taken him away. His long term relationship with her was softer than that of his sisters and it may have originated on these trips. It is worth remembering this when considering his stance when Bess married his father in 1809, although it hardened thereafter.

Hartington went regularly sea bathing when sea conditions allowed. However, the sky one evening was a new experience: '*you have seen Northern lights – it was this in red – but as red as blood... what added to the beauty was the moon appearance behind the hill and shedding that silver light that contrasted so admirably well... it was a long streak of red and even that bright yellow red a strong flame has and in this shape*' (it is shown inclined downwards from left to right, with four parallel streaks). *It was*, Bess wrote, '*a fine opportunity for you to write to or visit Mr* (Henry) *Cavendish* (the scientist). *Hartington is wild to know the cause of it*'. (9)

As the year drew to a close, the Duke learnt of the death of the Duke of Leinster. They had kept in contact since they had met as teenagers in Italy. He died on 20th October 1804. A further death on 28th November 1804 was closer to home. His personal valet (Mr. Brown) died after falling from his horse the day before. It would appear he had had a stroke. (10)

A small but interesting facet of aristocratic life is recorded in a letter from Haryo to her mother, as she travelled north to join Little G at Castle Howard in September 1804. She was travelling with Lady Elizabeth (Betty) Howard (she was Lord Morpeth's aunt), plus Lord and Lady George Cavendish, Haryo's uncle and aunt. Haryo wrote: '*Our etiquette is suprising ... we have disputes at every stage about the order of our procession and at the inns spend almost as much time at the doors of the rooms as we do in them*'. Presumably whether the daughter of a current Duke took precedence over the youngest son of an earlier, deceased Duke or whether the sister of their forthcoming host took it. (11)

Political Developments

In February, the King's madness returned and raised issues again about a Regency. On the 30th April 1804 Addington resigned, causing worries about an invasion with no Government in office. Pitt set about establishing a new ministry, all of which gave the Whigs plenty to think about, especially the extent that they could join a national ministry in a period of crisis. On 29th April 1804, the Duchess wrote to her mother to say that the Prince of Wales was '*arriving for discussions aimed at forming a new government including the Prince of Wales as Regent*'. It is interesting to note that this early meeting ahead of involving as many influential Whig friends as possible took place with the Duke. It would be easy to overplay the ability of the Duchess to contribute much, other than perhaps endeavouring to act as a facilitator to bring men like C.J.Fox to the table. The difficulty for those around that table were too many deep-seated divisions, for example, the king's deep dislike of Fox virtually precluded him for inclusion in any ministry, but that changed after the death of William Pitt two years later. An initial meeting took place at Devonshire House on the 11th May, with the Duke, Lord Morpeth, Generals Fitzpatrick and Walpole plus Messrs. Fox and Grey present.

Four days later, the Prince of Wales hosted a further dinner (the first since completion of recent building work at Carlton House). There were twenty there including six commoners, all men. [12] The Earl Fitzwilliam hosted a further three dinners on the 20th, 26th and 30th May at his house in Grosvenor Square. They were clearly not all at Devonshire House.

At the last one were the Prince of Wales and his brother the Duke of Clarence, plus the Dukes of Devonshire. [13] Despite their best endeavours, Pitt forged ahead, if only temporarily and the king recovered. At the end of June 1804, the additional Defence Bill, to raise an additional 24,000 men for the army, passed 154 to 69 votes against, confirming Pitt's position and divisions in the opposition with some siding with Pitt. The latter knew that the additional men could come too late and that the volunteer forces were, in the main, in disarray, with no effective system of control, discipline and defence. What saved him and England was not the sea, it was Austria entering the war, whereupon Napoleon turned his face to the east and away from a Channel invasion.

Although the Duchess may have been more than a fly on the wall at the Devonshire House dinner, there is no indication that she was at any of the others, although she did host a gathering of Fox and his friends at Chiswick on 29th May. The Duke held another dinner on the 5th June, but details of who was there were not recorded. [14] It will be noted that the above record of those present does not include any women. Had the Duchess or any other woman, for that matter, been formerly at meetings there, the Morning Post would have mentioned it. Moreover and more importantly, those there had a vote, or could rely on votes, and politics was very much a man's world in those days.

In 1805, at the end of September, Lord Holland gave a dinner for the Duke *and a party of friends* at his home, Holland House in Kensington. It was one of the largest houses in London and had one of the largest gardens at 32 acres. (It was lost, other than the East Wing, during The Blitz). This signalled the emergence of Lord Holland upon the political scene, at least as far as the Duke was concerned. He had succeeded to the title of 3rd Baron Holland on 26th December 1774 and was C.J. Fox's nephew. Thereafter, he appears to have been embraced by the Devonshire House circle. However, his political influence may have already been established.

He became a Privy Councillor in 1806 and served as Lord Privy Seal in the Ministry of All Talents. There is no mention of the Duchess being at that dinner. He had joined the Whig Club in 28th December 1799 and in 1805 was its Chairman. It was a literary club, engaged in high-level literary conversation although all *'discussions of opinion were studiously avoided'*. It met at the Crown and Anchor, Strand, over a good meal and wine. Its membership was small, deliberately so, and William and George Lamb became members, plus Earl Cowper, their brother-in-law. The Duke however, was not a member. (15)

Lord Holland married on 9th July 1797. It would appear that his wife, Elizabeth, succeeded the Duchess as the head of the ton: she *'played a very conspicuous part in society, political and literary. Her great attainments, lively wit, her grace and dignity decidedly placed her at the head of Whig fashion'*. (16) Early in 1806, Lord Stair was visiting her three times a day, according to the Duchess. (17)

Corisande and Lord Ossulston

By agreement with the Duc de Grammont, his daughter, Armandine Sophie Leonie Corisande, was brought up with the Duke's children at Devonshire House, apparently after her mother contracted TB. She was known there as Corise. With the Peace of Amiens, her parents came over to be reunited with their daughter in November 1802. Her parents were Antoine Gramont, Duc de Gramont and Louise, the daughter of Armand Jules, Duc de Polignac (18). The Polignacs were long established friends of the Duke and Duchess.

Corise's mother died on 4th April 1804 and shortly thereafter, Corise's name started to be linked with Lord Ossulston. He was the oldest son of the 4th Earl of Tankerville and was named Charles Augustus, born on 28th April 1776. He may have been introduced to the Devonshires (who had gone with Haryo) at the Marquis of Abercorn's Ball during Easter week 1803 or maybe a month later when he, the Duchess and Haryo were at Lady de Clifford's Assembly. A year later in mid-April 1804, he partnered Haryo in the first dance at Mr. M. P. Andrew's Ball, which suggests that he may well have become on good terms by then with the Devonshires.

In fact in 1804, he was part of the Duchess's party both at Devonshire House and when party-going. Lord O, as the Duchess referred to him, was her 'superintendent' on the boat trip to Richmond she organised in mid-July. By the end of that month Corise (the Duchess called her Corrie) was regularly being mentioned in the Morning Post.

Educated at Eton and Trinity College, Cambridge, Lord O had been returned as M.P. for Steyning in 1803. He was usually on the guest list when the family went to stay at Chiswick. It was clear that he and Corrise were in love. The

Duke and Duchess liked him, the Duke finding him *'sensible and pleasing'*. This might have been influenced by his interest in whist and being prepared to sit and play it until 2am, when they retired. However, thoughts of marriage were initially dashed by the Earl of Tankerville's refusal to agree to it. That July, he had refused to attend his daughter Anna's wedding let alone give her away, when she married the Rev. William Beresford. His objection was that the groom was Irish. There may have been another reason common to his son-in-law and Corise: they were possibly both Catholics. Haryo, writing to Little G in August from Chiswick, told her sister that *'Corise is in very good spirits and he seems so seriously and really attached to her'*. [19]

In late 1804 and throughout 1805, there appears to have been a news blackout on the couple, with hardly a reference to them. The Morning Post did note in August 1805, a Mr. Hill had left London to visit the Earl of Tankerville at Chillingham Castle in Northumberland. After Granville Leveson Gower left England as Ambassador to Russia, Harriet Bessborough caught a reporter's eye dancing with Mr. Hill. It makes one wonder whether he went as an intermediary to intervene on Lord O's behalf. The blackout continued into 1806, but the two were married on 28th July 1806 at Devonshire House. The Earl of Aberdeen wrote to Augustus Foster on 6th April 1805 to say *'Your old flame (Corise) is still in status quo, although Lord Tankerville, I understand, now consents'*. This would appear to have been wrong.

Also in 1806, Lord O was returned as M.P. of Knaresborough, one of the Duke's two representatives for Knaresborough, a seat he (Lord O) kept until 1818. He became, in 1806, the Treasurer of the Household in Lord Grenville's Ministry of All the Talents and also a Privy Counsellor. The 4th Earl of Tankerville died in 1822 and Lord O was elevated to the House of Lords as 5th Earl. Corise of course then became the Countess of Tankerville. She had two children, Corisand Emma and Charles Augustus, the 6th Earl. Corise died on 23rd January 1865. Lord O lived until 25th June 1859 and died aged 83. Corise's daughter married the 3rd Earl of Malmesbury. [20] As the daughter of a French Duke, Corise successfully integrated into the English aristocracy. Chillingham Castle is the home of the famous rare breed of white cattle.

The marriage of Caroline Ponsonby to William Lamb

The Duke would have found little amiss with the time it took Lord O and Corise to marry. He was never one to do much today if a decision tomorrow would do. He could and would rise to the occasion when expediency demanded it, sometimes changing his mind as a result – eg. his demand for a separation over the Martindale affair re the Duchess's alleged debt. What he thought of the speed of developments between Caroline Ponsonby and William Lamb was not recorded. Lamb was the 2nd son of Lord Melbourne – officially at any rate. He was actually the son of the 3rd Earl of Egremont. Lord Melbourne's oldest son Peniston died in January 1805. (Various dates are quoted, but the Duchess wrote to her mother on 24/01/1805 to say that he had died at Brocket Hall. (21) He was aged 34 and died of consumption on the lungs. This completely altered the financial prospects for William, who was 25 years old. The Melbournes returned from a stay at Brighton in the last week of April 1805 and he wrote to Caroline on 2nd May to say *I have loved you for four years, loved you deeply, dearly, faithfully*. (22)

Caroline had grown up as a teenager at Devonshire House. Gleeson suggests that Caroline may have been Charles Wyndham's child, he also being Lord Egremont's son. (in which case, with William Lamb, she was marrying her uncle.) Nonetheless, her mother believed she (Caroline) was her husband's daughter. (23) What a state for your patrimony to be in! The Duchess wrote to her mother that the two had met at the Opera *and when he came here to supper for the first time, I saw nothing remarkable*. This was probably on the 10th January 1805 when a Mr Lamb was noted by the Morning Post as being at a supper at Devonshire House. *The next opera* (and he had not seen her in the interval), continued the Duchess, *was decisive so that the first we knew was at once – his proposal and acceptance*.

On reflection she added *I do not wish Harriet* (Haryo) *to marry yet until she finds somebody she really likes and as yet it has not been the case*. (24) In a previous letter, the Duchess had told her mother that Caroline had been in love with William Lamb for some time, but had suppressed it. Now she knew his feelings for her, there was no holding her back. Both she and the Duke, she wrote, felt that any check on developments would produce serious consequences. She (Caroline) was going to see the Duke that day (4th May) following which it was announced that future developments would depend upon Lady Spencer's approval.

However, there was a problem, at least for the Marquis of Hartington and it was to be possibly a life changing moment. He could not handle the situation at all and had to be sedated by Walter Farquhar. It had been his intention to ask her to marry him and to ask his father for permission upon reaching eighteen. It was agreed that both he and Caroline would go to see their grandmother, Lady Spencer, who in a letter to Selina Trimmer, wrote *Hartington's behaviour has been quite affecting, he trembled and turned pale when she told him of it – cried bitterly and said you always was my wife and if you would have stood for me I would have married you – now, I shall never marry at all – at present he is most anxious for her happiness and never quits her*. He never did marry, true to his word. (25)

Lady Spencer did not quite give Caroline what she wanted, but it was near enough. Fortunately for Hartington, the Duke had been making other plans for him on leaving Harrow (see below). Initially, Harriet Bessborough was unhappy about Caroline marrying into the Melbourne family, because of *'their lack of social grace and hedonistic amorality'*. [26] There is no doubt that Lady Melbourne had a reputation as a predator of married men. The Devonshires, however, had continued their relationship with the Melbournes, if not with the Jerseys, which could indicate that she had not had a similar experience with the Duke, or at least one the Duchess knew about. According to Gleeson, Lady Melbourne did not have a better opinion of Harriet and there was of course good reason. [27]

The Lambs went to Brocket Hall for their honeymoon and the Melbournes prepared the middle apartment at Melbourne House in Whitehall, London for them to live in. [28] William had a sister Emily who married Earl Cowper and there are many references to them in the Duchess's correspondence. The Duke did not provide for Caroline Ponsonby on her marriage or for Corise for that matter (from surviving records). It appears he left it for their fathers to take the strain. On the other hand, the Duke paid for Caroline's wedding dress, which was of the finest muslin, with lace 'let in', the sleeves being 'very long'. The Duchess's present was a lace veil. With a nice touch of romance, William carried his wife-to-be in his arms into the church. [29]

In the case of Corise, her father did not have the money available to help his daughter. His money had gone to support two members of the French Polignac family. Bess Foster broached this with the Duke and found him (as usual, happy on such occasions) to match a contribution from Corise's father. However, as we have seen, that option was not available. The Duchess had felt unable to raise all of this with the Duke as he had just reached an agreement over paying her debts. She felt that she could not be seen to be using her money on a payment from herself. Bess felt that she could successfully press the Duke to pay £150 and was hoping that this could be lifted to £200 with a contribution from herself, Little G and Haryo. It is not known if this happened but it is likely that it did. Just prior to Christmas 1805, the Duke also agreed to settle £200 on Selina Trimmer. She had been paid £100 p.a. and it is likely that this was £200 pa. [30]

Caroline Lamb developed a talent as a writer and is also remembered as being the lover of Lord Byron, although their affair was short-lived and better known perhaps for her reaction upon it being ended. She became Lady Caroline Ponsonby in 1793 when her father became Lord Bessborough and died on 26th January 1828 aged 42 years. [31]

Caroline and the others benefitted from the sound education at Devonshire House, where the house curriculum included French, Italian and poetry. The children there developed a love of books, music (they regularly went to the family box at the Opera House and at Drury Lane Theatre) and were proficient at dancing, reading and poetry under the Duchess's direction. Only the boys went on to an independent school – Harrow for both Hartington and Augustus Clifford. Caroline's experience just prior to her marriage suggests that she was both determined and impetuous, which may go some way to explaining a similar behaviour when Lord Byron broke off their affair.

William Lamb was elected M.P. for Leominster in 1806 and became Home Secretary, 1830-34 and Prime Minister in 1834 and again in 1835-41. The city of Melbourne in Victoria, Australia was named after him in 1837. He also became young Queen Victoria's mentor, for which he is also remembered. He became Lord Melbourne on the death of his 'father' in 1828.

Upon the death of her husband, Lord Cowper, Emily married the 3rd Viscount Palmerston, with whom she had had a long relationship, on 16th December 1839. She became a noted hostess and at least one of Lord Cowper's children, Emily, was widely accepted as being Palmerston's daughter. (32) He became Prime Minister in 1855-58 and again from 1859-1865. He still is the last British Prime Minister to die in office. Prior to becoming the Prime Minister he held two other great offices of state: Home Secretary and Foreign Secretary. Palmerston received a State Funeral, only the 5th for a commoner in British history. Wellington was the intervening one after Nelson.

Consequently before he died in November 1848, ex-Prime Minister William Lamb, saw his brother-in-law reach high office as Foreign Secretary in 1846. (33) It must be unusual for the same generation of a family to have two Prime Ministers, with Emily having both her brother and husband occupying that office. The Devonshire's almost made it, with Dorothy Cavendish having her father (the 4th Duke) and her husband (the Duke of Portland) as Prime Ministers.

20

In Full Swing 1805

The Garter Knights Installation

Occasionally, State occasions demanded the presence of the Duke. He liked
the pomp and ceremony, as indicated by the Duchess when they were in
Paris in 1789 (see above). On 22nd April, 1805 the installation of four Garter
Knights occurred. It was the first time that this had happened since July 1771
when '*the heat of the sun was so oppressive that many of the Knights sustained
great inconvenience*'. The Morning Post of 15th April gave a long and detailed
description of the Garter robes (spared here). The Duke felt the need for
something new. The Devonshire House Accounts [1] includes 'Apparel', £421,
of which £251 was to W. Webb, Robemaker. The Post indicated that the plume
of feathers cost from 60-130 guineas. Presumably the additional £170 spent by
the Duke on apparel was largely for the feathers.

The main event was a Communion Service at the St. George's Chapel,
Windsor Castle. Thirty-five bed chambers had been knocked up in a week '*at
the top of the castle...all papered and furnished with tent bedsteads, the rooms
being about 12ft square. Over 600 labourers worked to have all the arrangements
ready on time, including the arrival of four heavily laden wagons with the new
bedroom furniture*'.

With the opportunity to make easy money, one modest householder in
Windsor was offering, the week prior to the Installation, a five-bed cottage for
'*three nights, covering the event at a cost of 200 guineas (£210), despite plenty of
accommodation being initially available*' only days previous. In Staines, Egham
and Eton, however, not a house or lodging was vacant for nearly a week before
the event, with a lot of guests ensuring they arrived early enough.

By the prior Sunday (the event was on the Wednesday) Windsor was clogged, *'every moment carriages of various descriptions arrived, some with four and others with six horses, all of them crammed with visitors and luggage. The windows of all the principal inns were crowded with company during the morning, principally ladies and those mostly of distinction'*. Arriving on the Monday morning were the Prince of Wales and the Duke who had gone early to cover the Chapel arrangements, the Duke being the most senior Knight. [2]

At the event, the Chapel procession, ahead of The King (amongst others), included the four new Garter Knights elect: Earls of Chesterfield, Winchelsea and Pembroke and the Marquis of Abercorn (the latter being a regular supper guest at Devonshire House). There then followed other Garter Knights: Dukes of Beaufort and Rutland (Duke's neighbour), then Earls: Camden, Spencer (Dukes's brother-in-law), Carlisle (Duke's son-in-law's father), Westmorland, Salisbury, Chatham and Marquis of Buckingham. Separately, in front of the Sovereign, came the Duke of Devonshire. [3] This edition also carried details of the dresses worn by the Queen and her party.

It is perhaps worthy of note here that the Morning Post always placed details of the Duke and Duchess immediately after announcements relating to the king and the Royal Family. At the Installation procession it was presumably because of the Duke's position as Senior Knight that he immediately preceded the king. It seems amazing now, but a lot arrived for the service intending to change on arrival in Windsor and finding nowhere available to do it. It was only after the Castle gates opened at 11am that rooms in town became available.

The Duchess was unable to be there. Presumably the problem with gallstones, which had occurred in March, had not improved enough to permit her attendance. Earl Spencer took the Marquis of Hartington (in the uniform of the Derbyshire Militia), Lord Althorp, the Earl's son and William Poyntz. Apparently, the Duke fluffed some of the ceremonials, having had no idea of how much he had to do in his position of Senior Knight (so wrote the Duchess to her mother), although the latter was probably at Windsor, going with her son. Lady Spencer said she grieved that her daughter was not well enough to go and it *'will really be a very fine thing altogether and such as is not likely to be seen again in this country'*. [4]

The four Garter Knights later held a celebratory Gala event at Ranelegh Gardens, expecting it to be better than the one given by the Knights of the Bath in 1803. A little sooner than that, the day after the Installation, the Duke relaxed over dinner at Chiswick with the Prince of Wales and his brother, the Duke of Clarence. [5] A few days later, on the 2nd May 1805, it was the Duchess's turn to mix with royalty. She went with the Duchess of Northumberland by chair to Court. Each chair was preceded by six liveried servants. The Duchess was followed by the chairs of Haryo, Lady Bessborough and Lady George Cavendish. The Duchess of Northumberland was attended by her three daughters. [6]

1805: Partying Apace

In January 1805, the Duchess had four supper parties plus a Comedy fete, featuring a comedy written by her and using some of the family as actors. She also went to Lady Perth's Ball, perhaps the first of the season, other than that which followed the Comedy, the dancing being opened by Haryo with Lord Duncannon, her cousin. The Duchess's last supper party in February was on the 12th, with her attending the Marchioness of Stafford's party on the 18th. She gave no suppers in March or April and although she is reported as being at the Marchioness of Salisbury's party on the 17th March, this may well be in error.

During March she was confined with another attack of gallstones, with her sister Harriet staying by the bedside during two nights. It was reported that on the 26th March the Duchess was extremely ill and doubts were entertained of her surviving. The paper described her illness as being yellow jaundice, which she may well have had at the same time, a symptom of a wider liver/gall bladder problem. [7] Although recovered during May, she suffered from an eye infection in June. On the 22nd, Harriet was called again and found her sister in agony and unable to bear to have any light at all.

At the end of 1804 a theatrical phenomenon started performing on the London stage. He was William Betty, whose stage name was Young Roscius. Although some were not too impressed, when Charles Grey informed William Pitt, when the House of Commons broke on 28th January 1805, that he was off to see Young Roscius with Charles Fox, Pitt replied that they could not spend a leisure hour better, for he was a prodigy. He was soon making even more money through his appearances on the fashionables' circuit. At the beginning of March, the Duke and Duchess were present at the Marquis of Abercorn's Entertainment when he sang, along with Lady Hamilton.

Despite troops having to be called out to preserve order in December 1804 at Covent Garden, because of the demand for tickets, the doubters persisted. 'Grey can see no merit in him and Mr Windham sees but little – while Mr Pitt has become a play goer and Mr Fox with whom I saw him in "Hamlet", thought his acting during the play better than Garrick'. [8] Fox and the Devonshires were of the same view: 'The Duke and all of us are going to see young Roscius tonight in the character of Richard the Third. It is a bold undertaking but his genius justifies his daring'. [9] It was reported in July 1805 that for the following season, he would be getting £100 per night at Drury Lane. Covent Garden would not match this (a rise of 100 per cent for the latter) and performances there ended. [10]

Even later into the year, the doubters were still peddling their opinion. The

Earl of Aberdeen (who had spent time trying to attract the attention of Haryo) wrote to Augustus Foster, Bess Foster's son, to say *'we are all bored this year by that wretch called the Young Roscius, who is the greatest imposter'*. There is no doubt that the young actor had his followers and objectors. One can only comment that at an early age, he retired on his earnings. [11]

The round of partying continued apace through the summer of 1805. Following the Duchess's Musical Subscription Concerts in May, she held a *'vocal and instrumental Concert'* at Devonshire House under the direction of Mr. Monzani on 17th June. It was held in the lofty Saloon with over 350 people present. Concluding at 12.30am, it was followed by supper for the select few, including The Prince of Wales. On the 5th the Duchess was at Lady Lambert's Masquarade in Little Argyle Street, where the Morning Post reckoned she was the best 'character'. She had gone in a Spanish dress consisting of brown muslin, trimmed with yellow satin vandykes. This suggests a brown dress with a series of yellow points forming a border. Haryo was dressed as a Swiss peasant and Corise was a Greek slave. The Duke was giving it a miss.

There is a possibility that the Duchess had had the dress made in Devonshire Brown. In January of that year, the Morning Post reported that the Duchess of Bedford had taken delivery of a new coach, which was painted in Devonshire Brown. This came a few days after the paper had reported that the Duchess of Devonshire's coach was 'most conspicuous by its elegance'. She usually went out in a white dress. Brown was unusual, so she was probably initiating something new. [12] If the Duchess was trying to introduce a new fashion, it is interesting on two counts: she chose to do so at a fancy dress party, where she would not lose face if it did not catch on and she also went in a Spanish style dress. Given below are the guidance notes for that season's fashions, which refers to large Spanish hats being very fashionable, viz:

'Fashions for April'

Full Dresses

A full dress of fine white muslin, embroidered pyramidically with gold, the dress made quite plain over the bosom, and clasped with a small miniature or medallion; the sleeves plain and embroidered to correspond with the dress. The hair dressed with a gold bandeau, white shoes – An evening dress of blue crepe or muslin over an under dress of white sarsnet; the blue dress made open in the back, to show the under one; the sleeves plain and looped up on the top of the arms with a brooch.

Promenade or Evening Dresses

Dress of plain white muslin, with long sleeves, a white muslin cloak, with lace let in all round. Straw hat turned a pin front and ornamented with a feather.

Head Dresses

The Savoyard cap of white crepe, ornamented with a bunch of roses on the top – A hat of yellow silk, looped upon the left side – a blue satin hat, trimmed with the same, turned up before and behind.

General Observations

The prevailing colours are pink, blue and green, all very pale. The large Spanish hat still continues very fashionable. The dresses continue to be made very short waisted, and very low over the bosom and back, lace is introduced into every article of dress'. [13]

No mention of brown, however, which may be why she did it – to be different and one step ahead. It was after all, the Duchess who had extended the season now starting in January and introduced the supper parties. She continually strove to introduce something different, in terms of room decoration, the French dancing etc.

A couple of nights after Lady Lambert's Masquerade, at Mrs. Du Pre's Grand Ball in Grafton Street, 300 people let their hair down. The Earl of Aberdeen, having taken a fancy to Haryo, partnered her at the dances. The ladies in general were wearing gold or silver muslin dresses *'with head dresses fully ornamented with diamonds'*. [14] The Duke accompanied the family to this one.

During the summer, the Marquis left Harrow for the final time. His tutor was to be the Rev. J. Smith who appears to have been engaged by the Duke from 1st June 1805. He resided near Sandwich, Kent. He came with the recommendation of the Bedfords, whose son Lord Tavistock was already being tutored by him. He was conveniently living by the sea, which Sir Walter Farquhar had recommended would be good for Hartington. His tutoring as a young man had begun. In the Devonshire accounts for the 4th quarter is a payment of £100 to the Marquis and £116.12s.6d to Rev. Smith. The Marquis had been previously allowed five guineas a quarter while at school. [15]

On the 8th May 1805, the Duke's Aunt Rachel Walpole died. She was the last surviving child of the 3rd Duke.

On the 29th June the Morning Post announced yet another claim that they knew of an attachment by Haryo. This time it was to a Mr. Lawley, (? Francis, later the 7th Baronet), the brother of Sir Robert Lawley the eldest son of Sir Robert Lawley, 5th Baronet. More seriously and accurately was a report that the Duchess had a 'slight' inflammation in her eyes. She was confined to her room from about 20th June and was not seeing visitors, except the family. She was being attended by Messrs. Wathen and Phipps (the latter being the king's doctor). A month later, she went to Chiswick with Haryo and Corise. Here she stayed until the end of August before returning to town *'to view the alterations at Devonshire House'*. [16]

However, it is probable that this was only a visit and she returned to Chiswick.

At the end of October, it was reported that she would remain there '*until Devonshire House has undergone a thorough repair*'. [17] Unfortunately, the house accounts for 1806 until the Duke's death are missing, so it is not clear what was in need of repair and how expensive it was. However, dinners there resumed in early January 1806. So, as the Duchess journeyed through the last full year of her life, fate and illness deprived her of enjoying a full season of her supper parties.

Devonshire House had been built some seventy or so years before, yet despite needing a '*thorough*' repair, it was back in service after several months. This does not therefore suggest major work in the reception rooms, where intricate moulded plasterwork would most likely have taken longer to complete. However, it did include 'modernisation' of the saloon and as a result, the Ball held there at the beginning of March 1806 did not include the usual adornment of artificial flowers. [18] No other detail was given. Several other major players in the party season had refurbished their properties, or even moved house (eg: the Abercorns (the former) and Duchess of Gordon (the latter). Each year, the Duchess strove to heighten the bar in the delivery of her parties, as indicated above. She would not wish to be seen to be playing second fiddle to anyone else. Hence going from Chiswick to see that the alterations were to her satisfaction seems to fit the bill.

There is however, a hint that the work was superficial rather than structural. In January 1806, the Duchess wrote to Hartington: '*By the by, the rooms are beautiful (at Devonshire House). I have got my red carpet on the stairs, my grey carpet in the rooms, a fine (?brown) Egyptian Lyon on red for my rug and my pink furniture. Old D(evonshire) House looks clean and gay, but to me it wants you to complete the gaiety. I run about picking up every bit of paper off the ground and have had all the spots on the passages painted. Your father says it is really very pretty but will not last long*'. [19]

Her health had improved by mid-August, 1805 and she was wearing spectacles. However, instead of glass they had black crape to take off the glare, which suggests she used them when at home. Lady Jersey was also using spectacles to read. The Duchess said she was as beautiful as ever but '*has given up all her old ways*', to the satisfaction of some ladies, no doubt. [20]

Having moved from Devonshire House during its refurbishment the Duke's gout returned in the autumn. '*We sent yesterday for all the apparatus of flannel shoes etc*' to Devonshire House, wrote Haryo to her sister. '*Papa has the gout settled in his knee and he says it is the most painful fit he ever had. He is confined to his room and of course we are all very triste and uncomfortable. Mama stays almost entirely with him*'. [21] As the Duke's health improved in December, the Duchess went, for some reason, to Sir Walter Farquhar's home for a consultation, complaining that she '*had so much more of that awkward pain in my good i.e. left side. I am so well in other respects*'. Her doctor diagnosed muscular pain, but was this associated with her liver/gallbladder problem? [22]

The family returned to Devonshire House for Christmas following completion of the work there (see above). Whether it was the new surroundings or a return of the gout which kept the Duke at home at whist parties in the evening is not clear. However, he was teased with being responsible for Brooks's Club being deserted in January 1806! [23]

Does '*Mama stays almost entirely with him*' not give the impression that the relationship between both the Duke and the Duchess with Bess Foster seems to have evolved into an arms-length sort, rather than a cosy, loving ménage, which history suggests was the case? This letter perhaps needs to be put into a wider context offered by Bess's visit to Paris a couple of years before. Despite several letters from the Duchess saying how much she was missing Bess, the latter seems to have been in no hurry to return. It was only when war threatened that she came back.

Suitors for Haryo

The year 1805 turned out to be a year for relationships for the younger generation at Devonshire House, although Hartington must have been sanguine about it all. Caro Ponsonby married in June and her new sister-in-law Emily Lamb the month afterwards (see above). Crusty and determined Lord Tankerville would not yield to the match between Corise and Lord Ossulston, which tested (favourably) that relationship. Little G was busy making babies, which left Haryo and Lord Duncannon, the oldest son of the Bessboroughs and Haryo's cousin.

He had managed to avoid the clutches of Lady Jersey to the relief of his mother and probably her sister, the Duchess. There was a loose understanding between the two sisters that the cousins might marry but with the ending of the relationship with Elizabeth Villiers, no romance blossomed for Haryo. The two had opened the dancing at Devonshire House after the Comedy play in January 1805, which was probably the Duchess's doing. They had also agreed to wait a year to see if they then wished to marry. [24] However, Duncannon started a relationship with a Mrs. Payne. She was married, but separated and a friend of the Abercorns.

This liaison caused Lord Abercorn to become infatuated with Haryo and according to her aunt Harriet, '*pretty near makes love*'. [25] By April, Haryo became the centre of attention for Lord Aberdeen, who was supposed to be marrying Lady Catherine Hamilton in July 1805, the daughter of the Duchess of Gordon. Although the Duke liked him and he spent a lot of time hanging around Devonshire House, Bess Foster thought that he would not be a good match for Haryo, despite him being *amiable and delightful*. (26)

Duncannon soon turned his attentions to yet another woman – heiress Lady Maria Fane, daughter of the Earl of Westmorland and granddaughter of Robert Child, of Child's Bank. Her mother had married at Gretna Green, without Robert Childs's approval and the latter's huge wealth would bypass her father (the Earl), going to Maria. All of a sudden, the dice had moved and Duncannon moved quickly to obtain the Earl's approval having proposed to Maria by letter. (27) It looks as though the Duchess had persuaded the Duke to go and see the Earl too, but in the event, his gout kept him at home.

When asked about her feelings for Duncannon, Haryo responded that marriage would depend upon him giving up these other liaisons, but Duncannon refused: he married Maria and the money. On the 16th November 1805, Haryo wrote to Little G: '*I gave up my ci-devant true love without a sigh and even Mr. Foster* (Bess's son) *congratulates me upon my wonderful command over my feelings... we expect nobody but Lord O*'. (28) Despite her '*dazzling beauty*', as the Morning Post had described her, it was 1809 before she married Lord Granville Leveson Gower. In 1805, he was still our Ambassador to Russia.

A month before Lady Maria Fane married Duncannon, she went to stay at Chiswick with Lady Villiers. Re the former, Haryo observed that '*she is certainly not a beauty but she has something so pleasing and feminine about her that nobody would think of regretting it. I hear the servants all thought her very pretty and Miss Keating* (the Duchess's dresser) *was in raptures about her elegance... Lady Villiers abated much of her usual loquacity upon the occasion and she ought to know what a blessing it is when she does*'. (29)

Staying At The Head Of Fashionable Society (The Ton)

The Duchess led London Society not because it just happened, although her charm and personality must have been a significant part of it. She projected herself in such a manner that it would have been difficult for anyone else to equal her, even if they tried to emulate her achievements. The cost would also have been a prohibitive factor. In the case of her jewellery, she ignored the cost and kept on spending with a ruthless determination (see below). There were several different facets to maintaining her dominance:

Fashion

A significant aspect of being the leader of the fashionables, or if you prefer, the French word, the ton, was the introduction of new fashions, chiefly in dress wear, cloaks, shoes and hats. The Duchess was instrumental in this although she must have wished that she visited Paris more often. She had been in Paris in 1772 and 1775, the year after her marriage. It was fifteen years before she went again. Although there in 1790, sightseeing and socialising was interrupted by revolution, from which they went to Spa, leaving two daughters (both illegitimate children of the Duke). Back again in 1791, following the birth of her son Hartington, she was ill and her daughter, Little G, became so ill that her life was in danger for some time. Back once more the following year, she was six months pregnant and wishing to keep the matter quiet. They were hanging about in Paris waiting for Bess Foster to join them. The Duchess never returned. Her mother advised her to stay away in 1777 because of her debts. It is amazing that she yielded so much influence in Paris with so little physical impact there. To recap, the Duchess only went to Paris in 1772, 1775 and in the three years 1789-91.

A leading hostess, Mrs Crewe (part of the Devonshire House set and lover of Richard Sheridan) found in 1783 that dress etiquette was different in Paris compared to London. In the latter, the figure and not the clothes mattered most, whereas in Paris, being decorated with grace and refinement was more important. [30] Equally, the interpretation of grace and refinement was somewhat subjective. One has only to think of Madame Recamier, dressed in a low cut dress with bare arms and shoulders, which caused a sensation in Kensington Gardens in 1802 and disgusted Bess Foster in 1803.

The Duchess picked up the mantle of wearing French fashions upon her return to London as a married woman early in 1775. It is likely that her thoughts were on such matters whilst she was at Londesbrough in late 1774, for Lady Clermont sent her a drawing of a new hairstyle-cum head dress on the 27th November. It showed a high coiffured style incorporating feathers and what appears to be a plant. [31] A Mrs. Harris, in a letter to her son, commented that the Duchess had been at a concert on 16th March 1775 wearing *two plumes sixteen inches long, besides three smaller ones; this has so far outdone all other plumes, that Mrs Damer, Lady Harriet Stanhope etc looked nothing*, Having arrived at Devonshire House, her influence on London fashion had begun. [32]

Reynolds painted her a year or so later with a high coiffure, which incorporated both reddish and white feathers. The Duchess wore longer and longer plumes, which eventually reached 4 ft/ 1.3m in length. However they were banned by Queen Charlotte at her assemblies, known simply as the Queen's Drawing Room, as she had to keep avoiding being slapped in the face by them as the wearer curtsied! Thereafter, they continued to be used but of a more demure length and within a year or so, they faded from further use. As one fashion lost support, another one succeeded it, often with some rapidity. Feathers were followed by puce, a purplish brown colour. [33] The latest French fashion was soon adopted in London and vice versa.

In 1783, the French Queen, Marie – Antoinette, posed for a portrait in a white chemise muslin gown. Although it provoked a scandal in France, the following year, she sent come of these dresses adorned with fine lace, which the Duchess chose to wear on the 18th August 1784 at a concert in Derby, wearing an 'English night gown (evening wear, not what we now call a nightie) of muslin with small silver sprigs' that evening at a Ball. (34) The chemise gown was soon the de rigueur item of fashion in both capitals. It was to be followed by other dresses, but the white muslin dress retained its popularity and appears to have been the favourite of the Duchess.

In the latter years of her life it would appear that the Duchess's formal dresses were white muslin with a brown spencer, a round straw bonnet and a white veil, worn with diamonds. A spencer was originally a woollen outer tail coat with the tails cut off, which was adopted as a mess dress by the British Army in the 1790s. It was worn as a cardigan and was soon popular with women as a fitted jacket. It was either cut to just above the waist, or in Empire style, cut to just under the bust and tailored to match the dress. Like a traditional jacket, it had long arms.

It is inconceivable that the Duchess would not embrace this new fashion: it was named after her brother George, 2nd Earl Spencer. In 1803, the Morning Post reported that in Paris the spencer was *now of a light cotton or linen stuff, richly trimmed with lace'*. It is persuasive to think that if the Spencer was originated by the Duchess's brother, it was his fashion conscious older sister who popularised its use. It is also interesting to note that refinements to the style made in Paris, were then highlighted in the Morning Post and no doubt subsequently adopted in London.

The dress wear for the girls living at Devonshire House, i.e. Haryo, the two Carolines and Corise, was a *'white cambric muslin dress trimmed with either lace or muslin with a montem bonnet of willow or muslin, plus nankeen shoes and open-docked silk stockings'*. (35) See also what would appear to be the introduction of a new style of Spanish dress in brown muslin which the Duchess wore on the 5th June 1805 at Lady Lambert's Masquarade, possibly in Devonshire brown colour (see above). With constantly changing variations of style, the Duchess effectively controlled the dress style of the London socialites, both with newly initiated French styles or others originated in Piccadilly, London.

Jewellery

The portrait of c. 1775 by Reynolds and arguably one of the finest portraits of her, shows her hair simply adorned with a string of pearls (other than the white and reddish feathers). Her white dress is decorated with gold frilled material on both shoulders, a gold gauze scarf over her right shoulder and with a gold sash. (36) It also shows her with brown eyes, although as a young girl, a portrait of her and her mother shows her with blue eyes. Surviving invoices reveal a later preference for diamonds as well as pearls.

An indication of the extent of the Duchess's spending on jewellery maybe gained by looking at her account with those to whom she was indebted at her death. Any other purchases paid for are excluded. It is clear from this that there is not a lot recorded as outstanding for 1801 and nothing here for 1802, 1803 and up to November 1804. See Chapter 18. Claims at her death from jewellers amounted to £15,714, including £416 to silver smiths. All this was money she did not possess. It shows how determined she was to maintain a position she could not financially sustain. (37)

Property

Devonshire House was situated in Piccadilly, on what is now the site of Green Park Underground Station, across the road from The Ritz Hotel. It was built to a design by Kent after its predecessor was destroyed by fire. It was truly opulent internally, although its Palladian front looked rather plain. It had six main reception rooms on the first floor, reached by a twin-set of external steps. This allowed for parties on a large scale, with 800 being accommodated without much difficulty. It was noted for its extensive collection of Old Master paintings. Its very large forecourt allowed for the parking of many carriages, with up to 400 making their way there for large events.

Its gardens at the rear were extensive, although by the 1780s were in need of refurbishment, as were those at Chiswick. Devonshire House was regarded as one of the finest properties in London and was a fitting backdrop to the glittering parties the Duke and Duchess hosted there.

Chiswick House is situated 12 miles from the centre of London and was in the Duchess's time out in the countryside. The house had an odd arrangement of buildings when the Duke and Duchess married in 1774. A large Jacobean building served as the main house but was regarded as being damp by the Duchess and with suspicion by the Duke after his wife developed 'putrid fever' there. The Duke's grandfather, the 3rd Earl of Burlington, had built next to it an early and very elegant Palladian villa, but its usefulness was marred by having no kitchen. The Duke demolished the old house in c. 1788 but left the service wing to act as the kitchen, with a very long external corridor to bring food to the villa.

Over the course of some seven years or so, two new wings were added, which gave more space and bedrooms. However it was not very large for the functions the Duchess held there. She achieved this by erecting marquees on the lawns and putting dining tables throughout the villa. Chiswick was ideal for this, with lovely lawned areas separated by hedges from others, several bands playing to regale the guests. Up to 900 people were invited to events here. Held in the afternoon, they were usually over by early evening.

The Parties, Assemblies etc

The Duchess continually strove to ensure that her parties were the best, but did not get away lightly. There was a lot of competition from some of her friends who were equally determined not to be left behind. They were continually being wrong footed. The Duchesses of Gordon and St Albans, the Marchioness of Abercorn and the Countess of Cholmondeley were among those endeavouring to keep up. The latter two were amongst those who even changed homes and refurbished the new ones in fashionable styles.

Many of the Duchess's gatherings had a theme to them, which maintained a spontaneity, even intrigue, such as when she 'borrowed' the Admiralty's barge and its compliment of rowers. Leaving their carriages at the West India Docks, they were rowed to Greenwich and Richmond, where they ate at a local inn. Probably only the Duchess would hold a party for French guests only and get the French Royal family to organise the guest list. Musical subscription concerts followed, although she did not have any exclusivity over that.

Private parties went to Ranelagh and Vauxhall Gardens (with up to 100 people in tow); she had large private viewings at the Royal Academy; top performing artists, eg Young Roscius, sang into the night. When Bess Foster returned from France in 1803, she brought back details of new dance routines – the French Cortillions, which also demanded a fashion change to emphasise the petticoats during the dances. The Duchess rose to the challenge.

Then there were all the little details in which the Duchess seemed to excel: use of scented blossom on a grand scale (eg. orange and lemon blossom; bigger and better use of lighting and decoration; top quality food with fruit etc especially grown in the Chiswick greenhouses, unusual fruits and those out of season etc. Not everybody would have the Prince of Wales dropping in with Mrs. Fitzherbert, let alone his younger brothers. No one else had the details of their to-ing and fro-ing immediately reported and always directly below the Court Circular in the top London newspaper, the Morning Post.

The family moved about in top quality carriages finished off with Devonshire brown, with a Devonshire boot, the coronet on the side and silver springs underneath. They were clothed in the finest material, Brussels lace and so on. It does not seem unusual to know that she sent a man to Paris to purchase the late Queen's harp. Despite the continuing waywardness with her expenditure, it helped that, once the Duke knew what was going on (she kept him very much in the dark for most of the time) he did not seem to mind about the fact she had done so, only the gravity of it. He treated his son the same.

The only exception appears to be when he was apparently egged on by Bess Foster to mutter something about a separation over the Duchess being swindled by Martindale. The Duke did not ever think about money, it was something that was always there to cover whatever he did. Although the cost of the parties does not always appear as a separate item in the accounts, the Duke must have agreed to cover the costs of much of the events held at home. It must have given the Duchess an edge over her friends who had shallower pockets.

All these various strands came together leaving the Duchess as the undisputed leader of the ton; no one really ever came near her. What has not been mentioned here is that other essential quality she possessed: her magnetic personality, which was priceless in itself, more so than even Devonshire riches could buy.

21

Final Days 1805-06

Trafalgar

For nearly 2½ years, the threat of invasion by France had been a real one, made worse by the inadequacy of the military defences if the Royal Navy could not hold its line. Naval successes bred a growing confidence in the ability of our naval commanders, especially Vice-Admiral Viscount Nelson. *'With Lord Nelson near us I think we need not fear our own shores'*, wrote Bess Foster to her son Augustus, then based in Washington, USA. [1] The threat of invasion and the confidence in Nelson played out in homes across the nation, not any less at Devonshire House.

Nelson had been at sea since the summer of 1803, when he had left Portsmouth on HMS Victory, bound for Malta. He was not just a war hero, but a legend in his own lifetime. In a sense, Nelson's Column in Trafalgar Square is not just a memorial to him, but a reminder of a nation that had the confidence to sleep securely, in the knowledge that he was at sea. If Earl Spencer and Admiral Jervis at the Admiralty had improved the efficiency, ability and ultimately the power to protect the nation beyond its shores, it helped to cover the inadequacy of our military owing to dithering and bad planning by Addington, the Prime Minister. For example, C.J. Fox wrote to the Duchess on 12th August 1803: *'I do not believe the French will come – if they do, by what I see they will find us as unprepared as ever owing to the last foolish manoeuvres of the Doctor* [Addington]'. [2]

Nelson, Commander in Chief of the Mediterranean Fleet, returned to England at the end of the summer of 1805 after more than two years at sea. On the 10th September he was seen dining at Tooting with Mr. Goldsmid (sic),

Lady Hamilton, his daughter (by her) Horatia and others. Writing to her son Augustus Foster, Bess Foster told him: *'when I dined with him* (Nelson) *in London he said to us...'* Just before he sailed for the final time, Nelson dined with both the Duke and Bess at 'Crawfords', which may indicate that the Duchess was ill again. He took a letter from Bess for her son Augustus Clifford. Nelson asked her to kiss the letter, responding that he would carry the letter and the kiss to her son. The dinner was a success, with both the Duke and Bess finding Nelson *'perfectly unassuming and natural'* rather than *'appearing vain and full of himself, as one had always heard'*.

Writing to Hartington, following a visit with the Prince Of Wales and Bess Foster to see a wax image of Nelson on 24th February 1806, prior to it being placed in Westminster Abbey, the Duchess wrote: *'I never saw him, but those who have assure me it is an exact represental* (sic) *of him'*. She must be referring to the wax image for she had seen him giving a speech and at a ball. Prior to Christmas, 1805, Bess Foster was still in despair over the death of Nelson: *'She has so much grimace about her grief that one can hardly present one's disgust of her operating upon one's pity for him. She sobs and she sighs and she grunts and she groans and she is dressed in black cockades, with his name embroidered on every drapery she wears ... whilst she is regretting that she could not have died in his defence, her peevish hearers almost wish she had'*. [3]

Napoleon's invasion plans needed naval supremacy in the English Channel, but his fleets were bottled up behind Royal Navy blockades. They consisted of a Combined Fleet of French and Spanish ships at Cadiz and others at Brest and Toulon. Many of the sailors lacked experience, especially in gunnery practice caused by the blockades. Eventually, the French admiral Villeneuve broke out of Cadiz with 33 ships. On 21st October 1805, Nelson was waiting off Cape Trafalgar with 27 ships and over 400 guns less than the approaching fleet.

Using the experience of the Battle of the Nile and confident of the quality of his gunners, Nelson sailed straight at the enemy line, intending to break through in two places, splitting it into three sections. His ships were initially open to enemy fire, lacking forward facing guns but taking advantage of poor accuracy from enemy fire. Slicing through the enemy line, British gunners then engaged. The stern of the vessel presented the ship's weakest point, and concentrated fire swept and smashed into the length of the gun decks, causing significant damage, loss of life and fire power.

Turning along the enemy line, the latter was then raked by fire from both sides at once. Within four hours, most of the Combined Fleet was sinking, disabled or captured. This and the storm which followed, caused havoc and loss of the enemy fleet, including many enemy prisoners, lifting enemy losses to c. 7-8,000. Also lost were Bonaparte's invasion plans, sunk like his ships.

It was a brilliant and bold battle plan in its planning and execution but the cost included Nelson, dead from a sniper's bullet. At the time never had so many of the enemy's ships been taken in one engagement without the loss of a single British ship. Nelson had lived for Britain's glory and he perished in her cause. After repairs at Gibraltar, HMS Victory broke sail for England, carrying Nelson's coffin to the Nore. It was then taken by yacht to Greenwich, the body preserved in brandy. HMS Victory was off Falmouth on the 29th November 1805, but the news has already arrived aboard HMS Pickle. Lying in state at Greenwich, mourners queued and eventually passed by and paid their final respects at the rate of 50 per minute. [4]

For the funeral, the coffin was rowed on the Admiralty barge, on the 8th January 1806, accompanied by three other official barges and dozens of private ones, to Whitehall Stairs, Westminster. Here it was landed and taken to the Admiralty, where the Duchess saw it arrive, having seen the water procession from a house in Whitehall. She wrote to her mother: *'Every house must be struck at considering that had it not been for this brave man, we now should have been trembling for the shores of Ireland and England. But he does meet with a grateful country.* [5]

The Admiralty Barge (the third in the procession) also conveyed Lord Hood, Sir Peter Parker (the Chief Mourner) and the Prince of Wales and was rowed by 46 seamen from HMS Victory. The procession included: His Majesty's Barge, (but without the king because of protocol), the Admiralty Commissioner's Barge, and the Lord Mayor in the City State Barge.

The celebration of the glory and relief over the threat of invasion was numbed by the grief of the death. The Duke wrote:

'To crown their merits but to check their pride
God gave them victory, but Nelson died'. [6]

From the Admiralty, on the 9th January, the official mourners proceeded from 11am to St Paul's Cathedral, with 681 carriages ahead of the coffin, which from Greenwich was carried on a representation of HMS Victory (demasted). It took so long for the procession to proceed and unload the mourners that it was going dark when the cortege arrived. The procession included the Duke and the Marquis of Hartington (Dukes and their oldest son only were requested). The interior of St Paul's dome was hung with captured flags from the Combined Fleet as Nelson's body was interred in the Cathedral. This four hour State Funeral was only the third given to a commoner. The previous two were for Admiral Robert Blake, (1657) and Sir Isaac Newton, (1727). Nelson was aged 47.

In the procession were 32 admirals, over 100 captains and there was an escort of 10,000 soldiers. Some 20,000 Volunteer militia lined the streets, two deep on each side. [7]

The logistics of parking 681 carriages and perhaps c. 2,000 horses takes some thinking about. Haryo rejoiced that she was not part of this: *'for it would have been the greatest fatigue and exertion and most likely to be able to see very little after all'.* [8] The procession itself was directed by the College of Arms and theatres were expected to be shut in the evening. For the State procession, Ticket No. 1 went to the Earl Marshal, the Duke of Norfolk. Ticket No. 2 went to the Duke of Devonshire. [9] Earl Spencer's son survived the action – he had been sent on a detail prior to the battle and missed it. Augustus Clifford missed it too. *'Clifford says he is happy enough to be with the inshore squadron ... the combined fleet* (the enemy) *are 36 strong and we 26, with which he says we are fully equal to them and with Nelson, to the whole navy of France'.* [10]

In 1835, Trafalgar Square, London was laid out in Nelson's memory and the column completed in 1843.

The Death of Pitt and the Ministry Of All Talents

With the death of Nelson, the country lost one of its finest sons. One that served the nation selflessly, in his case gallantly, and whose passing shocked the nation at its loss. There were to be two more occasions like this in 1806. Within a month of Nelson's funeral, William Pitt passed on, at 46, a year younger than Nelson. With no small sense of irony, his greatest adversary in the Commons, Charles J. Fox was to follow him in September.

Somewhat bizarrely, the date of Pitt's death is open to question although it is generally regarded as being 23rd January 1806. Never a friend of either the Duke or Duchess, they both, however, held him in high regard. So much so that the Duchess was awoken with the news of his death on the 22nd January, which had been conveyed to Lord Castlereagh by Lady Hester Stanhope. Castlereagh was then Secretary of State for War and Colonies and the only other member of the Government in the Commons following Pitt's death. He resigned shortly afterwards. Castlereagh sent the note on to the king.

Sir Walter Farquhar came into town to see the Prince of Wales. No doubt wishing to maintain anonymity, he had the coach window blinds down and went straight home again thereafter. Later in the day, it was put about that Pitt was still alive but unable to receive visitors. Earl Spencer, the Duchess's brother, was so certain that Pitt was dead, that his son, Althorp, went down to Cambridge *'to stand for the University* (as M.P.) *in his* (Pitt's) *place'.* The Duchess believed he was dead, but that the fact was being kept secret... *'a great indelicacy in keeping it secret for people are milling it about the streets with news like the last act of "School For Scandal"'.*

The following day she wrote to her mother letting her know that *'he is now allowed by all to have expired at half past four this morning'.* [11] In a letter to her son, she reflected: '*it is awful to the mind to reflect on a death of such magnitude...sorrowful indeed to think that this powerful voice of eloquence, so matchless, so beautiful is dumb forever...Mr. Pitt's fault as an Englishman and statesman* (was) *that he came into place against the constitution and supported himself in place, by increasing* [12] *the power of the throne – as a statesman he was chiefly brilliant, as a financier –in war he was a bad leader – not from his own want of powers but from his trusting too much to incapable individuals.*

But his eloquence was so great he could explain even any disaster with almost the contrary – his choice of words was perfect, his voice beautiful and his way of putting aside the question when he chose and fascinating the minds of men outstanding'.

The king asked Lord Grenville to form a government, but the latter would only agree if Fox was included. Thus the door to a Whig-ite government was opened. [13] In the end the king agreed and the coalition came in under Lord Grenville (Pitt's cousin) as Prime Minister, but it was to be some days before ministerial positions were agreed and yet several more before a reluctant king consented to it.

On the 31st January 1806, Caroline Lamb gave birth to a stillborn baby girl. [14] The Duchess was with her the following day – presumably at Melbourne House in Whitehall.

The distribution of offices fell to C.J. Fox. He filled the main posts with reasonable alacrity but was pestered by the younger lords all demanding positions which were not available or where the offer was considered lower than their expectations. Perhaps the worst was Lord Ossulston, who displayed similar characteristics to his father's intransigence over his son's plans for marriage. Offered different positions, and pushing Fox past the limits of patience (let alone the Duchess's), he appears to have ended up with no major position at all. Offered the post of a Lord of the Admiralty, he did not take it, [15] but he did take the minor post of Treasurer of the Household, then apparently associated with the now defunct Office of White Stick (c/f the Office of Black Rod). He was not taken very seriously in Parliament, primarily because he spoke so softly most could not hear him.

'*Dear Mr. Fox has had more trouble about this little man than the whole cabinet*', wrote the Duchess. Ossulston was soon at work and in July 1806 was at the Bar of the House of Commons acquainting the House that His Majesty had been waited on with several Addresses from the House of the 12th July and he had been graciously pleased to give directions accordingly. On the following day, the Duchess's son-in-law, Lord Morpeth, was also on his feet in the House of Lords moving the Order of the Day for resuming the adjourned debate on the East India Budget. [16]

Offered any position he wished was the Duke. The Duchess told her son, Hartington: '*Your father has been offered any place he chose but he declined saying that he always refused a place when younger and stronger and much more so now'*. He was then aged 57. It had been expected that Earl Spencer would return to the splendid work he had done at the Admiralty but he declined as the *'fatigue was too great'*. He therefore took the Home Secretary's job. There were many other appointments within the inner Devonshire House circle. The Duchess wrote to Hartington to say *'all my troubles are over, O has accepted'*. [17] Lord George, the Duke's younger brother refused a peerage, preferring to retain the name Cavendish. He accepted one in 1831 when he took the title Burlington (2nd creation). This peerage remains extant.

Pitt's debts of £40,000 were paid from public funds, despite a lowering of his popularity: there were quite a few who voted against his burial in Westminster Abbey and even the City Council voted only just in favour of a memorial to him. He had a military funeral (being a Colonel of a Volunteer Corp) following his body lying in State in Parliament House, on 22nd February 1806. The Duchess had tickets to the funeral but gave them to her sister. [18]

Britain's Best Bred Woman Passes On

If Devonshire House had opened its doors with the redecoration complete, it is strange that the Duchess was noted by the Morning Post as having only two events there in January 1806. Of course, there could have been events which went unrecorded but nonetheless, it was a slow start for the ebullient hostess. Two funerals may have forced the pace here with a need to exhibit periods of mourning. The funeral of Nelson was clearly one and the death of Mrs. Maria Duff the other. She had died just prior to Christmas, on 20th December 1805 aged 30 years. The sister of the Duchess of St. Albans, she was well known to the Duke and Duchess. The Morning Post reported that with her death, *'the families of Athol, Buccleugh, Argyle, Devonshire, Lansdowne, Bath, Bute, Spencer, Lauderdale and Caithness go into mourning'*. It could have mentioned Fife, Manners and St. Albans too. [19] Unfortunately, the Duchess had arranged a party for the evening of his funeral (22nd February 1806) and the number of attendees suffered as a result.

February gave the Duchess the opportunity for a better run at her supper parties, some following a visit to the opera etc. There were ten in all together with a Supper, Ball and Rout on the last day of the month, probably the first with dancing. The Morning Post reported that *Devonshire House once more takes the lead in the political as well as in the fashionable parties'*. [20] On Friday 7th February, there was a well attended Ministerial party, although not all were invited to supper; served in the now newly resplendent main dining room. *'Her Grace delighted the company by her wit, grace and beauty'*. The following night (8th February 1805) there was a larger gathering of friends and opposition guests, with 62 people sitting down for a hot supper at 1am. New and unfamiliar names on the published guest lists were the Duke de Berri and Viscountess Castlereagh.

On the 11th February, the Duchess, despite having 'been much tired lately', met 'Horatia Nelson, Lord Nelson's godchild, (she was actually his daughter by Lady Hamilton), to whom he left £9,000. She is a pretty child of 7 – when I gave her the anchor with Nelson, I said it was Nelson wrote on it and she said Nelson for ever?' (21)

These events were followed by what appears to be a further political party on the 17th February and another party two days later described by the paper as being 'the largest given by anyone this season'. Clearly the Duchess was keeping her competitors, the Abercorns and Gordons etc in check. At the party on the 17th February were the Prince of Wales with Mrs. Fitzherbert, Mr. and Mrs. Adair, Lady George Cavendish and the Greys, having been invited to the earlier part of the evening. No correspondence survives relating to a party on the 19th. These political parties followed the death of William Pitt (see above). They were, however, taking their toll.

On the 4th February, just ahead of the Ministerial party, she was 'weary and tired to death', not helped by a violent headache on the 5th and 'an abominable cold', the day after. On the 7th, she was so tired she was unable to maintain her regular (almost daily) correspondence with Hartington. She had described him in mid-January to her mother as being 'all my prudent wishes can hope'. Her correspondence indicates that she was especially proud of him and was already planning in her mind a trip with him back to their forsaken home, Chatsworth, 'next year'. (22)

The Duchess made no further comment on her health. However, a powerful indicator may be measured in her attendance at other peoples' parties. In 1805, she attended nine by the 17th February (when she stopped going through illness). Her first recorded attendance in 1806 was on the 23rd February when she went to the Marchioness of Salisbury's Party. She only went to one more – the Duchess of Gordon's Ball on the 6th March. Lady Salisbury's party impressed the Duchess as there was 'some fine dancing'. Grassini sang too; the Duchess remarked in a letter to her son: 'I find she is allowed to sing at all the places where Mr. Gould the manager is invited. A good plan of Mrs. Gould's to get invitations'. (23)

No report followed an advance announcement of Devonshire House of supper parties on the 4th and 8th or others on the 18th and 23rd March. Consequently, her last party may have been on the last night in February when she hosted a Rout, Supper and Ball. There were eight card tables and seven supper tables available. More people turned up than expected and two more supper tables were laid at 1am, with supper at 2am. A total of 110 sat down for the meal, with others (men) standing at side tables. The younger dancers were back on the floor by 2.30am and after an hour, the reels etc began the hour long conclusion, led by Mr. Thomas Sheridan and Corise de Grammont, still waiting leave to marry from Lord Tankerville, plus Capt. Macdonald and Caroline St. Jules. According to the Morning Post, the Duchess *never appeared in better health*. What she was feeling was perhaps another matter. [24]

It is fitting that at her last public appearance at a friend's party, the Duchess of Gordon's Ball on 6th March, and possibly the last party she ever attended, she displayed her compassion for others. Lord Kinnoul was taken ill after supper, *'but by some restoratives administered by the Duchess of Devonshire, he was entirely recovered before he departed'.* [25]

On the 5th March, unusually, the Duchess rested ahead of a busy day on the 6th when she and Haryo went to Court, followed by yet another Duchess of Gordon's Ball that evening. The latter was apparently calling the Duchess *'the head of the administration'*, which would have gone down rather well. She had also called her *'a most amiable person'* at a ballet she (Duchess of Gordon) had had on the 4th March, which points to the Duchess having been there too. [26]

The Duchess's Court dress was *'white satin and white crape with gold antique nails* (? – text illegible) *in a mosaic pattern'.* Haryo's was also white satin and crape with little silver Maltese filigree balls, similar to that of her friend Lady Emily Cowper. Following the Court, the Duchess returned home tired and went to bed for a couple of hours before heading for the Gordon's Ball. They blamed the Court Ball for giving Harriet a sore throat and the Duchess one of her worst headaches. [27]

Two days later (Saturday 8th March), she still had her headache. The next day, she was *'quite orange with the jaundice, but saved myself to dine at Ld* (unreadable), *where I was very ill and could not eat. I came home at 10 and found Harriet very ill and during the night we were both so. My pain and sickness did not yield till late – my pulse – 120... we both continued ill till yesterday. At night I had same... but today 14th believe it is much better'.* [28]

The improvement continued and her skin colour changed from deep orange to lemon. She was sufficiently well to write to her mother asking for a loan of £100 until Lady Day (24th March, when she received her quarterly allowance). *'You will save me a worry for Monday'*, she wrote. It appears her mother could only offer £20. There is some evidence to suggest that she may have also borrowed £500 from Lord Ossulston for the purchase of jewellery from Messrs. Flower & Mainwaring. In January 1807, the estate was endeavouring to get the firm to take them back. They had cost £2,018 10s 0d and the return was at a loss of £904. They were a *'brilliants; comb with gold teeth; Maltese cross; a butterfly and diamond necklace'.* [29]

A gallstone was expected to pass any day but it did not occur, perhaps a blockage being a measure of the extent of her liver/gall bladder disease. Haryo was now largely recovered. On the 19th, the Duchess's health had in fact become much more serious. She was extremely ill to the point of fears of her not surviving the night. The three doctors in attendance; Sir Walter Farquhar, Dr. Blaine and Dr. Walker summoned further assistance from a Dr. Bailey. With the whole family sitting up through the night (presumably Hartington, Lady Spencer and possibly Harriet Bessborough having been summoned), at 2am a hot bath was ordered in which the Duchess was immersed for about 30 minutes. This brought some relief and a better night's sleep for her.

On the 24th, following a further tranquil night, a return of a feverish state occurred around noon for some four hours. Amongst callers at the House were the Prince of Wales and his brothers. The fever came and abated on the next two days but became much worse on the 27th, when two more doctors, Pitcairn and Vaughan, were called in. The whole family were in tears for some time. The number of cards of enquiry left at Devonshire House was now over 500.

A Bulletin at 7.30pm at Devonshire House on Friday the 28th stated that the Duchess was 'now a little better'. There was 'not the most distant idea that her life was in danger'. On the Sunday night (the 30th), the Duke, Marquis and Haryo had all eventually gone to bed, leaving Lady Spencer at her bedside. The latter had just entered the Duchess's bedroom in the night when her daughter had a relapse and within four minutes was insensible. Calling only the Duke, the two were present as the Duchess slipped away at 3.30am. The three children were informed the following morning. (30)

The Duke had not been out of the house since the Duchess had been taken ill and on the 29th March had written to Selina Trimmer: 'If the worst should happen, I hope you will be so good as to stay at Devonshire House for the present for I shall not be in a state of mind to attend to anybody or to receive or give any comfort whatever'. (31)

Following the death, the front door of Devonshire House was locked for twelve weeks. Lady Spencer, at the behest of all, agreed to stay on at Devonshire House for a while. On the 1st April 1806, a post mortem took place at 7am in the presence of all five doctors who had been in attendance. However there was no agreement on the cause of death, although it must have been clear that she had liver disease. On the 6th April, at 5am, the Duchess's coffin left an emotively charged Devonshire House as she was carried down the entrance staircase to the courtyard and the awaiting hearse for the last journey to Derbyshire for interment at the family vault at All Saints Church, Derby.

The cortege was led by eight mutes on horseback (as was her father's coffin), then an attendant on horseback carrying her coronet. Behind came the hearse drawn by eight horses. It was followed by the Duchess's coach, and then two mourning coaches carrying the principal servants and Mr. Wilson the undertaker. According to practice at that time, the family did not accompany the body to the interment. It appears that the cortege was met at the county boundary of Derbyshire, probably at Swarkeston Bridge and given an escort for the 12 miles or so to Derby. Between 11am and 12 noon on the 10th April, the Duchess was laid to rest in the family vault. She was united with the Duke in 1811 and Bess Foster, then also the Duchess of Devonshire, in 1824. The latter had died on 30th March, exactly 18 years after the Duchess, with Madame Recamier and the 6th Duke at her bedside. It was a solemn and fitting end to such a colourful and entertaining life.

The Duchess's Final Years In Retrospect

Without question, the death of the Duchess saw the end of an era. The Prince of Wales said that they had lost *the most amiable and best bred in the land*. [32]

Although notionally at least the Duke and Duchess presided over the ton for over 30 years, much of this was in a benign manner compared to the golden age in the short period of 1801-06. Throughout her married life she dazzled those that met her, always with great dignity, kindness and consideration. In return, she was adored, admired and drew crowds to her presence wherever she went.

In July 1789, she left London for Paris with the Duke, not returning for over a year. Within a further year, she had left for a prolonged stay at Bath with her sister Harriet. Banished for a long period abroad because she became pregnant with Charles Grey's child, she eventually returned to London in September 1793 and stayed out of the limelight until 1800, when she went to Court to present her daughter, Little G, to the King and Queen. They were years dedicated to bringing up her children. The presentation was a catalyst for social re-engagement, socialising but chiefly on her own terms, at both Devonshire House and Chiswick. She usually restricted her party going to a small circle of close friends, despite the clamour of invitations elsewhere which must have become a feature of her popularity. Her grand ball, routs etc were the best in London, ever changing, ever reaching to a new theme, answering an ever growing and greater expectation.

Poor health at the end of 1803 saw a change of emphasis to smaller supper parties which ended earlier, allowing her to retire to bed earlier. The number of these increased in 1804-05. In 1806, the number of supper parties increased significantly in the weeks when better health permitted it. It must beg the question: did she know in herself her remaining days were short and was this her response; cramming as many in as she could before she finally wilted?

It was not just that her glittering parties were the best – and often the largest.

The acquiescence of the Duke regarding the cost and the backcloth of both Devonshire House and Chiswick House also counted significantly. The grandeur created at these two houses must have been rarely matched. She dressed with equal finesse in those final years particularly, usually in white, but adorned with her favourite diamonds. By the time of her death, she had been copied widely, much to the pleasure of jewellers, clothiers and hairdressers, let alone hire companies for the adornment of her balls etc. Whatever she did, whatever she wore, her practice soon became the norm. The London party scene continued within days of her death: she would have wanted nothing less.

Ever proud of her grandchildren, Little G was to give birth to Harriet Elizabeth Georgiana seven weeks after her mother's death. The baby's grandson was to marry Princess Louise, a daughter of Queen Victoria. Another descendant (through Little G) became the 9th Duke of Devonshire and his great grandson is the current, 12th Duke. [33]

With the death of the Duchess, the renaissance of Chiswick House as an icon for aristocratic socialising drew to a close. Its value as an exquisite and incomparable country retreat remained, but the catalyst who had breathed life and so much enjoyment and fun into the place had gone. She was 48 years old.

Chatsworth, it will be noted had receded into the background. Her last stay there was probably in 1801-02. In the 1790s her visits there may have been confined to 1794 and 1798.

Additional to the understanding we have of the Duchess's magnetic personality is the expression Haryo made of her feelings for her mother. It occurs in a letter she wrote from Castle Howard on an occasion when her mother had not travelled with her to see Little G: '*I cannot think of you, I cannot mention you, without crying like a fool and when I think of the happiness of seeing your dear smile, of hearing your beloved voice, I am almost mad with joy. I am sure you alone could inspire what I feel for you, it is enthusiasm and adoration, that for anybody else would be ridiculous, but that to deny it you would be unnatural*'. [34]

Perhaps her popularity and her personality is summed up by a story she apparently repeated often towards the close of her life: of all the compliments paid her, a drunken Irishman, who asked to light his pipe by the fire of her beautiful eyes, paid her the highest. He was probably more discerning than drunk.

The Duke and Duchess: an assessment

To this day, the Duchess has had no equal in the Cavendish dynasty. She enchanted all she met, except perhaps Lady Jersey who paid the price for her affair with the Duke and for dropping the Duchess during her (Lady Jersey's) affair with the Prince of Wales. From royal households in London and Paris to itinerant traders on street corners, noticeably butchers etc in the 1784 election, she charmed those that met her and fascinated many more.

Her relationship with the Duke is often wrongly presented in a negative way but it was the opposite. Here was the advantage of opposites attracting each other. He provided her with a platform from which she could express herself, especially from 1793 and her return from exile. He found her projects to get her teeth into. Then from 1800, she moved on to become the undoubted first socialite in London. To do what she did after 1793, let alone from 1800, she must have had the Duke's backing and encouragement, not least because he financed it. The essence of it all, however, was her personality, not just the glitter, the glamour and the number of her fashionable parties.

The Duke not only paid for these but also allowed her to go off partying. She was hardly going alone, however, with daughters, plus Carolines St. Jules and Ponsonby, Corisande de Grammont, Lords Morpeth and Ossulston, let alone the Bessborough family and other friends, all in tow.

The Duke also gave her the opportunity to enjoy the undeniable zest she had. His shyness worked to his wife's advantage. She enjoyed the party life. She turned her own into the best event in London – ever changing the back cloth, the theme etc., staying ahead of everyone else. Eventually, ill health reduced the number of all-night parties she could physically handle. This eventually forced her to switch to smaller supper parties which ended much earlier. No doubt to the relief of the servants too.

The dark side of her life was her compulsive problem with expenditure and the debt it created. Even here, once in the open (and this happened several times), her husband acted with equanimity and understanding. She would have bankrupted most households. The strength of Cavendish finances and ingenuity of John Heaton to handle it all saw off the difficulties she created.

This marriage worked. It survived the idiosyncrasies of two very different people. But then they were no ordinary couple, living in such an elevated manner. They gave each other the slack each of them needed. At the end of the day, it is too easy now to denigrate the Duke or castigate his wife's recklessness etc. Recognition of the reality of how they made their marriage work – and it did warts and all – is overdue. The passing of someone like the Duchess must have left an unfathomable gap for those she left behind. Not just her family, but all who fed off her indefatigable spirit, zest for life and the care and interest she took in other people whose paths had crossed hers.

22

The Duchess's Debts

An Overview

A lot has been written on this subject. Much of it seems to concentrate on her gambling debts as if that was the sole problem she faced; far from it. Georgiana was probably spending more than her pin money (initially of £4,000 p.a.) for most of her married life. Early excesses were paid off, initially by her parents (reimbursed by the Duke), with her mother exhorting her to protect her reputation by probity. This may have worked until the mid-1780s, with her mother writing to her in rather a heavy manner on what she expected of her daughter. She (Georgiana) preyed on friends for 'loans' – always it seems with the sincerity of promising repayment, with one loan repaying another or alternatively, never repaid. Only one thing is clear about the size of her profligacy: it has to be far higher than the position shown herein. To that must be added the pin money used to pay off old debt and now lost to history.

Following his marriage, the Duke soon left London for the country and did not return until 1775. The Duchess was very worried about the size of her debts by April, only three months after arriving there. Her parents paid the amount (it is unknown how large it was) and the Duke, on learning of this, repaid it. From the Duke's personal bank account, it would appear to have been £3,000, but no name is given, which is understandable. [1] The following year, she was £3,000 in debt again to Lady Day on figures seen by her mother. What happened thereafter to the end of the decade is not known. In August 1781, the Duchess of Portland wrote to her husband stating that John Heaton was *searching for money for 'G'*. On hearing this, Lord Frederick had openly wondered about calling in the £5,000 on loan to the Duke (see text above for

1781). This suggests that the Duchess had continued to exceed her allowance by a significant amount. [2]

In the autumn of 1783, the Duchess was suffering anxiety over the level of her debts, finally admitting the situation to her mother. In March 1784, she wrote to Bess Foster telling her the debt was *'many, many, many, thousands'*. [3] According to Foreman, [4] in April 1784 the Duke paid £1,500 and then £5,000. However she still had £3,000 of debt he did not know about. In fact this is probably the £2,900 she admitted to her mother later that year. Her mother continued to despair of her daughter's position: *'what will be the end of these terrible money matters if what you suffered last year has not been able to deter you. I have no right to expect that your promises to me or anything I have said or can say will be of any effect'*. [5]

On top of this was the election debt she ran up that year. It was stated by the Morning Post to be c. £30,000. The newspaper was probably exaggerating but the amount is not known. [6] Undoubtedly there must have been costs run up by the Duchess on drumming up votes, or at least endeavouring to. However much of this would have been in entertainment etc. at Devonshire House. Kisses to tradesmen etc. cost nothing, which is probably why she and Lady Duncannon etc. did it – the Duchess being unable to access cash for that purpose in the absence of the Duke and John Heaton, who were in York. The entertaining costs would be lost in the house expenditure accounts. This must be the reason why no separate item of expenditure is shown in the Expenses Book for 1784 for costs supporting C. J. Fox in the Westminster Election. The kisses for votes caused a media frenzy and much disapproval from the starchy element of the aristocracy.

If the Duchess did spend cash on the streets, it is not reflected in the accounts and there was no draw-down of cash to support it into the House account, so where did it come from? If it was on the Duchess's IOUs it must be reflected in the Duchess's debts otherwise considered to be gambling debts. Therefore, the payments by the Duke noted by Foreman [7] of £5,000 in 1784 could have related to election debt. In 1786 she was duped by a card shark called Martindale who claimed that she owed him £100,000. Martindale later agreed to accept a much lower amount. However in April 1787, John Heaton confided in his Hartington Manor Rent Collector, William Gould, that the Duchess had lost £30 – 40,000 at play the previous year and that he was going to have to borrow the same. [8]

Heaton did in fact borrow £40,000 on the London market, but if it was to pay Martindale, then it was not required in total. Perhaps there were other cash flow pressures he was facing on the estate. The Duchess was persuaded to face Martindale down; the fallen woman facing marriage separation etc. It worked and she wrote to her mother to tell her that he would take £10,000, although he was later to write asking for more. [9] In the last quarter of 1786 the Duke paid £14,932. 9s. 10d. to settle her debts, which appears to include the £10,000 agreed with Martindale. [10]

However there was no let up for the Duchess. In March 1787 she wrote to Thomas Coutts seeking a loan of £4,400 unsecured which he granted. She had also borrowed £4,239 from Richard Arkwright, son of the cotton industrialist. The repayment terms were for it to be repaid by several instalments in 1788 between February and September. He wrote to her, reminding her of the agreement and clearly expecting her to honour the repayment.

There was of course no chance of that happening. Following the Martindale crisis, the Duke had reduced her pin money to £2,000 per annum as part of a money-saving arrangement which also saw two of her staff being dismissed and some of her horses being sold. As seen above, she continued additional spending if only by the rouse of presumably agreeing it with the Duke first (see below). She never did pay Richard Arkwright. It was still owed when she died and the Duke paid it. [11]

In July 1787, the Duchess admitted to her mother that she owed Coutts £7,000 and in 1789 he lent her £6,000 more on Earl Spencer's bond just as she borrowed £2,000 from M. de Calonne (he had been Louis XVI's Controller General of Finance, 1783-1787, when he brought his family to England). In December 1790 she disclosed to Coutts that her total indebtedness had reached £60,000 (see below). Unable to stop, she borrowed £6,000 from the Duke of Bedford at 5% interest in 1800, despite the fact that she knew the Duke did not want her to borrow on agreed interest terms. It made it more difficult to negotiate a 'fairer' deal agreed in horse-trading with her creditors. [12] In 1789 the Duchess was obliged to draw £500 from her account to buy off Martindale again, and he demanded another £500 in 1807 and again 1810. [13]

At the end of 1790, the Duchess set out a list showing what was supposed to be all of her debt in a letter to Thomas Coutts. It included £16,000 due to Coutts, £8,000 due to M. de Calonne and £14,448 due to Denne & Co., the Duke's bankers. There was even £2,638 due to Mr. Scafe, the brother of her mother's servant (who attended the Duchess at the birth of the Marquis of Hartington). The total amount due was £61,697. The Duchess, knowing she was concealing more, wrote *'I don't know that this is exact, near, I think, there are a few more things of £100, 50 etc.'* [14]

She knew it was much more than that. There was £4,239 (plus interest) extra due to Richard Arkwright from 1788 and a sum she does not appear to have ever disclosed due to the Prince of Wales (or at least understood to be so). She seemed completely incapable of facing up to the full reality of her indebtedness. When she was pregnant with her son, the Duke asked what the full amount was. She wrote to him a long letter (they were living under the same roof and she could not even discuss it with him) to ask him not to ask her, pleading the stress it would place on her whilst pregnant – the Duke obliged.

In fact he seems to have kept his calm each time the issue of his wife's indebtedness came up. Even when he demanded a separation, there was no detail raised about his temper (unless the letter does not survive). In 1784, when she owned up to the extent of her debt after she had weaned Little G, she wrote to Bess Foster (who was in Rome): '*I would not tell Canis whilst I was with child and suckling … I told him without fear … every year of my life I have cost him immense sums, a mind he cd not trust in – and how do you think he has received the avowal – with the utmost generosity, goodness and kindness – his whole care has been that I may not vex myself and you would think he was the offender, not me*', letters to her mother and Bess Foster on the same day. To her mother she wrote: '*You can not conceve (sic) how good he has been and he knows everything*'. [15]

Gleeson's comment '*the Duke of Devonshire's angry reaction to Georgiana's disclosure of her debts*' is not substantiated and needs to be seen in this light. [16] This response from the Duke was highlighted by the Duchess on other occasions, it was not a solitary occurrence. It may have been better for the Duchess if he had been more robust in his reaction. In the event, shortly after demanding a separation, within days in fact, the Duke was behaving with great temper (i.e. without anger) and kindness to her, as mentioned above.

The Duchess's lack of discipline concerning her gambling debts reflected in her expenditure generally. Following the birth of Georgiana, on whom she clearly doted (born 1783) she spent £260 in 1785 on '*apparel*' (clothes and milliners' fees). In 1785, Harriet's bed linen cost £155 with a new nurse, Mrs. Aspy, paid from 1ˢᵗ October at £80 per annum. In 1786 clothing for the girls cost £511 and although this dropped to £100 the following year, she made up for it, spending £450 on toys. Her expenditure on the two girls in the three years 1785 – 87 was £1,656 plus food, incidental costs such as doctor's bills, clothes and bed linen and nursing costs prior to Mrs. Aspy's appointment (possibly at up to £80 per annum for Little G). The total cost would be at least £2,000 to the end of 1787. Little G was clearly being dressed as a Duchess's daughter: In mid-February 1785, she was described by her mother as looking '*beautiful in a white satin cloak trim'd with light blue fur and a little muff*'. [17] And why not?

Her hatter's bill (from Mr. Andre) in 1787 was £254 and linen drapery cost £403. She also took delivery of a new coach from Atkinsons, coachmakers, at a cost of £841. 10s. 0d. These items are in the household accounts with no indication as to whether these came out of her pin money, although the demands on the latter would suggest perhaps not. [18] In September 1790, the Duchess wrote to her mother stating that she had 'found' a diamond on her, making out that she had forgotten it, and for which she owed £1,500. [19]

The Crisis With Creditors

However not all her creditors kept up their patience with her. Between 1786 – 90, she spent £8,000 with Nathaniel Jeffries, a jeweller of Piccadilly, London. She had paid him £5,000 and he had even been to Brussels to obtain the remaining £3,000 (charging her £200 expenses). It is unlikely that she was there (in fact she had not been there since just prior to the birth of the Marquis in May 1790). [20] The Duke paid the £3,000 to Jeffries in December 1792 when the Duchess was in Italy. It is also not clear whether this was because court action was in the offing and the Duke did not want it disclosed that the Duchess was not at home, or he was now seeking a reconciliation with her. James Hare had been regularly having dinner with the Duke prior to July 1792 (when he wrote to the Duchess), but the Duke had never once mentioned about her being away and of course, Hare had not raised the matter. [21]

Thomas Coutts eventually confronted the Duke about her debts. In October 1792, the latter paid Coutts £4,400 plus 5½ years interest, amounting to £5,610 in all. Coutts wrote to advise that the Duchess still owed him £15,800 and £790 interest on this fell due on 13/12/1792. Coutts rote to the Duchess to advise her that *'There are a great many Bills of Yrs Graces and Lady Duncannons unpaid and waiting for money – I believe should the Duke hear of them the effect must be very prejudicial to you'*. [22] Coutts complained to her that he was trying to get in touch with the Duke, but getting no response. A year later, Coutts was at Buxton, taking the waters and the Duke (no doubt prompted by the Duchess), sent him a parcel of game. It consisted of 8 pheasants, 2 partridges, 5 hares, 26 snipe and 32 woodcock. [23]

It is almost as though the Duchess was in denial about her debts. This is perhaps best expressed in a letter from William Clulow, a lawyer who had given her more slack than he thought ought to have been necessary. In 1800, she had borrowed £600 from an 'honest clergyman' ... *upon a security which Your Grace in the most solemn manner assured me upon your House should be made equal to the money in a weeks time and guaranteed by your Mothers Note'*. This had not happened and the erstwhile lawyer, give him his due, had pursued her for both interest and the security. He had been to Devonshire House forty times, charging a guinea for most visits, many of them on appointments made by the Duchess, but she had been 'unable' to see him on all forty occasions.

He wrote seeking redress in the following seven days (in August 1802) with the threat of Court proceedings in the event of her ignoring this. Instead of doing something, she did nothing and the Bill was duly filed in Court against both the Duke and the Duchess. One presumes that at least something happened then, with the Duke's name on the summons. It was not the first time this had happened and it's a wonder that more creditors did not resort to law. [24]

The 'honest clergyman' was the Revd. E. H. Hoare (? of Lincoln) who was still owed his money in 1806. It amounted to £600 plus interest. The Duchess had given diamonds as security for the debts. [25] If this shows her lack of scruples, it was not a unique occurrence. In 1802, she leant heavily on Spencer Townsend for money and wishing to assist her, had lent her £200 of the Navy Office monies under his control. It was under strict agreement that it would have to be repaid within a few days, but she failed to do so. He eventually received his money, with interest only from the date of death on 13th February 1807. [26]

For a lot of creditors, family friendship prevented any precipitate action and they suffered most, some being owed money for many years. In fact at the Duchess's death nearly 50% of those owed money were either friends of the Duke or local people. The initial intention was to pay no creditors, but there was a change of mind. Here we probably see the reason for it. There was another reason weighing in the balance too: the volume of people owed less than £50: 173 of them. Having regard to potential media comment is no recent phenomena. Payments to these small creditors amounted to £2,263. [27]

Was it denial or deceit in the matter of the stock exchange debacle of 1791 (see below)? In the submission for payment of £13,000 following her death, the Old Worcester Bank asserted that the Duchess had pledged £2,000 of her alleged pin money of £3,000 per annum *towards the liquidation of the debt till it was discharged, with interest at 5%*. This was after solemnly swearing to the Duke that she would not take on loans with an agreed rate of interest and also only months after she had told Thomas Coutts that her debts amounted to £61,697. This being against the fact that she knew her list excluded the c. £5,000 owed to Richard Arkwright.

There was no possibility that she had a penny spare to pay the Old Worcester Bank (see below) let alone £2,000 per annum and she must have known this. It was probably neither denial nor deceit, it was desperation. We have to look at the last, sad, years of her life from the late 1780s in this light. The end of the tunnel would be, so she thought, when she gave birth to a son. She was denied even this. Plagued by creditors with an inability to stop spending, she compounded worry on worry, creating stress, desperation and continuing ill health. Her only relief was an early grave before she was fifty.

Towards the end of 1790 – or early in 1791 – the Duchess and her sister found another 'winner': gambling on the stock market. It seems to have quickly failed leaving increased debts. Once again the Duchess experienced a bad press, ever wide of the mark. Foreman quotes Lady Mary Coke (a neighbour at Chiswick) reporting that the failure, in February 1791, had seen the Duchess losing £50,000. [28] The reality would appear to have been much lower.

The Stock Exchange crash had seen her lose £11,500. She seems to have adopted the tactic recommended for her action against Martindale, with the bottom line being that she had no money. A threat to expose her brought out the Martindale technique: '*Her Grace then in the most earnest measure requested him [Mr. Pilliner of the bank] to procure the money somewhere for that the consequence of the transaction being known would infallibly be a separation from the Duke from her children and family, as he had paid many of her debts before but accompanied with threats which she dreaded being put in execution as the greatest calamity that could possibly befall her*'. (29.)

The Old Worcester Bank had lent the money and the Duchess, together with her sister, had signed a declaration '*acknowledging the debt as a debt of honour*'. Jewels were provided as security and she promised to pay £2,000 per annum out of her pin money to pay it off. She later asked to borrow the jewels '*for a Court day saying that the Duke not seeing her wear them would suspect that she had disposed them*'. She returned them but later repeated the process and failed to return them. The Bank sought £11,500 plus interest from 31st December 1799 at her death. So much for the debt of honour. John Heaton and the other trustees established to pay off the debts were determined not to pay it.

She used this ruse on other occasions too. An undated letter to Mr. Anthony Calvert, a jeweller at 8, Hatfield Street, Blackfriars Road, survives which states that she was going to Court the next day (i.e. the Royal Court, not a Court of Justice) and wished to borrow a diamond butterfly for a day or two and also pay £20 to have back temporarily a diamond necklace which she had provided him as security for debts due. Between 29/12/1804 and February 1806, she had purchased jewellery from him to the value of £2,519. The most valuable was in May 1805 when she bought '*a watch and chain diamonds and 3 rows of pearls £315*'. He presumably took some of the many items back for he was eventually paid £1,144 in November 1808. He must have agreed to wait for his money as he was paid interest on this half yearly. (30)

In 1801, there seems to have been an attempt to resolve the crisis of the Duchess's debts. In the years 1800 – 1803, the Duke paid a total of £13,300 to Thomas Coutts. This is most probably payment of the monies due to Coutts by the Duchess. A letter she sent to Thomas Coutts indicated that something was afoot to structure debt repayment. Certain of her creditors had agreed to wait for payment. (31) These included the Duke of Bedford, her brother, her friend John Crauford and Sir Richard Arkwright, the son of the late inventor and cotton manufacturer. The Duke of Bedford ended his friendship when he learnt that she had no money to repay him. His early death compounded her misery over this.

At the time of the advance he had indicated that Arkwright had made it owing to special circumstances affecting the Duchess, but without giving the detail. The letter to Coutts gives the gist of it. The Bessboroughs (sister and brother-in-law) had frequently put themselves in the position of being exposed (probably with threats of bankruptcy). The Duchess had paid off some of their creditors. However this seems to have usually been on such onerous terms that a lot of her money was used to buy some of them off, in excess of the principal money owed. *'I was obliged to pay to keep things quiet'* she wrote. The money she borrowed from Arkwright was part of this, she advised, it had not been to pay off her own debts

She also goes some way to admitting to Coutts her lack of understanding of her own situation: *'The debts of honour amounting to £1,500 are some that pain me because at the time of borrowing I had no idea of not being able to repay very soon and I should, had not the annoying cheating* (re) *Ld. B ... taken all my money'*. She does not, however, appear to have learnt from this experience.

With her income static at c. £2,000 per annum, rising to £5,000 in 1805 [32] the Duchess continued spending, which had only one outcome, her debt increased annually. She was borrowing to pay off creditors and using items she owned for security against other purchases. At James Edwards' sale on 18th March 1791, her brother George bought lot 328 for 111 guineas. It was a rare and beautiful book, richly decorated and dating from 1514. It was Le Cose Volgari by Francesco Petrarca. It was given by George to the Duchess. He had given it to her in acknowledgement of the books given by the Duke to him. At the time of her death, the Duchess was using it as security for purchases unpaid for at White's Bookshop in Fleet Street, London, where she owed £326. 7s. 6d. The book by 1806 being worth considerably more than she owed, it was returned in 1807 on settlement of the debt.

The Duchess was still being urged to tell all in December 1804, but by mid-month it had been agreed. The terms are unknown, but agents were appointed and it appears that the backlog of the debt would be paid over a period of years, hence the first payment of £5,000 in 1805. This principle was adopted for debt payment after the Duchess's death. [33]

Because much of the Duke's possessions had been handed down to him on settled terms, he could not sell them. He could borrow against his massive land holdings, even if settled, because he had significant resources of cash and unsettled property to stand as security against losing any settled land. It was different in a high street shop where she was buying stock. It was the same as going to a pawn broker which she clearly did with her jewellery. With this in mind, the Petrarca was clearly her possession. At her death, she was using her Vatican prints as security at Faulder's Bookshop in Bond Street, London, where she owed £136. 13s. 0d. These had been another gift to her by her brother.

In 1805, the Duke increased the Duchess's allowance to £5,000. In the Autumn of 1804, she was encouraged to tell the Duke the extent of her debts by various friends. She told him everything, except the total amount and it came with a suggestion that her affairs be put into the hands of agents, rather than have Heaton control it. The Duke was under the impression that the amount owed was £5-6,000. He was unhappy about Heaton losing control over her expenditure and for a while it looked as though any deal might be lost on this issue. The Duchess was still being urged to tell all in December 1804, but by mid-month it had been agreed. The terms are unknown, but the agents were appointed and it would appear that it was likely that the back log of debt would be paid over a period of years – hence the first payment of £5,000 in 1805. However with the amount per annum being so low, it is doubtful that she told the Duke the true story. (34)

Payments Following The Duchess's Death

It is often represented that her difficulties stemmed from her gambling debts, but the true situation finds that wide of the mark. An initial estimate of her debts due at her death shows gambling debts to be £13,898 (14%). (35) Table 5 lists her creditors at her death. The noticeable exception is the Prince of Wales. Even the amount of his generosity remains unknown. On her death bed the Duke promised the Duchess that he would pay her debts. (36) Following her death, the estate tried, not without some success one suspects, to return some of her jewellery, even at a discounted rate, to the value of £4,000 of debt. It initially promoted that the Duke, not being responsible for his wife's debts, would decline acceptance. Whether this was with his approval is not known, but in the event, he chose to do the honourable thing.

Trustees were appointed to sort out the mess. The initial total due to creditors came to £93,657. Some were proved spurious, others were not pursued, but still more had to be added to the total. In an endeavour to stem the tide, the Trustees would only agree to pay interest from the date of death. The Duke appointed four trustees including his brother, Lord George and John Heaton. He did not recognise liability for any of his wife's debts. Creditors were required to sign a deed accepting payments over five yearly instalments to be paid on 31st January each year, with interest from the date of death only. Other conditions were that the creditor would not go to law to speed up the process, or refuse to produce proof of the debt. Certainly at least some of those under £500 were paid in one payment. (37)

Additionally, paid from the Duke's account, was £4,396 to Sir Richard Arkwright and £2,300 to Earl Fitzwilliam. Arkwright was in the process of funding a mortgage by the Duke of Portland for £11,000 'of the Estate which His Grace has lately purchased at Bulstrode'. He linked this to his claim, saying that he would make it up to £11,000. His claim, including interest prior to death, was £5,441. The decision not to pay the interest was directed by John Heaton; whether he was making decisions for the Trustees or just acting as a messenger is not clear. [38]

By August 1811, the amount paid out to creditors stood at £80,548 (but it is known that the 6th Duke paid out additional claims, some of which were still arriving a decade later). This amount included interest from the date of death. (c/f Earl Fitzwilliam's claim was £2,000; the payment was £2,300). The total amount claimed eventually rose to at least £111,325 which included the 173 claims for amounts under £50. This included Thomas Coutts who was paid £5,237 for interest in 1811 plus £1,000 which the Duke paid personally to Martindale and a further £1,000 which was paid to a Devaynes, which may also have been one of the Duchess's debts. [39] Even after the agreement, shortly prior to her death, that the Duke would increase her allowance and agents would dispense the sum per annum to her creditors (the actual detail is not known), she continued spending. At least c. £2,000 was owed after this agreement to a jeweller and the estate lost £900 in getting the firm to take the jewels back. She had borrowed £500 from Lord Ossulston, presumably a down payment.

However this amount grew on amounts unpaid after the date the list was compiled, to cover interest. Perhaps the strangest amount owed was £400 to an occultist. Finally, it is unclear if any of the French debts are included in the list, or more to the point, what was paid, as they may have used English agents to claim on their behalf. All the accounts seem to ignore debts from France. Fortunately one invoice from France survives listing jewellery purchased by the Duchess in Paris. It amounts to over £3,200. One item cost £1,200. Intriguingly the purchases include a gold box with 'lapis'. The current Devonshire Collection includes such an item. Is this a reminder of the Duke's and Heaton's nightmare of family expenditure out of control and seemingly beyond control?

One claim which must have been anticipated, however spurious, and was paid, probably without too much investigation into its genuineness was £1,000 to Martindale. He had milked what he could over the years and knew a soft touch from time to time. Not claimed but listed in an inventory of unpaid bills owing to Richard Cosway, the miniature portrait painter, at his death in 1820 was £311.

First to be paid were all the bills under £50, amounting to £2,055. It is likely that much of the difference between the total claims and actual payments outlined above remained unpaid. It remains most probable that the Duke had initially no idea of the extent of her debt. In 1791 he wrote to Thomas Coutts stating that his wife was not incurring debts through play. He had been told by his wife that this was the case. Coutts knew differently. [41]

Given the steadfast probity and disciplined life chosen by her mother, who survived her daughter, one can only speculate on her feelings of disappointment on how she had been let down and with good reason.

Perhaps one of the most interesting debts accepted for payment was to Duesbury & Kean, a bill of 6th December 1799. It was for a pair of wine coolers *'very richly enamelled and silk, in honour of Lord Nelson's Victory of the Nile £42. 0s. 0d.'* It is endorsed *'Given by Her Grace to Lord Spencer* (then First Sea Lord) *to present to Lord Nelson'*. She regularly wrote to her brother at the Admiralty, this time she sent him the coolers to send on to the famous Vice Admiral of the Fleet. Nearly a year later she bought a tea service at Derby for £21. 1s. 6d., also for Lord Nelson, on 7th November 1800. [42]

There was no claim from Lady Spencer, or the Prince of Wales. Lord Spencer, her brother, also did not put a claim in for the £500 he was owed by his sister, claiming that he had no document to prove it. However, his other sister, Harriet, put in a claim for £400, which was paid. Given the monies the Duchess had provided for Harriet's creditors over the years, this must have been a somewhat rich to the Trustees. [43] In 1804, debts due to *'servants and dependants'* amounted to £1,097. [44]

This included £80 from Toussaint Bertrand and £160 from William Beard (Devonshire House French Cook and House Steward respectively). It was more than a year's salary for Beard. A further sum of £240 due to him was settled by an annuity of £40 per annum. From December 1804 to March 1806, Georgiana borrowed £11,420 from Thomas Coutts' bank and repaid £10,579 of it. [45]

Adding on the known debts that had been paid during her lifetime, a total amount of debt in excess of her pin money reveals the enormous sum of £230,465. It is most likely that the exact sum is much higher.

One aspect about her debt crisis was the personal effect it had on the lenders. Letters survive which indicate the difficulties some found themselves in, some situations being profound. One letter showed a more general view, one supposes, but one not many would express. It was sent a year before her death: *'Your Grace then gave me her word of honour that you would send for me in the month of October last to settle everything with me – not having been send* (sic) *for to this hour increases My anxiety of course – in case of Death I should loose that money and could show no title to it.'* [46] He received £451. 12s. 0d. on 4th February 1807.

The wife and daughter of a deceased creditor, Mr. Hunter, were *'in very great want of it'* and still no decision to pay it had been made in 1811. This related to a loan made in February 1789 of £1,400, following the Duchess successfully securing a post for a Mr. Alexander Stratton in one of our Embassies. The one depressing aspect of the Duchess's inability to stop spending was her blindness to the distress she created to those she took in; her obvious deceit to people who relied on her to honour her word and suffered as a result. Over the years there were clearly hundreds of them, including those who did eventually get paid.

The Estate managed to avoid many claims (and those conveniently who did not claim). One has only to think of Philip Reinagle, the painter at Chatsworth in 1783, accepting a commission in good faith from a patron not in a position to hand out the commission and with no money to pay it. More to the point, she knew she could not pay it. It shows a side to her character that needs to be recognised in any judgement about her, for she did it frequently.

How was repayment financed?

No statement has been seen which shows how John Heaton financed the payment of the Duchess's debts. However it is possible to provide a potential, if unproven, solution.

Upon her death, her pin money would stop and her domestic expenditure also. This would cover her household entertainment expenses, purchases for the house and the odd debt she could palm off on the household accountant. This could have amounted to £2,000 a year. The Duchess initially received £4,000 per annum. This was increased by £2,000 extra and for some reason, an extra £50 per annum: This was reduced with her agreement when the Duke paid off a lot of her debt in 1786. In 1799, her pin money was £1,500 per annum, rising the following year to £2,000. In 1803 she received £2,811 and the following year £1,500. However from 1805 she received £5,000 and the same rate in 1806 up to the date of death, 30th March, was £2,210. [47]

What is clear is that there was little immediate prospect of it being financed from Estate income. However revenues were rising and there were occasional one-off large receipts of what Heaton called 'casual' income. An example of this was the value of lead ore unsold at the time of the Duke's death in 1811. Chiefly from Yorkshire, this amounted to 420 tons (67 from Derbyshire) valued at £23 per ton – worth £9,650. [48] Money was however needed more quickly. Therefore on 28th November 1807, the Duke took a loan of £20,000 from Earl Cholmondeley, secured on the Wetherby Estate, plus on 29th October 1808 a further loan of £30,000 from E. F. Fitwell and E. D. Fitwell. [49] This was probably a loan on the money market.

Although the Duchess's death and the payments which flowed brought some degree of closure, there must have been a lot of people who wished that the outcome had been different or that they had not made the advance in the first place. At the top of such a list must have been one man who in all probability personally lent her nothing: John Heaton.

Table 4 Additional Known Debts etc

Date	Amount £	
1775	3,000	Paid by the Duke
1776	3,000	Due by Lady Day
2/4/1779	500	Borrowed from John Dingwall[1]
1784	6,500	Paid by the Duke
1786	14,932	Paid by the Duke
1789	500	To Martindale
12/1790	69,850	Debts owed
4/1795		Dss's account at Coutts in the black
1801/2	150	Borrowed ex T.Knowlton. Paid by Duke
12/03-3/06	7,271	Creditors paid through Coutts Bank
1807	500	To Martindale
1810	500	To Martindale
1811	5,237	Paid by the Duke to T Coutts
	4,000	Jewellery returned
	500	Not claimed by Earl Spencer
	3,200	? Not claimed by French Jeweller
Total	119,640	

Excludes Pin Money
[1] D MSS DF4/1/10. Borrowed plus interest

Table 5

Duchess of Devonshire debts at date of death (L/24/112) plus other known debts

Creditor	Comments	Claim
Arkwright Esq		4239
William Adam		1050
JJ Angerstein	Pall Mall, 16/2/1804	350
Ditto sent to Bath		150
Lady Barker	through Cockeril	900
Bulle		100
Earl of Bessborough		1725
Duke of Bedford		1700
Mr Beauclerk		1100
Ditto	Duke gave security but Beauclerk induced induced to give it up	2500
Mr Bosanquet	deceased	1050
Biddulph Cocks & Co		300
Earl of Cholmondeley		1100
Mrs Cuthbert		200
John Crauford		900
Charles Ellis		1500
Earl of Egremont		2300
Earl Fitzwilliam		2000
H Foster		50
P Francis		150
Greville		1000
Thomas Garde	Dublin, [Irish estate lawyer]	277
Mess's Hammersley	q.if due	1000
Mess's Harries & Co	of 1801 on Coutts & Co	200
Mr Hare's 4th		185
Macdonald		49

Madox		100
A L Maynard Esq	Chesterfield	477
F Moore	War Office	75
Col. MacMahon	was 150, £50 paid	100
Lady Palmerston		25
Earl of Peteborough		570
Baron de Rolle		700
Lord Stair		400
Earl Spencer		500
R Sidebottom	Sutton Court	200
Robert Stevenson	Chiswick	315
Rd Thompson	Grosvenor Square, lent 1800	470
MT Vaughan		500
T ? (perhaps Thompson)		500
W Wall	[Banker, Worcester]	11500
Isaac Wilkinson	[Banker,Chesterfield]	100
Michael Ashley	70 Wardour Street	94
E Andrews	Cornhill	123
William Andrew	at Rundill & Bridge	50
Thomas Briggs	Paulton, near Preston	150
Jos Briggs, Attorney	Greys Inn law bill, son of above	10
Birkett & Dockway	Princes St pawnbrokers	2573
	secured by Duke's bond	
Bennett		330
Barker	42 Broad St Golden Square	115
Brown & Mawe	5 TavistockSt Covent Garden	62
	minerals etc	
Barker	St George's Row Tyburn	2650
Buttall	230 Oxford Street	120
Wm Beard	Haldon House, Exeter	412
Broadwater	Old Cavendish Street	300
Bearcroft	41, Pall Mall	450
Mrs Bunting		55
Bromehead		100
Barlow		300
Benwell		100
Wm Blackmore's Exors	14,Henriettaa St	160
Baker	2, St Pauls Churchyard	260
	for Danvot & Co, Brussels	
Chas. Bourchier	Hadley, Barnet	200
Beaman & Abbott	61 New Bond St	71
John Blaxland		650
Baker	142, New Bond St, Haberdasher	163
E Byers & Co	24 Bow Street	250
Canningham Evans & Rowe	St James St	365
Calvert & Parker	mostly due to Parker the	2519
	Pawnbroker, Crane Ct, Fleet St	241
John Camsell Chiswick		565
Coward	Bath	306
Cocker	Nassau Street	916
Clulow	? Paid	300
Christie Pall Mall		100
Crook & Eyston	Milliners	398
Cierlans & Mattos		241
Collinsons		
Cockeril		50

Coward, Cornhill		406
Jos Cator	Buckingham, Kent	125
Cierlans		94
Cockayne	Lyons Inn	100
Carbery	Conduit St, artificial flowers	54
Davis	Sackville St, Jeweller	1859
Davies	Jermyn St., agent for ye Duchs.	
	He holds some china jars	450
Druce	India House	94
Dorants		750
Dingwall	Croydon	3000
Dunage	Philpot Lane	600
De Baffe	Gerrard Street	97
Dauthemare	Hair dresser	148
Duesbury & Kean	Old Bond Street, China men	79
Eddes	194 Strand, Jeweller	250
Edwards	Beaufort Buildings, wine bill	108
James Edwards	Pall Mall, Bookseller	220
Faulder	Bond Street, Bookseller	137
	F. hols the Vatican Prints as a security	
John Freer	Money Hill, Rickmansworth	1700
	For Salmon	
Fosbrock	Drury Lane Theatre	141
Flower & Mainwaring	Chichester Rents, Chancery Lane	758
	Jeweller	
Francillor	24 Norfolk St	8000
	? Most jewels returnable	
Founkeroy		150
Ferrari	Concert tickets	168
W Gillman	Laleham	117
Griffin	Brookes's, St James Str	200
Gray	Sackville St, Jeweller	360
Graham	Gt Queen St	300
Gosling		150
Wm Greensell		150
Sir John Gallini		200
Godfey		200
Francis Goold	Dover Street	415
Gardinier	90 Pall Mall	130
HiginsonDavison & Co	24 New Bond St	250
Hillhouse		111
Jourdan Hansler	11Charles St Grosvenor Sq	464
Robert Hodgson		100
Re Mr Hoare		726
Mrs & Miss Hunter		2472
Horn & Ash	St James St, Jewellers	78
Jeffries Jones & Gilbert	Cockspur St, Jewellers	211
George Jeffries	86 New Bond St	141
Kirkup	Apollo Buildings, Walworth	250
Kennibal		500
Wm Laver	119 Chancery Lane	270
Benj'n Laver	Burton St, Silver Smith	66
Mrs Lamb	15 Gresse St, Rathbone Place	200
James Lawton	Servant to the Duke	331
Mines Royal Copper Co	Bridge Row	250
Miller	23 Marylebone St	1300
Mortimer		400

Masters, Stafford		334
Milnes's Exors		412
Hilton Morrison		80
Marsden		200
Monchet	70 Great St, St Martins Lane	50
Nichols		89
Nunn & Barber	[Haberdashers]	295
Nardine		68
I & H Newman	re Miles Watkins, Cheltenham	50
Ovey,	Linen Draper, Tavistock St	155
Phillips,	Auctioner, Bond St	100
Pelisie	Baker Street	211
Phillips,	Bookseller, Bridge St,Blackfriars	80
Wathen Phipps	Occulist, Cork St	400
Mrs Peterson		76
Parish & Smith		78
Peartree		2200
Mr Phillips	Grosvenor Place. Jewels held as security worth ? £250	900
Edward Russell	Biscuit Baker, 455 Strand Russell holds some books	210
Rock	85 Cornhill	200

Rock supposeses other agents owed:

Godfrey		200
Baker	St Georges Row,Tyburn	200
Fosbrook	Box Keeper	200
Cunningham & Co		250
Birkett		200
Rundle & Bridge	Jewellers, Ludgate Hill	1464
Robson & Hale	Paper Hangers, 213 Piccadilly Work done in Bolton Row	133
Richardson		234
Reeve	Linen Draper,	200
Rauze	Hair Dresser	85
Sheen Snr		180
Sheen Jnr	For Costs	93
Wm Stewart	194,Piccadilly, Bkseller/auct'eer	300
Stones & Shelton	Chandos St	100
Mr Scott	Cash lent by Mrs Scott	145
Mrs Scott's first husband	School bills paid by Duchess for Mrs Scotts Daughter to be deducted	467
Sapio	Musician	55
Sutton		800
Stoddart		128
Mrs Smith		282
Scafes Exs (sic)	[Brother of Ann Scafe]	1320
Sizeland		110
Salmon	arrears of annuity of £150	500
Smith & Keys	Upholsterers	836
Stewart	Milliner, Albermarle St	336
Townsend	Cleveland Row	263
Ralph Travis	Chatsworth	50
James Travis		100
Toussaint & Co	9 Pall Mall	220
Mrs Thoman	19 Eagle St, Red Lion Square	230

	Late husband was a jeweller	
Turner		60
Vardon	Silversmith	350
G Warriner	Linen Draper, 24 New Bond St	360
Myrry Wilson	35 Davis, St Berkley Sq	100
Wirgman	Jeweller, 67 St James St	327
Willis & Co	Thatched House, St James St	268
	Subscription Tickets	
White	Bookseller, Fleet St	326
	Petrarch (sic) held as security	
	returned 1807	
John Wicks	Gunsmith, West St, Soho	345
Whitaker		170
Wilkinson		100
Willerston		129
Williams & Hovill		160
Whalley	for Gibbon of Bath	150
Wakelin & Garrard	Panton St, Haymarket	120
Wilson		475
Thomas Williams	41 Pall Mall	208
Mrs Weddell	Exc of husband, agent for Dss	450
Thos. Weeks		99
[Amounts under £50	Total: 173 claims]	2,262
Total		110514
Richard Cosway	not claimed	311
Lord Ossulston		500
Lifetime Debt Payments	see table 4	119,640
Excluding purchases with her pin money		
		230965

Notes

Rock was an agent for money lenders

? £1000 paid to Devaynes needs adding

List excludes any interest paid from date of death of the Duchess or items paid by 6th Duke

Eg ?payment to Reinagle of £210 22/2/1814

Total claims: 373, of which 205 for less than £100; 27 for £1000 and above

In 1808, there was an Indiaman (ship) called the Devaynes (to Madras)

23

Affairs and Mistresses

In the spring of 1775, on their arrival in London, the Duchess went completely off the rails. It was clearly quite profound. Some eighteen months later upon the prospect of her daughter returning to London, her mother wrote to her:

'Does the Duke go up for the meeting of the Parlt (Parliament) *if he does and you do I hope my sweet girl you will consider very seriously how much is in your power and consult me on your future conduct. A very little steadfastness may regain you everything you have lost but a very little imprudence may sink you past recovery'.* [1]

Perhaps it was in part the discovery that the Duke had a mistress and child which precipitated the dissipation the Duchess enjoyed for several years. With the destruction of the Duke's correspondence and presumably much of the Duchess's which was perceived by the 6th Duke or his successors to be indelicate, little survives which gives a hint of any affairs outside the Duke's marriage. Although Foreman suggests that the birth of Charlotte Williams coincided with the Duke's marriage, care needs to be taken here. Lord Bessborough was of the view that she was born earlier, possibly in 1772 or the year after. This was his perception drawn from indirect comments in the Duchess's correspondence. [2]

However, the comment in a letter to the Duchess from Lady Clermont *'I do love you my dear child most sincerely why don't you name Lady Jersey'* [3] could relate to the discovery of another relationship, that between the latter and the Duke during 1775. [4] Having no children of her own, Lady Clermont's affection for the Duchess, expressed frequently in the surviving correspondence, was likely to have been heartfelt.

Lady Frances Jersey was 22 years old, her husband was aged 40 and she was a month over 17 years old when she was married. One can understand her being drawn towards the younger Duke, just a little over four years older than she was. She had performed her duty in delivering her husband his heir on 19th August 1773. The son was later to marry Sarah Sophia, the daughter of the 10th Earl of Westmorland. (5) The family home was Middleton House, Middleton Stoney, north east of Oxford.

For her own reasons, the Duchess put up with this and even seems to have kept her relationship with Lady Jersey on an even keel for some time. It showed fortitude at least.

Lady Melbourne

The other close and life long friend of the Duke and Duchess was Lady Melbourne In fact the Duchess's niece Caroline Ponsonby married William Lamb, Lady Melbourne's son and Bess Foster's daughter by the Duke, Caroline St. Jules married William's brother, George. Lady Melbourne was more than gracious with her sexual favours and it is probably no coincidence that her presence in the Devonshire social circle saw the 3rd Earl of Egremont on the same guest list. Three years later in 1778 he made her pregnant, possibly at Coxheath Army Camp, or more probably in nearby Tunbridge Wells, although no mention of him survives in the remaining letters as being present at the latter. Uncomplicated liaisons beyond marriage were a feature, if an unwanted one in many instances, in aristocratic social life at that time. It was often overlooked so long as it did not make any waves.

Two surviving items in correspondence to the Duchess around this time may show both aspects of this. Lady Melbourne wrote to her in August 1776: 'I wish you could play a little, a proper de play is the D of D with you. I don't mean your husband'. The 'D of D' was possibly/probably the Duke of Dorset. Gambling was often referred to as 'play' but this quotation is not in that context. The second quote is more difficult to interpret but is considered to refer to an unequivocal rejection of advances: 'when my second and third are added to my first, half the world are running after it, yet there is nothing more hated by everyone than my tout'. This quote came from Lady Elizabeth Pembroke, wife of the 10th Earl of Pembroke and the Duchess's aunt (daughter of the 3rd Duke of Marlborough). She was later a Lady of the Bedchamber to the Queen Consort from 1783 to 1818, living to the age of 93 years (died 30th April 1831). It is unlikely that she would have held this position if her marriage had knowingly been blemished by her. (6)

As noted above, Lady Melbourne was also pregnant in 1778 by the 3rd Earl of Egremont. Both Lady Melbourne and Lady Jersey were there too. The following day the Duchess and Ladies Jersey and Melbourne went out for a ride, the latter in her own phaeton. She fell on getting out and two days later sought a consultation about pain she had developed. However this pregnancy certainly survived.

The fall did no lasting damage and the child was brought up in the Melbourne household at Brocket Hall. The birth was on 15th March 1779 and the baby boy was christened William Lamb.

The second son, he actually inherited, his older brother, Peniston Lamb, (half-brother in reality), dying of tuberculosis in January 1805 at the age of 24 years. Nonetheless, William was a frequent visitor to Petworth in West Sussex to see the Earl of Egremont; he looked like him and it was generally known that the latter was his father. Five years later, Elizabeth Melbourne gave birth to another son, George. The father was the Prince of Wales (see below). William Lamb married Caroline Ponsonby and became Prime Minister as Lord Melbourne. George was to marry the Duke's daughter with Bess Foster, also called Caroline. The boys' sister Emily married Earl Cowper but was soon in a relationship with Viscount Palmerston and had two of the latter's children. She was to marry the latter after the death of her husband.

The Earl turned liaisons with women (both married and unmarried) into a fine art. He is alleged to have had 15 mistresses and 40 children by them in all. Petworth was like a commune with polite conversation continually interrupted by the din of children who had the run of the place. Clearly his ability to melt a lady's heart was impressive but he appears to have travelled alone to social gatherings of the Cavendish inner circle. His abilities and success (if that is the right word) were clearly a match for the raw sexual designs of Ladies Jersey and Melbourne. It does beg the question of whether the two had a long-term, casual relationship with him. Their attitude towards it would seem to have been largely similar and it filled a gap between other liaisons.

Lady Jersey

On the other hand however, Lady Frances Jersey's promiscuity seemed to be continuing unabated. On 11th September 1777 the Duchess rose early (a phenomenon in itself) and set out for Matlock with Lady Clermont to meet Lord and Lady Jersey. The latter looked *'extremely well'* and his Lordship was in *'pretty good humour'*. However over the next twelve days he had been *'two or three times out of humour and has threatened the old story of parting but she has put him in good humour and he is in great spirit now.'*[7] Whether this was as a result of her activities at Chatsworth or earlier was not recorded.

Her activities had been the centre of attention by an over-indulgent Morning Post (a London based paper, but often quoted by the provincial press) and it had been a while before Lord Jersey had caught up with what the media frenzy was saying. The Duchess told her mother that he *'has behaved very handsomely (sic) about them* (i.e. the Morning Post articles) – *for he told Lady Jersey he should think it right to be the more indulgent to her, to show the world he did not believe them'.* Everybody knew her reputation. Francis Villiers simply wasn't discreet enough, if at all, relying on her charm and bedside manner to smooth away domestic difficulties.

A month later (i.e. 24th September 1777) while at Chatsworth, she appears to have turned the charm offensive on to Sir Harry Hunlock of nearby Wingerworth Hall, but one suspects he was a different kettle of fish. There is no apparent indication that the Jerseys were at Chatsworth in the August when the Morning Post was revealing all it could. (8) Had they been so, Lady Jersey would have been better able to keep the gossip away from her husband, but maybe she was past caring.

Lady Jersey became pregnant, possibly around the beginning of the year, having a miscarriage early in April 1778. The Duchess couldn't resist telling her mother: '*... you must not own you know it even to Ld J as it is to be kept a secret. I have seen Ly Jersey I spoke to her about yr knowing of his being here, and I think will be of use for the future'.* (10)

A little later, in further correspondence, it was revealed by Lady Spencer '*Ld Jersey came about four o'clock he told me Lady Jersey was ill. I ask'd what was the matter with her and he said she had a little fever so I said no more'.* (11) So who was it who had been to see Lady Jersey and why would knowing the information be of value? The answer may lie in the completely open affair of the Duke with her about five months later, but intriguingly, perhaps not.

There is a pointer in a different direction. Only two weeks or so after the miscarriage, Lady Jersey was at a party attended by Lady Spencer. '*Was it not very imprudent in Lady (Jersey) to go to The Oaks so soon after the illness she has had* (use of coded language here) *and to meet such people, surely she must be infatuated. I have said nothing of all that here you may be sure'.* (12)

Surely the father was there at the party and the Devonshires (at least the Duke) appears not to be there. If he had been, would the letter have been destroyed? The Duchess clearly was not there and had the Duke been, it's likely that Lady Spencer would have indirectly mentioned it. Nonetheless, there is a nagging thought that could point towards Lady Spencer using the information to coerce Lady Jersey to end her relationship with the Duke at that time. The Duchess mentioned deliberately to Lady Jersey that she had written to her mother mentioning that '*he*' had been to see her (Lady Jersey). She added that it might be '*of use for the future*'. This means that it put both the Duchess and her mother in receipt of information which could be usefully used against Lady Jersey's best interests, whoever '*he*' was.

As it turned out, Lady Jersey fell straight into the trap when her charm offensive turned into an open affair with the Duke at their tents at Coxheath Camp in 1778. It was, according to Foreman, [13] ended by Lady Spencer. It appears convincing that Lady Spencer linked knowledge of Lady Jersey's affair and pregnancy to her ending the affair with the Duke in the face of the detail being revealed. As much as anything else, it shows vividly much about Lady Spencer's character.

In 1805, Harriet, the Duchess's sister, went to see Lady Jersey when she was ill. She wrote (28th August 1805) *'I went and found her rather ill and very much affected; I expected it tho' everybody laughed at me for saying so, for she certainly used him* (Lord Jersey) *very ill. I do not mean only in infidelities* (*Heaven knows bad enough*) *but she made him unhappy – teaz'd and turn'd him into ridicule'.* [9] Virtually all of the letters written by the Duchess the following year are missing, except those to her son, Hartington, probably destroyed because of their content.

The relationship between the Duchess and Lady Jersey cooled over the years, but never ceased. This was even when the latter became the mistress of the Prince of Wales and wanted little to do with the Duchess. That relationship lasted about five years, when the Prince dropped her and had a reconciliation with the Duchess, which lasted until she died. They were firm friends, but it was at arms length.

Charlotte Williams

There is some evidence to suggest that the Spencer family knew about Charlotte, the Duke's illegitimate daughter, before she went to live at Devonshire House. Lady Cowper wrote to her grandson, George Spencer (the Duchess's brother), in 1778: *'Miss Williams has been ill all ye winter. She may have great blood in her veins, but I fear not good blood, w'ch is a better thing'.* [14]

At about the time of the Duke's marriage, the date is not known, the Duke had a daughter by a milliner called Charlotte Spencer (no relation to his future wife's family). In 1780, it appears that her mother, for some reason, was unable to continue looking after her. It was not as a result of her death, which came almost a decade later. A carer, Mrs Garner, had been appointed before Charlotte was taken for the first time to Devonshire House, where she met the Duchess, on 21st or 22nd March 1780. The Duchess initially liked Mrs. Garner: *'I have made her take a ready furnished lodging for ten days as she could not find one unfurnished that suited her'.* Charlotte had no surname and the Duchess was thinking of William. She was eventually given the name Williams. The Duke was quite sure she had been inoculated (? against smallpox and the Duchess understood that she had had measles).

The Duchess described Charlotte as being *'a very healthy good humoured looking child. I think not very tall, she is amazingly like the Duke, I am sure you would have known her anywhere, she is the best humoured little thing you ever saw, vastly active and vastly lively, she seems very affectionate and seems to like Mrs Garner very much – she has not good teeth and has often the toothache but I suppose that does not signify as she has not changed them yet – and she is the most nervous little thing in the world'.* [(15)]

Mrs. Garner let it be known to those enquiring that Charlotte's father was dead and whose mother was out of town and a distant relative of the Devonshire's. The lodgings were not good and a move elsewhere was needed. On 8ᵗʰ May 1780, Charlotte went to live at Devonshire House. No sooner had she arrived and the Gordon Riots erupted. She was sent to stay with the Melbournes at Brocket Hall until the disturbances were over. [(16)] When the Duke and Duchess left for the Duke's Militia duty at Plymouth in late July 1780, Charlotte went to stay with Lady Spencer. She, like the Duchess, was quite fond of her. [(17)] Charlotte grew up with the Devonshires, but her personality, especially in relation to her manners became unacceptable to the Duchess, who saw it becoming a bad influence on her daughters. While the Duchess was in exile abroad, the Duke permitted her to marry the nephew of John Heaton, the Duke's Agent or Auditor and Charlotte dropped off the Duchess's radar after that.

Lady Clermont

Another dark horse at this time was Lady Clermont. Ever stern in her letters to the Duchess about probity etc., the occasional comments from the latter to her mother give a whiff of scandal and further expressions of loose morality fostered by a sterile marital relationship. This time the Duchess was more open and very specific. Into her sights had drifted Lady Clermont: *'Lady Clermont has miscarry'd after a retard of some days and to tell you the truth as it is pretty certain Mr. Marsden the apothecary was the father, I fear some wicked method was made use of to procure abortion, and this is more likely as Mr. Marsden might bring the drogue from his own shop – you will allow her toothach was very symptomatical tho' she carry'd the affair off with her usual art'.* [(18)] 'Usual art' smacks of familiarity.

Lady Duncannon (Harriet Bessborough)

It was not unusual for the aristocratic parent to take in the children of an extra-marital relationship and this happened with the Duchess's sister, Harriet, Lady Duncannon (later Countess Bessborough). She had married on 27ᵗʰ November 1780. Within a year, on 31ˢᵗ August 1781, she bore her husband Frederick Ponsonby, Lord Duncannon, his heir, John William Ponsonby. She had another child by him on 6th July 1783. Despite outward appearances, she was having an affair with Lord Granville Leveson Gower, 1st Earl Granville (widely known as Granville). She had two children by him who were brought up in the Ponsonby family (and one other that was adopted). The extra two were Harriette Emma Arundel Stewart (born in 1801-02) and George Arundel Stewart, who was born in c.1804. Intriguingly, on 8th December 1782, Lady Spencer wrote to the Duchess having just learnt that she was pregnant saying that she thought that Harriet was pregnant too and added: *'your situation and your sisters differs'*. Was Harriet's second child, Frederick, really a Ponsonby? [19]

Haryo wrote in early 1803 that Granville and Lord George Villiers (Lady Jersey's son) were laying siege to Lady Sarah Fane, *'the great heiress'*. She could not have been too impressed with Granville's background for she married Lord Villiers in 1806. [20]. Gleeson states that Granville, had another secondary affair with Lady Hester Stanhope in 1804 but this ended when Hester's uncle William Pitt, with whom she lived, offered Granville the diplomatic post of Ambassador to Russia in 1804. [21]

Harriet also had a secondary, if albeit a short affair with Charles Wyndham in July 1786. He was the 24 years old son of the 2nd Earl of Egremont and younger brother of George, the 3rd Earl who was a close friend of the Duke; she was 25. The Spencers managed to curtail this liaison, which happened virtually at the same time as Georgiana Fawlkner, nee Poyntz (Harriet's and the Duchess's cousin) had gone off with Jack Townshend one of the Devonshire's inner circle of friends. This was more serious and her husband tried to blame the Duchess for being involved, which the Duke strongly denied. [22] Fawlkner divorced his wife and she married Jack Townsend (later 1st Marquis Townsend) in 1787. He was a Privy Councillor from 1806 and Paymaster of the Forces, 1806-07, in the Ministry of All Talents. [23]

Granville married the Duke's daughter Haryo in 1809. Having left Harriet Bessborough for Haryo (her niece), Harriet Bessborough then had an affair with Richard Sheridan (see below).

Granville was initially disliked by the Duke's children, despite his long association with their aunt Harriet. Haryo wrote that *'in their long correspondence* (i.e. Granville and Lady Duncannon) *he shows himself to return her selfless devotion with a rather heartless egotism'*. [24]. Duncannon also initially treated his wife rather heavily, but she still retained what may have been a cause of it: her happiness with two men in her life.

A curious phenomenon at the time was the practice of a couple having an affair and being welcomed without reserve. Yet if they later married, the lady would be dropped like a hot potato. This was highlighted by Haryo when C.J. Fox announced his forthcoming marriage to Mrs. Armistead, who had been his mistress for many years. She was suddenly dropped from the guest list of many people who had welcomed her for years.

Haryo pointed out that this had also happened to Lady Holland after her divorce from Sir Geoffrey Webster and her marriage to Lord Holland (C.J. Fox's nephew), despite the Devonshires supporting her. So far as Fox was concerned, he had the last laugh. He eventually owned up that he had bucked the system. They had been married secretly eight years previously in 1795. [25] Haryo wrote: *'I hear the Hollands and all his friends have taken it amazingly well'.* [26] Not much option really, with hindsight, but whether it was viewed as that by some at the time is a different matter.

This reluctance to engage with newly weds also extended to civil partnerships on occasions. In 1795, a Mr Williams and Lady Barriemore moved to Dallington House, having leased it for six years. *'They appear to be a pleasing excellent couple – her ladyship happening to be the widow of Ld. B., and niece of lady Ladde, the ladies in the neighbourhood are shy of visiting her, tho' apparently without reason'.* [27]

The Prince of Wales

Having a reputation for having many affairs, this section concentrates on those, or at least some of those, ladies in the Devonshire circle. However to set the scene first:

Shortly after he reached the age of 21 years, 12th August 1783, the Prince of Wales commenced a relationship with Maria Fitzherbert, illegally marrying her on 15th December 1785. Prior to this he had a relationship with Mary Robinson – as early as July 1780: *'she wears his picture about her neck and drives about with four nag tail'd horses and two servants behind her'.* The Duchess described her as *'en maitresse declose vest tout a faiture & tablissement'.* [28] After this affair ended, the Prince apparently gave her a painting of himself endorsed on the back: *'gage de mon amour'.* She had it framed incorporating both these words into the frame plus £700 worth of diamonds.

In 1781, according to the Duchess, the Prince began *'an attachment to Mrs Armistead, who was already the mistress of her brother in law, Lord George Henry Cavendish'.* She records that *'Lord George was returning one night to Mrs Armistead's rather drunk. In going into her room he perceived some unaccustomed light in another and much against her entreatys* (sic) *went in – the room seem'd empty but willing to examine every where he soon found there was a man behind the door – he stretched out his arm with the candle in his hand close to the persons face, and to his great surprise found that it was the Prince of Wales'.* Lord George burst out laughing, made a low bow and withdrew.

She goes on; *'Mrs Armistead finding the P of W would not be constant to her ... soon broke with him'*. This may be because he was already seeing Lady Melbourne. It is held that her husband's peerage and appointments came as a result of her liaison with the Prince. As Lord Melbourne was created a Viscount in 1781, the date may give some indication of when the affair began. She bore a son by the Prince, who was called George Milbanke Lamb, in 1784. In 1809, he married the Duke's daughter by Bess Foster, Caroline St. Jules. This birth confirms that the liaison was extant in 1783. It possibly followed a brief flirtation with Lady Jersey, but if so, he dropped her in favour of Lady Melbourne and this later relationship may have continued until Maria Fitzherbert came onto the scene.

Maria Fitzherbert, nee Smythe, was a Catholic and had been married twice, both husbands leaving her widowed within a few years of marriage. Her second marriage was to Thomas Fitzherbert of Swynnerton, between what is now Stoke-on-Trent and Stafford. She was born on 26th July 1756. Upon the death of Thomas, (c. 7th May 1781), she inherited a house in Park Street, where the Duke's oldest daughter, Little G, was living as Lady Morpeth in 1806, together with an annuity of £1,000 pa. She was introduced to London society in 1783 by Lord Sefton, her uncle, who was a friend of the Duke and Duchess. It may well have been at Devonshire House therefore that she was introduced to the Prince. This would explain perhaps why the Duchess became sucked into a situation she did not approve of.

The Prince fell hopelessly in love with Maria but she would not marry him, A legal marriage was not possible under the Act of Settlement, 1701, which excluded marriage to Catholics by the heir to the throne and under the Royal Marriages Act, 1773, which required the consent of the king to any marriage. He would not give consent to any marriage to a catholic let alone a woman who had already been married twice.

None-the-less, the Prince had obtained, under pressure, a promise to marry from Maria, which the Duchess had witnessed, even providing one of her rings for Maria to slip onto one of her fingers and which was soon returned with a determination not to submit to further pressure. However on the 6th July 1784, a party at Devonshire House was interrupted by messengers from the Prince advising that he had attempted suicide, the inference being that Maria was there at the party.

It would appear that Maria and the Duchess went to Carlton House to see the Prince because of a threat from the latter that he would tear off his bandage if he did not receive a promise of marriage. Keate, the Prince's surgeon swore that a knife had barely missed the Prince's heart and further pressure applied as *'Ld Southampton was sent for as there was an idea of informing the (kin)-g for if the P died they might all have been tryd for their lives...'*

The Duchess was frightened by all this and informed the Duke of the events. Presumably on advice from friends (including the Duke and Duchess) Maria left the country for France the following day. The attempted suicide turned out to be a sham but none-the-less, the Duchess (presumably taking advice from the Duke) told the Prince on 12th July that she insisted on his lessening *the intimacy between us and he is not to come to Chatsworth unless I write him word ... He knows the Duke is acquainted with every thing and submits his whole conduct to him*. Within a week, ignoring all of this, the Prince sent her a four-page flattering letter buttering up to her, his *ever dearest friend and sister*.

Eventually Maria was persuaded to return in December 1785, the Prince maintaining liaisons with other ladies in the interim, despite undying love for her (see below). Despite the illegality, they were married on 15th December 1785, the witnesses being her uncle Henry Errington and brother Jack Smythe. Clearly the Duchess gave it a wide birth but the Pope approved it. The Prince lived with her until 1794, when he yielded to pressure from the king and a bribe of the payment of his enormous debts.

His marriage to Caroline of Brunswick was doomed from the start and he went back to Maria in 1798, having an affair with at least Lady Jersey in the interim. However Maria ended the relationship in 1809, dying on 27th March 1837. She was buried at St. John the Baptist's Church, Kemp Town, Brighton. (29)

The Duchess also records that the Prince was *supposed to be attached to Ly Augusta Campbell, whose beauty manner and amiable qualitys (sic) authoriz'd such a supposition, but if that was the case, it was soon put an end to as there is no appearance of it now*.

Following his 21st birthday and the unshackling of oppressive parental control, the Prince started to assert himself. By February 1784, he had given several parties and was minded to give them every week, although *the Duchess seemed to think they were rather formal and dull. His flirt, Mrs Hodges is gone out of town*, so maybe there was at least one amour while Mrs Fitzherbert was abroad. This letter was written by an unknown author, who was clearly out of favour with the Prince (and was therefore probably a woman) and also it might appear, with Lady Jersey, whose parties *as you may suppose were very stupid*. (30)

There does appear to be a list of several other ladies who more than caught his eye, but the one most germane to this account is the Duchess herself. (31)

Wraxhall relates that the Duchess succeeded Lady Melbourne as the Prince's favourite, *but of what nature was that attachment must remain a matter of conjecture. I know, however, that during her pregnancy in 1785, HRH manifested so much anxiety and made such frequent morning visits on horseback to Wimbledon as to give umbrage to her brother Lord Spencer, and even, it was supposed to excite some emotion in the phlegmatic bosom of the*

Duke her husband... (Her beauty consisted) *in the amenity and graces of her deportment, in her irresistible manners and the seduction of her society ... her face though pleasing, yet had it not been illuminated by her mind, might have been considered ordinary... The Gainsborough portrait* (of 1785), *with the hat and feather probably does not represent any Dss of D at all...'.* [32] Her son, the 6th Duke, was the Bearer of the Orb at the Prince of Wales' Coronation as George IV in 1821. [33]

The Complete Peerage states that Lady Jersey was sometime mistress to George IV and was succeeded in this post by Isabella, Lady Hertford. Farrington in his Diary, 6th July 1803, refers to her (Lady Jersey) as 'now quite out of favour with the Prince of Wales '*and adds that having apologised to him for inadvertently blocking his way on the stairs of the Opera House, she received a call the next day from his Private Secretary, who informed her that it was the desire of the Prince that she would not speak with him'.* It would appear that the Prince had an affair with Lady Jersey, possibly after he broke with Mrs Fitzherbert in 1794 but it had ended by 1799. The friendship he had with the Duchess had cooled, but a reconciliation had occurred by August 1799. [34]

The Prince found his male friends in the younger element that frequented Brooks's Club. These consisted of Charles Fox, Mr. Fitzpatrick, Mr. Hare, the Duke of Devonshire, Lord Egremont, Lord Carlisle, Mr. Fawkner, Mr. Greville etc. Most of them shared the same politics as the Prince – opposition to the Court and firm Whig principles. There was a second group of younger men with which the Prince also associated. This group included Lord Euston, Lord Althorp (the Duchesses younger brother), William Pitt, Mr. Pratt, and Lord Chatham. If accurate, it was a cross-party group. [35]

The Duchess also provided a pen portrait of the Prince: '...*the POW is rather tall and as a masculine figure which tho' striking is not perfect – he is inclined to be too fat and looks too much like a woman in mens cloathes (sic), but the gracefulness of his manner and (h)js height certainly make him a pleasing figure, his face is very handsome and he is fond of dress even to a tawdry degree... his person his dress and the admiration he has met and (illeg.)still more than that he meets from women takeup his thoughts chiefly – he is good natured and rather extravagent'.*

She mentions about '*some shabby traits to his mistresses*' and '*two or three generous things to his friends in distress do him the highest honour'.* Presumably the last comment was against the background of his generosity to her and her creditors. The episode recounted above about Lady Jersey may be an example of the Duchess's description of the Prince's '*shabby traits'*.

The closeness of their friendship set tongues wagging concerning a potential liaison between the Prince and the Duchess. John Heaton was sufficiently concerned to advise the Duke that stories about a relationship between the

Prince and the Duchess were circulating in London, together with another rumour that the Duke and Duchess *'liv'd ill together'*. Although the Duchess felt that this was an unprovoked attack upon her, the Duke felt differently, telling her that he did not believe that Heaton had meant to hurt her. [36]

If the hint of an affair between the two was not enough, it was followed shortly afterwards by an accusation that she was having yet another one with C.J.Fox and the Duke was also having one with Lady Jersey. [37]

This had come from the Duchess's sister Harriet. She had been with Lady George Cavendish (the Duke's sister-in-law) at Compton Place, her family home. *'Ly George teaz'd her cruelly with telling her all manner of things which she s'd (said) she knew from the D and Dss* (Duke and Duchess) *of Rutland ... so blended with some truths that my sister was quite hurt'* [38] The story was garnished with an assertion that the Duke's liaison with Lady Jersey was because he was angry with the his wife because of her association with Fox. There is no doubt that they were good friends but doubt about the statement's validity. Probably another example of not allowing the truth to get in the way of a good story and in this case from close family (Lady George) and sometime only good friends, the Rutlands.

This was probably gossip being used to wind up Harriet. It is worth noting that affairs, liaisons, intrigues (all the same) feature commonly in the 18th century records of all kinds. What does not occur so often – rarely in fact in comparison – was the record of opportunistic encounters especially between friends, when a lady dropped her modesty and her hand onto her room key, leaving her male companion to fight his way through voluminous underskirts for a quick romp on her bed. For the Duchess, no such implication is suggested. This could, at this stage in her life, have been a line in the sand she did not cross. One aspect of the probity Lady Spencer sought from her daughters, which the Duchess heeded, at least until she delivered the Duke his heir.

Suggestions that the Duchess had a relationship with Bess Foster are probably relying on the language the Duchess used in her correspondence with her: *'I adore and love you beyond description'* plus *'Canis sends a thousand loves'* being just two examples. However she frequently used the word love in her letters with her mother when describing men in the family, let alone other friends and acquaintances. In this context, no physical attachment was implied or construed.

Perhaps the Duchess's probity was best summed up by Horace Walpole relating to her relationship with C.J. Fox during the 1784 election: *'she certainly procured the greatest part of Mr Fox's votes for him; though the Court partly endeavoured to deter her by the most illiberal and indecent abuse, yet they could not fix the smallest stain on her virtue'*. [39]

Richard Sheridan

In April 1780, the Duchess went to the opera, probably with Lady Melbourne, and afterwards they went to Mrs. Crewe's for supper. The Duke was there along with others including Richard Sheridan. He had had a great deal of success as a playwright and was part owner of Drury Lane Theatre. His play for the 1779 season would have had a particular resonance for both the Duke and the Duchess. It was the The Camp, a satire on the ongoing threat of French invasion and on military matters. It was very successful, running to 57 performances – a lot at the time.

Mrs. Crewe was the Whig society hostess, Frances Anne Crewe who was married to John Crewe but was later to have an affair with Sheridan, which lasted until the mid or late-1780s, tolerated by Mrs. Eliza Sheridan. Following the end of this affair, Sheridan developed a deep relationship with the Duchess's sister Harriet, who had been involved with Lord Granville Leveson Gore (see above).

In 1789 Harriet's husband, Lord Bessborough, decided to divorce his wife and to sue Sheridan. However he was persuaded by the Duke to abandon the idea in early 1790. Memories would still have been relatively fresh over the Duke's own plan to separate from his wife over her debts, although he quickly had changed his mind. However Eliza Sheridan seems to have abandoned all hope for her own marriage. She had initially forgiven him, having been persuaded by C.J. Fox, no doubt worried about its effect upon the Whigs in general and Sheridan's voters in particular.

She certainly appears to have has her admirers. Apparently the Prince of Wales found the need to persuade his younger brother, the Duke of Clarence, to stop pestering her. While her husband was pleading for forgiveness, he was found locked in a bedroom with a governess at Mrs. Crewe's house. Casting him to the wind, Eliza fell in love with Lord Edward Fitzgerald and bore his daughter, born in Spring 1792. However the birth was followed by an attack of TB and Eliza died on 28th June 1792, the child being brought up by Sheridan as one of his own. (40)

Back in 1780, Sheridan stood successfully for Stafford (probably in a seat which was the patronage of the Marquis of Stafford) in the general election held between 6th and 18th September, it not being held on a single day as now. His election campaign was orchestrated by the Duchess, but whether she paid the expense of it, said to have been £1,000, is not clear. (41)

The Duchess quite clearly had a soft spot for him. She wrote to her mother in April 1783: *'in the mens box at the opera t'other night Ld Cholmondeley and some of them were talking of Sheridan and one of them s'd they thought Benedick as good as anything he had ever written, guess how proud I am.'* (42)

24

Life At Chatsworth

Getting There

It usually took about three days to reach Chatsworth from London. The family for years used it for their main holiday, coinciding with hunting and attending the races at Derby, Chesterfield and sometimes Nottingham. Other family members also went to York, but the Duke and Duchess tended to give it a miss. The movement of so many personal possessions and other essential requirements to avoid anguish and disappointment required much attention to detail. All the goods going with the family were loaded onto a wagon, which took a week to reach Chatsworth. It usually had three staff, with two never leaving it, all three sleeping on it.

It was not always without mishap either. In 1784, the driver was probably drunk by the time he reached Chatsworth Park and ran off the road, upturning the wagon. Two valuable pier glasses costing £500 were smashed as a result and two servants travelling with him were sadly and badly hurt. One servant hurt his/her head and a maid broke her arm. Three weeks later, it turns out that one of the maids called Fanny Cook, a nursery maid, had a spinal injury. It had been initially thought that she was not on the wagon (i.e. she was walking alongside), but that unfortunately was not the case. She was sent to Buxton for treatment on the advice of Dr. Denman. In May 1795, George Canning was returning to London *with no other hazard than that of being robbed on the road or overturned by a drunken postboy*.[1]

No note has ever been found to indicate that the wagon was ever robbed. John Heaton purchased a gun for the house, but whether the staff on the wagon could use it was another matter. There were separate groomsmen to bring the

Duke's and the Duchess's riding horses the 160 miles/256 km to Chatsworth. Once Hartington was old enough, he travelled with his sisters. The servants travelled separately, with a senior staff member bringing the lower servants – the maids, kitchen staff etc with them. There were generally about 24 people involved including the family

The Duke would have had top quality, well sprung carriages and many of the main turnpiked roads to the north of the country would have a comparatively good surface, elsewhere, surfaces could be uneven and uncomfortable. Dust was another problem, making the surfaces suffocating and intolerable, according to Lady Spencer [2]. The same was also the case in London and Piccadilly was wetted to keep down the dust towards the end of the 18th century.

Food and Drink

Although the house was well aired ahead of a family visit, with good and plentiful fires lit before arrival, the place took some time to respond to the heat the fires applied. Chatsworth was a prodigious user of coal, as one would expect of a house of that size. Good quality household coal was obtainable nearby from the Derbyshire coalfield. During a 14 week stay to the end of the year, some 300 tons or more were required.

The family ate well, as may be expected. In 1798 in the 14 weeks they were in residence, 14 tons of meat was consumed, with the poorer cuts going to the servants and local poor people. The diet was varied with a lot of fish, caught locally in the River Derwent, which flowed past the House. Even a brace of pike were purchased from a local angler for the family table. On the 1798 visit, they also enjoyed 23 barrels of oysters brought in from Sheffield, 30 lbs of eels, and also 229 dozen, (that is 2,748) crayfish.

They drank well of course: 6 dozen bottles of East India Madeira and German Moselle plus 2 pipes (284 gallons) of port. They even managed to get Belonia sausage but were never able to produce enough milk or eggs for their needs. They borrowed cows from neighbours to ensure they had enough milk. The grocery bill came to c. £500 and other wines, foreign cordials and hops cost another £236. An apothecary looked after their health, presumably to the resident doctor's advice, and also provided medicines for servants.

Amongst the supplements to the regular diet of meat and fish were oranges, essence of lemons and other fruits, olives, ginger, best refined sugar, seltzer water, cockles etc. Although the House produced its own beer, employing a brewer, to fill 12 very large barrels in the cellar with the family crest carved on them, cider was also well liked. The family got through about 70 gallons of it on a visit. It cost about twice as much as the price of beer, being 2s 10d (about 14p) per gallon in 1800. [3]

A remarkable surviving document lists the alcohol in the cellars at Hardwick in 1795. Bearing in mind that the house was only in use as a home for a few weeks a year, the quantities seem excessive. The ale cellar contained 17 pipes (a pipe – 108 gallons) and 72 hogsheads(i.e. 72 half-pipes). This amounts to 5,724 gallons. Much of it was supplied by two local brewers, Hardys and Smiths. The beer dated from 1793 and included malt beer (most of it) plus small beer and one hogshead of oat beer. The wine cellar contained 954 gallons of wine and spirit. The majority of it was port (705 gallons) and white wine (144 gallons). Although there were some small quantities of rum, madeira and Lisbon (?sherry), there was no brandy or whisky. [4]

The following year (1799), the family did not return to Chatsworth. The Duke wrote to his Chatsworth doctor (Dr. Denman, who was paid a retainer of £30pa), to tell him that it was beyond his power to go there. His problem was that the proposed Act of Union (which created the United Kingdom) was making a tortuous journey before Parliament. The Duke espousing the Whig cause, needed to be in the House of Lords to try and protect the interests of the Irish Catholics. It would be autumn 1800 before he saw Chatsworth again.

Notwithstanding this, the Duchess had her own reasons for not wishing to go there. This needs to be seen against the almost certain fact that this was the first visit in at least ten years. Now however, the two new wings and other work were finished at Chiswick and it was only 12 miles away, not 150 or so.

A Guest At Chatsworth

In September 1786, Lady Spencer was staying at Chatsworth. She had Lady Clermont for company. It isn't clear how much company was in the House, but the Duke of Dorset is recorded as being there a few days later (14th September). She wrote to her close friend Caroline Howe in Mayfair almost daily and on the 9th gave details of how she (Lady Spencer) was spending her time. [5]

Rising early as usual, she read a chapter of the Greek testament and then other works until 10am when she met Lady Clermont in the breakfast room. She usually sat there until the post arrived, which was seldom before noon. She then retired to her room to read any letters for her, write letters and generally waiting *until the world is about*. Basically, waiting until the Duke, Duchess (in that order) and other guests rose. This procession altered, presumably, later when the Duke and Duchess slept together. Whilst waiting, she would take advantage of fine weather to go for a walk or drive. For clarity, the other guests arose when they liked, but the Duchess was usually formally woken when the Duke got up.

If the weather was bad, she would *wander about the house and often fine nobody – or rather those I would rather not find till 4 o'clock*' when she went back to her room to dress for dinner. This latter comment was probably with Bess Foster in mind. Lady Spencer kept her thoughts about Bess largely to herself. However she was not too worried about commenting that on account of Bess's cough, the sooner she left for a warmer climate, the better! Now that Bess was back in England, Lady Spencer intended leaving Chatsworth (ostensibly to see Dr. Warren) just as soon as she knew Bess was heading there. She seems to have been well informed about Bess's movements in London, even to the point of enquiring at Devonshire House about it through a 3ʳᵈparty.

Lady Spencer made it a rule to be in the Drawing Room at at 5pm. This was the notional hour for dinner, although this could be delayed if the Duke had not returned from hunting, shooting etc. or something else occurred, which could delay dinner until 6pm or even later. Over the years, the time for dinner gradually progressed to 7pm. Lady Spencer found dinner longer than she preferred, but enjoyed her evenings which passed into the night with cards and music until 11pm when supper was delivered and she went to bed. Sometimes a musician would be hired in London and sent up to Chatsworth to provide, presumably, background music during the day as well as perform at night. Most guests would stay, perhaps be expected to stay, up after supper.

All was not quite right however, for she wrote: *'with all the Luxeries (sic) that Riches can give, fine house numerous Company, excellent Eating and delightful Musick, I know no place where time is so often near hanging upon ones hands and I really think there is not either the Comfort or the Society of poor little Holywell (her home in St Albans). However I am well aware that I shall like it better, as I grow more used to it. I only hope I shall not get the habit of liking it too well for that would be the worst thing I could do'.* [6]

A couple of weeks later (25ᵗʰ September 1786) it was the second of the two annual Public Days (which meant dinner at 3pm) followed by a Great Ball in the evening. The guests included the Duke of Dorset, Lords Thanet, Duncannon, and George Cavendish, and several other men. The Ladies included Clermont, Bess Foster, Duncannon (the Duchess's sister), Spencer (her mother) plus Mrs St. John and Miss Lloyd. It would appear that Richard Sheridan and his wife arrived shortly afterwards. Lady Spencer noted that a Mrs Musters was exceedingly pretty and with Mrs. Sheridan, Bess Foster and the Duchess 'made a fine group of pretty women'.

Lady Spencer found stimulating company and conversation when Lord Chancellor Thurlow came to stay at Chatsworth following a visit to Buxton. This had coincided with a similar visit by the Devonshires with a large party of the Chatsworth guests, going to look at the recently opened spa resort. After his health had improved he left Buxton for Chatsworth. The Buxton waters must have done the trick.

A year later, in September 1787, Lady Spencer was back at Chatsworth. She wrote to Caroline Howe to say that the evenings were short, with dinner often not being before 6pm and sometimes 7pm, lasting two hours until they were done with coffee. Then they played billiards for an hour and then whist until supper was on the table at 11.30 – 12pm, when she went to bed. She was quite a good billiards player, equal to the Duke and habitually with a bet on the outcome. The Duchess does not appear to have taken up the game, although her daughter, Haryo, was to do so about two decades later.

Lady Spencer described the Duke of Dorset and Lord Thanet as being the most indefatigable billiards and whist players she had ever seen, ideally matching the Duke and his mother-in-law. Occasionally, the Duke managed to persuade her to play whist after supper, when she had not managed to get to bed until after 2am. Despite this, the Duke and Duchess were rising much earlier than previously. Generally being down by 11am. The Duke was being *remarkably attentive and kind to me, which adds greatly to my satisfaction of being here, and Georgiana's behaviour in many respects gives me much comfort,* she wrote.

It was all part of a charm offensive: ideally, the Duke wanted her to live with them more often if not permanently. From his point of view, it was the best way of keeping his wife under control, at least where her socialising and spending was concerned. The Duchess miscarried in late November 1787. This was one characteristic of her mother she could manage without. The latter could not agree to moving in so long as Bess Foster remained there. Studiously intent on being civil when she had to be, Lady Spencer was not going to be intimate, as she put it. [7]

In May 1788, they were back again at Chatsworth and the cordiality was still extant: *'We live most comfortably here and if it was not for the idea of their going abroad (which I cannot like) when we go back, I should feel happier about them than I have done in a long time'*. Not only were they still getting up at a reasonable hour (at least for the Devonshires) but the Duke had started to be 'constantly employed' in his park, stables and paddocks each morning. If he could get the others to join him he did so, as in fishing the river with nets. Otherwise the Duchess went walking and riding with him, and read and wrote a great deal. They strolled around the garden or between tea and coffee in the evening.

The Duke and Duchess were clearly getting along much better; *'I have scarcely ever seen them so long almost alone and it is impossible to describe the pleasant kind of confidential ease and unaffected playful fondness that subsists between them'*. Domestic bliss, good weather and exercise all combined to the benefit of both the Duchess and the Duke. For Lady Spencer there was the additional good news that they had received permission to open the Buxton mailbag at

Bakewell so that they could take out their letters. [8]

The Duke's keenness to have a bet was reciprocated by Lady Spencer and her husband the Earl. A good example of this survives albeit at Althorp, the Spencer's Northamptonshire home. She and the Earl had been playing billiards and she had lost 34 guineas. Ever optimistic, she rose the next day: *as it rains dogs and cats* (sic) *today, I reckon they cannot hunt and we shall be able to have some good billiards this morning (against the Duke and Lord Lucan) before we start reading*.

Play started with all the other ladies watching with the Duke soon ten guineas down, when he proposed playing double or quits. The other ladies asserted that Lord Lucan would beat Lady Spencer. They played two games and were even. In the third (and presumably the final game), she bet the Duke ten guineas and Lord Lucan another two that she would win. At 5-love down, the Duke had another bet with her at 7 to 2. When the score reached 10-2 down, the Duke betted her 15-1 on the outcome. After this she won the game and 34 guineas, recovering her losses. This however was controlled betting for small amounts. The Duchess's gambling at cards in London had been out of control and she had been losing significant amounts.

In London, John Heaton supplied the Duke with his needs for cash. At Chatsworth, the Steward, the manager of the House, did the same, with sums of £150 not unknown .He did not like to Derbyshire 'fogs'; he described them as being 'unwholesome'. The Duchess advised the children and Bess Foster not to leave the House in the winter months unless the sun was out. In such days she would sometimes take the children on an outing, no doubt muffled up to keep them warm. On one such occasion they went through Bakewell to White Watson's black marble mill at Ashford. They looked around his mill and bought black marble egg cups. Keeping the children occupied indoors when the weather was poor meant much time spent on games, when they were not being schooled. On one occasion, Little G spent time making petticoats which were given to local girls.

For the men, in addition to billiards, there were the shooting parties, a skittle alley and no doubt an opportunity to have an eye for the ladies. For the latter, a regular feature was taking the air in a chaise with a 'ring' around the park or further afield especially on a sunny day. The stables had up to 90 horses in it, but the Duke was not a keen breeder of racing stock like his younger brother George Henry. On occasions, guests would be taken to neighbours or there would be trips to Races at Derby, Nottingham and Chesterfield, as mentioned above. As an alternative, there would be running or horse racing during the day in the park. On some of these trips, the Duchess, joined by the Duke, would return on horseback together.

The visit in 1798 cost some £2,000, excluding the trip back to London. By comparison, the cost of family expenses for a 21 week stay in 1757-58 cost £14 per week.

A Decade On

In late November 1798, Louisa Ponsonby was staying at Chatsworth for the first time in some years. A letter she wrote to a Louisa O'Callaghan in Dublin gives us a rare detailed description of bedroom furnishings and other detail. She was sleeping in the Chintz Room, on the West front of the second floor. Louisa O'Callaghan married the Duke's nephew, William Cavendish on 18th July 1807.

She wrote that her bed was 16 ft/4.9 m high and covered with the finest chintz, lined with green silk. The frame of the bed was carved with festoons of fine cut flowers and gilded. The chairs in the room were carved to match the bed frame and also gilded. In 1792 there were four of these elbow chairs and they were covered with a chintz fabric to match the bed. The latter had three mattresses, four blankets, a bolster and two pillows with a green silk quilted counterpane.

A common feature to the principle bedrooms was a fire place; a four post bed with three mattresses; curtains matching the bed or the chairs; elbow chairs; a chest of drawers; dressing table; a large gilt framed mirror over the fireplace; and Wilton carpet. The House had a lot of white furniture.

There was a dressing room on either side of her bedroom, one serving her bedroom, the other being *'your uncle's Dressing Room'*. Both were furnished to match the bedroom *'and every sort of comfort in them'*.

She confirmed that the Dining Room was on the first floor, along with the Drawing Room and the Music Room, all enfiladed. Breakfast was however on the ground floor, next to the library. It was served from 10am and until 3pm or even later if required, *'so that one can go to it when one pleases'*. There was a piano in the room *'and all kinds of pleasant books besides those in the library, which is always open'*. It is thought that this Breakfast Room may be the room in the north east corner of the House, formerly the Billiard Room, the Library then being next to it below the Gallery.

In late November 1800, Bess Foster confirmed that the Library was still on the ground floor. She had just arrived at Chatsworth from Devonshire House: *'With what delight I enter'd the park gates, and through the snow frozen on our windows shew'd* (accompanying guests) *the gardens, then the House with its cheerful lights and blazing fires … Then the Dss came flying down to the Library to see us'*. [9]

Dinner was more formal, taken in the Dining Room on the south east corner of the first floor and with *'such a multitude of servants'* in the room in attendance. Supper however, known to have been served at 11pm, *'is brought into the Drawing Room and is quite comfortable. There are blazing fires in all corners of the House of that charming Derbyshire coal. In short, I never saw any fireplace that was half so comfortable'*. Outside, the plantations had grown markedly since her previous visit and *'a vast deal of bad ground reclaimed and made quite green. Altogether I do think it by far the most magnificent place I ever saw'*. Given the state it was in when the Duke married, clearly the House had had a remarkable make-over. (10)

This contrasts with a letter sent two months earlier by Sir Philip Francis to his wife: *'Events never happen at Chatsworth except a public dinner every Monday'* (he happened to stay on the two Mondays in the year when Public Days were held). The House was as quiet as a mouse and he saw nothing of his hosts until dinner at 7pm. *'I have all the comforts and enjoyments compatable with a state of uninterrupted solitude. The best of breakfasts, riding, walking, reading and fine weather. As for silence, the Abbaye of La Trappe is a mere babel to this House. I asked the gardener how long he had lived here and who he conversed with. He replied 40 years and seldom spoke to anybody'*. His experience does not appear to have been the norm. None-the-less, he was persuaded to stay an extra night before he sought a higher level of social activity at Buxton. (11)

The Chatsworth account book for 1810 may show the taste of the new Duchess being reflected in the furnishings of the Dining and Drawing Rooms etc. At the end of the year, John Orchard was paid his bill for '4 new curtains for the Dining Room (i.e. one set for each of the four windows) of red silk with yellow silk drapes and muslin curtains within, also for Fringe and ornaments for the Music Room and Drawing Room curtains £274.12.0d' (12)

This must have been initiated by Félicité, Lady Scarsdale, who wrote to Lord Hartington from Kedleston Hall near Derby in August 1810. She had taken a House party into the Peak District, calling at Chatsworth. The House, she wrote, was beautiful from the outside, but she complained of the state of the wallpaper in the Music Room and *'the flanel'* (i.e. the curtains etc) in the Drawing Room. With so little use since 1801 and the lack of heat in family rooms, the dampness was taking hold.

Whilst at Chatsworth she (Lady Scarsdale) packed her guests off to dine at the Edensor Inn' *and took the liberty to ask some bread and water for myself I was so sick of Buxton and Castleton eating that I could not bear it any longer.* Clearly the refined dining at Kedleston was preferred to the more basic food for those less fortunate. She was the second wife of the 2nd Baron Scarsdale.

There was a twist in the tail of this correspondence: *how glad I am that you came back so soon, we are here like fish out of water without you and can hardly persuade myself that we are at the races* (at Derby). *Your regiment of men would have done famously for my regiment of women, you never saw such a thing of them together ...'.* And was she hoping to hook the Marquis at the same time? [13]

To cater for all the guests, the Housekeeper had, in 1792, the following in her store cupboards: 388 table cloths; 1,514 assorted napkins; 202 pairs of sheets; 208 pillow cases and 801 towels and cloths of various descriptions. Some of the latter were of coarse towelling called huckerback which was made locally, all carefully noted down in the House Inventory.

The Duchess must take much of the credit for turning the sombre, old fashioned appearance of the House at the time of her marriage (1774) into a welcoming and more comfortable place to stay, despite the initial changes made by the Duke. As mentioned above, the House under the 5th Duke was never more than this. It was used even less once the extensions to the Palladian villa were made at Chiswick from the mid-1790s.

After the death of the Duchess, the house was hardly used at all until the Marquis found it to his liking a few years later. Indeed, it was the intention of the Duke to give it to him on his 21st birthday, but his death shortly afterwards saw the Marquis inheriting it. The remarks by Lady Scarsdale emphasise this point: what she found was probably the effect of damp and lack of use. The Duchess had successfully used the House as its hostess in the years following her marriage but it was eclipsed by Chiswick until the 6th Duke breathed fresh life into his main Derbyshire home.

25

Problems of Poverty

There is plenty of evidence in the Devonshire accounts, for Derbyshire and Ireland particularly, to point to many tenants living at a subsistence level, or just above it, and for many years. Poor summers or winters, or both, could materially affect their ability to fill empty stomachs and keep the family warm and dry. This chapter looks at the involvement of the Devonshires and Lady Spencer in poverty relief for the benefit of their tenants and others.

In exceptional circumstances one-off payments were made to tenants in parishes, on the recommendation of that parish's Devonshire rent collector. It seems likely that these were paid without a quibble. However, there was no plan for ongoing aid and tenants unable to keep up with rent payments did not appear to have been tolerated for long.

Rent increases clearly would have an effect on the poorer tenants and also any land tax which may have been due from them. The Duke generally paid the land tax (or a portion) for his tenants but it is not clear if this was for poor relief. In August 1757 following nearly a year of high food prices, there were food shortages and much discontent. This caused considerable unrest at least in the Bakewell and Crich areas, made more difficult by the demands of the new Militia Act on local men, ironically brought in by the 4th Duke of Devonshire when he was Prime Minister. A hungry mob marched from Bakewell to Chatsworth, but their fury was vented on being met by tables groaning under the weight of food and ale. Apparently the quality of the ale was not as good as had been anticipated! [1]

Underground Homes

There were some people living in the Hartington parish who could ill afford to pay rent. Pilkington in 1789 records ten 'dwellings' dug out of the ash waste adjacent to the Grin lime kilns. These were not unique to the area, for Daniel

Defoe described one on Brassington Moor in the early 1720s. It was in 1811 and stated that over 200 people lived in these dwellings at Grin, which is either wrong or the result of many more being created.

In May 1783, Lady Spencer spent much of her time in Buxton going on walks with Lord Frederick Cavendish. One of these was to the south of the village to Grin Hill. There were two limestone quarries here, worked for at least a century and each by a different family until a few years before when the Duke bought out their interests in lime production and in their separate collieries a little to the west high on the Axe Edge moors. Considerable amounts of lime was being spread to the south of Grin Hill in the Duke's Hartington manor both to sweeten existing pasture and arable fields and to reclaim moorland to make more land available for cultivation.

The huge waste heaps from lime production were soft and easily cut away. Lady Spencer went to see the homes which had been created in the heaps, making underground places to live. She described these homes [2]: *'they make very comfortable habitations... and most of them are filled with a man and woman and a whole brood of fine healthy looking children – all they want is a door which some of them have not, a little window and a chimney composed of a few stones and a little turf. I quite long to settle some remarkable near ingenious poor family in one of these... one woman has got an inch of garden, where she has planted a few potatoes but, the earth of which it is composed, was all brought up the hill by her children in buckets'.*

Presumably much of their water was brought the same way and the family she had in mind were installed there.

Previously unrecorded it would seem were others at Peak Forest lime works, where rent was charged by the estate in 1801 for *'a cott erected on the waste'*. There were three of them, one erected $3\frac{1}{2}$ years previously, one 3 years and one 2 years. [3] Yet even these crude and simple homes were a big improvement over the mud and straw cabins in Ireland.

A letter written by Geoffrey Heathcote, dated 29th November 1766 [4] indicates that: *'the poor miners, men, women and children, have been always allowed to pick and dress lead ore out of the old castaway deads (waste rock) and hillocks after the owner of the mine had got what they could in the ordinary way of dressing'*. It was initially without payment, but a small payment had been made for ore obtained *'in later years'*.

Problems created by the weather

There is no doubt that severe winters caused problems for the poor and in the main, this would have centred round hunger and the effects of the cold. The problem would have existed equally for farm animals too. In the winter of 1794-

95, the winter must have been especially bad. The Hartington accounts record payments '*for the relief of the Poor during severity of last winter*' amounting to £23.0s.4d., a significant sum of money. The same accounts record payments in five other parishes. A payment to Sir Robert Needham '*for meals and coals distributed to the Poor of Peak Forest £33.9s.81/2d*' may have been a late payment. [5]

Matters were worse in Wetton, however. This must have been exacerbated by the failure of the nearby Ecton Copper Mine in 1790. An account of 10th February 1795 records that 18 households involving 76 people received, free from the estate, 456lb. of oatmeal per week from Wetton Mill for four weeks in all (over 16 cwt or 0.8 of a ton). Thirty-two households received 1 cwt of coal per week, also for four weeks (6.4 tons). [6] This came from the Duke's colliery at Kingsley, near Cheadle.

Unfortunately, it was not just bad weather in winter that was causing the problem. In 1793, rain had damaged the harvest and drought the following year saw yet another bad one. On top of this there was a hard winter over 1794-95 followed by frost damage to the wheat crop in spring 1795 just as it 'bloomed'. [7] No wonder the estate was under pressure to assist the tenants. The 1794-95 winter was so cold for so long a period that both the Thames and Severn completely froze over allowing 'Frost Fairs' on the ice.

Before memories had faded there was another poor winter in 1800 when Thomas Fogg received £14 expenses for '*His Grace's Subscription for relieving the Poor in Hartington during the Severity of the Winter*' (1799 – 1800). Life in the parishes must have been wretched for some. The severe winter of 1799-1800 and perhaps other problems had affected the poor well into 1800. The account for the Chatsworth Estate carried annual payments for the poor assessment for Edensor, clergy widows and orphans in Derby etc. However, in 1800, there was a series of payments which indicates something much more serious. Payments started in April and continued until September. It is clear that the list is not the totality either, for the Hartington payment of £14 mentioned above is in the Hartington Accounts and others may lie in other collection accounts.

Nonetheless, the following gives some indication that the area's poor were suffering in a profound and more serious way:

'*April 23*	*Towards the Relief of the Poor of Little Longstone*	£ 15.0s.0d.
Ditto	*Ditto the Poor of Wardlow*	£ 10.0s.0d.
May 20	*Ditto the Poor of Ashford*	£ 42.0s.0d.
Ditto	*Ditto the Poor of Sheldon*	£ 25.0s.0d.
May 23	*Ditto the Poor in the Hamlet of Newbold*	£ 10.10s.0d.
June 18	*Ditto the Industrious Poor of Beeley*	£ 8.0s.0d.
Ditto	*Ditto Ditto of Pilsley*	£ 10.0s.0d.
Ditto	*Ditto Ditto of Edensor*	£ 15.15s.0d.

July 26	*Ditto the Poor of Gt. Longstone*	£ 25.0s.0d.
Sept. 18	*Ditto the Poor of Brampton*	£ 10.10s.0d.
	Total	£171.15s.0d.

Other Payments to the Poor

A surviving document records the existence of a Charity Estate situated at Hollington and Rodsley, south and south-east of Ashbourne, Derbyshire. It yielded a rental income annually of c. £500 for use in poverty relief. It had been purchased with £1,020 left by Bess of Hardwick and her husband, the Earl of Devonshire in 1687. [8]

Requests for relief seem to have usually been met, especially if it came through the Rent Receivers, but these were anticipated to be a one-off ex-gratia payment. Because of the nature of the problem (i.e. continuing distress through poverty) some payments were repeated to parishes on a more frequent ad hoc basis. Other payments were made annually as a gratuity. Many of these were around £5 p.a. Similarly payments for teaching '*poor children*' to read/write were of a similar amount. For example, at Tideswell in 1809, the schoolmaster was paid a yearly amount at Lady Day of £ 6.0s.0d. '*for teaching 20 poor children to read*'. In 1793 and in 1806 it had been £10 p.a. [9]

There seems to be little doubt of the Duke's willingness to dispense ad hoc and gratuities but there was no overall strategy for relieving poverty through any modern-style social scheme. Insufficient is known today of the extent of appreciation the aristocracy had of the extent of the poverty experienced by their tenants. There was also the difficulty of non-provision to people who were not tenants. Nonetheless it is difficult not to consider the plight of villagers with half-empty stomachs and the Devonshire family and their friends getting through a ton of meat per week for a 14-week stay at Chatsworth and 296 gallons (two pipes) of port ordered to cover requirements. Another comparison would be the £10-£20 sent to a parish in dire circumstances and the £50 plate donated annually to each of the Derby and Chesterfield Races and the £52.5s.0d., to Buxton Races which commenced later, in the 1820s.

Other payments were usually sent to aid subscriptions for a new church, chapel, school or even a gaol with the amount set at £10-£25 or thereabouts. An exception to this was at Hartington Manor where £100 was sent for a school at Brand Side on Axe Edge in 1831 and a new church at Earl Sterndale in 1828. [10]

Ironically, the alterations to the park, stables, kitchen etc at Chatsworth by the 4th Duke provided 'the means of subsistence to some hundreds of families'. His death and the fact that the work was almost complete in 1764 was 'to the inexpressible concern of many families, whose sole dependence for so many years had been upon his service'. This was not alleviated locally by the 5th Duke, whose capital expenditure on buildings and parks, i.e. excluding furniture and refubishing, was chiefly at Buxton, Chiswick and in Ireland. Fortunately for the tenants and other workers in the Staffordshire moorlands, developments at the Ecton copper mine saw the total number of employees reach c. 700 by the mid-1780s. [11]

Assistance was usually provided for larger schemes too, such as repairs at Derby Hospital in 1807, [12] when £ 60.13s.6d., was paid. What must not be overlooked however, is that a lot of tenants, albeit those with larger properties and probably better off, also had a proportion of their property tax assessments paid by the Duke. His decision to do this cost a fortune annually. Regrettably this was no consolation to those in greatest need with small cottages.

The dozens of minor payments made out to individuals (usually the schoolmasters and clergy) plus payments 'to the poor' was described by one of the book-keepers as being similar to a tax on the nobility and perhaps that was how it was viewed by the Duke. The document is a list of Burlington House expenses in 1807. [13] In 1774, Georgiana enquired for someone known to her about the possibility of a clergy living. The Duke responded that none were currently available but most of those he had 'are bad ones'. This may account for his additional payments of up to £40 p.a., to some clergymen. The Duke had some 45 livings in his gift. [14] It was customary, upon the internment of a family member in the vault at Derby (in what is now the Cathedral), to make a donation of £100 for the poor of Derby. [15]

Examples of the Problems

On the other-side of the coin, there did not appear to be a consistent policy concerning eviction for non-payment of rent where poor people were concerned. Lawrence Wardle of Hartington Upper Quarter held on to his home for ten years despite not paying rent albeit of £1.50 p.a., only. It was probably because it was of little or no value, for it was demolished once it was vacated in 1822. On the other hand, two valuable properties (from a rental point of view) were a different matter in Chesterfield.

'Eliza Bradley died and left several daughters very much distressed and who proved very abandoned. Neither rent nor possession could be got until an ejectment was brought'. The house was subsequently let at £10 p.a. In another case, in the same area, 'Edward Lawton was a very respectable man but was ruined by his own family, the son was imprisoned a long time for aiding French prisoners to escape and has since gone to France along with his sister and the old man brought to the parish (i.e. ? sent to the workhouse). The premises have been let from Lady Day 1812 to Mr. W. Smith an advanced rent (i.e. increased) £10 per year'. [16]

For many workers on the Duke's estates, particularly in Derbyshire and in Ireland where there is plenty of documentary evidence (and it could have been little different on his other estates except the aristocratic homes in Burlington

Gardens in London) that poverty was never far away. It was a thin line between having enough to eat or having a half-empty stomach.

The payment for relief of the unemployed workers of Dublin in 1797 mirrors the problem particularly well, although the Duke's estates were several miles to the south of there. The Duke, not wishing to appear extravagant at the expense of other benefactors contained his donation to £100. That paid for 3,700 meal tickets when 20,000 tickets were needed every week. He had matched the donation of his neighbour, Lord Shannon who was married to the Duke's cousin, but £550 per week was needed. Compare this to the debt run up by Georgiana in 1785-86 of c. £40,000 according to John Heaton. Those seeking meal tickets were rising in numbers every week and she was possibly increasing her debts at the rate of c. £400 per week.

In many cases each week, women would cower in a corner when the man called to give the meal ticket for that week. Many were virtually or entirely naked, having sold their clothes, bed lined etc. See below for the threat of this at Chiswick. Other than the well-off, women tended to not wear many, if any, underclothes.

Of course war and economic conditions was shouldering much of the cause rather than the aristocracy and it's highly likely that the Duke had not much idea of the depth and scale of the poverty on and around his estates. Nonetheless, it begs the questions of why the Duke's contribution to poor relief was not higher. By contrast, the 2nd Earl of Egremont was noted for his good record relating to poor relief, even providing the cost of emigration to the New World.

Matters were not helped when commons were in-closed, for the land was usually carved up between the landowners. The ability to pasture a cow on the common meant a lot to many cottagers who could make butter and cheese to sell on local markets to raise the money towards the following week's food bill. The Duke was allocated 8,000 acres of freehold land in 1808 from the inclosure of Hartington common. It is not clear how the parishioners with no land of their own or access to the former common maintained their cow after that time, if they did at all.

Of course, if the estate was not working hard to offset Georgiana's extreme extravagance, it would not have seen that sum or any large part of it directed to filling tenant's stomachs. The march on Chatsworth by a posse of hungry workmen in 1757 wishing to express their discontent and anger was assuaged by tables groaning under the weight of food and ale. There is no evidence to suggest that that march was ever repeated or anything positive resulted from it.

Even in Ireland, there was no civil unrest on the Duke's estate in the rebellion of 1798. However, here a shipload of free coal to keep their stove hot and their stomachs full during the winter ensured that, coupled with a steady replacement of the so called 'cabins' – hovels would be a better description – slowly saw a restoration of dignity, let alone reasonable living conditions.

Civil projects created work, such as the Lismore Canal and Dunvagen Bridge. People turning up for work at Ecton copper mine were usually found a job before the mine failed. At least one project at Buxton's new church ironically was bedevilled by a shortage of skilled masons but on the whole would have created and met a demand for workers. However, there was no structured plan to achieve worker placement targets. There does not appear to have been a desire to create capital projects to increase demand for labour. The latter was a result of work/expenditure to satisfy other objectives such as profit generation and improvements at Chatsworth. Perhaps, however, Dunvagen Bridge and to some extent the Lismore Canal in Ireland could have been exceptions.

Although this, over two hundred years later, seems to be the reality of the situation, there is another dimension: at the time that money could have been used to create more capital projects in the years immediately after the death of Georgiana, the English estates suffered from a lack of available resources to spend hardly anything. Exceptionally, work continued on Buxton church, eventually costing £ 6,758.00. (17)

All available funds were being used to pay off much of her debts over a period of several years (see Chapter 22). This was on top of the fact that running costs were severely eating into available net revenue.

The Position of the Duchess

The Duchess seems to have a reputation for her support for the poor. However, her lack of discipline in managing her pin money meant that her ability to help others with money from that source was limited. In August 1781, she was focussed on a Sophy (sic) Newton who had become totally dependent on others as a result of an illness which developed as a result of her brothers 'being lost'. The Duchess settled £40 p.a., on her. *'I can't well afford it, but I could not help it – I have not seen her yet'* she wrote to her mother (18)

From time to time, to be fair, the Duchess did allow her heart to rule her head and good for her that she did so. In a box full of many documents relating to claims against her at the time of her death is a note of a matter completely separate. It seems it must relate to an example of a family at Chiswick in dire circumstances and possibly a case of where she had given support. The note draws attention to a Mrs Ashforth, where the bailiffs had taken all of her furniture and were threatening to take Mrs Ashforth's *'and her childrens clothes the next time'*. (19) Although they would not take clothes being worn, it readily focuses one's mind on the many completely destitute ladies in Dublin in 1797, bereft of clothes, some perhaps sold, but others perhaps taken by distraint, leaving the only clothes available for sale being those that were worn on that day.

It seems today, looking at the note re Mrs Ashforth, that in the absence of the Duchess, the prospect of her receiving assistance from the estate would have been slim.

Georgiana's Charity School

Following the birth of Little G, in 1783, Georgiana established a charity school in Edensor in her honour. She provided £100 p.a., to clothe ten boys and girls and to school them, the excess being invested to yield 1½%, to be used in helping to finance apprenticeships, the cost of marriage or training them for a career in service. The first twenty children were invited to dine at Chatsworth. *'My girls have dark blue jackets, long blue coats, white aprons and handkerchief and black silk hats. The boys had a blue coat with silver buttons, buff waistcoats and breeches plus round hats'.*

The schoolmistress was proficient with both fine as well as plain needlework (essential training for young women). There was a schoolmaster too, who had lost an arm. The meal at Chatsworth was the usual roast beef and plum pudding. Thereafter the children are described as having walked back in procession, the ages being 9-10 years. It appears that the Chesterfield Charity School was founded in honour of Little G too, also with ten boys and ten girls. [20]

The Work of Lady Spencer

Following the death of her husband, Lord Spencer, in 1783, Lady Spencer adopted a daily regime starting and ending with prayers and embracing so much social work. It also included a determination to continue her love of cards in a more moderate fashion after she lost 'a great deal of money' one night. She seems to have had the strength of character to succeed too. One year she stumbled upon several people living in wretched circumstances, worse than anything recorded in the Devonshire estate archives by the Rent Receivers, although the two instances recorded in Chesterfield may have been something similar. No other record has been found which suggests this personal involvement in alleviating dire need of relief was undertaken by anyone else in the Devonshire family. An assumption that she told her daughter Georgiana is acceptable here; it is not so the case of the Duke.

It is likely that Lady Spencer was encouraged in her poor relief work by the Lord Egremont. They met in August 1785 at Devonshire House, for instance and may well have both been staying there on other occasions. Although she may well have frowned upon the excesses of his sex life (and indeed all aspects of his liberal way of living with his many wives and forty children at Petworth) he had a deep sensitivity to the plight of many poor people and had all sorts of schemes to try and alleviate poverty and/or its worst excesses. It is entirely plausible that they discussed such matters and she gained by his encouragement. [21]

That Christmas (1785), she saw the good and the bad side of trying to be benevolent. She had given away a dozen cloaks and bonnets and promised a dozen more (costing her £6). However, it had created more *'jealousy than gratitude and satisfaction'*. She had also bought an ox *'which I am going to make into soup and meat for the poor – 200 portions – 100 in my own parish and 50 in each of the others'*. [22]

Her diary records: *'January 1st 1788, Holywell House – went to the abbey and passed the rest of the morning in walking to see different poor people – among which the most interesting were a poor Irish woman – whom we rented out a few days ago perishing in an outhouse without fire – with Cold and Hunger – I have placed her at Mitchels where she is well taken care of and with the help of food and medicine will I hope soon recover – the next was a travelling shoemakers wife just brought to bed* (i.e. expecting a baby) *without a farthing* (¼ of a penny) *to furnish her or her child with neccessary's, the stench and dirt of the place she lay in was Dreadful – but by a trifle to the Midwife and to a granny woman to take care of her and sending her a few of the lying in things I trust she will soon be well - but the most shocking scene I saw was poor Philby's family in Daynil Lane – in a small room which could just hold two beds was a wretched mother who had just fainted away with supporting a lovely girl of 14 who was insensible and expiring of a consumption and close to the bed sat her eldest daughter of 16 in a deep decline – panting for breath and moaning over her dying sister, I never was more overcome than with the misery of this poor woman – all I could do was to tell her she should want for nothing – and to send Langford around which I did immediately in hopes of saving the eldest daughter who has been ill but three weeks – how thankful ought I to be that God Almighty has given me the means and the inclination to be as service – able* (sic) *as I can to some of my fellow creatures –*

January 3rd

Walked about the Town to see some of the sick people ... Poor Philbys Daughter died the morning before and the rest of the wretched family were forced to sleep on the bed next the dead body close to it and without any Curtains between ... Langford gives some hope of saving her (the other daughter) *... the lying in woman is much better'*. [23]

This had followed on from Lady Spencer's involvement in dispensing meat and broth to the poor on the 29th December, when over *100 'poor families'* were fed. *Word quickly went around the parish and on the following night many more people arrived: 'such crowds came for it* (the food) *that there was great confusion in finding out those who were upon the lists'*. [24]

Lady Spencer was involved with a Sunday School near Holywell House, St. Albans plus a Spinning School for girls. In May 1788 she was at Chatsworth where she 'got a good deal of information from Sir Wm. FitzHerbert concerning my Spinning School and an order for 200 yds of coarse cloth'. In mid-July, she was distributing clothes to 'a good many poor children belonging to the Sunday School'. She had taken Little G with her: 'showed Lady Georgiana a little Girl almost naked whom on her Birthday (two days previous) she was promised she should cloath. (sic) ... (I) was delighted with the astonishment and distress expressed in her countenance when she saw the poor little thing walking about here'. The following October, the Duchess wrote to her mother that Little G was making 'petty-coats for poor children' at Chatsworth. (25)

It would seem that the girls at the Spinning School were making cloth, which Lady Spencer was selling to finance the clothes given away to the Sunday School children. No doubt Tissington Hall was not the only place which saw lengths of it arriving. One can imagine Devonshire House and Chiswick being recipients, for example. In September, 1788 she records that there were 'multitudes (of children) ill with eating Walnuts and Trash'. Clearly they were scavenging, although the illness 'in their bowells' could have been dysentery resulting from poor sanitation rather than eating rotting food (the trash). She also went to see 'the Blacksmiths Child who is dying of the violent complaint so many children have in their Bowells (sic) and to see Fletcher the Bakers twins who I fear are far gone to recover for want of a breast', (both died).

This is one of the last entries in her surviving journal, other than a Grand Tour to Italy. Her entries regarding the effects of food shortages etc which the country was suffering could not be better described and show the background to why the Duke's estate accounts are peppered with payments to parishes to augment poor relief, especially amongst his poorer tenants. It also explains why there were often arrears in rental payments. However, as has been indicated above at Chesterfield, long term non-payment resulted in eviction.

Lady Spencer's social work was a result of a determination, expressed in her diary, after her husband's death, to lead a quieter, more meaningful life. It was in the same way that she was prudent about her play at cards and moved a little closer to The Almighty, especially on Sundays, in her religious beliefs and her expression of it. Foreman states that 'religious fanaticism (which) later overshadowed her life'. (26) There were certainly times when she was prepared to express her strong views but whether this should be judged as fanaticism is subjective. The extent that some of it was motivated by such abject poverty she found on her doorstep also needs to be remembered.

Many of the social problems outlined above did not improve much for many years. A symbol of the wretchedness being suffered was the breadline: people queuing for the handout of free bread and this became a feature of village life in Hartington in the 1820s.

Printed Sources

Anon, *An Interesting Letter To The Duchess Of Devonshire*, 1778

Barker, N., *The Devonshire Inheritance, Five Centuries Of Collecting At Chatsworth,* 2003

Burton, M., *More Wingerworth Recollections*, 1996

Bentley Smith, D., *A Georgian Gent & Co: The Life & Times Of Charles Roe*, 2005

Bessborough, Earl Of, & Aspinall, A., *Lady Bessborough And Her Family Circle*, 1940

Bessborough, Earl of, edit, *Georgiana, Extracts from the Correspondence Of Georgiana, Duchess Of Devonshire*, 1955

Bickley, F., *The Cavendish Family*, 1911

Bond, M. & Beamish, D., *The Gentleman Usher Of The Black Rod*, 1976, 1981

Boswell, J., *The Life Of Samuel Johnson, 1884 edit.*, Vols.1-5

Burke's Peerage, 107th edit, Vol. 3

Butterton, H., *Bonnie Prince & Burning Rebel*, 2012

Camp, AJ., *Royal Mistresses & Bastards, Fact and Fiction, 1714 – 1936*, 2007

Cannadine, D., *Aspects Of Aristocracy*, 1994

Capes, R., *Poseidon: A Personal Study of Admiral Lord Nelson*, 1947

Clegg, G., *Chiswick House & Gardens, A History*, 2011

Colvin, H., *A Biographical Dictionary Of British Architects, 1600-1840*, 1995

Cunningham, P., *The Letters Of H. Walpole, 4th Earl of Orford*, 1891

Devonshire, D., *The House*, 1982

Devonshire, Duchess Of, *Memorandums Of The Face Of The Country In Switzerland*, 1799, D MSS, Notes & Transcripts Series

Dodd, A E., & EM., *Peakland Roads & Trackways*, 2nd edit, 2000,

Douglas, P., *Lady Caroline Lamb, a Biography*, 2004

Draper, W., *Chiswick*, 1923

Farey, J., *General View Of The Agriculture Of Derbyshire*, 1811, Vols. 1 & 2

Featherstone, P., *Biggin & Hartington Nether Quarter*, 1998

Foreman, A, *Georgiana, Duchess Of Devonshire*, 1998

Foskett, D., *British Portrait Miniatures*, 1963

Foster, V., *The Two Duchesses*, 1898

Gibbs, V., *The Complete Peerage*, 1913

Gleeson, J., *Privilege And Scandal*, 2007. (USA edition on sale in UK) Originally published as *An Aristocratic Affair: The Life Of Georgiana's Sister, Harriet Spencer, Countess Bessborough*, 2006

Graves, A., *The Royal Academy Of Arts, Dictionary Of Contributors& Their Works, 1769 – 1904*, 1905, Vol. III

Gunn, W.T.J., *Harrow School Register, 1571 – 1800*, 1934

Haines S., & Lawson L., *Poor Cottages and Proud Palaces*, 2007

Hall, I., The Burlington Magazine, June 1980, *A Neoclassical Episode at Chatsworth*

Hammond, P. & C., *Life In An Eighteenth Century Country House*, 2012

Hanson, M., *Wm Gould's Diary*, Derbys. Record Soc. 2001

Hattersley, R., *The Devonshires, The Story Of A Family and A Nation*, 2013

Haupman, W., Brit Art Jnl, 22/3/2010, *Brandon & Gibbon in Lausanne, c.1787*

Healey, E., *Coutts & Co: The Portrait Of A Private Bank*, 1992

Hitchins, F., *The History Of Cornwall et al*, 1824, Vol. 2,

Ingamels, J., *A Dict'y Of British & Irish Travellers In Italy, 1701- 1800*, 1997

Jackson, P., *The Last Of The Whigs*,1994

Jeffares, N., *Dictionary Of Pastellists Before 1800*, on line edition

Jerome P., *Petworth from The Beginnings to 1600*

Jupp P., (ed) *The Letter-Journal of George Canning, 1793-1795*, 1991, Royal Hist. Soc., Camden 4th Ser., Vol. 41

Kennedy,A., *Nelson, An Anthology Of Poems etc*, pr. pub.

Langham, M., & Wells, C., *The Baths At Buxton Spa*, 2005

Langham, M., *Buxton, A People's History*, 2001

Lees Milne, J, *The Batchelor Duke, 6th Duke Of Devonshire, 1790-1858*, c.1990

Leveson Gower, Sir G., & Palmer, I., *Hary-O, The Letters Of Lady Harriett Cavendish*, 1949

Lloyd, S., *The Cosway Inventory Of 1820*, 2004, Walpole Soc., Vol. 66

Lord Orford's Voyage Around The Fens In 1774

Manning D., *Sir Joshua Reynolds, A Complete Catalogue Of His Paintings*, 2000

Masters, B., *Georgiana*, 1981

Namier, ed. *The Hist. Of Parliament: The Hse Of Commons, 1754 – 1790*, 1964

Naylor, D., *The Chatsworth Villages: Beeley, Edensor & Pilsley*, 2005

Neave, D., Garden History, Spring 1980, Vol. VIII, No. 1, *Lord Burlington's Park And Gardens At Londesborough, Yorks,*

Neave, D., *Londesborough*, 1977

Oxford Dictionary Of National Bibliography, 2004

Oxford Magazine, The, Feb. 1770

Paine, J., *Plans, Elevations and Sections of Noblemen and Gentlemen's Houses*, Part 1, 1767, p. ix

Pearce, C., *Cornish Wrecking, 1700-1860*, 2010

Pearson, J, *Stags and Serpents*, 1983

Pevsner, Sir N., *The Buildings Of England: Derbyshire*, 2nd edit. 1979

Porter, L., & Robey, J A., *The Copper & Lead Mines Around The Manifold Valley, N. Staffordshire*, 2000

Porter, L., *Ecton Copper Mines Under The Dukes Of Devonshire, 1760-90*, 2004

Porter, L., *The Duke's Manor, Georgian Hartington & Buxton Under The Dukes Of Devonshire*, 2012

Porter, R., *English Society in the 18th Century*, 1991

Ramblers Magazine, 1783

Samuel Rogers And His Correspondence, 1889, Vol. 1

Simond, L., *A Visitor to Chatsworth & Chiswick in 1811*, pub. History Book Club, 1968,

Sotherby's Collection Sale Catalogue, Castle Howard, 1991

Sotherby's, Attic Sale Catalogue, Chatsworth, 2008

Sotherby's, Collection Sale Catalogue, Stanstead Park, 1999

Spencer, C., *The Spencer Family*, 1999

Stapleton, M., *Cambridge Guide To English Literature*, 1983

Stewart, B., & Gitten, *Dictionary of Portrait Painters in Britain*, 1997

Survey Of London, 1963, Vol. XXXII, *The Parish Of Westminster*; Vol. XXX, Pt 1, *South Of Piccadilly*, 1960

Switzerland, 1799, (photocopy D MSS, Notes & Transcripts Series)

Thompson, F., *A History Of Chatsworth*, 1949

Thompson, F.M.I., *English Landed Society In The 19th Century*, 1963

Treasure, G., *Who's Who In Late Hanoverian Britain*, 1997

Trethewey, R., *Mistress of the Arts, The Passionate Life of Georgina, Duchess Of Bedford*, 2002

Watson, J.S., *The Reign Of George III, 1760 – 1815*, 1960

Wheatley, H., *The Hist. & Postumous Memoirs Of Sir Nath.Wraxhall*, Vol. III 1884

Winstanley, RL., *The Diary Of J. Woodford, 1981*, Vol.1

Wood, E., *The South – West Peak: History Of The Landscape*, 2007

Woods, J.A., *The Correspondence Of Edmund Burke*, 1963, Vol. IV

Woolfe & Gandon, *Vetruvius Britannicus*, 1767, Vol. 4

www.pastellists.com

Yale Univ. Press, *Farrington J., The Diary Of*, Vols. 3-4, 1979

Manuscript Sources

B.L., Additional Series, Althorp Papers, 76062 – 72 (for 1766 – 94); 75610 – 67, Corres. Hon. C. Howe & Countess Spencer

B.L., Derby Mercury Newspapers, 1800 – 11

B.L., Morning Post Newspapers, 1801 – 11

Castle Howard Archives

Chesterfield Library, 1788 Celebration of the Glorious Revolution

College Of Arms Archive re Nelson

Devonshire Archives, Chatsworth

Friends Of Chiswick House Archive

Harwarden R.O., D/E1177, 3/10/1775

Nat. Lib. Of Ireland, Collection List, 129, Lismore Castle Papers

Univ. of Nottingham Archives, Portland Papers,

References and Notes

Abbreviations :
BL. Add., – British Library Additional Series
BP – Burke's Peerage
CP – The Complete Peerage
D MSS – Chatsworth Archives. D MSS plus a number refers to the number of a letter in the 5ᵗʰ Duke's Group of correspondence
DNB – Dictionary of National Bibliography
GD – the Duchess
LS – Lady Spencer
EF – Lady Elizabeth Foster
MP – Morning Post
MH – Morning Herald

Chronology

1 Hanson, Wm Gould's Diary
2/3 ibid
4 Jupp, P., The Letter Journal Of George Canning 1793 – 95, Royal Hist. Soc., Camden 4ᵗʰ Series, Vol. 41, p. 42
5 ibid, p.54, 66
6 D MSS, C7

1 Introduction

1 Stock, J.E., Memoirs of the Life of Thomas Beddoes, M.D. with an Analytical Account Of his Writings, 1811, p.100, quoted in Bergman, N.A., Journal of the Royal Society of Medicine, Vol., 91, 1998, pp. 217-19

2 The Spencers, the Dukedom and the Duke

1 D.MSS Letter to F. Thompson from Earl Spencer, 1925, Archive Office file: G. Spencer
2 Spencer, C., The Spencer Family, 1999, pp. 89, 101, 106
3 Pearson, J., ibid, p.93
4 D MSS 918, 23/10/1788
5 D MSS 902, 15/9/1788
6 Leveson- Gower, Sir G., & Palmer I., Hary-O The Letters of Lady Harriet Cavendish, 1796 – 1809, 1940, p. 43: 15/1/1803. Hary-o not Harry-o was used
7, ibid, pp. 35 – 36
8 ibid, pp. 36, 38
9 Devonshire, Duchess of, 'The House: A Portrait of Chatsworth', 1982, p.110
10 Porter, L., Ecton Copper Mines under The Dukes of Devonshire, 1760 – 90, 2004
11 Kennedy, A., 'Nelson, An Anthology of Poems etc.' privately publ., p. 29. Copy in 5ᵗʰ Duke's file, Chatsworth
12 Leveson- Gower, Sir G., & Palmer I, ibid, p. xiii
13 Burke's letters to Lady Rockingham, 25/8/1778, Woods, J.A., 'The Correspondence of Edmund Burke', Vol. IV, 1963, p. 141. Woods states incorrectly that the camp was at Warley, Essex
14 D MSS 331, 16/2/1781
15 D MSS 1257.1, (breakfast time reading), 14/10/1794; 128, 3/8/1776

16 D MSS 123, 30/7/1776

17 D MSS Chatsworth, 174, 30/7/1777; Londesbrough, 156, 2/10/1776; Devonshire House: 163, 30/10/1776

18 Joseph Farrington, The Diary of, 1/8/1796 – 31/7/1801, Vols. 3 & 4, Chapter LXXXII under the heading: Expense of Education at Eton, a Good Scholar. Thanks to Charles Noble for finding this important reference

19 D MSS 622: 19 – 23/6/1784

20 D MSS 508, 18/6/1783

21 Hattersley, R., The Devonshires, The Story of a Family and a Nation, 2013, p. 282

3 The 1770s: Marriage and Married Life

1 D.N.B. 1st Earl Spencer, Vol.51, p. 864; The Peerage/Surname Index online; Bessborough, Earl of, edit., Georgiana, Extracts From The Correspondence of Georgiana, Duchess of Devonshire, 1955, p. 1; D MSS, DF4/2/2/9 The Diary Of Lady Georgiana Spencer, transcribed by the 6th Duke. Previously catalogued as the diary of her mother.

2 D MSS 12, 31/1/1774

3 Wheatley, H.B., Historical & the Posthumous Memoirs of Sir Nathaniel W. Wraxhall, Vol. III, pp. 343-44

4 D MSS 43, 7/11/1774; re Longleat: ibid, 1750, 13/12/1803, LS to GD

5 Also protected were payments to members of the Duke's family which he had inherited. These were: To the Duchess of Devonshire (The 3rd Duke's widow, Dowager Duchess Dorothy) £2,500 per annum; £500 per annum each to the following Cavendish members: Lord Charles, Lord George Augustus, Lord Frederick, Lord John; Mrs. Cavendish £3,000; Mrs. Fitzwilliam £1,022. 16s. 0d; Lord Richard £1,000 and Lord George Henry £1,000, all per annum, amounting to over £10,500) Earl Spencer put £10,000 into trust for the benefit of Georgiana, although if it was to yield 4% it would have brought her only £400 per annum. Upon the death of the Earl, this sum would pass to the Duke. The £4,000 payable to Georgiana was to be paid by four equal instalments and the £1,000 was to be paid during the joint lives. (D MSS L/114/37)

6 D MSS C166; University of Nottingham Archives, Portland Papers, PWF 10650, u.d.; Porter, L., Ecton Copper Mine Under the Dukes of Devonshire, 1760 – 1790, 2004, pp. 224-25

7 What this meant was that the income from certain estates had a first call on it from the settlement of a sum of money on an individual so that the payment was secure. The settlement terms could include the land being held by trustees acting independently of the Duke. There also appeared to be a right for the Duke to switch the security (for example to remove it if the beneficiary had died or upon marriage as in the case of the Duke's sister where an annual payment under her father's will of £6,000 per annum was terminated upon her marriage). This also included allowance for the Duke's obligations to the family members who received an annuity from him each year (detailed above) under the will of his father and grandfather.

8 D MSS 17, 10/7/1774; Georgiana Devonshire Misc. Box 2, item10

9 BP, 1999, 106th edit., Vol. 2, p. 1871

10 D MSS 16, Countess of Clermont to G.D., n.d., but Sunday following the wedding

11 ibid

12 D MSS 14, 15/6/1774

13 D MSS 37.1, n.d. but ? October 1774. It is one of only a few of his letters to survive

14 D MSS C166

15 D MSS 20, 22/9/1774, a Thursday

16 D MSS 2014.176

17 BP, 105th edit., 1980, p.1016; William FitzHerbert had borrowed £3,000 from the Duke at 4% per annum interest from 30th April 1773. This is confirmed by the Duke's Personal Bank Account (D MSS Uncatalogued)

18 D MSS 30, 27/10/1774) Georgiana and

her mother regarded themselves as very close friends

19 D MSS 146, 23/9/1776

20 Boswell, J., The Life of Samuel Johnson, LLD, edit Napier, A, 1884, Vol. IV, p.390

21 Butterton, H., Bonnie Prince and Burning Rebel, 2012, pp. 118-19

22 Boswell, J., ibid, Vol 2, p. 288

23 D MSS 18, 17/9/1774

24 D MSS 28, dated 9/10/1774 but added to for several days later

25 D MSS 50, 24/11/177

26 D MSS 43, 7 &8/11/1774

4 Early Days

1 Hattersley, R., The Devonshires et al, 2013, p. 235

2 Foreman, A., Georgiana, Duchess of Devonshire, 1998, p/b edit., pp. 30-31

3 Hattersley, ibid, pp. 235-36; D MSS 433, Sept 1782, Duchess to her mother; Chapman C., & Dormer J., 2003, Elizabeth & Georgiana, p. 80

4 D MSS 62, 14/4/1775

5 D MSS 58, 9/12/1774

6 Re charity to the poor: D MSS 80, 11/8/1775, Lady Spencer to Georgiana; re 1774 poem to the Duke: D MSS 59.2, ud; re going to her mother in her polonaise: 60, Feb. 1775

7 Easter Ball at Devonshire House: D MSS 60.1, ud & Univ. of Nottingham, Portland Papers, PWF 10680, ud

8 D MSS 61, 13/4/1775

9 D MSS 62, 14/4/1775

10 D MSS 64, 22/4/1775 and 63, 18/4/1775; D MSS Uncatalogued, the Duke's Personal Account Book, 1770-84; Re 1st Earl Spencer: Spencer, C., The Spencer Family, 1999, pp. 113-119

11 Univ. of Nottingham Archives, Pw F 10671, 15/4/1775

12 D MSS AS/1717, John Heaton's Account with the Duke, 1772-74

13 D MSS 85, 26/8/1775;

14 D MSS 86, 28/8/1775 and 93, 10/9/1775

15 Foreman, A., ibid, p.48; D MSS 89, 92, 94, 2 – 16th/9/1775

16 D MSS 97, 1/10/1775

17 Harwarden R. O., D/E1177, 3/10/1775

18 Univ. of Nottingham Archive, Pw F 2700-01, 3 & 10/10/1775, the Duke of Devonshire to the Duke of Portland

19 D MSS 95, 103, 107

20 D MSS 109, 5/11/1775

21 Re Lady Spencer: D MSS 80, 11/8/1775, from Spa; 54 D MSS 111, 26/11/1775, Lady Clermont from Paris to GD; D MSS 112, letter re. Xmas 1775 to GD. There is an historical problem here. It is recorded on www.ancestry.com, that a child called Georgiana was born on 24th June 1776 at Middleton Hall, Middleton Stoney. She would hardly be 'monstrously big and rather fat' about ten weeks into a pregnancy. Georgiana's birth is not recorded on-line on The Peerage: Jersey. Nor does it list Elizabeth Catherine born 30/12/1792 or an eleventh child, Mary Anne, born c. 1790 which are listed on www.ancestry.com.)

22 D MSS 118

23 The 10th Earl was born on 16th July 1734 and died in his 60th year on 26th January 1794 at Wilton. The Pembrokes had celebrated twenty years of marriage earlier in the year and the Countess was 40 years old on 29th December the following year, 1777. (CP, 1945, Vol. X, p. 426)

24 The Duke and Duchess were not there in 1774 and the book on the event (Lord Orford's Voyage round the Fens in 1774) does not record him being a member of the party. The 'Voyage' was held between 16th July and 6th August. The 3rd Earl was used on occasions as a trustee of parts of the Duke's settled lands, held in trust for his heir etc. The Duke's Aunt Rachel was married to the 1st Earl of Orford

25 D MSS 120, 28/7/1776

26 D MSS 120, 123; Details of this eclipse are rare. The Met Office Archive quotes Winstanley, R. L. The Diary of J. Woodford, 1981, Vol. 1, 1776-1777 (The 1st Six

Norfolk Years 1776-1981) pub. The Parson Woodforde Soc.

27 Craven, M., & Stanley, M., The Derbyshire Country House, 2001, Vol. 2, pp. 239-240

28 CP, Leicester, Earl of

29 D MSS 159, 17/10/1776

30 Re Lord Frederick: D MSS 151, 6/10/1776; D MSS 148; 151, 6/10/1776

31 CP: Carlisle

32 Fitzgerald, B., edit., Correspondence of Emily, Duchess of Leinster (1731-1814), Vol. III, 1957, p. 524

33 CP: Bessborough; Fitzgerald, B., edit., ibid, p. 313

34 DNB, 2004, Vol. 52, pp 943-44

35 Manning, D., Sir Joshua Reynolds, A Complete Catalogue of his Paintings, 2000, pp 242-43

36 D MSS 168, 15/12/1776

37 D MSS 125, n.d.

5 A Social Life 1777-79

1 D MSS 170, 20/1/1777

2 CP: Clermont

3 D MSS 176, 178

4 D MSS 180, 12/8/1777 to her mother at Spa

5 Foreman, A., ibid, p.57

6 D MSS Duke's Personal Account Book, uncatalogued

7 D MSS 181, 20/8/1777; BL., Add.MSS, 75923

8 7th Baronet, born 4th March 1745 – 6 (Julian Calendar)

9 Boswell, J., ibid, Vol. 2, p. 403

10 D MSS 189, 17/9/1777; Ford, T.D., Castleton Caves, 2008, pp. 43-46

11 D MSS 190, 28/8/1777 Georgiana also told her mother in this letter that she was a 'great player' at cribbage

12 D MSS 199, 21/10/1797

13 12 Brit.Lib., Add. Series 76062, Letters, 27/2/1778 & 4/4/1778; 75923, Letters, 12/3/1778

14 D MSS C166 (Devonshire House accounts); BL., ibid, 75923, 4/5/1778

15 CP, Vol. 111, p. 480

16 Dailly, T & W, Biographies of People who worked in British India; D MSS 216, 17/7/1778

17 Woods, J. A., The Correspondence of Edmund Burke, Vol. IV, July 1778 – June 1782, 1963, p. 20

18 Anon, An interesting Letter to the Duchess of Devonshire, Printed for J Bew, 28, Paternoster Row, London, 1778, pp. 99-100

19 From the poem 'The Meteors, the Comet and the Sun', written by C.J.Fox, see Fox, C. J., The Life of the Right Honourable C.J.Fox, 1807, p. 363

20 Bickley, F., The Cavendish Family, 1911, pp. 240, 242-43, 257

21 Brit. Lib., Add. 76064, letter 29/8/1788

22 Foreman, ibid, p.71

23 D MSS 246, 3-6/10/1779; the Duke's expenditure at Warley camp was £493 (D MSS C166 – note that the annual summary shows a lower figure)

24 (D MSS 248, 259. All of Lady Jersey's older children had just recovered from putrid fever

25 Spencer, C., The Spencer Family, 1999, p.138

6 Changing Times 1780-85

1 Chapman, C., and Dormer, J., Elizabeth and Georgiana, The Two Loves of the Duke of Devonshire, 2002, p. x. Unfortunately, the work suffers from virtually no references being quoted and equally frustratingly, insufficient dates

2 D MSS 279, 24/4/1780

3 D MSS 280, 20/4/1780

4 D MSS 289, 12/5/1780

5 D MSS 297 & 301; Watson, JS, The Reign of George III 1760-1815, 1960, pp 236-38; Wheatley,H.., edit, The historical and the posthumous memoirs of Sir Nathaniel William Wraxall, 1772-1784, p. 241

6 D MSS 304, 12/6/1780

7 D MSS 350, 28/8/1781

8 D MSS 297, 301-03

9 Wheatley, ibid, Vol. I, p. 248

10 Wheatley, ibid, pp. 238 – 39

11 Wheatley, ibid, pp. 236 – 37

12 Namier, L., edit., The History of Parliament: The House of Commons 1754 – 1790, 1964 Admiral Keppel later became Lord Keppel

13 D MSS 207, 25/7/1780; 321, letter to Miss Shipley

14 Univ. of Nottingham Archives, PWF 10736, 5/9/1780

15 D MSS 326-331

16 B. L., Additional Series 76071, Aug – Dec. 1794. There are more in the files covering later years up to Add. Ser. 76087. His time at the Admiralty was entirely in wartime and he did much to introduce efficiencies and improve management of the Service; DNB, Vol. 51, pp. 842 – 43

17 CP, 1910, Vol. XII/I, pp. 154 – 55

18 Univ. of Nottingham Archives, PWF 10758, 6/8/1781

19 D MSS 341 – 5, 348, 351; 331, 16/2/1781

20 Watson, J.S., The Reign of George III, 1760 – 1815, Oxford Hist. of England, 1960, p. 241

21 D MSS 342 – 3, 27/8/1781

22 www.bbcnews: The wreck that found the Mary Rose, 4/9/2011; In June 1782, the fleet was laid low at Portsmouth and the French had done nothing towards it: the crews were all affected by the fever epidemic which swept across the country. It was described by the Duchess as causing violent pain in the bones plus violent headaches, D MSS 400-01

23 Boswell, ibid, Vol. 3, p. 244

24 D MSS C. 166, Household Accounts Book, p. 46

25 D MSS 374, 8/10/1781

26 Pearce, C., Cornish Wrecking 1700 – 1860, Reality and Popular Myth, 2010, pp. 115-16; Hitchins, F., The History of Cornwall etc., 1824, Vol. 2 & Wikipedia

27 D MSS 372, 5/10/1781

28 D MSS 426; Boswell, ibid, Vol. 2, p. 361; Walpole, H., Letters Of Horace Walpole, Earl of Orford, Vol. 8, p. 90, 9/10/81

29 D MSS 377, 16/10/1781; L/13/5 (re the marriage settlement)

7 A Time Of Change 1780-82

1 Walpole, H., ibid, pp. 138, and also letter of 14/4/1782

2 Foreman, A., ibid, p. 97; D MSS C. 166, p. 68

3 D MSS 388, 390-1, 397-98; re EF: Chapman, ibid, pp. 23-24, 138-39

4 D MSS 407, 408 and 412 (29/7/1782 to 6/8/1782)

5 D MSS 400, 13/6/1782

6 D MSS 392-93, 30/5/1782 and 1/6/1782; CP, 1910 Vol. XII / I, p. 155; Lady Spencer disliked her daughter-in-law, Lavinia, according to the DNB, Vol. 51, p. 846

7 D MSS C 166, p. 68

8 D MSS 496, 10/5/1783

8 Meddling and Maternity

1 D MSS L/75/29; for references to Hervé etc (see below in Ch. 8): Green Vellum Book of 1837 compiled by George Spencer Ridgeway

2 D MSS 504, 22/5/1783 re Lady Spencer's letter; 523 of 1/9/1783 from Chatsworth

3 D MSS 528, 8/9/1783

4 Ramblers Magazine, 1783, p. 318

5 D MSS L/75/29

6 D MSS 533, 15/9/1788

7 University of Nottingham Archives, PI F5/15/3/1-9

8 D MSS 533, 15/9/1788

9 D MSS 533

10 D MSS 533; 534, 17/9/1783

11 D MSS 576

12 D MSS 576. Ironically and unknown to the Duchess, the final payment the Duke had been made prior to September 1783, in the sum of £1,791. It was held in a special account, which was running with a balance of c. £16,000. This was used for the purchase of an estate at Chesterfield subject to a lease for the length of three lives. So much for the Duchess trying to stain the character of John Heaton. D MSS AS/1717/9

13 D MSS 595, 6/2/1784

14 D MSS 555, 1/11/1783

15 D MSS 606 and 607

16 MP 27/5/1783

17 D MSS 496, 10/5/1783

18 Boswell, J., Life of Johnson, ibid, Vol. 4, p. 390

19 Pub. History Book Club, 1968, edit: C. Hibbert

20 D MSS 492 – 492/1

21 D MSS 499, from Geneva, 23/7/1783

22 D MSS. 508.1, July 1783; Walpole, H., The Letters of Horace Walpole, Earl of Orford, Vol., 8, p. 388, 23/7/1783

23 Fitzgerald, B., (edit.) Corres. Of Emily, Duchess of Leinster (1731-1814), 1957, Vol. III, p. 360

24 D MSS 549, 21/10/1773; 551, 23/10/1783

25 Spencer, C., The Spencer Family, 1999, p. 124; D MSS 576, 6/1/1784

26 D MSS 568, 29/12/1783, 569, 31/12/1783; 569, 1 u.d.; 573, 3/1/1784. 27 D MSS 572, 2/1/1784

28 D MSS 587, 22/1/1784

9 Complications 1784-85

1 D MSS 576, 6/1/1784

2 D MSS 603, 25/2/1784; Miss Lloyd on Charlotte: Chapman, ibid, p. 57

3 D MSS 625, c. end of June 1784

4 D MSS C 166

5 Foreman, ibid, p. 200

6 D MSS 639-40, 14-19/8/1784

7 Wheatley, H. B. (edit), 'The Historical and the Posthumous Memoirs of Sir Nathaniel Wm. Wraxall, 1772 – 1784, 1884, Vol I, p. 113

8 Boswell, J., ibid, Vol.2, pp 201-02; re nightingales: D.MSS, L/91/4/4. The birds cost £1. 16. 2d

9 D MSS 645, 13/9/1784. It is worth noting that in letter 646, Lady Spencer gives a long description of her views of Johnson

10 D MSS. 666, 14/2/1785

11 D MSS 665, 31/1/1785

12 D MSS 835 and 837, 27 & 29/10/1787 It should be noted that his citation on Wikipedia states that he died of liver disease induced by a heavy consumption of claret

13 D MSS 672, 15/4/1785

14 D MSS 682, 4/8/1785

15 Correspondence: D MSS 737, 16/5/1786; 739, 22/5/1786; EF's baby: Chapman C., et al, Elizabeth & Georgiana, 2003, p. 65

16 D MSS 683, 11/8/1785

17 D MSS 682, 4/8/1785

18 D MSS 679, June 1785

19 D MSS 2014.150, 3-5/8/178

20 D MSS. 2014.150

21 D MSS 679.1

22 D MSS 2014.151

23 D MSS 2014.152 from Chiswick

24 D MSS 2014.153

25 D MSS 2014, 153, 3/4/1785

26 Fletcher, J., edit. Where Truth Abides, Diaries of the 4th Duke of Newcastle-under-Lyme, 1822 – 50, 23/8/1833

27 D MSS 2014.155

28 D MSS 2014.142, 29/3/1785

29 Bickley, F., The Cavendish Family, 1911, pp. 250, 253

10 Upheaval 1786-90

1 D MSS 704, 717B, 729

2 Foreman, A., ibid, p. 184

3 D.N.B., ibid, p. 612

4 Foreman, A., ibid, p. 185

5 D MSS 764; re Martindale: Bickley, F., The Cavendish Family, 1911, p. 247, quoting Sichel, Sheridan, Vol.2, app. 4 & Vol.1, p. 72

6 D MSS 795, 14/1/1787

7 BL Add., 75610-67, 5/10/1786

8 D MSS 777, 21/12/1786. It was the best Christmas present they could have wished for

9 D MSS 791

10 D MSS 799.1, admission to EF in letter of 28/2/1787

11 D MSS 811, 10/5/1787

12 Gleeson, J., Prejudice & Scandal, 2006, p. 110-11

13 Mannings, D., Sir Joshua Reynolds, A Complete Catalogue of his Paintings, 2000, pp. 201-02

14 D MSS 1672, 19/11/1802

15 Kitson, M., 1977-78 Exhibition Catalogue

16 D MSS 1672, 19/11/1802

17 Re the Crescent: B.L. Add. 75610-67, Lady Spencer to C. Howe, 9/12/1786; re Chatsworth: Wm Gould's Diary, transcribed by M Hanson; at Buxton: D MSS 765

18 D MSS ibid. 765, 25/10/1786

19 D MSS 778, 23/12/1786

20 D MSS 765, 15/10/1786; 778, 23/12/1786

21 D MSS L/93/49

22 Hanson, M., Wm. Gould's Diary, 7/11/1786

23 BL Add., 75610-67, Corres. C. Howe to Lady Spencer, 1st and 6th/2/1787; Sir Wm Boothby may have been living at Edwinstowe House, Edwinstowe (now demolished)

24 Gleeson, J., ibid, p. 97

25 BL Add., 75610 – 67, 30/7/1787

26 D MSS 828, 20/8/1787

27 D MSS 835, 29/10/1787; 843, 14/12/1787

28 BL Add., 75610-67, Lady Spencer – Caroline Howe, 14/9/1787, 24/9/1788

29 BL Add., 76064, 8/7/1787

30 D MSS 432, 24/9/1782

31 BL Add., corres. 2 & 6th/10/1787; 16/10/1787; 21,24,26,28/11/1787

32 Wm Gould, ibid, 25/12/1787. However, Zonneveld states that he died on 18th March 1787, aged 68 years, leaving Mansfield Woodhouse to Sir Brooke Boothby. He is probably wrong in assuming that the friend of the Devonshires was Brooke Boothby rather than the older William of Mansfield Woodhouse. See Zonneveld, J., Sir Brooke Boothby, Rousseau's Roving Friend, ud, priv. pub., ISBN 90-77032-23-1. The Peerage (on line) states that he died 15/4/1787, unmarried, aged 66 years and is buried in Bath Abbey, so care needs to be taken

33 D MSS 858, 19/2/1788 – seeing EF off on 21/2/1788; Foreman, A., ibid, p. 198

34 Foreman, ibid, p. 201

35 DA., ibid, 1421, 30/12/1797

36 Foreman, ibid, pp. 200; BL Add., letter 14/7/1788, C. Howe to Lady Spencer. The Wikipedia entry for Augustus states that he was wet nursed in England by Louisa Augusta Marshall, wife of Rev. John Marshall, curate of Clewer, near Windsor. This cannot be true because James Hare went to see him in Normandy in 1789. Chapman et al state that Augustus was at Clewer in 1794 but her index reference refers to Clewer in Somerset: Chapman, C, ibid, pp. 133 & 277, col. 2

37 Bond, M., and Beamish, D., 'The Gentleman Usher of the Black Rod, 1976, 1981. Only one person has held the position longer since 1361: Sir Francis Molyneaux from 18th September 1765 – 11th June 1812, just a little longer than Sir Augustus Clifford's term of office.

38 D MSS 2014.164, 25/2/1788; 2014.168, 30/3/1788; 2014.169, 20 – 21/4/1788

39 D MSS 877 and 879, 3 & 7/7/1788

40 D MSS 905, 19/9/1788; 922, 1/11/1788

41 D MSS 2014. 174; 2014. 179

42 BL Add., 75923, letters 11/8/1788 and 6/11/1789

43 The Earl of Bedford was conferred his Dukedom on the same day. The 5th Duke of each title were good friends.

44 Porter, L., The Duke's Manor, p. 88

45 Derbys. R.O., 'Account of the Celebration of the Revolution Jubilee'; Porter, L., The Dukes Manor, p.88; D MSS 923, 4/11/1788; Porter, L., The Ecton Copper Mine Under the Duke's of Devonshire, pp. 77-86

11 Family Matters Abroad

1 BL Add., 75923, letter u.d. but June 1789

2 D MSS 960; for previous detail on the journey see 956 – 59

3 D MSS 968, 10/7/1789. Copy of the letter to the French Banker, D MSS Archive office file: G Spencer

4 D MSS 991, 8/9/1789

5 D MSS 956, 19/6/1789 'hopes of Spa entirely curing one'; BL Add., 75610 - 67, Lady Spencer to C. Howe, 20/8/1789, 'I hear nothing yet of the Duke & Duchesses return'

6 BL Add., 75610 – 67

7 D MSS 993, letter to Lady E. Foster, 15/9/1789; 991, to the Duchess, 8/9/1789. both from Charles Street, London, after Hare had left Paris

8 BL Add., 75923, 11/10/1789

9 ibid., MS. 75610 – 67, Lady Spencer to Hon. Caroline Howe, 31/8/1789

10 ibid, Lady Spencer – C. Howe 1/10/1789

11 Was this Anthony Storer whom they had invited to parties in 1776?

12 BL Add., 75923, letter to brother 27/10/1789

13 D MSS 1009, 2/11/1789

14 ibid, Duchess to her mother

15 Gleeson, J., *Privilege & Scandal*, ibid, pp. 106-07

16 D MSS C. 166 Book B, adjoining payments for teachers etc. again *'for the ladies'*

17 D MSS 1038, 12/2/1790

18 Jeffares, N., *Dictionary of Pastellists before 1800*, online edition, www.pastellists.com. The Duke took the picture of Little G back to Brussels with him. Both drawings passed down to Haryo which seems strange. One would have expected the two daughters to have had their own likeness. This may suggest that the wealthier Little G passed hers over to her sister. Both images were later sold on into the art world. (Pers. Com., J. Jeffares – C. Noble, Chatsworth, 2013)

19 The party seems to have been: Duke, Duchess, Ladies Foster, Duncannon, Lord Duncannon, Selina Trimmer, four daughters, Messrs. Marsden, Beard, Bertrand (senior staff) plus a few servants of the Duke, Duchess and the Duncannons. The doctor arrived in Paris direct from England just prior to the birth as did Lady Spencer, her few personal servants and apparently a maid for Charlotte. Other travellers in the party were William Beard, Steward of Devonshire House, Mrs. Smith (who had responsibility for the children), Miss Trimmer and a couple of nursery maids. It was the Duchess's intention to send Louis Rossi from Brussels to Calais because of his knowledge of the route, inns on the way, etc. Mr. Vigoreaux travelled too as a teacher for the girls. He seems to have been a relative of the Spencers and Lady Spencer may have pushed for him to be there, especially as the Duke had initial doubts as he thought Vigoreaux might be *'troublesome'*.

As Selina Trimmer was employed as the girls' teacher, his exact role is unclear (as his employment in England).

20 Richard Croft succeeded his brother as 6th Baronet in 1816. The following year he was appointed to attend Princess Charlotte in her confinement. However there were complications which caused her death. Croft was blamed for this by the public and took his own life as a result. (Bessborough, Earl of, edit. *Georgiana et al*, ibid, p.171); leaving England: D MSS C 166; arriving at Brussels: D MSS 1050; Duncannons following: BL Add., 75610 – 67, letter Hon. C. Howe to Lady Spencer, 25/3/1790

21 D MSS 1041, 18/2/1790. This letter sets out much of the Duchess's thinking re the children's travelling arrangements

22 D MSS 1041

23 Re Alleyne FitzHerbert: Catalogue of Christie's Sale of the FitzHerbert/Tissington Collection, 22/1/2008; re Ann Scafe's diary: D MSS 1054.1

24 BL Add., 31/5/1790

25 ibid, 19/6/1790

26 ibid, 75923, Ldy Spencer to Caroline Howe, 4/6/1790

27 ibid, Lady Spencer to C. Howe, 17/6/1790

28 ibid, 11/7/1790

29 There seems to have been a reluctance on the part of some doctors (including Dr. Warren) to travel to Paris. Dr. Pitcairn was 79 years of age and died the following year. He had been physician to St. Bartholomew's Hospital, London, 1750 – 80 (Bessborough, Lord, edit., 'Georgiana', 1955, p. 173)

30 D MSS 1054.1; BL Add.. 76066

31 BL Add., 75923, 28/8/1794; La Fayette was in an Austrian prison and the Duchess was hoping to at least improve his conditions which were rather bad

12 Weary of Errors, 1790-93

1 D MSS 1064, 10/9/1790, Dss to Lady Spencer

2 D MSS 1078, 9/9/1790

3 She was the niece of the Duke of Beaufort

and Duchess of Rutland, D MSS 1078.1, March 1791

4 Bessborough, Lord, ibid, p. 183

5 D MSS Devonshire House Accounts, C 166, 4th Qtr, p. 109

6 Gleeson, ibid, pp 117 – 124; Foreman, ibid, pp. 255 – 56; Bessborough, ibid, pp. 183 – 4

7 Gleeson, J., ibid, p. 130

8 D MSS 1115

9 Bessborough, ibid, pp. 183 – 84

10 Bessborough, ibid, p. 188; D MSS 1104, 8/1/1792

11 Aspinall, A., & Lord Bessborough, Lady Bessborough and her Family Circle, 1940, p. 68; Bessborough, ibid, p.294; re spar and coral: D MSS Archive office file G Spencer

12 D MSS 1120, 4/3/1792; Bessborough, ibid, p.188

13 Bessborough, ibid. p. 190

14 D MSS 1124, 3/4/1792

15 D MSS 1754.1, ud but ? Jan. 1803

16 D MSS 1132, 29/9/1792. Elizabeth, Countess of Sutherland in her own right, succeeded her father the 18th Earl when she was only a year old. In 1785 she married George Granville Leveson Gower, then Viscount Trentham, succeeding his father as Marquis of Stafford in 1803 and created Duke of Sutherland in 1833, the year he died. They purchased the house of M. de Callonne at Wimbledon in 1792. She described Lady Melbourne in D MSS, letter 1132 as 'much handsomer than when I saw her (there) formerly, and dresses in the most becoming way you can imagine'. Bessborough, ibid, p.194

17 D MSS 1129, 17/7/1792 from Foley House; 1147 ud. This last letter also includes a note from Hare saying that Devonshire House 'is incredibly dismal and dirty'. Care needs to be taken over the assessment of this letter's perceived date. Did the marriage take place so soon after her arrival from Paris?

18 Gibbon: Foster, V., The Two Duchesses, 1898, p.115; Going to Spa: D MSS 1131, 30/8/1792; Duke to Lady Spencer. Lausanne and Gibbon would have been known to the three Spencer ladies: The two sisters' brother, George, (2nd Earl Spencer) and his wife Lavinia had stayed there with Gibbon in September – October 1785 when Lavinia drew his portrait (Hauptman, Wm., British Art Journal, 22/3/2010, 'Brandoin & Gibbon in Lausanne', c. 1787). Perhaps more importantly, EF had also met Gibbon, being introduced by John Holroyd, later Lord Sheffield, and had stayed with him in July 1784 at Lausanne (the house was a regular stopping point for many British travellers), Chapman, C., ibid, pp. 8, 50-51). Staying at Ouchy: BL Add., MSS, 75641

19 D MSS 1137 – 38

20 Watson Library, Metropolitan Museum, New York, NB497.W47 A3 1800 V.1, Volume 1; Roscoe I., on-line dictionary, A Biographical Dictionary of Sculptors in Britain re R Westmacott

21 The Duke writing in May: Foreman, A. ibid, p. 282, quoting Connell, B., 'Portrait of a Whig Peer', compiled from the papers of the Second Viscount Palmerston 1739 – 1832, 1957, p. 383; Leaving in June: letter to Coutts, D MSS 1152.3, 4/5/1793

22 D MSS C 166, p. 186. In this year, 1793, Devonshire House employed 60 staff and household expenses were £9,376

23 Coutt's letter: D MSS 1137.1; 1142.1; legal action: D MSS AS/1717

24 D.N.B., Vol. 10, p. 673

25 D MSS 1200.1

26 D MSS letters 11154, 1165A, B, 167

27 D MSS 1300.1

28 D MSS 1157, 1159 – 60, 1164 – 65A & B, 1167

29 D MSS 1169

30 Wikipedia, which quotes many of the works on him

31 D MSS 1171, 22/8/1793

32 D MSS 1179

33 Wikipedia: The Flanders Campaign 1793/ Dumouriez's invasion of the Dutch Republic, quoting Fortescue, J., British Campaigns in Flanders, extracts from A History of the British Army, Vol. 4

34 Foreman, ibid, p. 283. As this detail is not part of the letter used as the reference, where is it from?

35 D MSS 1179. They landed at Dover on 18th September 1793. They had left England late October/early November 1791

36 D MSS 1176, 9/9/1793, letter to her mother

37 D MSS 1180

38 D MSS 1180, 18/9/1793; Ingamells, J., National Portrait Gallery, Mid-Georgian Portraits 1760 –1790, 2004, pp. 144 – 45. An unfinished sketch of this is still in the Chatsworth Collection and is possibly the item purchased by the Duke. However the Reynold's sale had been cancelled and not held until the end of 1794 but perhaps, being away, she had not realised this. It is likely to have been a private purchase from Reynold's estate, following his death

39 D MSS 1180, 18/9/1793

40 D MSS 1206, 25/1/1794

13 Building Bridges

1 D MSS 1191, 28/10/1793

2 D MSS 1201

3 D MSS 1210, 1/2/1794; 1223, 17/4/1794

4 D MSS 1206, 20/1/1794

5 Watson, J.S., ibid, 1960, p. 360

6 Re Chiswick: pers. comm. Dr. E Whittaker: author; furniture payments from D MSS, C 166. Re Chatsworth: D MSS 1223

7 D MSS 1246, 20/7/1794; Water Closet/Miss Lloyd: Chapman, ibid, p. 53; Porter, L., *The Duke's Manor*, 2012, p. 63, re Buxton water closets

8 D MSS 1215.2, 5/3/1794

9 D MSS 1284.1, 2/4/1795; 1268.1, 11/1/1795; 1263.1, ud

10 Improved relations, D MSS 1215.2, 5/3/179453; headache: D MSS 1214 from Lady Spencer to G.D., 22/2/1794

11 D MSS 1220, 10.4.1794. Duchess to her mother

12 D MSS 1256 – 57, 7/10/1794

13 Butler L., & Morris, R., Derbys. Arch.

Jrnl., 1994, Vol. CXIV, 'Derby Cathedral: The Cavendish Vault', pp.14-28; BP, 106th edit., 1999, Vol. 2, p. 2673

14 Lavinia: Farington Diary, quoted by Cockayne, CP, Vol. Xii/1, pp. 154-57; death of Charlotte: Gleeson, J., Privilege & Scandal, ibid, p. 13

15 D MSS 1232.1 (undated, but within a few days after the Duchess's death); re size of the ovary; 1233, 5/6/1794; Jupp P., (ed) The Letter-Journal of George Canning, 1793-1795, 1991, Royal Hist. Soc., Camden 4th Ser., Vol. 41, p.118

16 D MSS 1243 & 1245

17 D MSS 1250 – 51, 1253

18 (D MSS 1290.1, 1/5/1795, Little G to S. Trimmer

19 D MSS 1293, 9/5/1795

20 D MSS 1303, 26/8/1795

21 D MSS 1323, 7/1/1796

14 Family Life 1796-97

1 D MSS 1064, 10/9/1790

2 Gleeson, J., ibid, p.139: Foreman, A., ibid, p. 272

3 D MSS 1326, Selina Trimmer to Lady Spencer, 14/1/1796: 'Lady Elizabeth is come to town'; re Duke of Richmond: Foster, V., ibid, p. 153

4 D MSS 1232.1, c. June 1794

5 D MSS 1330.1, 6/4/1796

6 D MSS 1258.3, 18/4/1794

7 D MSS 1258.2, 1/11/1794; 1324, 8/1/1796

8 (D MSS 1327.1, 31/3/1796

9 D MSS 1284.1, T. Coutts to G.D., 2/4/1795; 1290.1, Little G to S. Trimmer, 1/5/1795

10 D MSS 1330.1, 6/4/1796. G. Cavendish – S. Trimmer

11 D MSS 1344.3

12 D MSS 1339, 3/6/1796, GD – LS

13 Bessborough, ibid, pp. 219 – 20

14 Schraibman, I.G., Jnl. Of Medical Biography, 2002, Vol. 10, '*A dead disease, as illustrated by the illness of Georgiana, Duchess of Devonshire*', pp. 105–08

15 Bessborough, ibid, p. 221
16 D MSS 1355,
17 D MSS 1356, 1358 – 59, 1361
18 D MSS 1603.1, 15/9/1801
19 Farington, J., Diaries, Vol. IV, p. 1239, 16/6/1799. The Duchess had her sister and Lord and Lady Melbourne for company at an exhibition at the Royal Academy
20 D MSS 1365, 19/8/1796
21 D MSS 1366
22 D MSS 1603.1, 15/9/1801
23 D MSS 1373, 20/9/1796
24 D MSS 1326, 14/1/1796
25 Bird traps: D MSS 1362.1, 12/8/1796; Clifford: Harrow School Register 1571-1800, Compiled & edit. By W.T.J. Gun, 1934, p. 53
26 D MSS 1377, 1381 – 82
27 D MSS 1391, 1394
28 Farington Diaries, Vol. III, pp. 846 – 849, Yale U.P. (Copy in the National Portrait Gallery, Heinz Archive/Library); D MSS 1400.1 (re headaches)
29 D MSS 1404
30 D MSS 1406.1
31 D MSS C166, Book C, pp. 13, 20, 22
32 D MSS C.166, Book C, p. 19
33 D MSS 1409, 16/9/1797
34 D MSS 1416, 1420
35 D MSS 1412, Haryo to Selina Trimmer
36 D MSS 1414, Hartington's deafness; 1415 – 16, Duke's humour: 1415; D MSS Chatsworth Accounts, 1798

9 D MSS 1477
10 D MSS 1479 (re. civility) and 1787 (re. maid)
11 D MSS 1489 – 90; accounts: D MSS C 166, Book C
12 D MSS 1492
13 D MSS 1478
14 D MSS 1515, Haryo to Lady Spencer, who was not at the event, 22/5/1800
15 D MSS 1519, 2/6/1800
16 D MSS C166, Book C
17 D.A., ibid, 1520
18 D.A., ibid, 1521B, 14/6/1800
19 Derby Mercury, 19/6/1800. The paper reported the date as the previous day (a Wednesday) incorrectly. It was the Wednesday of the previous week. It also had the company numbered at 1,200 and the cost at £4,000. Even the Duke would have baulked at that
20 The Oracle, 7 – 8/7/1800 and Morning Post 7 – 8/7/1800
21 re bread: Watson, J.A., 'The Reign of George III 1760 – 1815', 1960, p. 520); total cost: D MSS L/60/25. An unforeseen payment was to a Mrs. Strong who was hurt by a carriage needing medicines and surgery
22 D MSS 1495, Gleeson, ibid, p. 200
23 D MSS L/24/112, ibid, 1494 – 95, 1500 – 02
24 D MSS 1463, 31/1/1799
25 Sotherby's Sale Particulars for the Stansted Park, Rowlands Castle Sale 5/10/1999, p. 9

15 1798-1800

1 D MSS 1275, letter from Thos. Pelham, 2/2/1795
2 D MSS 1443, 9/7/1798
3 D MSS 1450, 8/10/1798
4 D MSS 1454; re Haryo's dress: Leveson Gower & Palmer, et al, p. 7
5 Mineral collection: D MSS 1466, 1468, 1477; pain in her eye: D MSS 1469, 6/5/1799
6 D MSS 1469
7 D MSS 1450, 8/10/1798
8 Bessborough, p. 232

16 1801-02

1 D MSS Chatsworth Accounts, 1800
2 D MSS 1533, 1539 – 40, 1543
3 D MSS 1567, 291/1/1801
4 D MSS 1554 & 1559 of 7/1/1801
5 D MSS 1562
6 BP, 2003, 107th edit., Vol. 3, p. 3335
7 D MSS 1558
8 D MSS 1611.3
9 D MSS L/75/29
10 D MSS Green Box, uncatalogued
11 D MSS Duke's Bank Account, Green

Box, uncatalogued; Lamb Indenture of Settlement, 1809: L/114/73

12 D MSS L/52/8. The 6th Duke was rather fond of Caroline apparently, as well as Blanche Howard, his niece

13 D MSS L/21/2, L/52/8

14 Trousseau: D MSS 1592.1; Accounts: D MSS C.166, Book C, pp. 104 – 05

15 D MSS 1548, 24/12/1800

16 CP, Vol. III, pp. 36, 302

17 MP 23, 25/3/1801

18 Castle Howard, Sotheby's Sale Catalogue, 11- 13/11/1991, p.9

19 Through careful living, Earl Spencer had reduced mortgage debt from £128,900 to £72,800 by the end of 1794. (BL Add., MSS. 76071)

20 MP 9/3/1802

21 In 1804, the MP reported that the *'fashionable campaign'* closed with Lady Heathcote's Ball on 16th July at her house in Grosvenor Square. (MP 14/7/1804). This was perhaps premature, for both the Duchess of St. Albans and Mrs. Marten-Pitt held a ball in the last week of July. The former was a particularly well attended masquerade

22 Bessborough, ibid, p.56. Letter dated 10/9/1803

23 MP 20/5/1801

24 D MSS 1675, 20/11/1802; 1675.3, ?4/12/1802, both letters to EF in Paris

25 MP 2/6/1802

26 MP 5/5/1802; 12/8/1802

27 Bessborough, ibid, p. 254). One of her daughters became the Duchess of Manchester and another, Charlotte, married the 6th Duke of Bedford

28 MP 28/6/1802, 29/6/1802, 1/7/1802

29 First ever balloon flight: Wikipedia, 6th Duke d' Arenberg; MP 4/4/1803

30 MP 20/5/1805; Jupp, P., The Letter –Journal of George Canning, 1793 – 95 , 1991, p. 238

31 Harrow School Register 1571-1800, comp. & edit., by W. T. J. Gun, 1934, p.53; D.N.B.; Wikipedia

32 MP 8, 25, 26/2/1801

33 Chiswick events: MP 22/6. 11 & 14/7/1801; payments to clubs and daughters: D MSS C. 166, Book C

34 D.A. ibid, 1611.3; MP 9/11/1801

35 D MSS 1605, 22/10/1801

36 D MSS 1611.1

37 MP 27/2/1802 re the Duke; Bessborough, ibid, p. 245 re Lord Besborough

38 Bessborough, ibid, 247

39 D MSS 1627 and 1629, 19 & 20/4/1802; Jane, Duchess of Gordon, was the 2nd daughter of Sir William Maxwell, Bt. She married the 4th Duke of Gordon in 1767 and died in 1812, aged 63

17 Two Beauties In Town & Relaxing Ramsgate, 1803

1 MP 29/4/1803; 25/3/1802

2 MP 29/4/1803, 21/4/1804

3 Lecture: Bessborough, ibid, p. 76; Duncannon: Bessborough, ibid, p. 251

4 MP 11/7/1803. Granville had been on the Duchess's guest list per the MP articles of 22/6/1801; 4/1/1802; 4/2/. 9/4. 30/4. 17/6. 9/7 of 1803; a trip to the West India Docks and then on to Chiswick on 16/7/1803

5 Bessborough, ibid, p.58. Haryo to Little G, u.d., but ?Sept. 1803 from Holywell, which Haryo found to be very cold

6 Bessborough, ibid, p. 59, letter dated October 1803; p. 76

7 Re Haryo at Chiswick: Bessborough, ibid, p. xiv; at Castle Howard: D MSS 1781, 24/9/1804

8 Bessborough, ibid, p.248

9 D MSS 1675, 26/11/1802; MP all dates 1802: 26/4. 29/4. 4/5, 10-13/5. 17, 19, 24, 27/5

10 Foreman, A., Georgiana, ibid, p. 350

11 MP 1/4/803; the 'rout' was held on 20/3/1803. The Duchess of Devonshire was not present, but it was very well attended with c. 400 guests, including the Prince of Wales

12 MP 10/4/1805

13 D MSS 1645, 1/9/1802; 25/5/1802; re

Coleridge, see Bickley, F., The Cavendish Family, 1911, p. 241

14 D MSS 1635, 21/6/1802; C.166

15 D MSS 1648, 28/9/1802. See also 1645 and 1647

16 The cost of the Ramsgate holiday was £2,111 (of this cost, provisions cost £1,027, wine £189, beer £81, stables £160 and lodgings £214; MP 29/9/1802

17 D MSS 1648, 28/9/1802

18 1803

1 D MSS 1672, 19 – 22/11/1802; 1730, 2/5/1803

2 D MSS 1708, 18/1/1803; 1711, 25/1/1803

3 e flu: MP 9/6/1803; MP 9/6/1803. Strictly speaking the paper stated that these two ladies caught a cold which settled on their chest

4 MP 11/3/1803

5 D MSS 1731, 23/5/1803

6 In addition to the two parties of the 3rd and 10th May given by the Duchess, advance notice of the 'Duchess Concert' was given for the 25th, but this could have been a public concert under her patronage. No report of it was given

7 D MSS 1733, 8/7/1803, letter to her mother

8 Foreman, ibid, p. 359. The comment appears to be unsupported by any evidence

9 Quote: D MSS 1625, 26/11/1802; lumbago: D MSS 1675.3, ? 4/12/1802

10 Quote: D MSS 16901.1, Dec. 1802; D MSS 1685, 18/12/1802

11 D MSS 1675.2 (?1)/12/1802

12 MP 4, 6, 8/1/1803; D MSS 1700 and 1701, both 5/1/1803 and 1704, 8/1/1803

13 Denon, D.V., Voyage das la Basse et la Laute Egypte, 1802, two vols

14 D MSS 1754.1, u.d., but probably January 1803

15 D MSS uncatalogued, kept in Green Box

16 D MSS 1724-24, 2nd and 25/3/1803

17 MP 16/3/1803

18 D MSS 1736, 16/9/1803

19 MP 2/5/1803

20 MP 22/4/1803

21 MP 2/5/1803. Amongst his patients was an expression that he killed more than he cured and the Morning Post repeated it after the death of the Duke.

22 MP 2/6/1803

23 MP 17/6/1803

24 MP 18/6/1803; Cotillion is French for petticoat, which would flash as the ladies turned, their ball gowns acting as an overskirt with the petticoat in view.

25 Wikipedia: Jane Gordon, Duchess of Gordon; MP 23/6/1803

26 Various copies of the Morning Post for May/June 1803

27 MP 16/7/1803, 18/7/1803, 21/17/1803

28 MP 22/7/1803

29 D MSS 1747.1, 1/12/1803 and Bessborough, ibid, pp. 261-62, 271

30 D MSS 1741, 12/10/1803

31 .D.A, ibid, 1742, 21/10/1803; MP 24/10/1803

32 D MSS L/114/48, pp. 55 & 60

33 Bessborough, ibid, pp. 74 & 79, letters of 16 & 19/11/1803; D MSS 1747.1, 1/12/1803

34 Bessborough, ibid, pp. 71, 73, 74

35 Bessborough, ibid, p.79

36 Bessborough, ibid, p.84 Letter to S. Trimmer, 24/11/1803)

19 1804-06

1 D MSS C 166 Book C

2 MP 23/01, 11/02, 27/02/1804

3 MP 17, 20, 22/03/1804

4 MP 21/04/1804

5 MP 29/06/04

6 MP 14&16/07/1804

7 D MSS 1761, 13/03/04

8 D MSS 1777, 02/08/1804, Duchess to her mother

9 D MSS 1785.1, 22/10/1804. Letter written the same evening. They had returned to Devonshire House by 08/11/1804. (MP 08/11/1804)

10 MP 01/12/1804

11 Leveson-Gower, ibid, p. 97

12 These included Messrs Fox, Grey, Sheridan, Windham and Grenville plus the Dukes of Bedford, Devonshire, Marquis of Buckingham, Earls Fitzwilliam, Derby, Carlisle, Spencer, Caernarvon, Darnley, and Lords Grenville, Minto, Dundas and others.

13 Also there were the Dukes of Bedford, Leinster and Richmond, the Marquis of Buckingham, Earls of Lauderdale, Egremont, Caernarvon, Carlisle, Derby, Earl of Dundas, Lords Morpeth, Minto, plus Messrs. Grey, Windham, Ponsonby, Sheridan and T. Grenville.

14 MP 12, 17, 22, 26, 30, 31/05, 6/06, 16/06/1804; Watson, ibid, pp 416-18

15 Lord Byron & His Times, Ch. XIV, 'The King of Club' by W.P. Courtney, pp 334-38

16 Foster, V., ibid, p. 481

17 D MSS 1850, 30/01/1806. Duchess to Hartington. Why she felt the need to convey this tittle tattle to her 16 year old son is mystifying

18 Bessborough, ibid, p. 247

19 Leveson Gower, ibid, p.94; MP 02/04/1803, 05/05/03, 21/04/04, 27/07/04; BP, 107th edit., Wikipedia for 5th Earl of Tankerville; D MSS 1781, 24/09/1804

20 Foster, V., ibid, p. 213

21 D MSS 1796

22 Bessborough, Earl of, Lady Bessborough and Her Family Circle, 1940, p. 129

23 Gleeson, ibid, pp. 86, 270, 267

24 D MSS 1808, letter of 09/05/1805; MP 14/01/1805

25 D MSS 1807, 08/05/1805

26 Gleeson, ibid, p. 268

27 Gleeson, ibid, p. 270

28 Foster, V., The Two Duchesses, 1898, p. 224;'Caroline Ponsonby is to be married tomorrow – she is very nervous', EF to her son, Augustus, 02/06/1805. She wrote again on the 15th July: 'Emily Lamb is to be married next Saturday (i.e. 20th July 1805) to Lord Cowper'. (Foster, V., ibid, pp. 223 & 230

29 D MSS 1812. This letter from the Duchess to her mother includes a list of other wedding presents

30 D MSS 1834.1, EF to the Duchess, undated; re Selina: D MSS 1832, 16/12/1805

31 Douglas, P., Lady Caroline Lamb, A Biography, 2004, p. 360

32 The country seat of Lord Cowper was Passanger House in Hertfordshire

33 CP, Vol. VIII, pp. 635-36

20 In Full Swing 1805

1 D MSS 166, Book C, 2nd Quarter

2 MP 08, 19, 22/04/1805

3 MP 24/04/1805

4 D MSS 1800, from Lady Spencer; 1801 from the DSS. Presumably Lady Spencer was thinking of the number of her family members at such an event

5 MP 29/04/1805; Foster, V., The Two Duchesses, 1898, p. 218

6 MP 03/05/1805

7 Bessborough, ibid, p. 271; MP 29/03/1805; MP 29-30/03/1805

8 Samuel Rogers and his Corres., 1889, Vol. 1, pp. 18-19, 24/03/1805, Letter S. Rogers to H. MacKenzie

9 Foster, V., ibid, EF to A. Foster, 29/05/1805, p. 220

10 MP 13/07/1805

11 Foster, V., ibid, p. 241

12 MP 18/01/1805), 07/01/1805; in addition to carriages being painted in Devonshire brown, there existed a type of Barouche Coach with a Devonshire boot (MP 27/1/1807)

13 MP 10/04/1805

14 MP 06, 07, & 19/06/1805

15 D MSS 1803, 04/05/1805; C 166, Book C, 1805

16 MP 29/06, 04/07, 23/07, 29/08/1805

17 MP 31/10/1805

18 MP 03/03/1806

19 D MSS 1843, 22/01/1806 GD to Marquis of Hartington

20 D MSS 1815, 14/08/1805; 18/07, 09/09/1805 re Lady Jersey

21 Leveson Gower, ibid, pp. 129-30,

10/11/1805; p. 130, 17/11/1805

22 D MSS 1829, 06/12/1805

23 D MSS 1841, 19/01/1806

24 Gleeson, ibid, p. 274

25 Letter Lady Besborough to Lord Granville Leveson Gower, 26/02/1805, see Bessborough, ibid, pp. 115-16

26 Foster, V., ibid, p. 210, letter to her son Augustus Foster, 05/04/1805

27 D MSS 1819, 20/04/1805

28 Bessborough, ibid, p. 130, letter of 17/11/1805, sent from Chiswick

29 Leveson Gower, ibid, p. 119, letter Haryo to Little G, 10/10/1805

30 BL Add., 37926, fol. 55

31 D MSS 52, 27/11/1774

32 Mannings, D., Sir Joshua Reynolds: A Complete Catalogue of His Paintings, 2000, p. 124, quoting Malmsbury, 1st Earl of, Letters ... 1745 – 1820, Vol., 1, 1870, p. 296

33 A good article on fashions of the late 18th century has been written: Chrisman-Campbell, K., Dress Journal, 2004, Vol., 31, French Connections: Georgiana, Duchess of Devonshire and the Anglo-French Fashion Exchange, pp. 3-13. However some care is needed, for instance, the Duchess's visits to Paris are overstated

34 D MSS 639, 14-18/8/1784, GD to LS

35 Spencer jacket: Wikipedia: Spencer jacket; in Paris: MP 4/4/1803, p. 3; girls' dress wear: MP 5/10/1802

36 Mannings, ibid, p. 124

37 D MSS, L/24/111

21 Final Days 1805-06

1 Foster, V., The Two Devonshire Duchesses, 1898, p. 221, letter dated 02/05/1805 from Devonshire House

2 Foster, V., ibid, p. 185

3 Foster, V., ibid, pp. 256-57, letter dated 01/12/1805; After only a stay of three weeks or so, Victory sailed off again. MP 12/09/1805. On seeing Nelson: D MSS 1863, 26/2/1806. This is odd, as she heard him speak and was present at another gathering when he was there, as noted above. On EF's grieving: Bessborough, ibid, Haryo to Little G, 25/11/1805. This piece of prose illustrates well Haryo's command of English. Her written English far outshines her mother's. For a good description on setting the scene and the battle itself, see Adkins, R., Trafalgar, 2004

4 D MSS 1835, 06/01/1806

5 D MSS 1837, 18/01/06

6 D MSS 1820.2, the last two lines of the poem are quoted. The Duchess also wrote a poem on his death

7 MP 09/01/1806

8 Leveson Gower et al., ibid, p. 146

9 Pers. Com., C. Vane, Portcullis Pursuivant, College of Arms, to author

10 D MSS 1822, 06/10/1805) letter to her mother; re Augustus Clifford: Foster, V., p. 243, his mother (BF) to his half brother Augustus Foster, 30/9/1805

11 D MSS 1844, 22/01/1806; D MSS 1846, 23/01/1806

12 Bessborough in 'Georgiana', p. 276 says this word is 'exercising' but a careful check on the Duchess's use of the letter x leads this author to the belief that 'increasing' is meant. It reflects failing eyesight and probably health affecting her handwriting. The context in which it is used is historically important

13 D MSS 1844, 23/01/1806

14 D MSS 1849, ud but? 01/02/1806

15 D MSS 1853, 1854A, 1855

16 MP 15/07/1806; MP 16/07/1806

17 D MSS 1854B, 12/02/1806. If so, his position has not been identified

18 D MSS 1863, 26/02/1806

19 MP 09/01/1806

20 MP 10/02/1806

21 D MSS 1855, 11-13/02/1806

22 D MSS 1852, 4-7/02/1806; Chatsworth: 1850, 30/01-04/02/1806

23 D.A., ibid, 1863, 26/02/1806; opera singer Giuseppina Grassini was to leave London later in 1806 for Paris, where she sang at the Tuileries Palace and became first Napoleon's and second, Wellington's lover (when the

latter was British Ambassador to France) – Wikipeadia
24 MP 03/03/1806
25 MP 08/03/1806
26 D MSS 1863, detail of 24/02/1806;
27 D MSS 1870, 4-6/03/1806; 1873, 08/03/1806
28 D MSS 1878, 14/03/1806
29 D MSS 1880, 15/03/1806 (letter to her mother); L/24/111 re jewellers
30 MP 28/03 and 31/03/1806
31 MP 28/03/1806; D MSS 1887
32 MP 31/03/1806; re death of Bess Foster: D MSS diary of the 6th Duke
33 The 9th Duke was the grandson of Caroline Georgiana, born 24th June 1803
34 Letter of 18/10/1804, Leveson Gower et al, ibid, p.107

22 The Duchess's Debts

1 D MSS Green Box, uncatalogued
2 Univ. of Nottingham Archives, PwF10758, 6/8/1781
3 D MSS 607, 8/3/1784
4 Foreman, A., ibid, p.168
5 D MSS 630, 10/7/1784
6 Foreman, A., ibid, p.171
7 Foreman, A., ibid, p.168
8 Porter, L., The Duke's Manor, ibid, p. 85
9 D MSS L/51/35, Bond taken 15/6/1787 from Wm. Mellish: appears to have been transferred to Wm. J. Denison on 15/8/1812, L/75/29. The initial loan was taken out at the same time as Heaton was sorting out the Duke of Portland's finances; D MSS 765, 25/10/1786
10 D MSS C166. 1786 Accounts, Devonshire House
11 D MSS 800, 802.2, re Coutts; 851, 21/1/1788 re Arkwright
12 Bessborough, Earl of, (edit), Georgiana, Extracts from the Correspondence of Georgiana, Duchess of Devonshire, 1955, pp. 5-6, 8
13 ibid, p.151; D MSS Dukes Account Books 1797 – 1811, uncatalogued

14 D MSS 1076.2, 25/12/1790
15 D MSS 606-607, 8/3/1784
16 Gleeson, J., ibid, p. 154
17 D MSS., 667
18 D MSS Devonshire House Accounts, C 166
19 D MSS 1060
20 D MSS 1079.5. The letter is of May 1791
21 D MSS re. the Jeffries payment: 1142.1; re. Hare: 1129
22 D MSS 1142.1, 30/11/1792
23 D MSS 1136.2 re Coutts; L/91/8 Chatsworth Estate Account book. The vouchers relating to this are in the Chatsworth Estate Voucher Box, 1792-92; in the period 1800 – 1803, Coutts was paid £13,267 by the Duke and £5,237 in 1811. Although this may however been off his own account rather than that of the Duchess, the Duke used Denne, Snow and Co as his bankers. (D MSS Duke's Account Books 1797 – 1811, uncatalogued
24 D MSS L/24/111
25 D MSS L/24/110
26 D MSS L/24/111., Wm. Bromehead's Account of Payments
27 D MSS L/24/112
28 Foreman, ibid, p. 253, quoting Scottish National Register of Archives, Douglas-Home MSS TD 95/94, diary of Lady Mary Coke, 27/2/1791. Lady Mary was a neighbour at Chiswick
29 D MSS L/24/105, bundle of vouchers etc
30 D MSS L/24/111
31 D MSS 1603.1, 15/9/1801
32 D MSS Duke's personal account book, Green Box, uncatalogued
33 Re The Petrarca: D MSS 1115; Advice to the Duchess: ibid, 1789, 11/12/1804, C.J. Fox to the Duchess; Bessborough, ibid, pp. 268-69
34 D MSS letters, ibid, 1115; increased allowance: 1789, 11/12/1804, CJ Fox to the Duchess & Bessborough, ibid, pp. 268- 69
35 These drawings, by Volpato and others are still in the Collection at Chatsworth and may be seen in the Guest Bedroom suite (formerly known as the Scots Bedroom. These formerly hung at Compton Place, Eastbourne, and are

believed to have gone there from Chiswick, possibly in 1892.; D MSS L/24/112, Account book listing creditors at date of death; Statement of Duchess's account at Coutts Bank in the same box; Barker, N., The Devonshire Inheritance, Five Centuries of Collecting at Chatsworth, 2003, pp. 256-57

35 D MSS L/24/105

36 Joseph Farrington, quoting Julius Angerstein, father of the National Gallery. Farrington Diaries, Vol. X. A copy of these diaries is held by the National Portrait Gallery, Heinz Archive

37 D MSS L/24/106

38 D MSS L/24/11

39 D MSS L/24/112 and Duke's Personal Accounts, not catalogued, filed with Green Box

40 D MSS Duke's personal accounts, ibid

41 Coutts' Archive 3101, letter Duke to T. Coutts, 15/3/1791

42 D MSS L.24.108

43 D MSS L/24/104,111 (Wm. Bromehead's Account of Payments)

44 D MSS L/24/105

45 D MSS Uncatalogued notebook, Box L/24/110 – 114

46 D MSS L/24/111, 26/2/1805

47 D MSS L/52/8

48 ibid

49 D MSS L/75/29

23 Affairs and Mistresses

1 D MSS 160, 18/10/1776

2 Bessborough, Earl of, edit., ibid, p. 2

3 D MSS 111, 26/11/1775

4 Lady Clermont was about 40 at the time (born c. 1734) and married to William the 1st Earl of Clermont and lived into her 80s. She died on 3rd December 1820 at Hastings. She became Countess of Clermont on 2nd February 1777. (CP, Vol. 111, p. 277)

5 CP, Vol. VII, pp. 90 – 91

6 D MSS 136.1; 168, 15/12/1776

7 D MSS 189, 23/9/1777

8 D MSS 182, 21/8/1777; GD to LS; 188,

11/8/1777

9 CP, Vol. VII, pp 90 – 91

10 D MSS 203, 12/4/1778

11 D MSS 205, 18/4/1778 to Georgiana at Devonshire House

12 D MSS 209, 22/4/1778

13 Foreman, A., ibid, p. 65

14 BL Add MSS. 76062, 1763-83, letter dated 4/4/1778

15 D MSS 286-87, 289

16 D.MSS 304, 12/3/1780

17 D MSS 350, 28/8/1780

18 D MSS 233, 28/10/1778

19 LS's letter re Harriet: D MSS 472; A date on www. The Peerage of the birth of Harriette of 1781 cannot be correct with John William being born on 31st August, but there was time in 1782 prior to the second Ponsonby child, Frederick, being born on 6th July 1783

20 Besborough, ibid., p. 41

21 Gleeson, ibid, p. 250; Granville took with him Harriet's son William, who was taken seriously ill whilst they were away

22 D MSS 748, ud

23 DNB, John Townsend

24 Besborough, ibid, pp. 21-22

25 Bessborough, ibid, p. 141

26 ibid, pp. 21-22

27 BL Add., 76072, J.J. Rye to Lord Spencer, 23/1/1795. The reference to Lord Spencer suggests this was Dallington House, Northamptonshire, and near to his home, Althorp

28 D MSS 304.2, GD to Lady Spencer

29 Wikipedia: Maria Fitzherbert; D MSS 621-22, 629, 631, 634

30 D MSS 607.1, to Bess Foster

31 ibid, 433, Sept. 1782. Clamp asserts that the Prince has a total number of liaisons in excess of 75, Clamp A.J., Royal Mistresses and Bastards, Fact and Fiction, 1714 - 1936, 2007, self published, ISBN 978 095033 0822

32 Wraxhall, The Hist. & Posthumous Memoirs of Sir Nathaniel, 1884, Vol. III, pp. 343-44

33 CP, Vol. IV, p. 348

34 CP, Vol. VII, p. 91; re reconciliation: D

MSS 1486

35 D MSS 433, September 1782

36 D MSS 533, ?15/9/1783

37 Foreman, ibid, p/b edit., p. 129

38 D MSS 547, 18/10/1783)

39 Walpole, H., The Letters of Horace Walpole, Earl of Orford, Vol. 8, p. 469, 11/4/1784

40 D.N.B., 2004, Vol. 50, pp. 298-99

41 The Oxford D.N.B. states that Sheridan funded it, the Cambridge Guide to English Literature, Stapleton, M., 1983, p. 803, states that the Duchess did

42 D MSS 490.1

24 Life At Chatsworth

1 D MSS 637, 12/8/1784; 644, 3/9/84. Fanny returned to work and was paid £20 pa plus her board. Re Canning: Jupp, ibid, p.256

2 D MSS 672,15/4/1885

3 D. MSS Chatsworth Account Books

4 D MSS L/60/22, 8/7/1795 (beer) and 20/8/1799 (wine). No valuation was given. For quantities, www. simpson.uk.com/beers/uk/measures.htm was used

5 BL Add., 75610-67

6 ibid, 9/9/1786

7 ibid, 75610-67, 14-18/9/1787

8 ibid, 24/5/1788

9 Chapman and Dormer, ibid, p.147)

10 D MSS 1453.1, 23/11/1798

11 D MSS 1448, 18/9/1798

12 D MSS Chatsworth Account Book, 1810

13 D MSS 1985, 5/8/1810; Hartington was used to the attention he received from eligible young women as well as their mothers trying to progress the interests of their daughters

25 Problems of Poverty

1 Derbys. Arch. Jnl., Vol LXXII, 1952

2 D MSS 497, 11/05/1783

3 They were occupied by George Barnsley (the first two) and David Pearson (the latter). The rents per annum were 3s.0d, 2s.0d and 2s.6d respectively; a clear indication of a

nominal payment for an underground abode. (Dev.Coll., T-Series Bundle 2. There was no further charge up to 1806

4 D MSS AS/1353

5 D MSS, T-Series, Bundles 2&3

6 D MSS, AS/917

7 Watson, J.S., ibid, 1960, p. 360

8 D MSS, L/114/22

9 D MSS, T-Series, Bundle 2

10 Much of this material is from the D MSS Chatsworth Accounts for the year concerned

11 Paine, J., Plans, Elevations & Sections of Noblemen and Gentlemen's Houses, Part I, 1767, p. ix

12 D MSS Shottle Collection accounts, Dev. Coll., T-20

13 D MSS., L/114/27/9

14 D MSS L/114/67

15 For example on the 26/06/1793: 'Pd. Gift to the poor people of Derby on account of Miss Ponsonby's Funeral there this day £100'. (D MSS, L/91/8) This is also confirmed in Lord George Augustus's will. (D MSS L/43/23, proved 12/07/1794)

16 D MSS, T-Series, T-38, Account for 1811

17 Porter, L., The Duke's Manor, ibid, pp. 60-61

18 D MSS 351, 21/08/1781

19 D MSS, L/24/111, note dated July 1806

20 D.MSS 548, 19/10/1783. Joseph Machin was the teacher on £12 p.a., in 1783. D MSS, Chatsworth Estate Vouchers, Box 1792-93. Voucher No. 314; Re Chesterfield School: see Bickley, F., The Cavendish Family, 1911, p. 267

21 Haines S. & Lawson L., Poor Cottages and Proud Palaces, 2007 or Jerome P., Petworth from the beginnings to 1600

22 D MSS 699, 27/12/1785

23 D MSS 2014.160

24 D MSS 2014.159

25 D MSS 2014.176, 14/07/1788; 915, Oct. 1788

26 Foreman A, ibid, p. 12

Appendix 1

Thoughts on the Duke: Comments by the Duchess etc

Letter 58, 9/12/1774 (D MSS 5th Duke's Series)
The Duke has been so attentive so good natured and has shown so sincere an attachment to me that I am sure it must have won any bodys approbation who had been indifferent to him and then judge of mine.

Letter 63, 18/4/1775 re payment of her debts
It would be unjust to dwell too long on his goodness in this as it is so like everything he does.

Letter 331, 16/2/1781
The Duke is very proud of what you (Lady Spencer) say of him and indeed he deserves it.

Letter 390, 22/5/1782
I hope Bath will do me good for it ought, it is amazingly disagreeable I only am surprised at the Duke's bearing as much as he does but he is so good natured he bears everything well.

Letter 606/7 8/3/1784 re her debts
You can not conceive how good he has been and he knows everything. He has received the avowal with the utmost generosity, goodness and kindness – his whole care has been that I may not vex myself and you would think he was the offender not me.

Letter 755, 12/8/1786
The Duke has certainly got the gout … I am almost always with him.

Letter 777, 21/12/1786
I am afraid going to Buxton is very disagreeable to him (the Duke) but he is set on it for me.

Letter British Library, Add. MS,75610-67, 24/5/1788, Lady Spencer to Hon. Caroline Howe
I have scarcely ever seen them (the Duke and Duchess) so long almost alone and it is impossible to describe the pleasant kind of Confidential Ease and unaffected playful fondness that subsists between them.

Letter 1421, 30/12/1797, Lady Spencer to S Trimmer
I have not for many years seen the D and Dss seem so happy in each other – she looks extremely well and he seems delighted with her Civility to the neighbouring families who occasionally come, he listens often with attention to her conversations with other people and I often see a cheerful whisper between them which is very pleasant and in her last head ache he was in and out of his room perpetually to know how she did – all this and the acquaintance he is making with his children…

Letter from Bess Foster: Mr Hare often says that he thinks the D.D. has the best sense & judgement of any body he knows – and added to that good taste & much real humour.

Appendix 2

The Duke's Creative Endeavours

Hattersley (1) states that in 1775, the Duke 'embarked on building the Crescent in Buxton' (clearly wrong, it was in 1780). He then states that it was 'one of the few creative endeavours in which he ever engaged'. Here are a few more:

- The Classical Bridge at Chiswick, 1774 'a better example – fine in line and rich in detail – does not exist in England of the Classic treatment of this kind of structure (2)

- The elegant Lismore (Co. Waterford) Bridge with its 109ft/11.7m span built in 1778-79 (washed away in the mid 19th century)

- The East and West Wings, Chiswick, 1788-1794

- Garden alterations, Chiswick, 1784

- Refurbishment of the private rooms, Chatsworth, 1783

- The first to commission Anglo-French craftsmen to manufacture furniture (3)

- Investment Plan, English Estate and capital expenditure of c. £700,000

- Management Plan, Irish Estate and capital expenditure of over £88,000

- St Johns Church, Buxton. Pevsner states: the domed top of the tower has no parallel in the normal neo-classical church types of 1810 – 20. The church cost over £6,000.

- The Square, Buxton, 1806. Middle class colonnaded housing development next to the Mineral Baths

- Purchased one of the first (the 4th) of James Watt's rotative steam engines for haulage in shafts, 1788

- First mine in at least Britain to pass 1,000 ft/ 305 m deep

- Construction of the Lismore Canal, Ireland, 1790s, plus one of Britain's first underground canals in a mine (Ecton Copper Mine)

- One of the very few Irish absentee landlords who clothed his many distressed tenants to keep them warm. He also gave them a ship load of free coal delivered up the canal to Lismore

Index